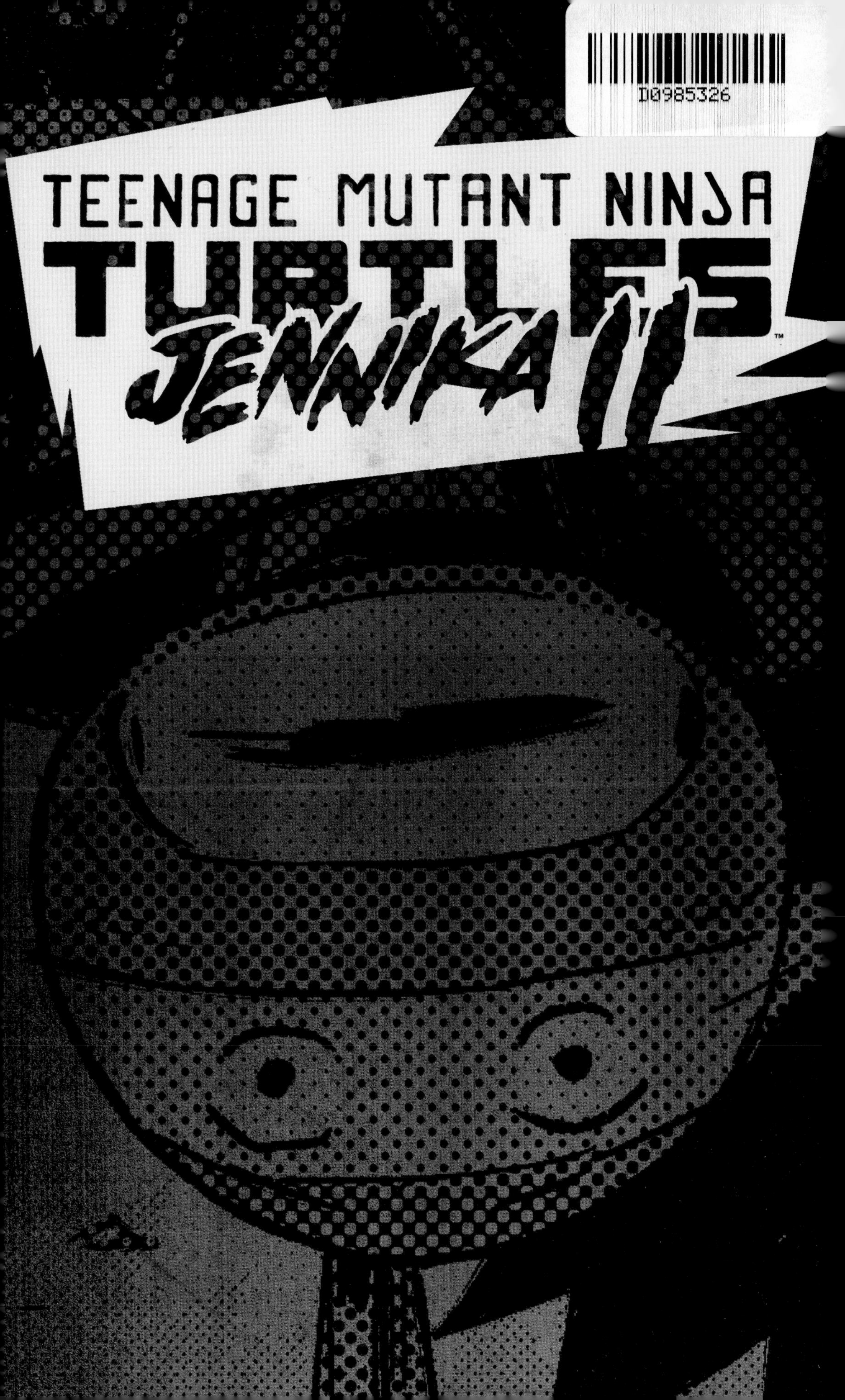
TEENAGE MUTANT NINJA
TURTLES™
JENNIKA II

Special thanks to Joan Hilty & Linda Lee
for their invaluable assistance.

Cover Artist: **Brahm Revel**
Series Editor: **Bobby Curnow**
Collection Editors: **Alonzo Simon** and **Zac Boone**
Collection Designer: **Shawn Lee**

Nachie Marsham, Publisher • Blake Kobashigawa, VP of Sales • Tara McCrillis, VP Publishing
Operations • John Barber, Editor-in-Chief • Mark Doyle, Editorial Director, Originals
Justin Eisinger, Editorial Director, Graphic Novels and Collections • Scott Dunbier, Director,
Special Projects • Mark Irwin, Editorial Director, Consumer Products Mgr • Joe Hughes, Director,
Talent Relations • Anna Morrow, Sr. Marketing Director • Alexandra Hargett, Book & Mass Market
Sales Director • Keith Davidson, Senior Manager, PR • Topher Alford, Sr Digital Marketing Manager
Shauna Monteforte, Sr. Director of Manufacturing Operations • Nathan Widick, Sr. Art Director,
Head of Design • Neil Uyetake, Sr. Art Director Design & Production • Shawn Lee, Art Director
Design & Production • Jack Rivera, Art Director, Marketing

Ted Adams and Robbie Robbins, IDW Founders

www.idwpublishing.com • Facebook: facebook.com/idwpublishing
Twitter: @idwpublishing • Instagram: instagram.com/idwpublishing
YouTube: youtube.com/idwpublishing

TEENAGE MUTANT NINJA TURTLES: JENNIKA II. AUGUST 2021. FIRST PRINTING.
© 2021 Viacom International Inc. All Rights Reserved. Nickelodeon, TEENAGE MUTANT
NINJA TURTLES, and all related titles, logos and characters are trademarks of Viacom
International Inc. © 2021 Viacom Overseas Holdings C.V. All Rights Reserved. Nickelodeon,
TEENAGE MUTANT NINJA TURTLES, and all related titles, logos and characters are
trademarks of Viacom Overseas Holdings C.V. Based on characters created by Peter Laird
and Kevin Eastman. © 2021 Idea and Design Works, LLC. The IDW logo is registered in
the U.S. Patent and Trademark Office. IDW Publishing, a division of Idea and Design Works,
LLC. Editorial offices: 2765 Truxtun Road, San Diego, CA 92106. Any similarities to
persons living or dead are purely coincidental. With the exception of artwork used for review
purposes, none of the contents of this publication may be reprinted without the permission
of Idea and Design Works, LLC. IDW Publishing does not read or accept unsolicited
submissions of ideas, stories, or artwork. Printed in Korea.

Originally published as TEENAGE MUTANT NINJA TURTLES: JENNIKA II issues #1–6.

ISBN: 978-1-68405-832-7    24  23  22  21    1 2 3 4

**MONSTERS**
story, art & letters
# BRAHM REVEL

**REDEMPTION**
story & colors
# RONDA PATTISON

art **JODI NISHIJIMA**

**SHAWN LEE** letters

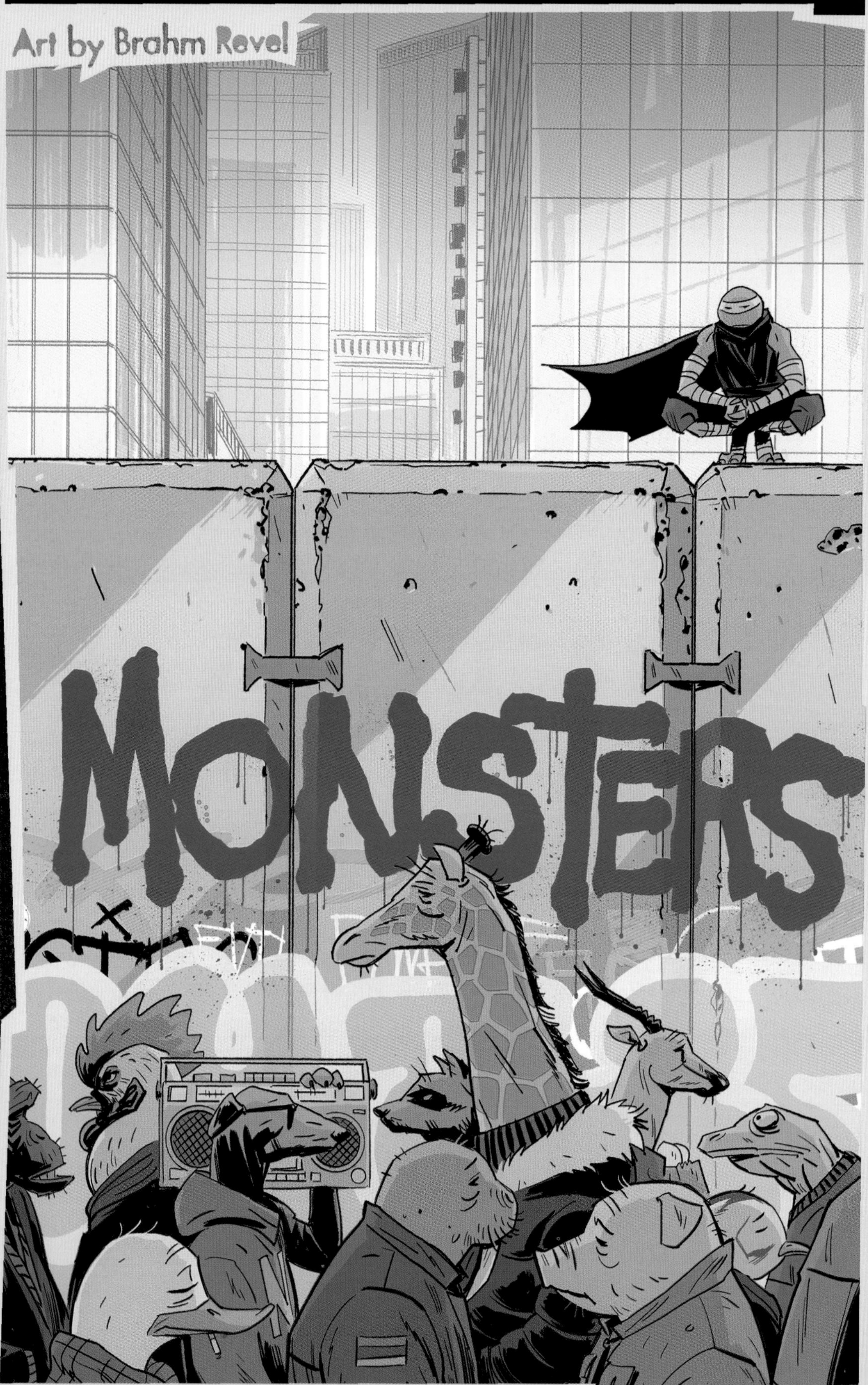
Art by Brahm Revel
MONSTERS

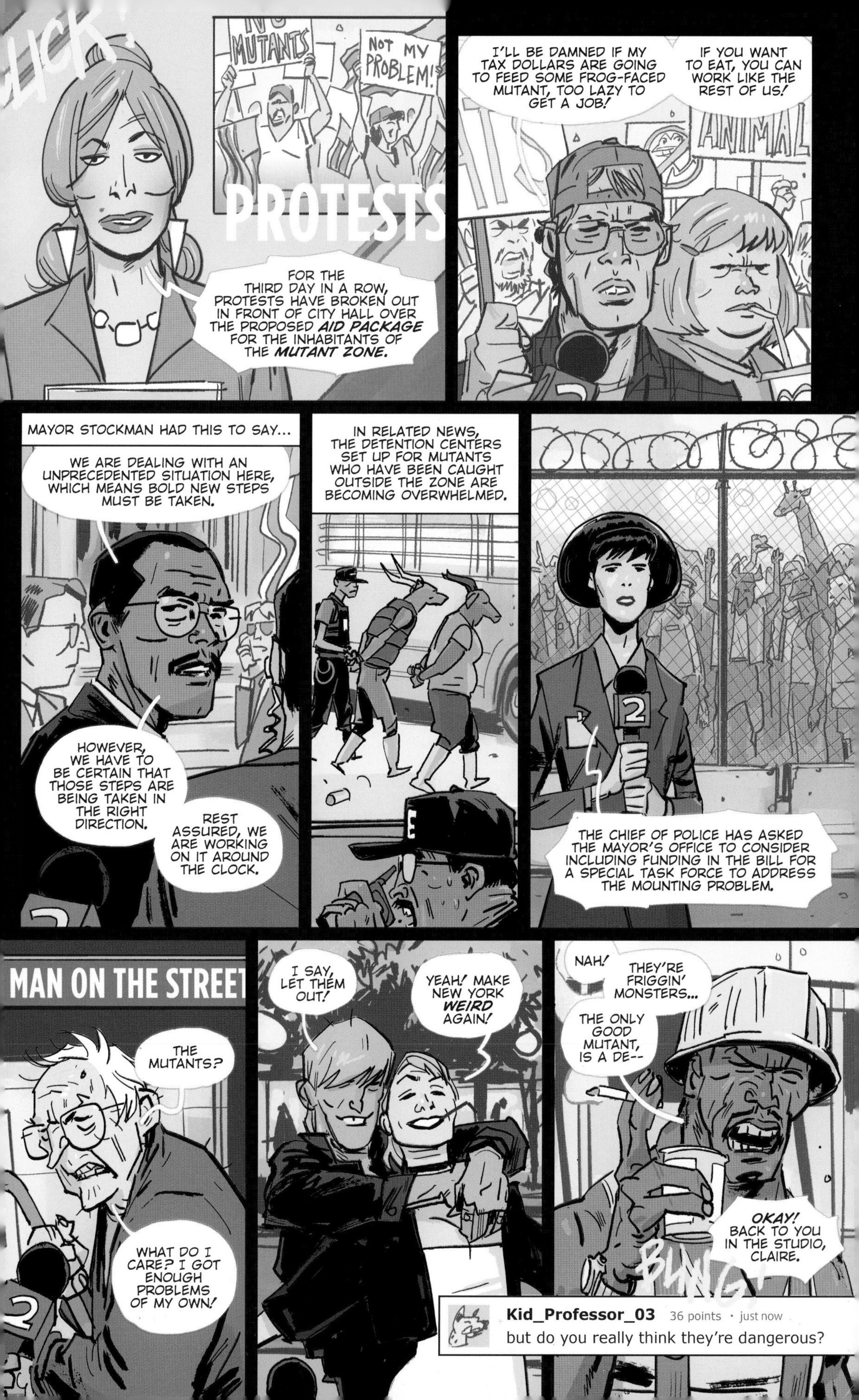

CLICK!
NO MUTANTS
NOT MY PROBLEM!
PROTESTS
FOR THE THIRD DAY IN A ROW, PROTESTS HAVE BROKEN OUT IN FRONT OF CITY HALL OVER THE PROPOSED AID PACKAGE FOR THE INHABITANTS OF THE MUTANT ZONE.
I'LL BE DAMNED IF MY TAX DOLLARS ARE GOING TO FEED SOME FROG-FACED MUTANT, TOO LAZY TO GET A JOB!
IF YOU WANT TO EAT, YOU CAN WORK LIKE THE REST OF US!
ANIMAL
MAYOR STOCKMAN HAD THIS TO SAY...
WE ARE DEALING WITH AN UNPRECEDENTED SITUATION HERE, WHICH MEANS BOLD NEW STEPS MUST BE TAKEN.
HOWEVER, WE HAVE TO BE CERTAIN THAT THOSE STEPS ARE BEING TAKEN IN THE RIGHT DIRECTION.
REST ASSURED, WE ARE WORKING ON IT AROUND THE CLOCK.
IN RELATED NEWS, THE DETENTION CENTERS SET UP FOR MUTANTS WHO HAVE BEEN CAUGHT OUTSIDE THE ZONE ARE BECOMING OVERWHELMED.
2
THE CHIEF OF POLICE HAS ASKED THE MAYOR'S OFFICE TO CONSIDER INCLUDING FUNDING IN THE BILL FOR A SPECIAL TASK FORCE TO ADDRESS THE MOUNTING PROBLEM.
MAN ON THE STREET
THE MUTANTS?
WHAT DO I CARE? I GOT ENOUGH PROBLEMS OF MY OWN!
I SAY, LET THEM OUT!
YEAH! MAKE NEW YORK WEIRD AGAIN!
NAH!
THEY'RE FRIGGIN' MONSTERS...
THE ONLY GOOD MUTANT, IS A DE--
BLNG!
OKAY! BACK TO YOU IN THE STUDIO, CLAIRE.
Kid_Professor_03 36 points • just now
but do you really think they're dangerous?

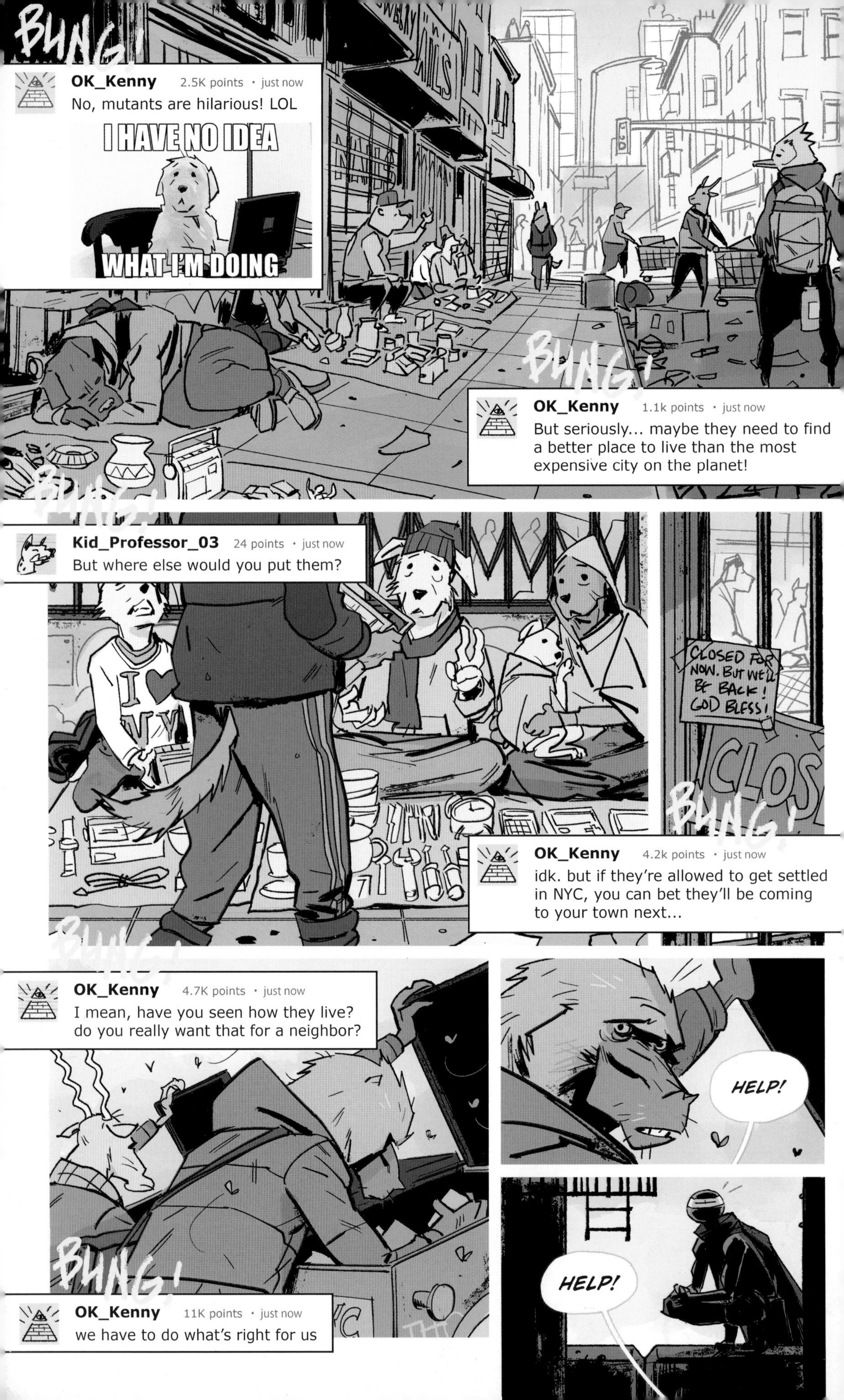
BUNG!
OK_Kenny 2.5K points • just now
No, mutants are hilarious! LOL
I HAVE NO IDEA
WHAT I'M DOING
BUNG!
OK_Kenny 1.1k points • just now
But seriously... maybe they need to find a better place to live than the most expensive city on the planet!
BUNG!
Kid_Professor_03 24 points • just now
But where else would you put them?
CLOSED FOR NOW. BUT WE'LL BE BACK! GOD BLESS!
BUNG!
OK_Kenny 4.2k points • just now
idk. but if they're allowed to get settled in NYC, you can bet they'll be coming to your town next...
BUNG!
OK_Kenny 4.7K points • just now
I mean, have you seen how they live? do you really want that for a neighbor?
BUNG!
OK_Kenny 11K points • just now
we have to do what's right for us
HELP!
HELP!

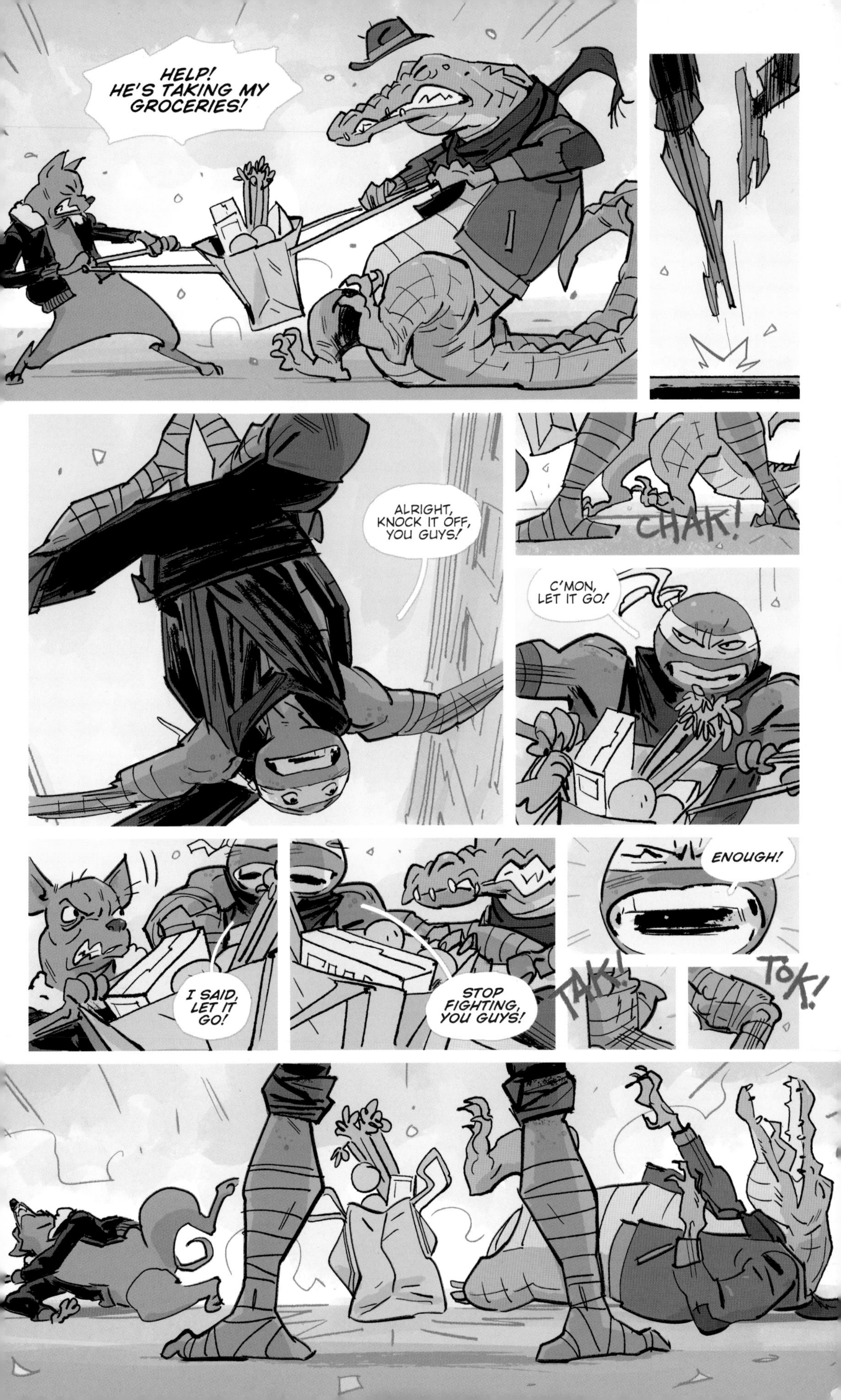
HELP! HE'S TAKING MY GROCERIES!
ALRIGHT, KNOCK IT OFF, YOU GUYS!
CHAK!
C'MON, LET IT GO!
I SAID, LET IT GO!
STOP FIGHTING, YOU GUYS!
ENOUGH!
TAK!
TOK!

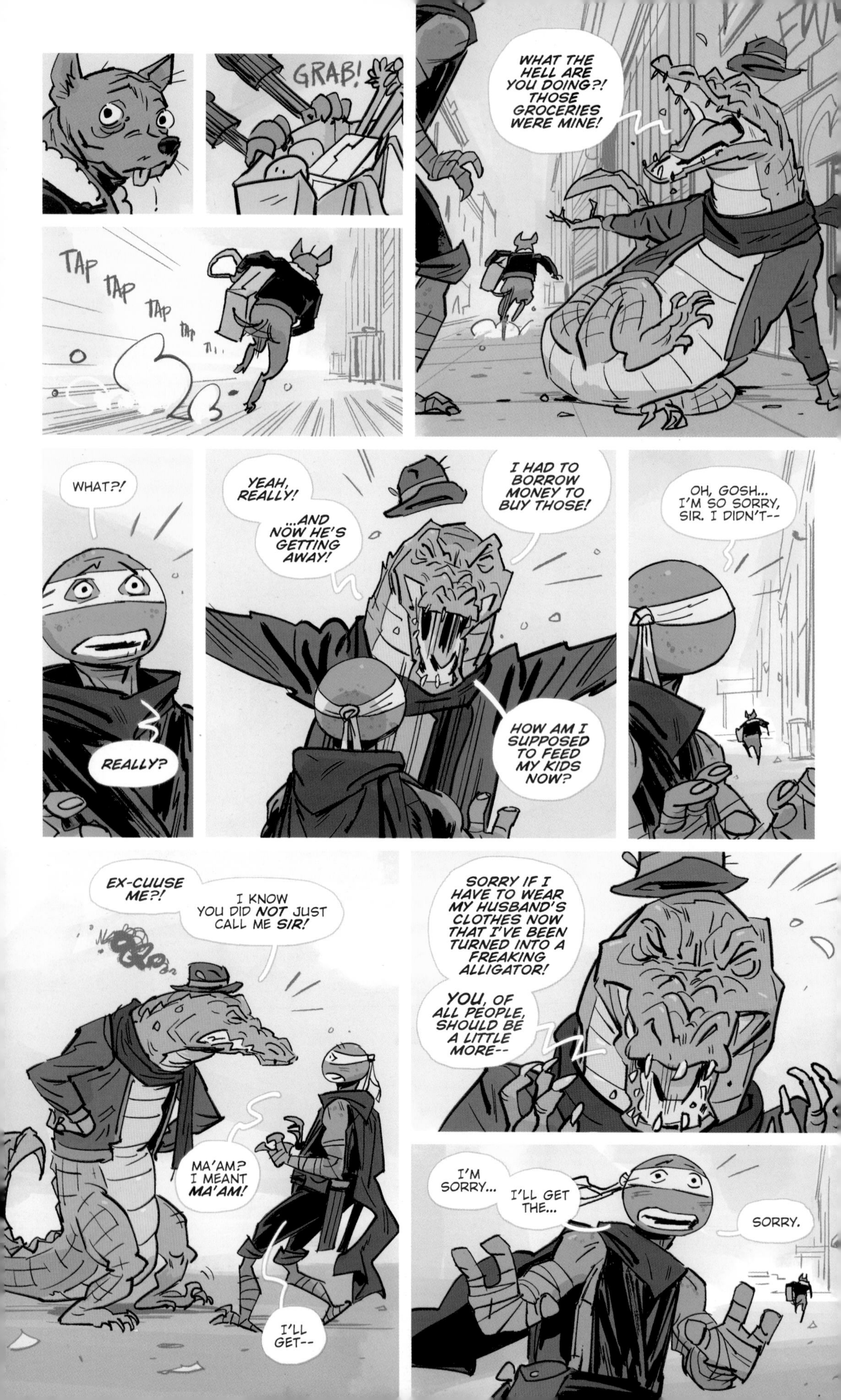
GRAB!
TAP
TAP
TAP
TAP
WHAT THE HELL ARE YOU DOING?! THOSE GROCERIES WERE MINE!
WHAT?!
REALLY?
YEAH, REALLY!
...AND NOW HE'S GETTING AWAY!
I HAD TO BORROW MONEY TO BUY THOSE!
HOW AM I SUPPOSED TO FEED MY KIDS NOW?
OH, GOSH... I'M SO SORRY, SIR. I DIDN'T--
EX-CUUSE ME?!
I KNOW YOU DID NOT JUST CALL ME SIR!
MA'AM? I MEANT MA'AM!
I'LL GET--
SORRY IF I HAVE TO WEAR MY HUSBAND'S CLOTHES NOW THAT I'VE BEEN TURNED INTO A FREAKING ALLIGATOR!
YOU, OF ALL PEOPLE, SHOULD BE A LITTLE MORE--
I'M SORRY...
I'LL GET THE...
SORRY.

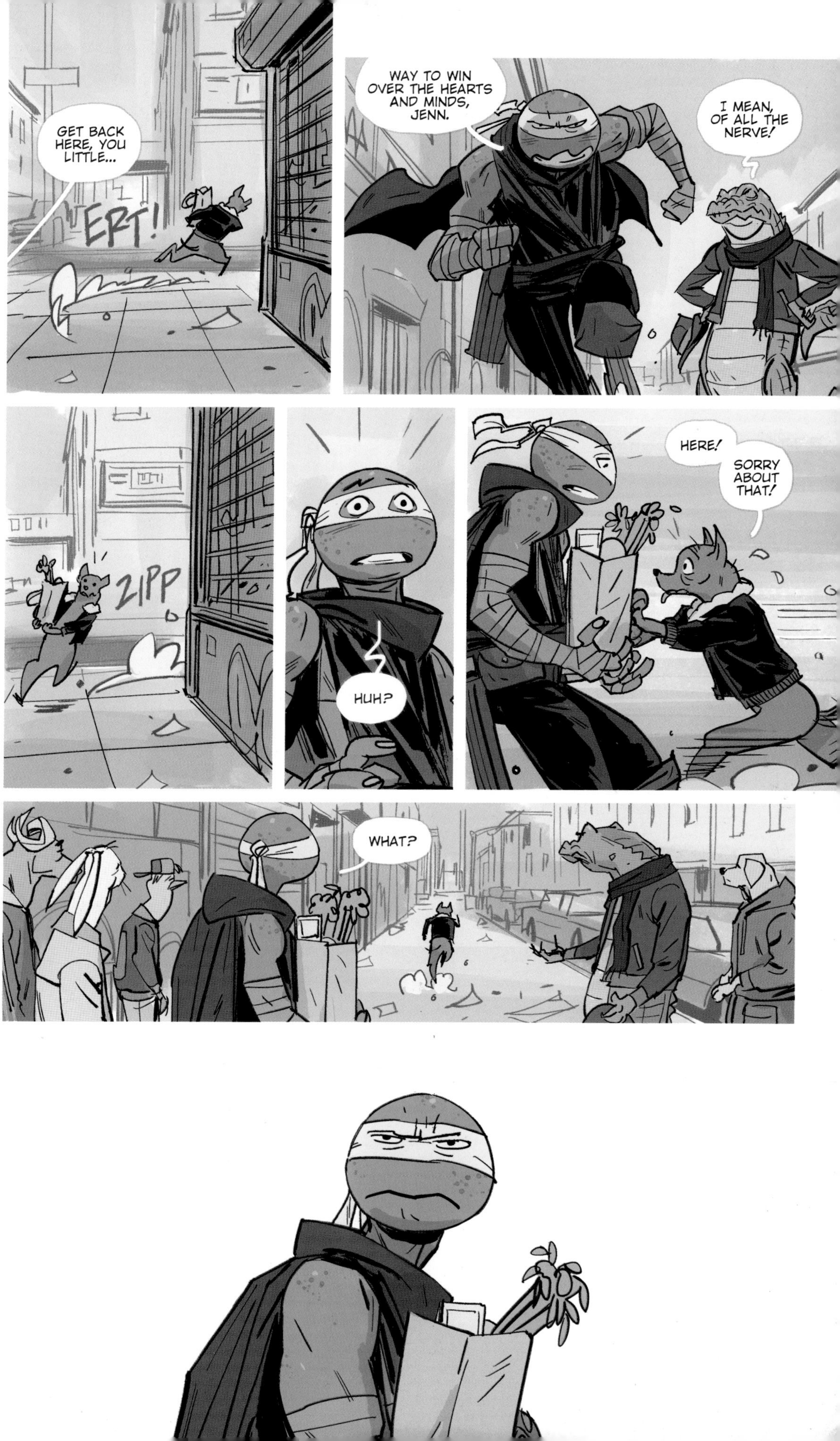
GET BACK HERE, YOU LITTLE...
ERT!
WAY TO WIN OVER THE HEARTS AND MINDS, JENN.
I MEAN, OF ALL THE NERVE!
ZIPP
HUH?
HERE!
SORRY ABOUT THAT!
WHAT?

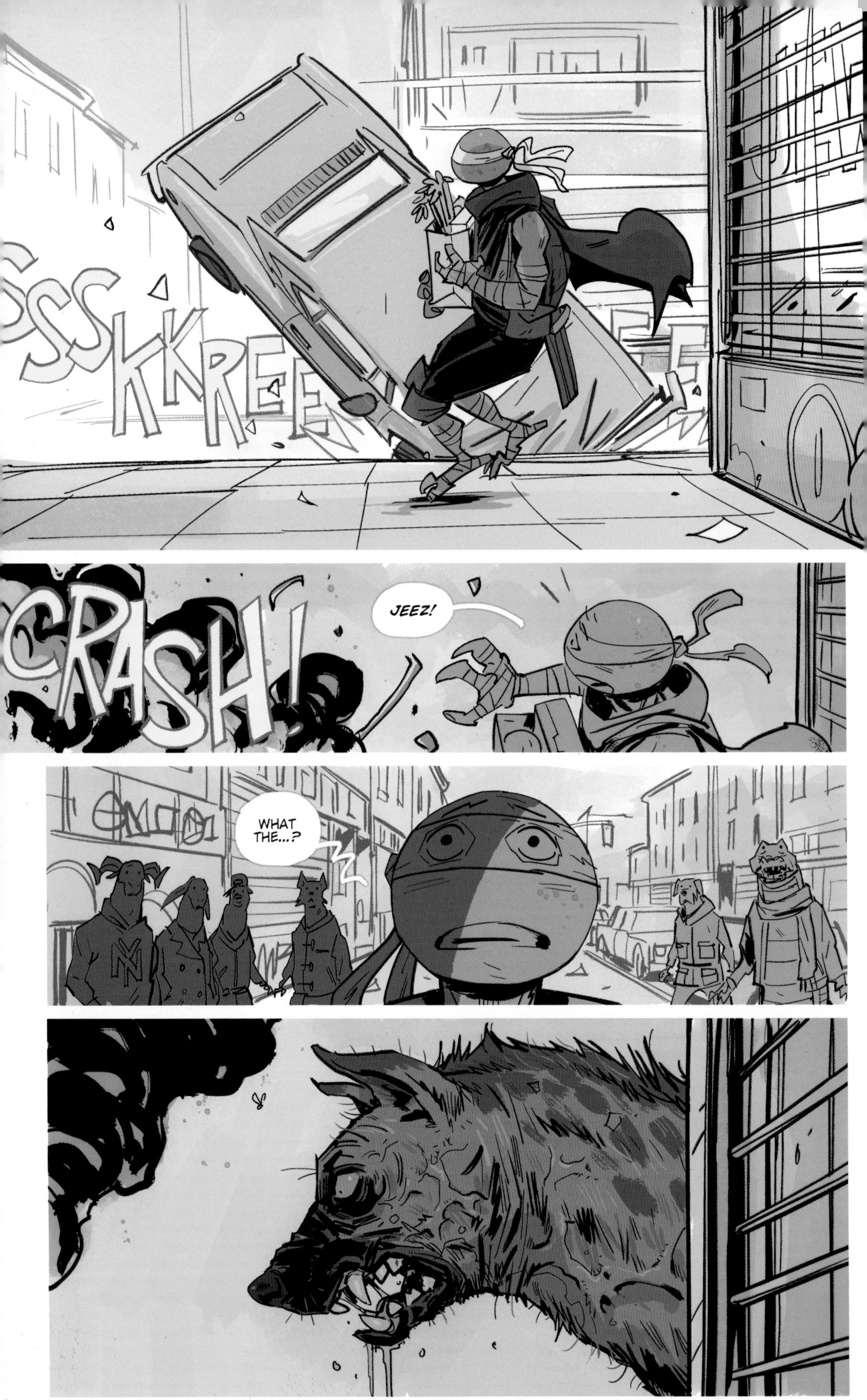
SSKKREE
CRASH!
JEEZ!
WHAT THE...?

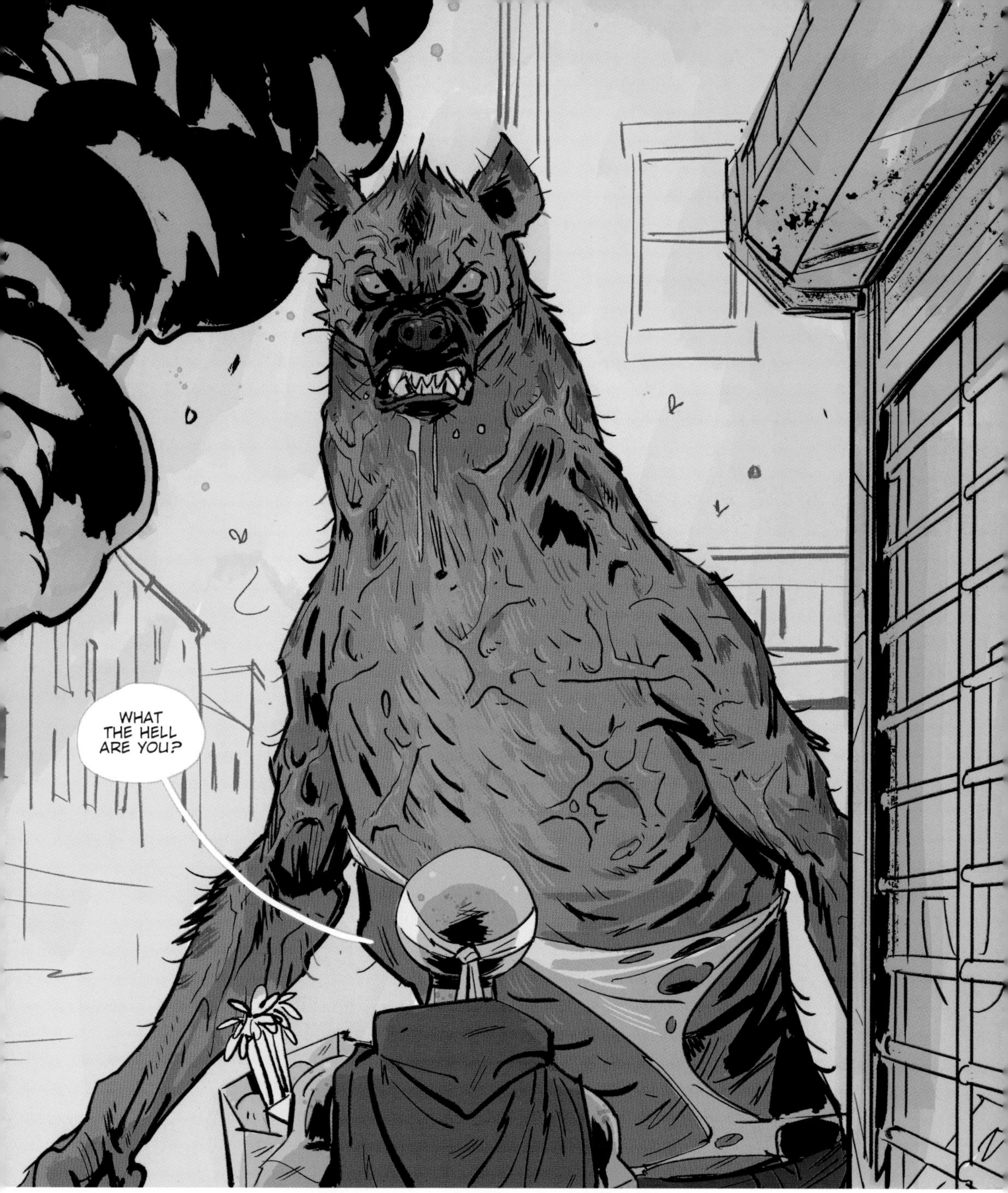
WHAT THE HELL ARE YOU?

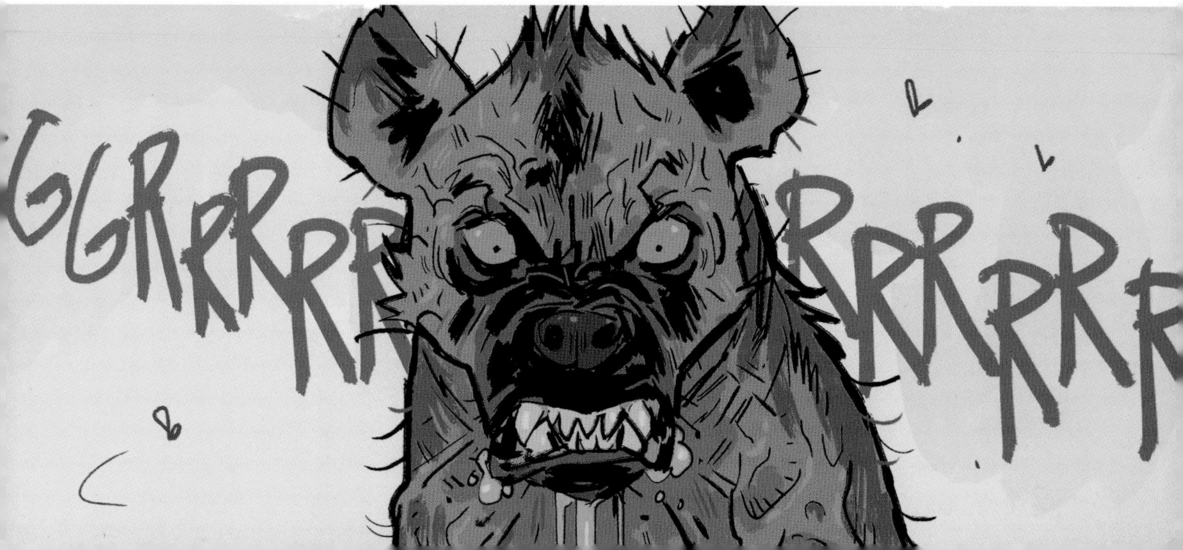
GGRRRRRRRRRRR

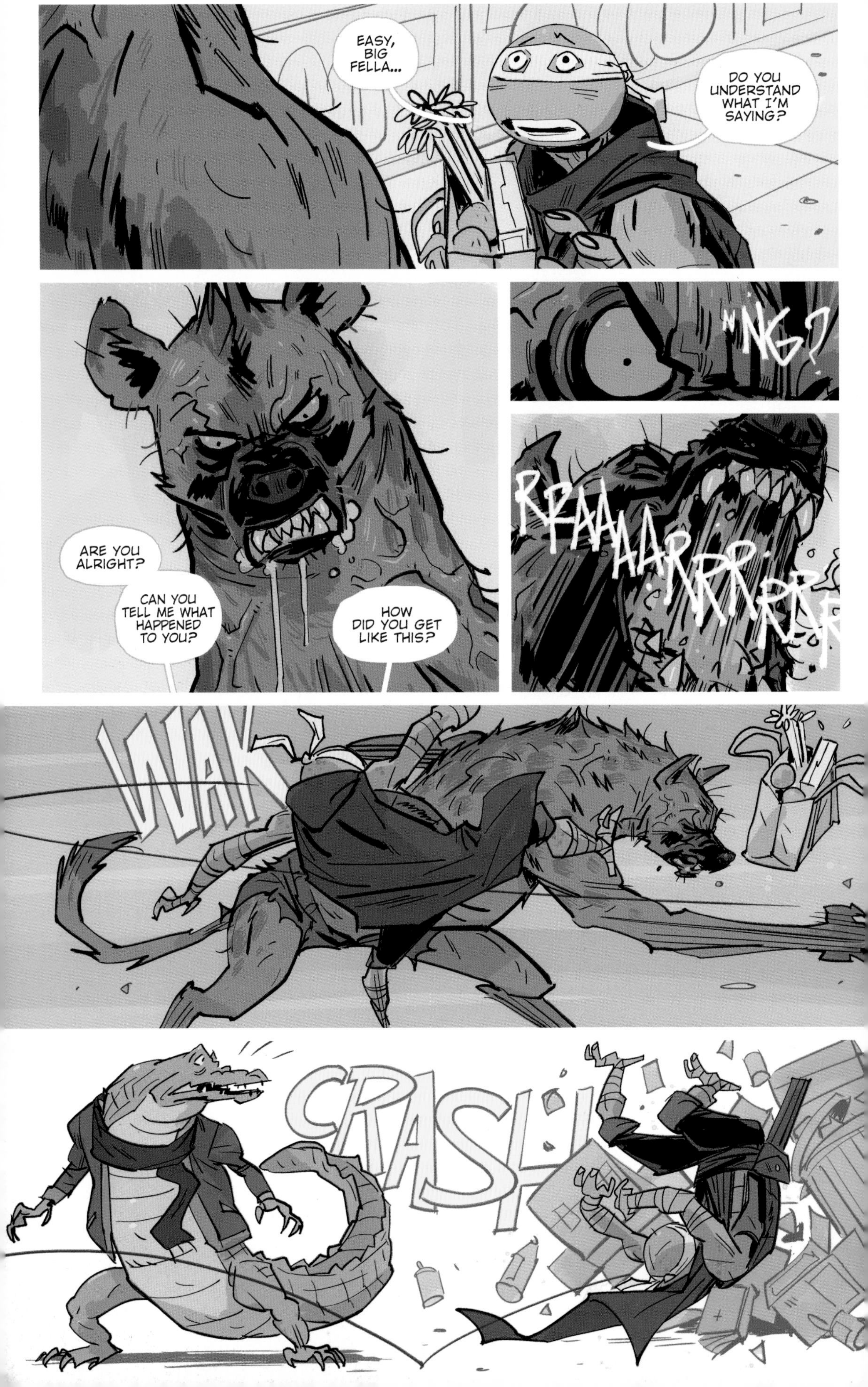

EASY, BIG FELLA...
DO YOU UNDERSTAND WHAT I'M SAYING?
ARE YOU ALRIGHT?
CAN YOU TELL ME WHAT HAPPENED TO YOU?
HOW DID YOU GET LIKE THIS?
"NG?
RRAAAARRRRRR
WAK
CRASH

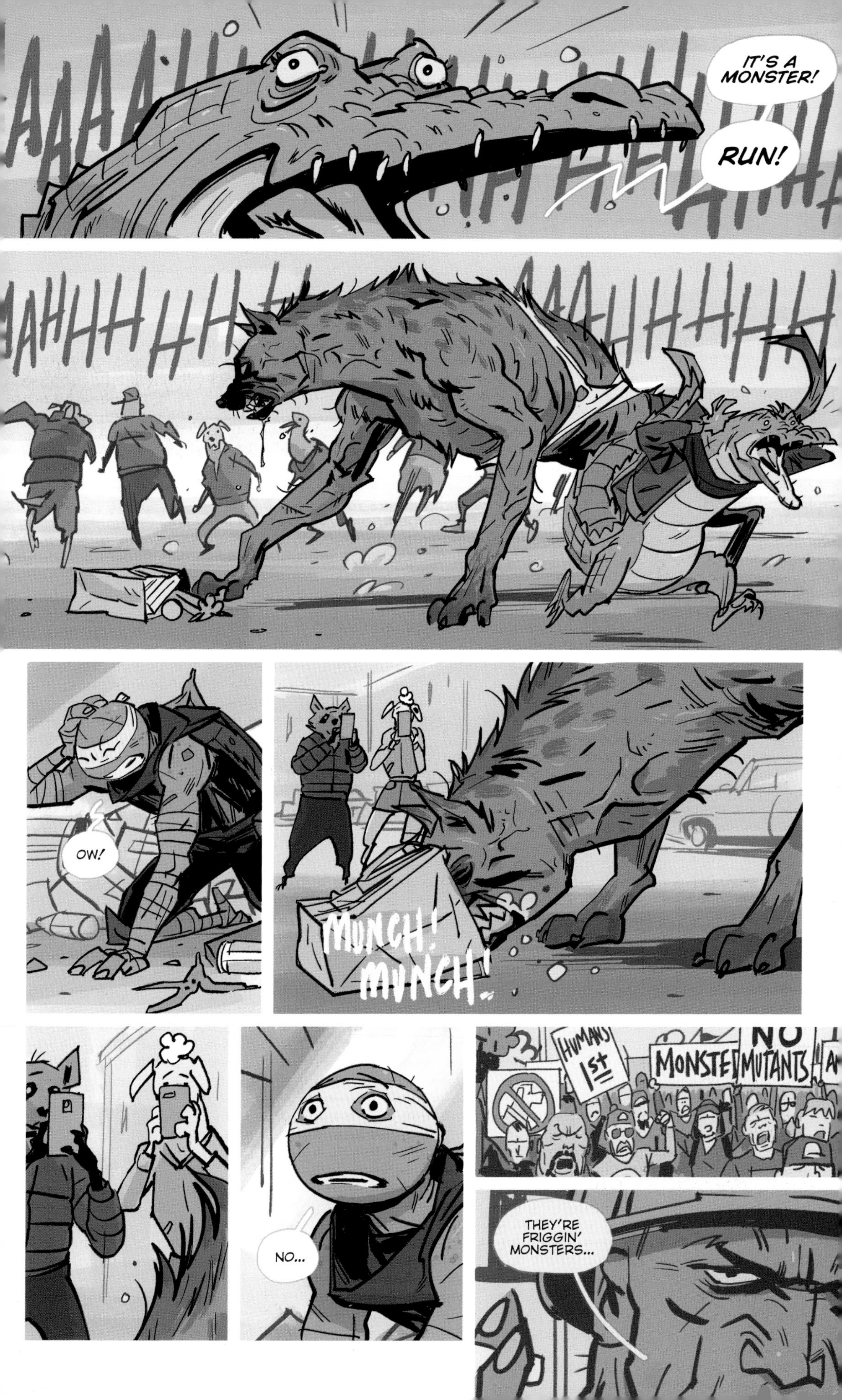
AAAAHHHHHHHHHHHH
IT'S A MONSTER!
RUN!
AHHHHHHH AAAHHHHHHHH
OW!
MUNCH! MUNCH!
HUMANS 1st
MONSTE
NO MUTANTS
NO...
THEY'RE FRIGGIN' MONSTERS...

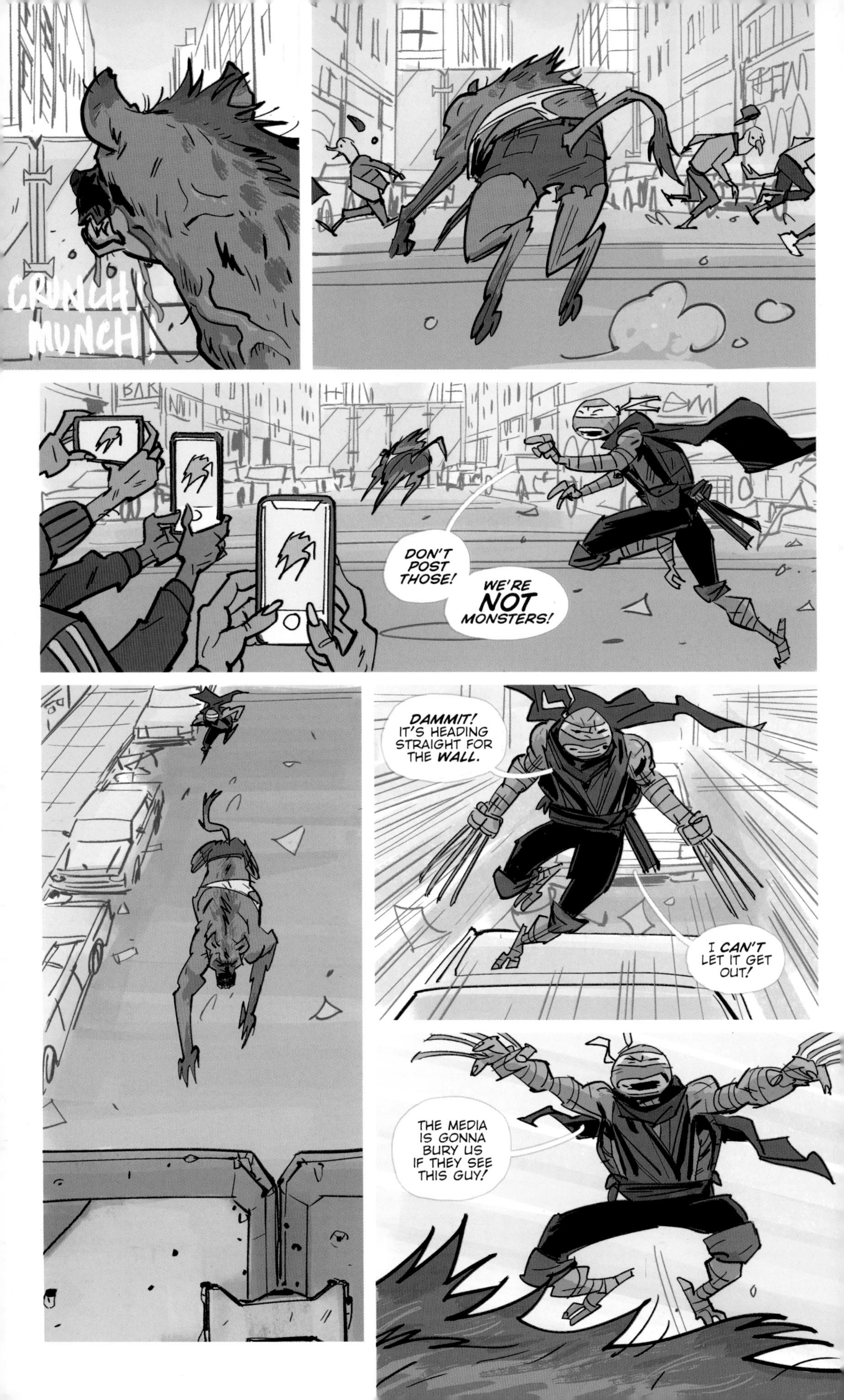
CRUNCH! MUNCH!
DON'T POST THOSE!
WE'RE NOT MONSTERS!
DAMMIT! IT'S HEADING STRAIGHT FOR THE WALL.
I CAN'T LET IT GET OUT!
THE MEDIA IS GONNA BURY US IF THEY SEE THIS GUY!

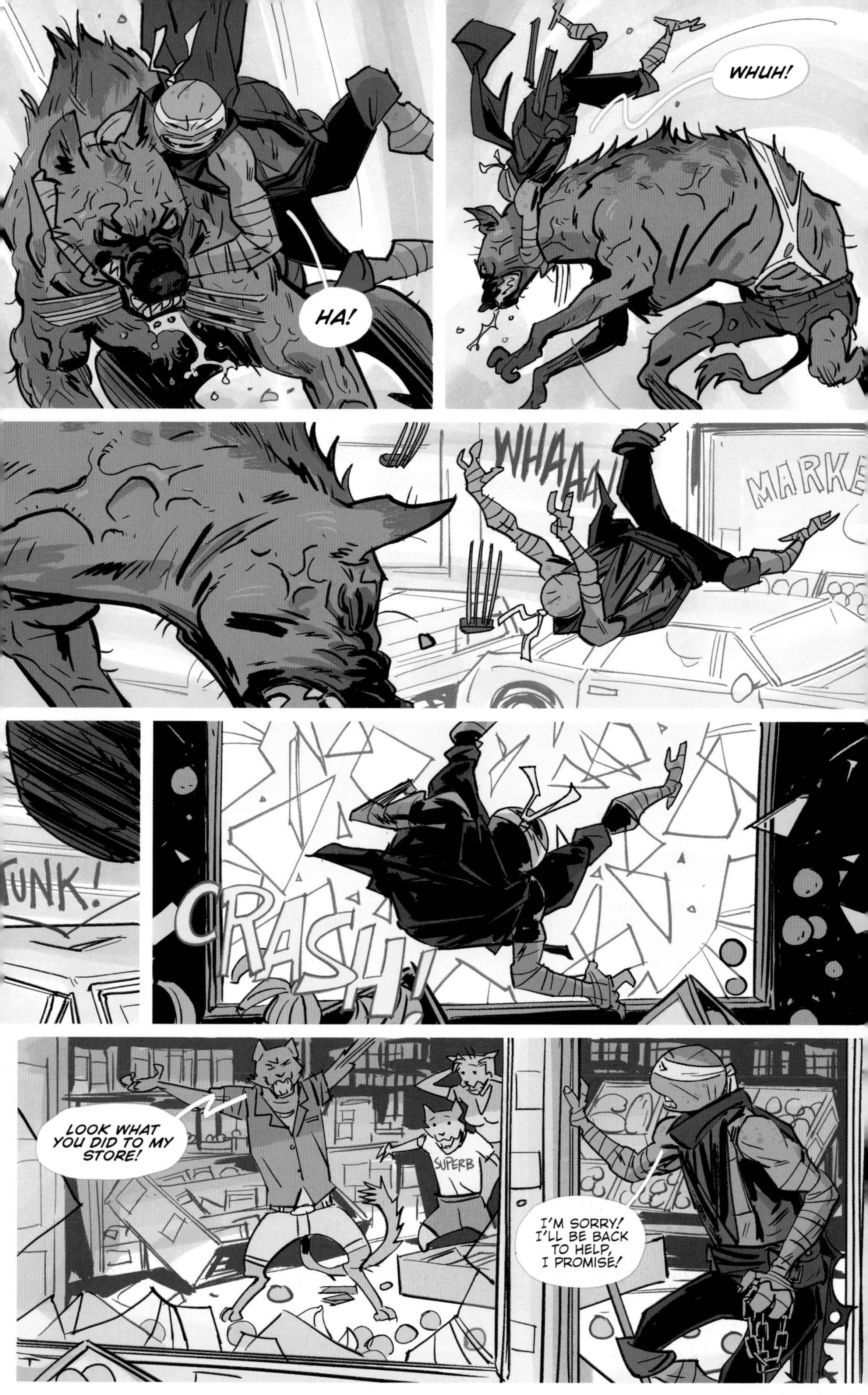
HA!
WHUH!
WHAAA
MARKE
TUNK!
CRASH!
LOOK WHAT YOU DID TO MY STORE!
SUPERB
I'M SORRY! I'LL BE BACK TO HELP, I PROMISE!

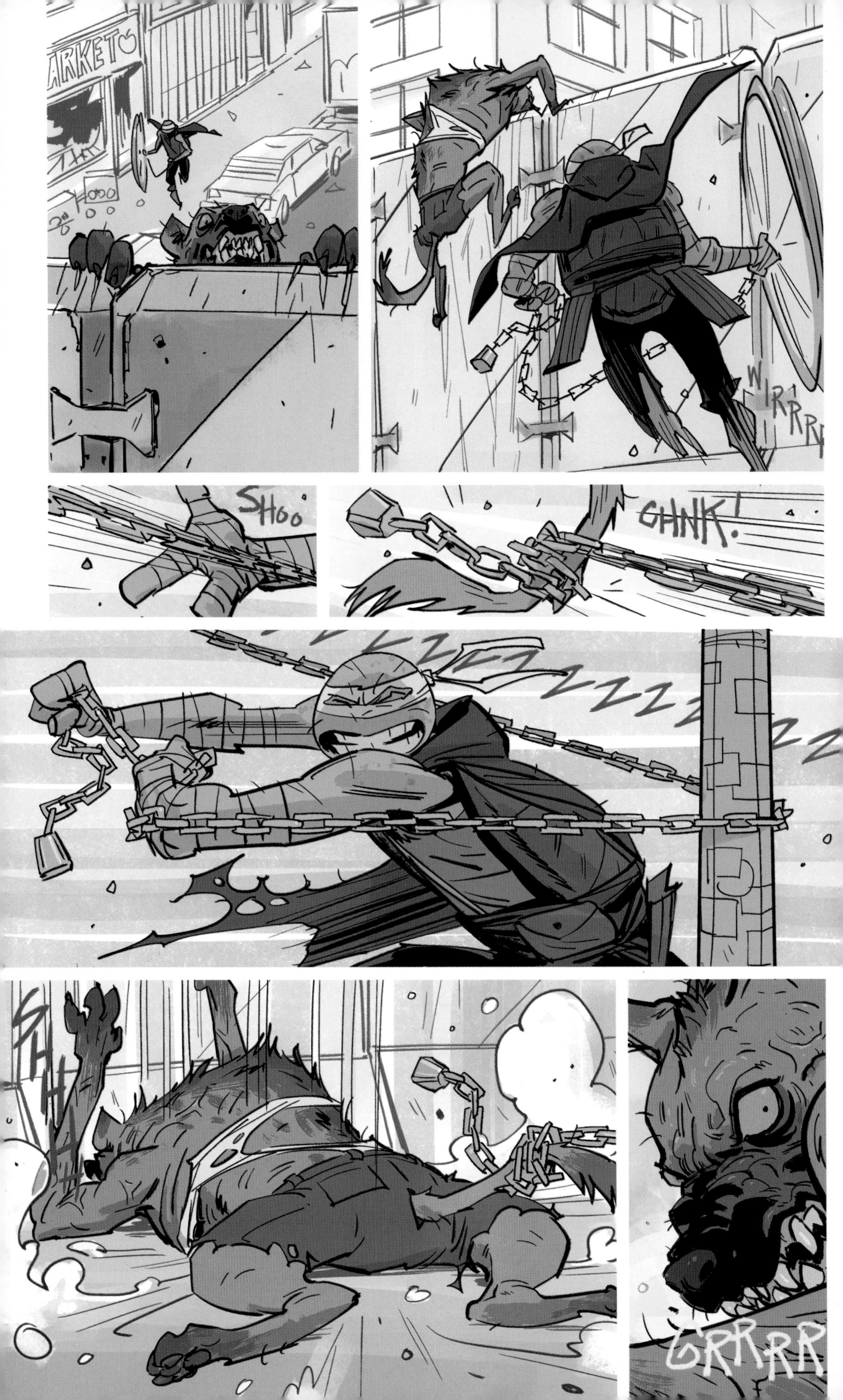
ARKET
WIRRRR
SHoo
CHNK!
ZZZZZZZ
SHHH
GRRRR

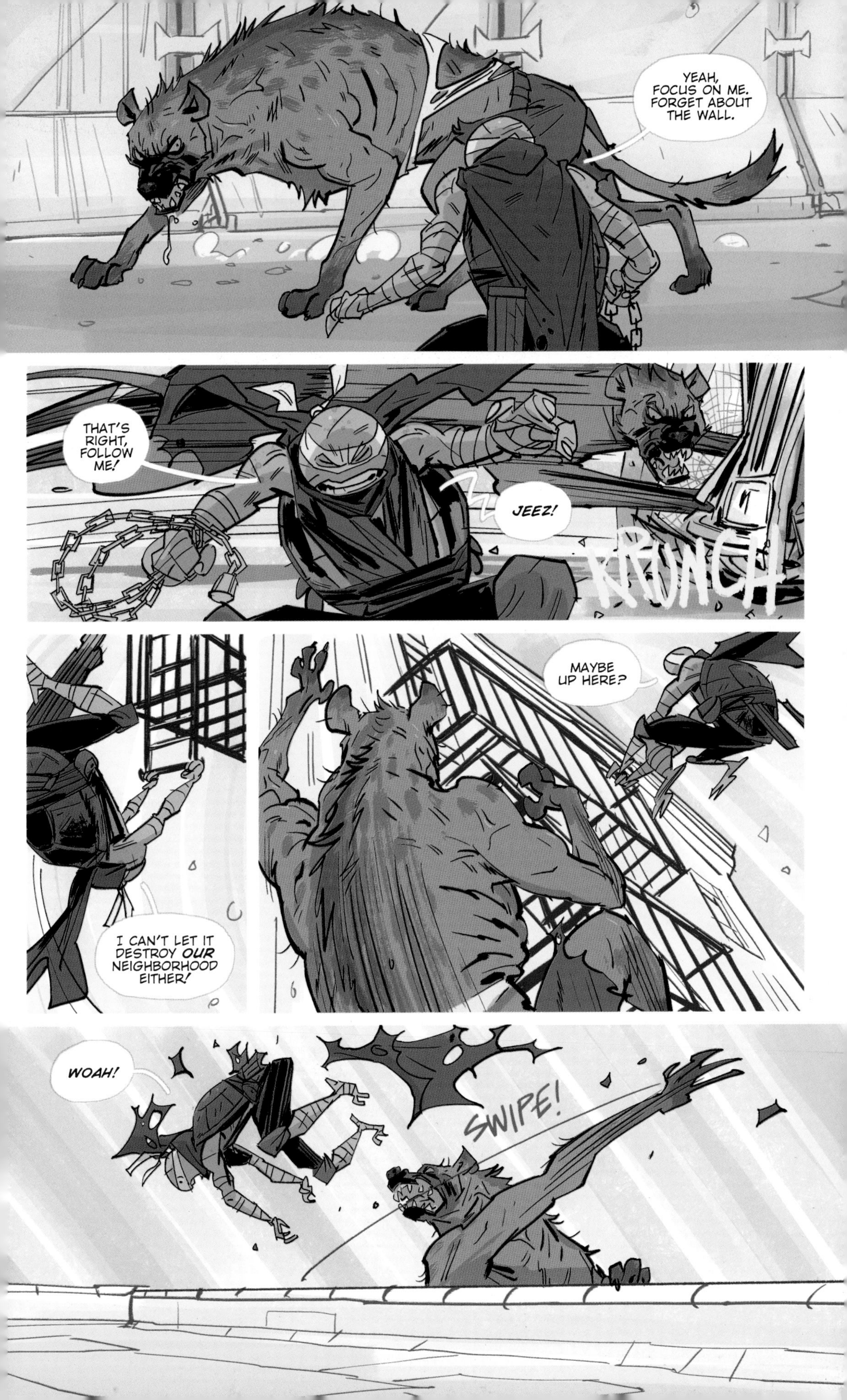
YEAH, FOCUS ON ME. FORGET ABOUT THE WALL.
THAT'S RIGHT, FOLLOW ME!
JEEZ!
KRUNCH
I CAN'T LET IT DESTROY OUR NEIGHBORHOOD EITHER!
MAYBE UP HERE?
WOAH!
SWIPE!

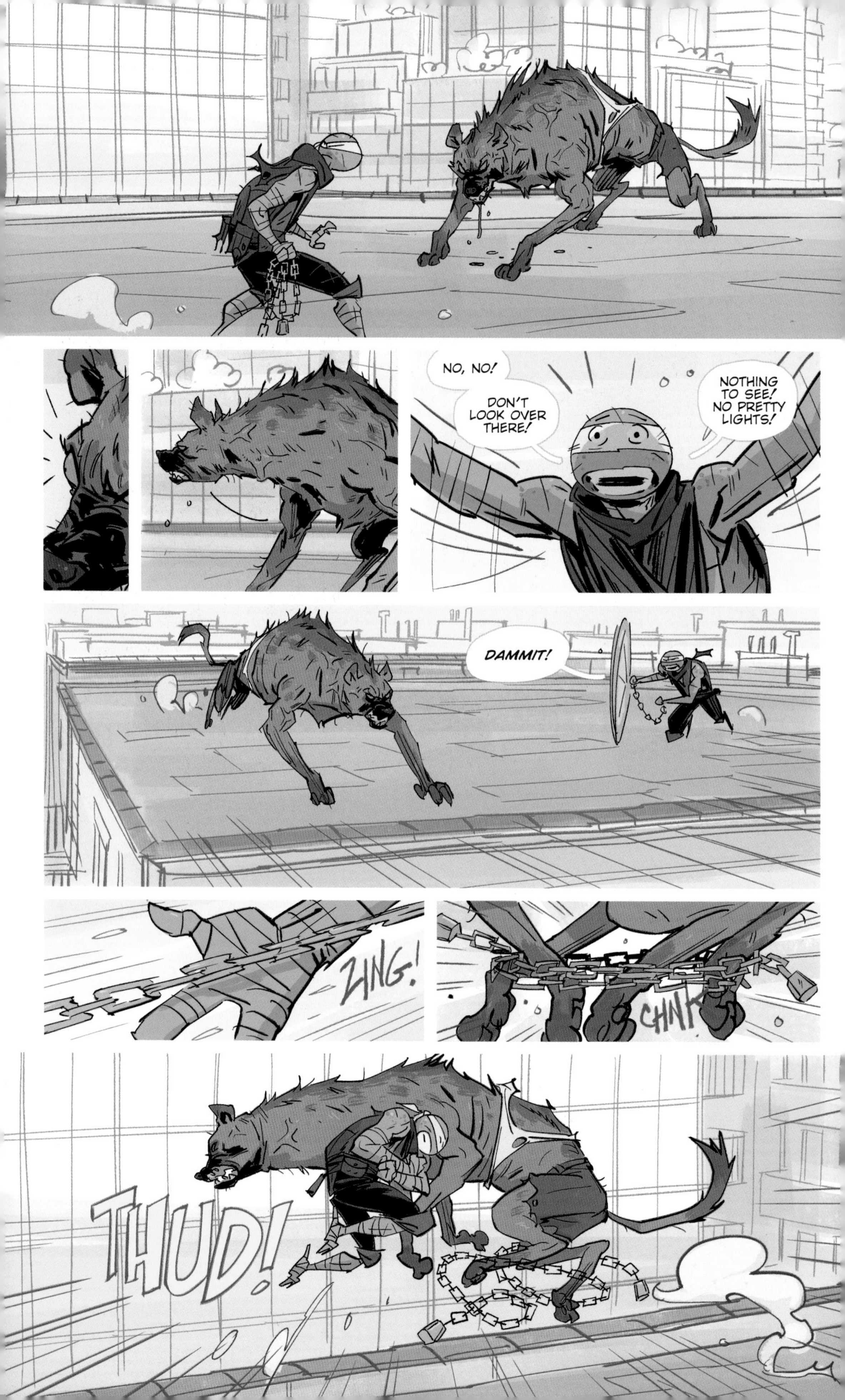

NO, NO!
DON'T LOOK OVER THERE!
NOTHING TO SEE! NO PRETTY LIGHTS!
DAMMIT!
ZING!
CHNK
THUD!

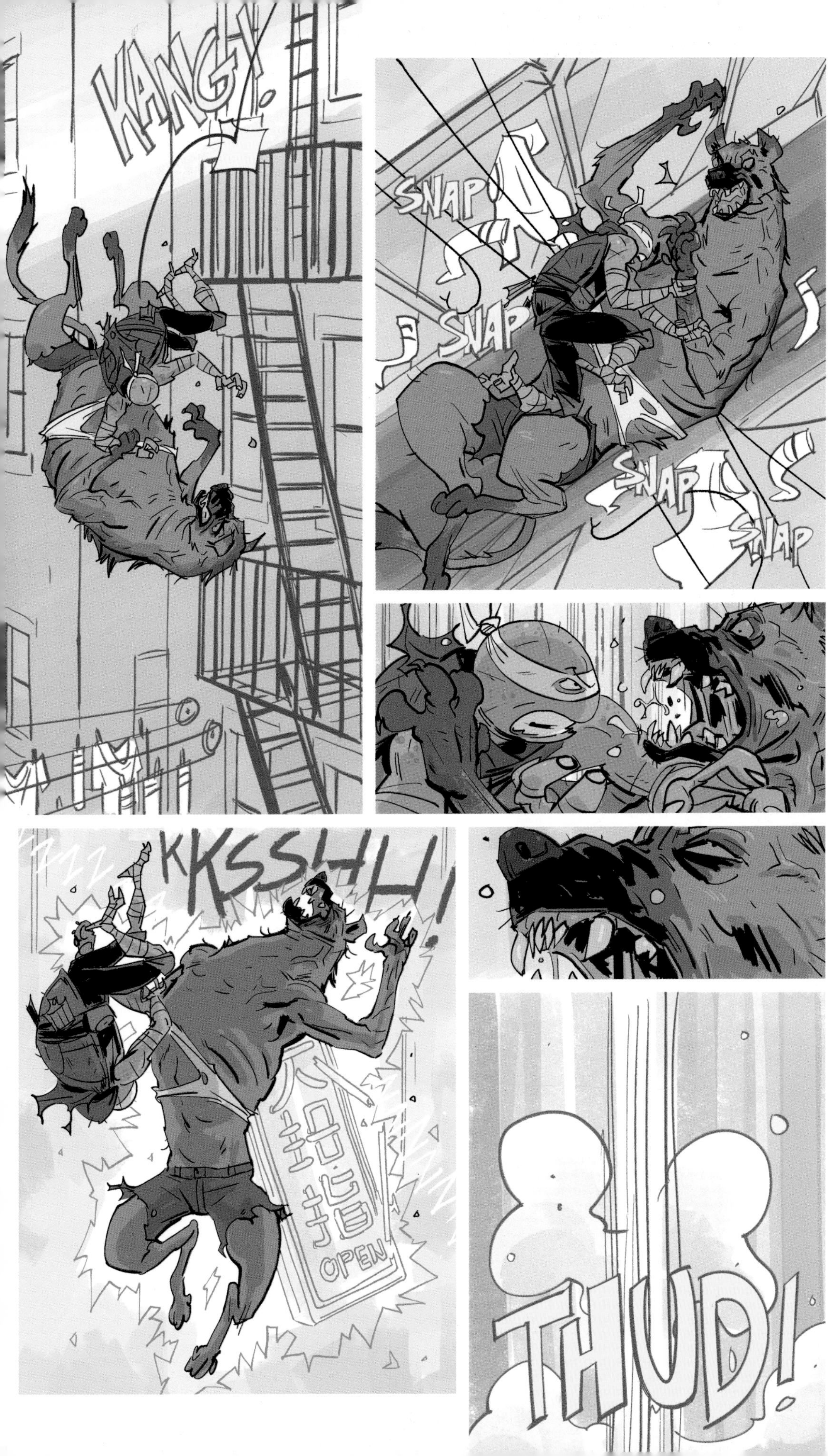

KANG!
SNAP
SNAP
SNAP
SNAP
KKSSHH!
OPEN
THUD!

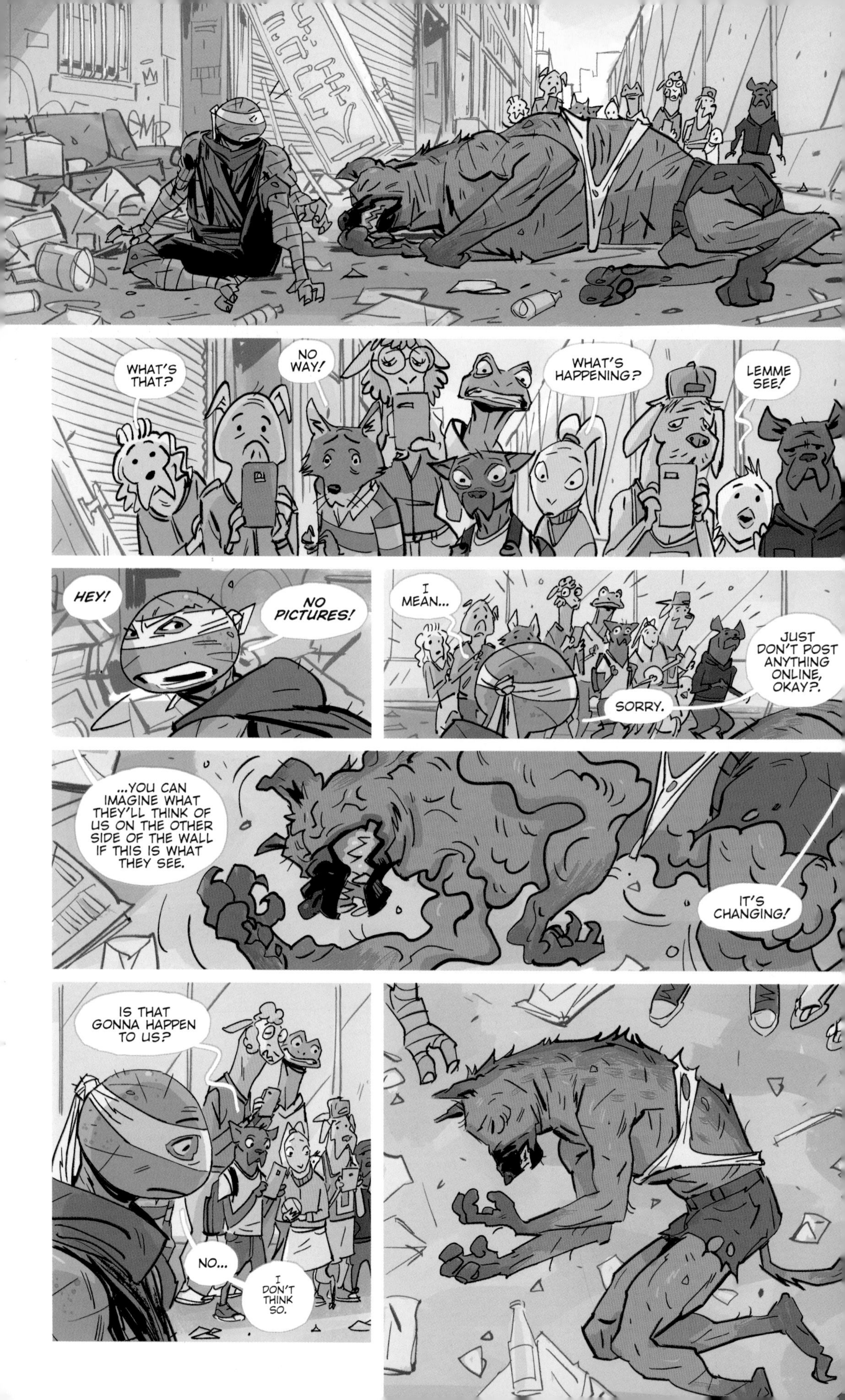
WHAT'S THAT?
NO WAY!
WHAT'S HAPPENING?
LEMME SEE!
HEY!
NO PICTURES!
I MEAN...
JUST DON'T POST ANYTHING ONLINE, OKAY?.
SORRY.
...YOU CAN IMAGINE WHAT THEY'LL THINK OF US ON THE OTHER SIDE OF THE WALL IF THIS IS WHAT THEY SEE.
IT'S CHANGING!
IS THAT GONNA HAPPEN TO US?
NO...
I DON'T THINK SO.

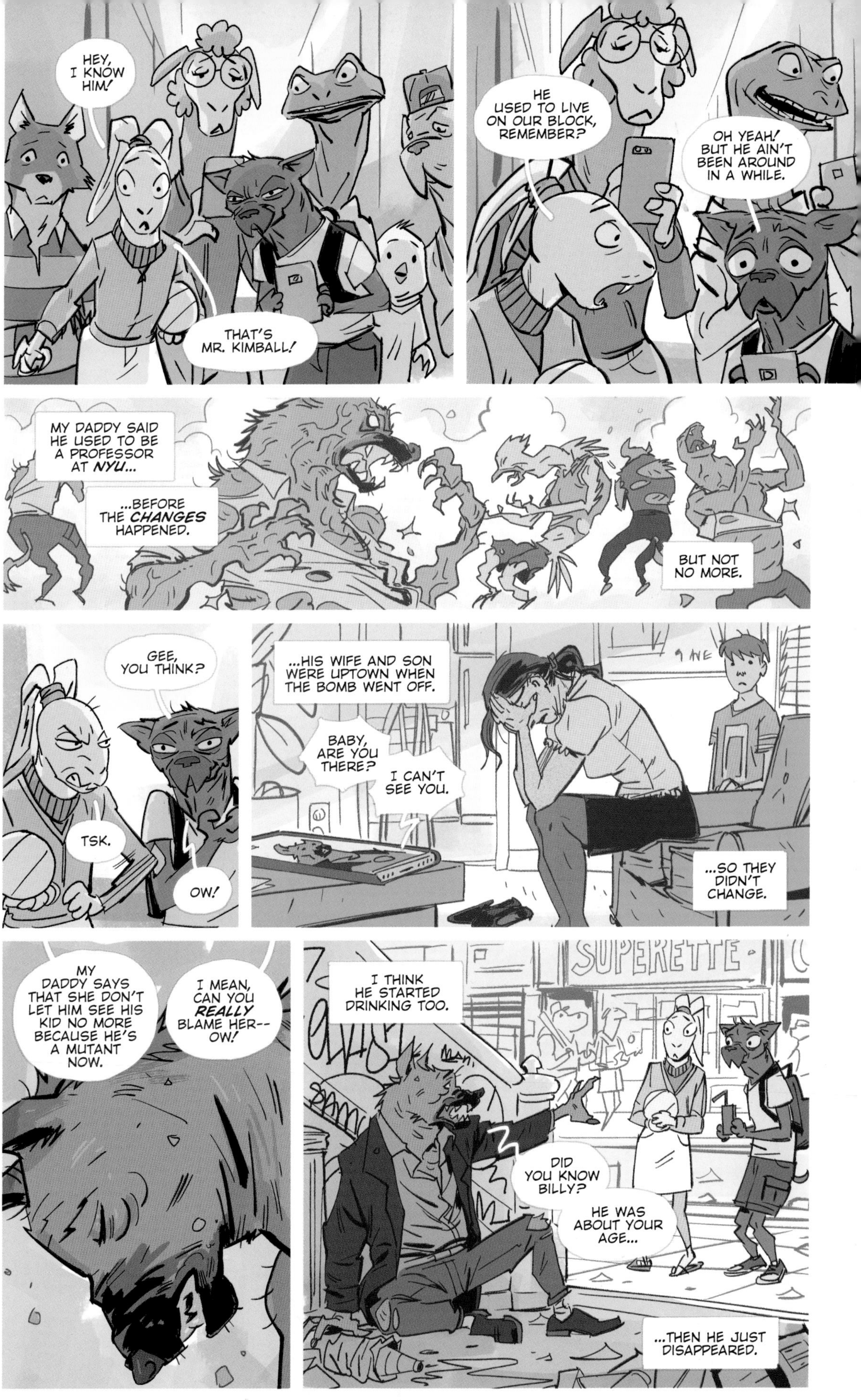
HEY, I KNOW HIM!
THAT'S MR. KIMBALL!
HE USED TO LIVE ON OUR BLOCK, REMEMBER?
OH YEAH! BUT HE AIN'T BEEN AROUND IN A WHILE.
MY DADDY SAID HE USED TO BE A PROFESSOR AT NYU...
...BEFORE THE CHANGES HAPPENED.
BUT NOT NO MORE.
GEE, YOU THINK?
TSK.
OW!
...HIS WIFE AND SON WERE UPTOWN WHEN THE BOMB WENT OFF.
BABY, ARE YOU THERE?
I CAN'T SEE YOU.
...SO THEY DIDN'T CHANGE.
MY DADDY SAYS THAT SHE DON'T LET HIM SEE HIS KID NO MORE BECAUSE HE'S A MUTANT NOW.
I MEAN, CAN YOU REALLY BLAME HER--OW!
I THINK HE STARTED DRINKING TOO.
SUPERETTE
DID YOU KNOW BILLY?
HE WAS ABOUT YOUR AGE...
...THEN HE JUST DISAPPEARED.

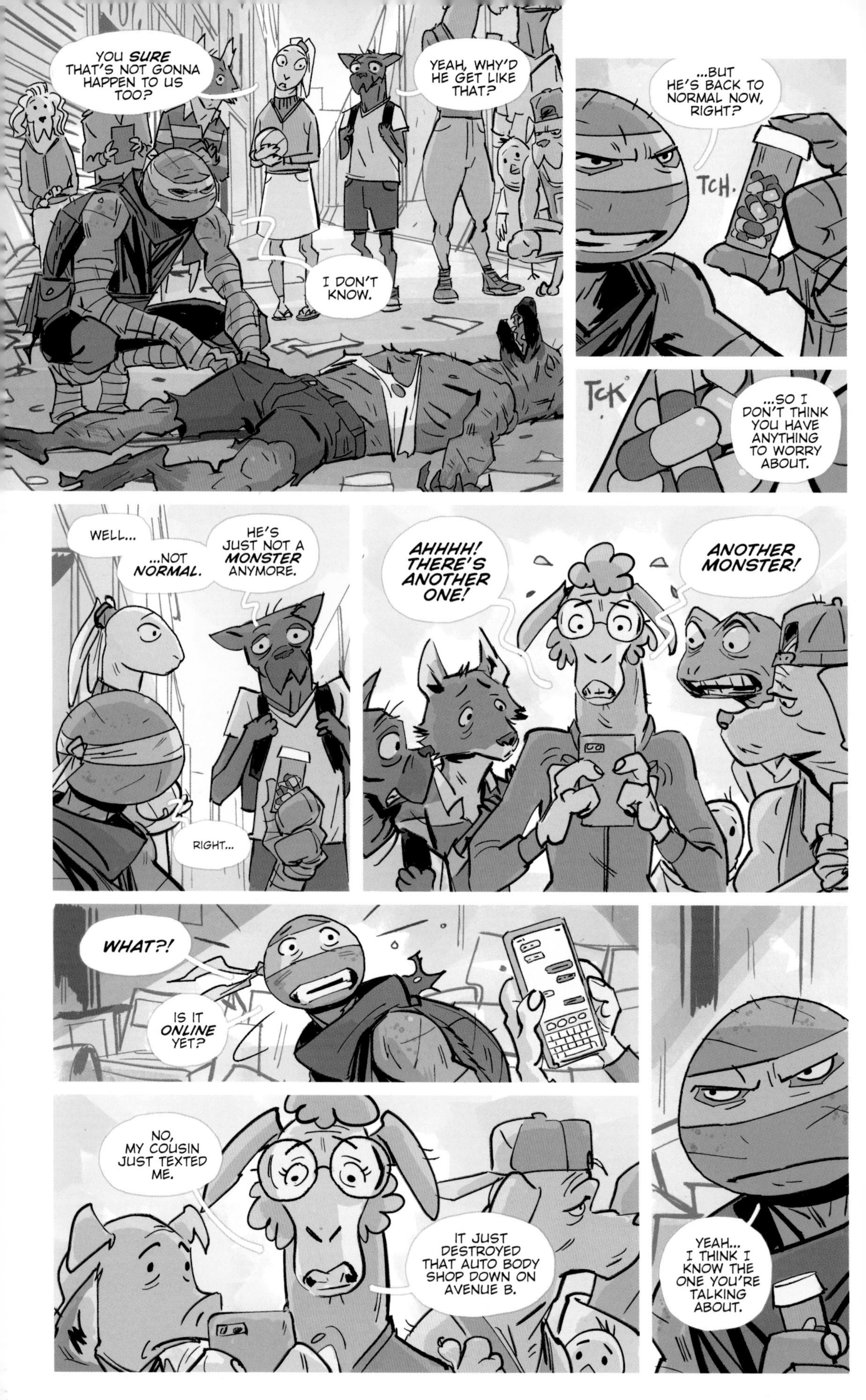
YOU SURE THAT'S NOT GONNA HAPPEN TO US TOO?
YEAH, WHY'D HE GET LIKE THAT?
I DON'T KNOW.
...BUT HE'S BACK TO NORMAL NOW, RIGHT?
TCH.
TCK
...SO I DON'T THINK YOU HAVE ANYTHING TO WORRY ABOUT.
WELL...
...NOT NORMAL.
HE'S JUST NOT A MONSTER ANYMORE.
RIGHT...
AHHHH! THERE'S ANOTHER ONE!
ANOTHER MONSTER!
WHAT?!
IS IT ONLINE YET?
NO, MY COUSIN JUST TEXTED ME.
IT JUST DESTROYED THAT AUTO BODY SHOP DOWN ON AVENUE B.
YEAH... I THINK I KNOW THE ONE YOU'RE TALKING ABOUT.

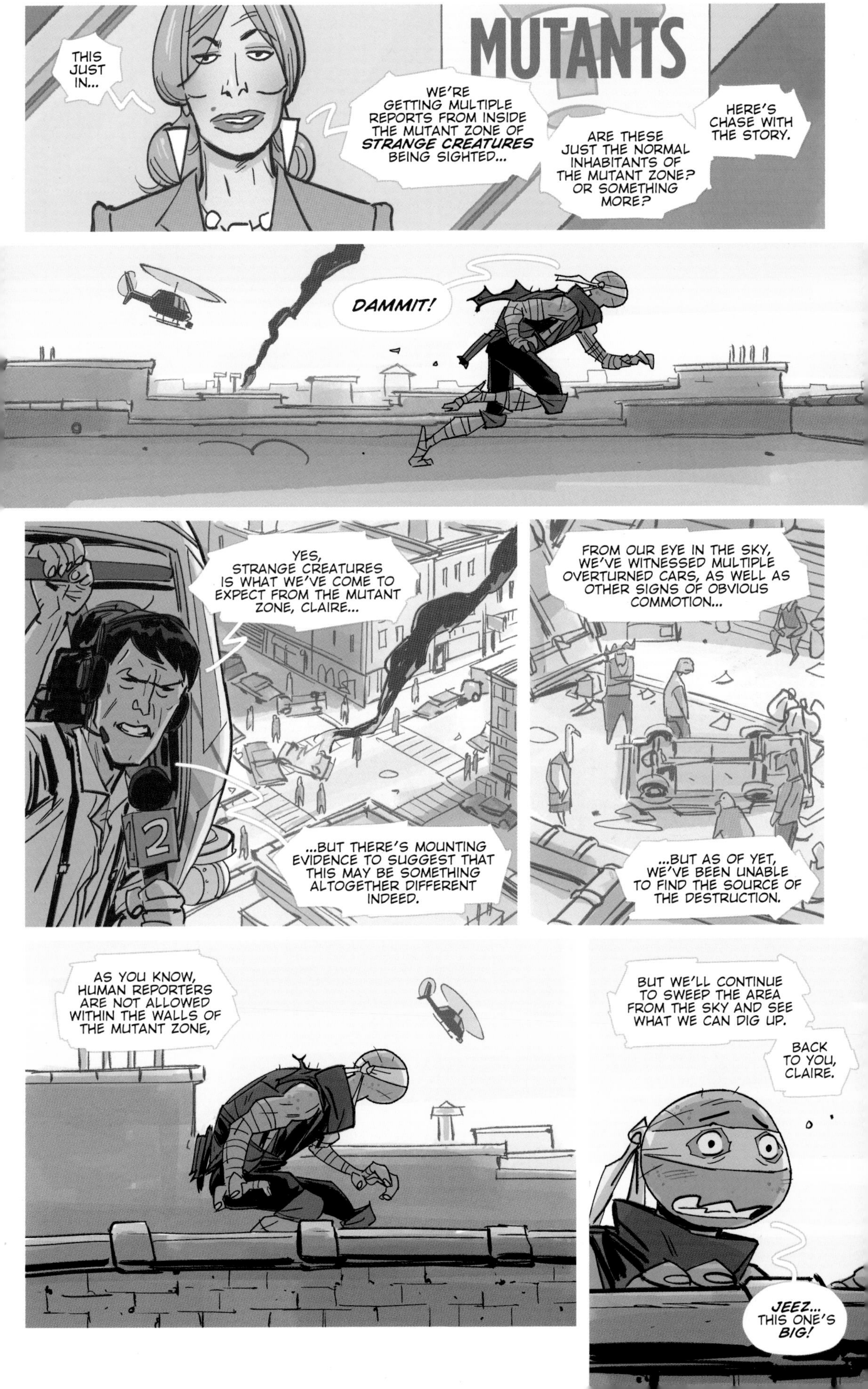
MUTANTS
THIS JUST IN...
WE'RE GETTING MULTIPLE REPORTS FROM INSIDE THE MUTANT ZONE OF STRANGE CREATURES BEING SIGHTED...
ARE THESE JUST THE NORMAL INHABITANTS OF THE MUTANT ZONE? OR SOMETHING MORE?
HERE'S CHASE WITH THE STORY.
DAMMIT!
YES, STRANGE CREATURES IS WHAT WE'VE COME TO EXPECT FROM THE MUTANT ZONE, CLAIRE...
...BUT THERE'S MOUNTING EVIDENCE TO SUGGEST THAT THIS MAY BE SOMETHING ALTOGETHER DIFFERENT INDEED.
2
FROM OUR EYE IN THE SKY, WE'VE WITNESSED MULTIPLE OVERTURNED CARS, AS WELL AS OTHER SIGNS OF OBVIOUS COMMOTION...
...BUT AS OF YET, WE'VE BEEN UNABLE TO FIND THE SOURCE OF THE DESTRUCTION.
AS YOU KNOW, HUMAN REPORTERS ARE NOT ALLOWED WITHIN THE WALLS OF THE MUTANT ZONE,
BUT WE'LL CONTINUE TO SWEEP THE AREA FROM THE SKY AND SEE WHAT WE CAN DIG UP.
BACK TO YOU, CLAIRE.
JEEZ... THIS ONE'S BIG!

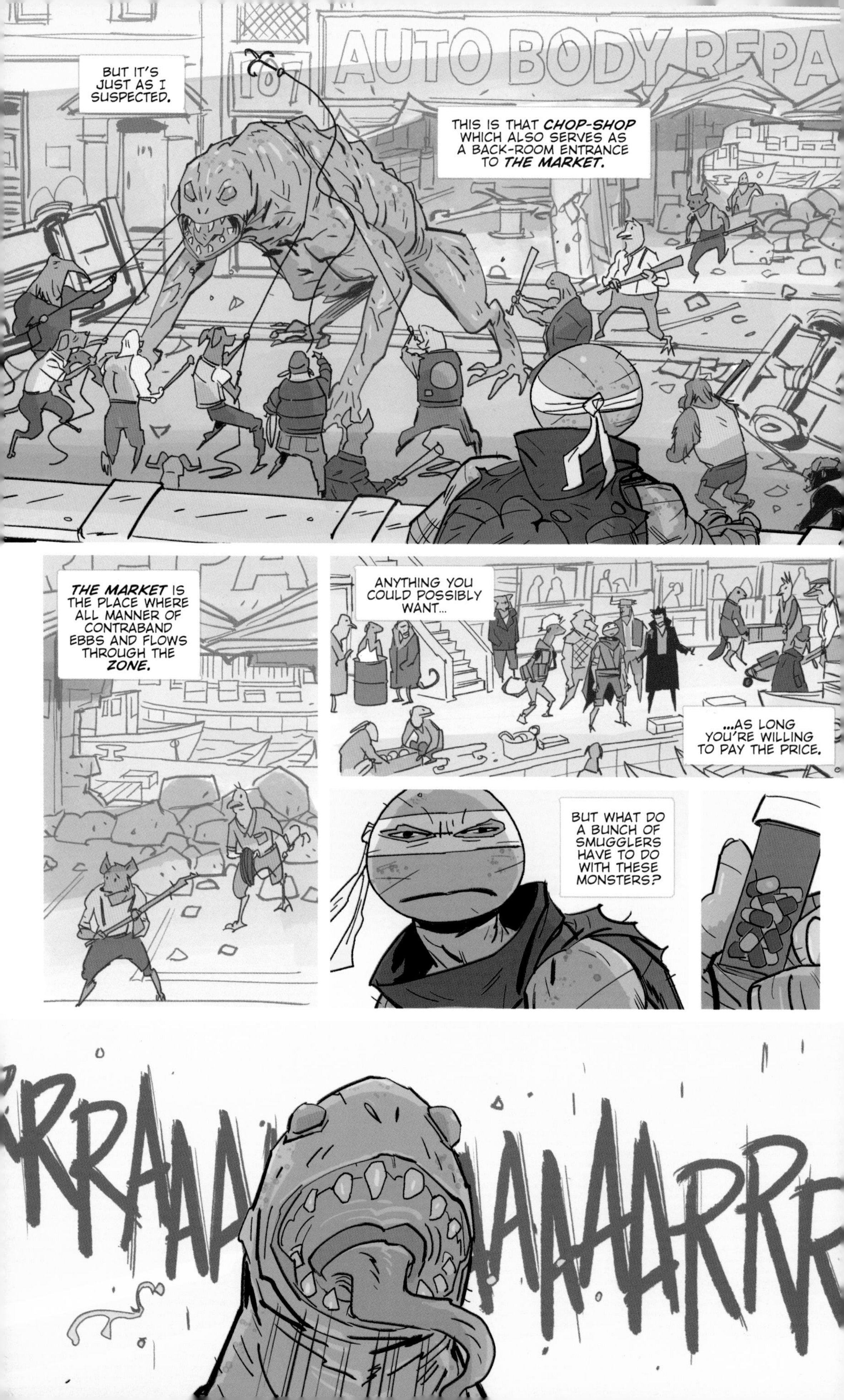

AUTO BODY REPA
107
BUT IT'S JUST AS I SUSPECTED.
THIS IS THAT *CHOP-SHOP* WHICH ALSO SERVES AS A BACK-ROOM ENTRANCE TO *THE MARKET.*
*THE MARKET* IS THE PLACE WHERE ALL MANNER OF CONTRABAND EBBS AND FLOWS THROUGH THE *ZONE.*
ANYTHING YOU COULD POSSIBLY WANT...
...AS LONG YOU'RE WILLING TO PAY THE PRICE.
BUT WHAT DO A BUNCH OF SMUGGLERS HAVE TO DO WITH THESE MONSTERS?
RRAAAAAAAARRR

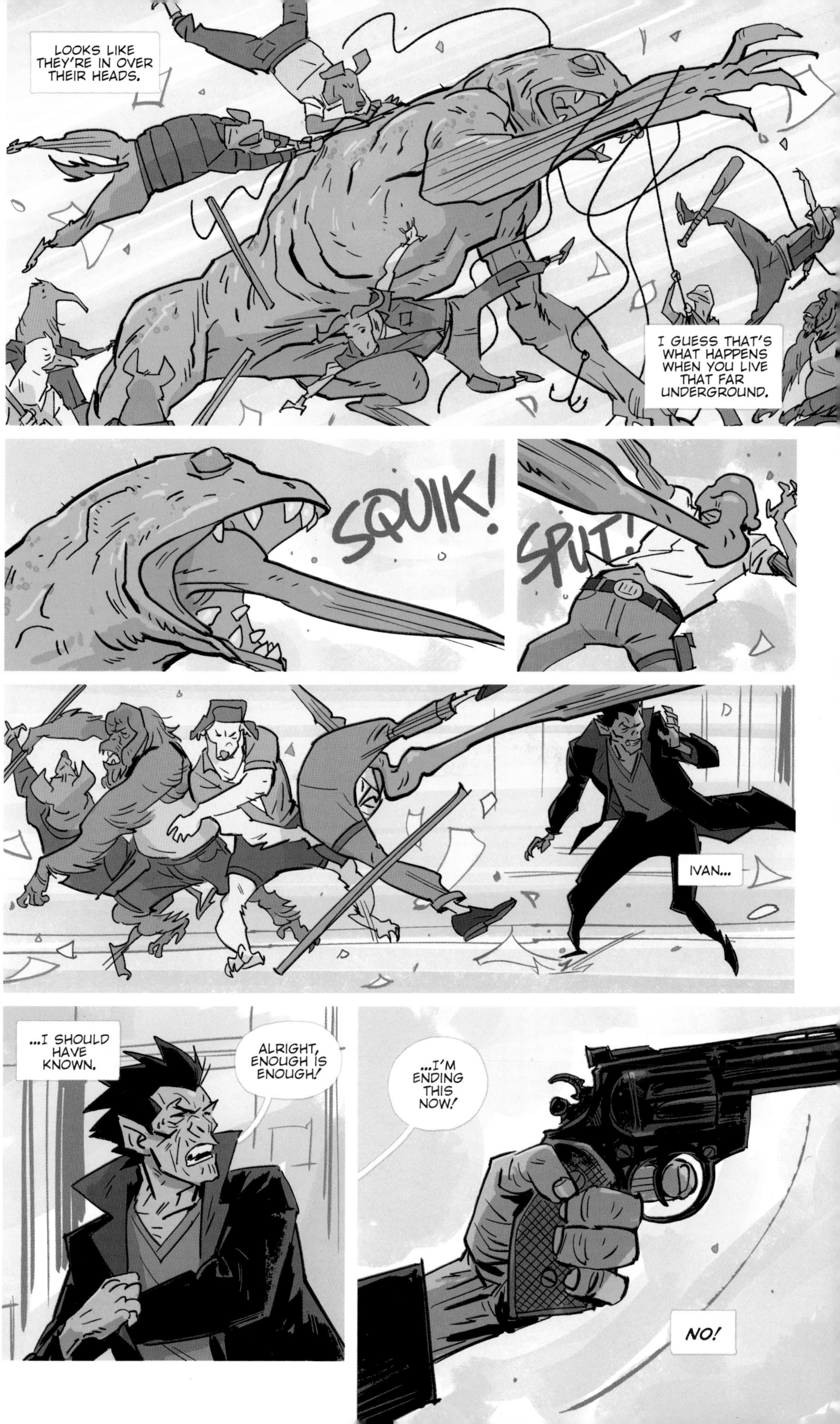
LOOKS LIKE THEY'RE IN OVER THEIR HEADS.
I GUESS THAT'S WHAT HAPPENS WHEN YOU LIVE THAT FAR UNDERGROUND.
SQUIK!
SPUT!
IVAN...
...I SHOULD HAVE KNOWN.
ALRIGHT, ENOUGH IS ENOUGH!
...I'M ENDING THIS NOW!
NO!

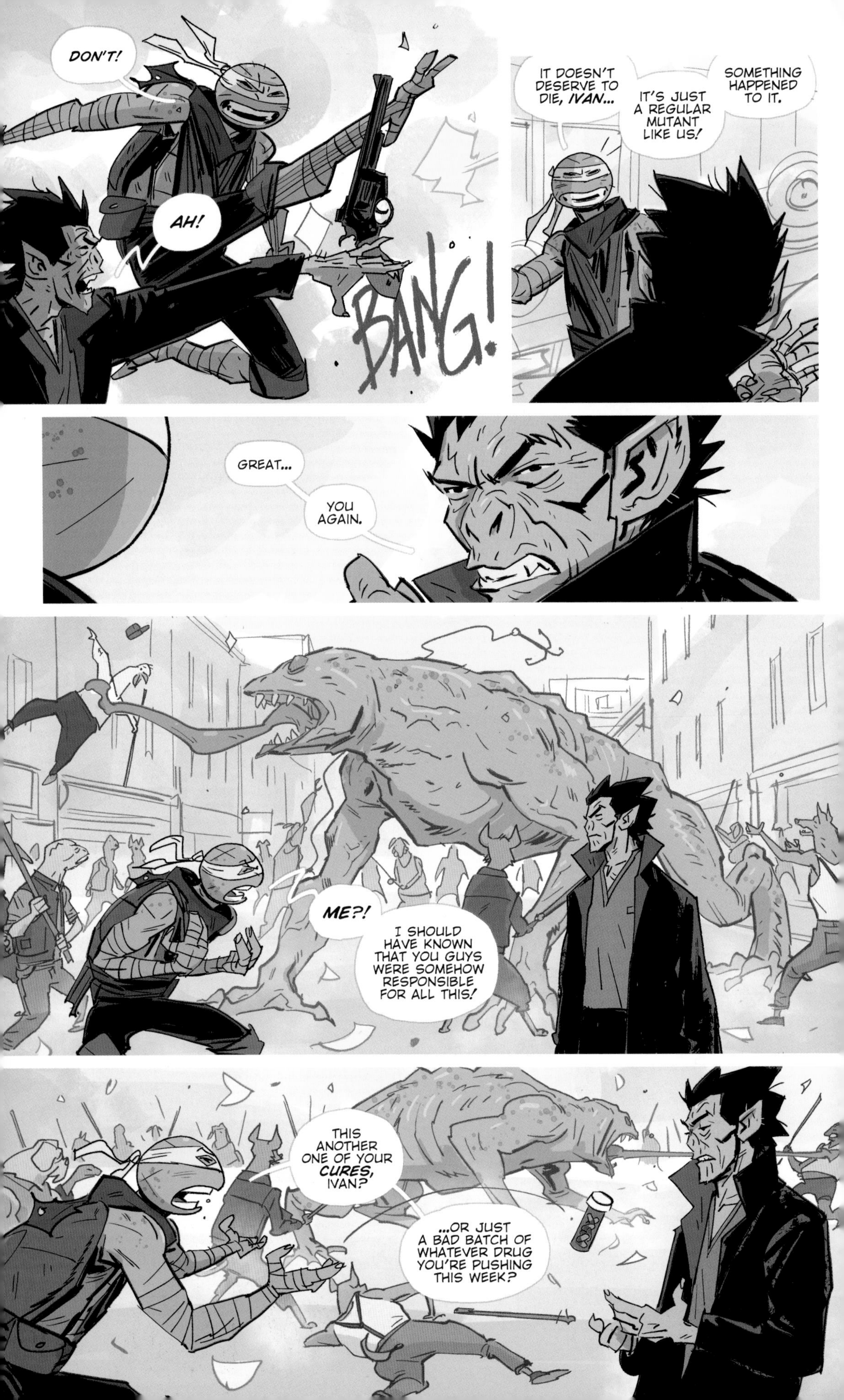
DON'T!
AH!
BANG!
IT DOESN'T DESERVE TO DIE, IVAN...
IT'S JUST A REGULAR MUTANT LIKE US!
SOMETHING HAPPENED TO IT.
GREAT...
YOU AGAIN.
ME?!
I SHOULD HAVE KNOWN THAT YOU GUYS WERE SOMEHOW RESPONSIBLE FOR ALL THIS!
THIS ANOTHER ONE OF YOUR CURES, IVAN?
...OR JUST A BAD BATCH OF WHATEVER DRUG YOU'RE PUSHING THIS WEEK?

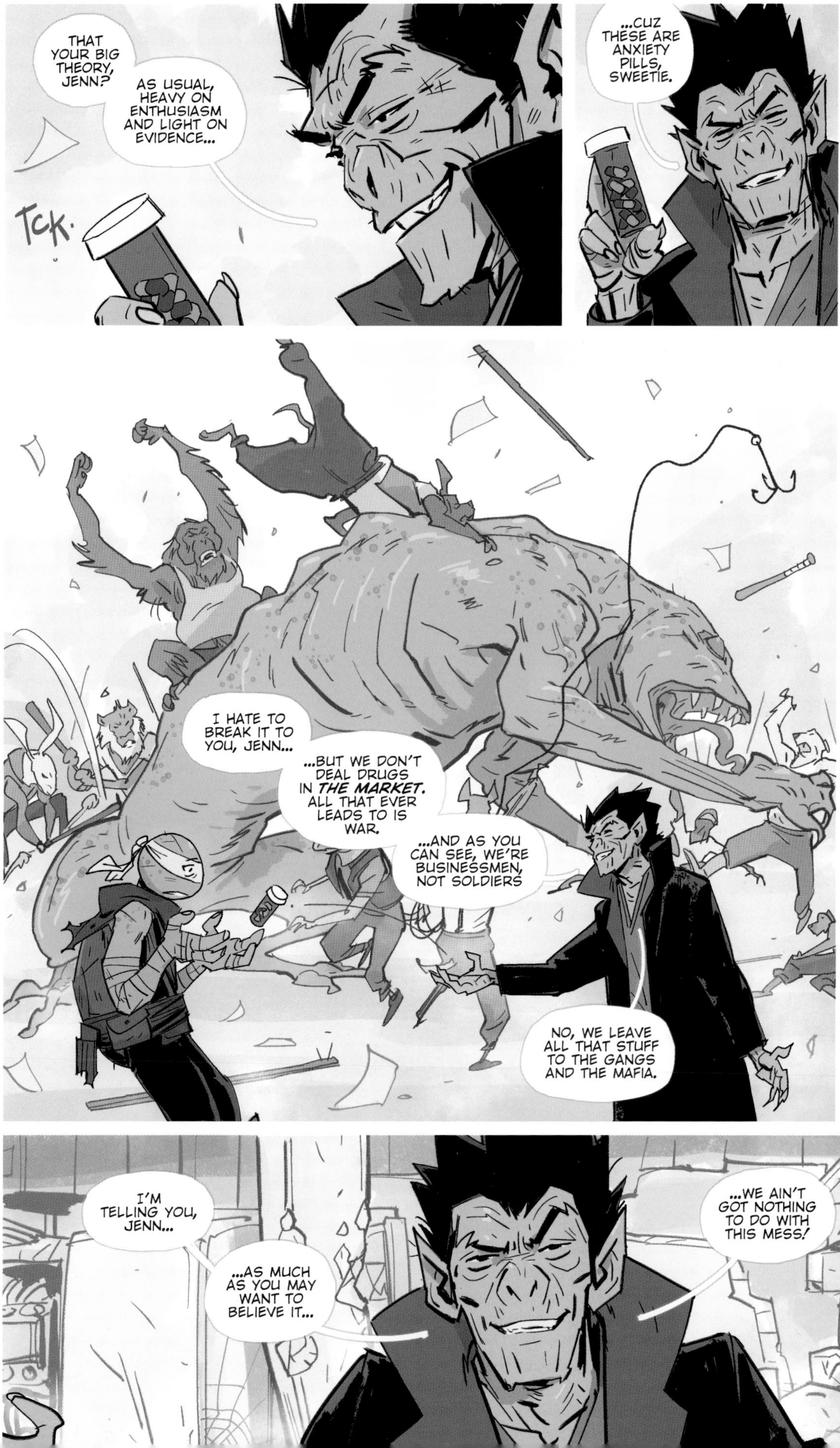
THAT YOUR BIG THEORY, JENN?
AS USUAL, HEAVY ON ENTHUSIASM AND LIGHT ON EVIDENCE...
TCK.
...CUZ THESE ARE ANXIETY PILLS, SWEETIE.
I HATE TO BREAK IT TO YOU, JENN...
...BUT WE DON'T DEAL DRUGS IN THE MARKET. ALL THAT EVER LEADS TO IS WAR.
...AND AS YOU CAN SEE, WE'RE BUSINESSMEN, NOT SOLDIERS
NO, WE LEAVE ALL THAT STUFF TO THE GANGS AND THE MAFIA.
I'M TELLING YOU, JENN...
...AS MUCH AS YOU MAY WANT TO BELIEVE IT...
...WE AIN'T GOT NOTHING TO DO WITH THIS MESS!

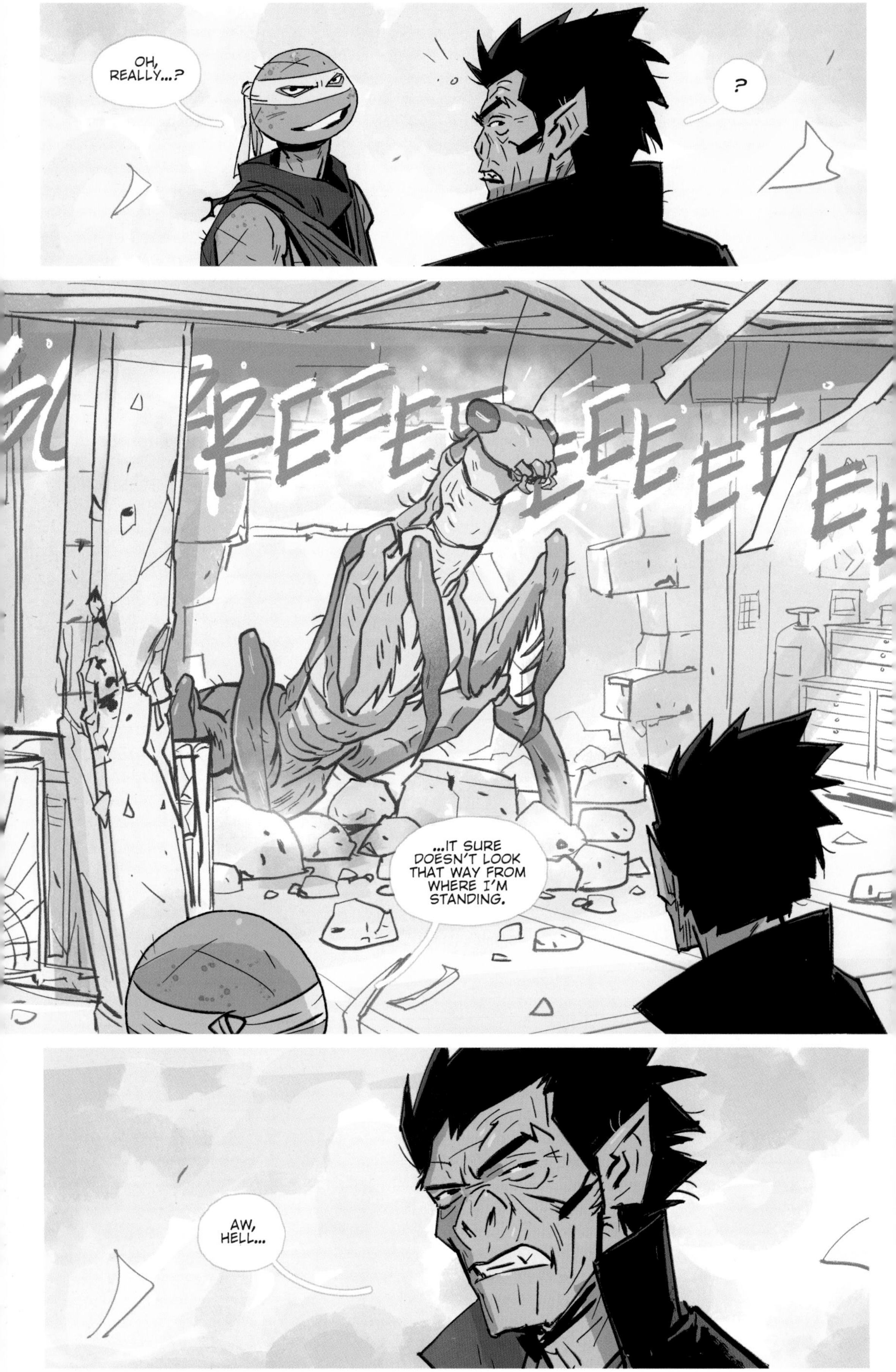
OH, REALLY...?
?
SKREEEEEEEEEE
...IT SURE DOESN'T LOOK THAT WAY FROM WHERE I'M STANDING.
AW, HELL...

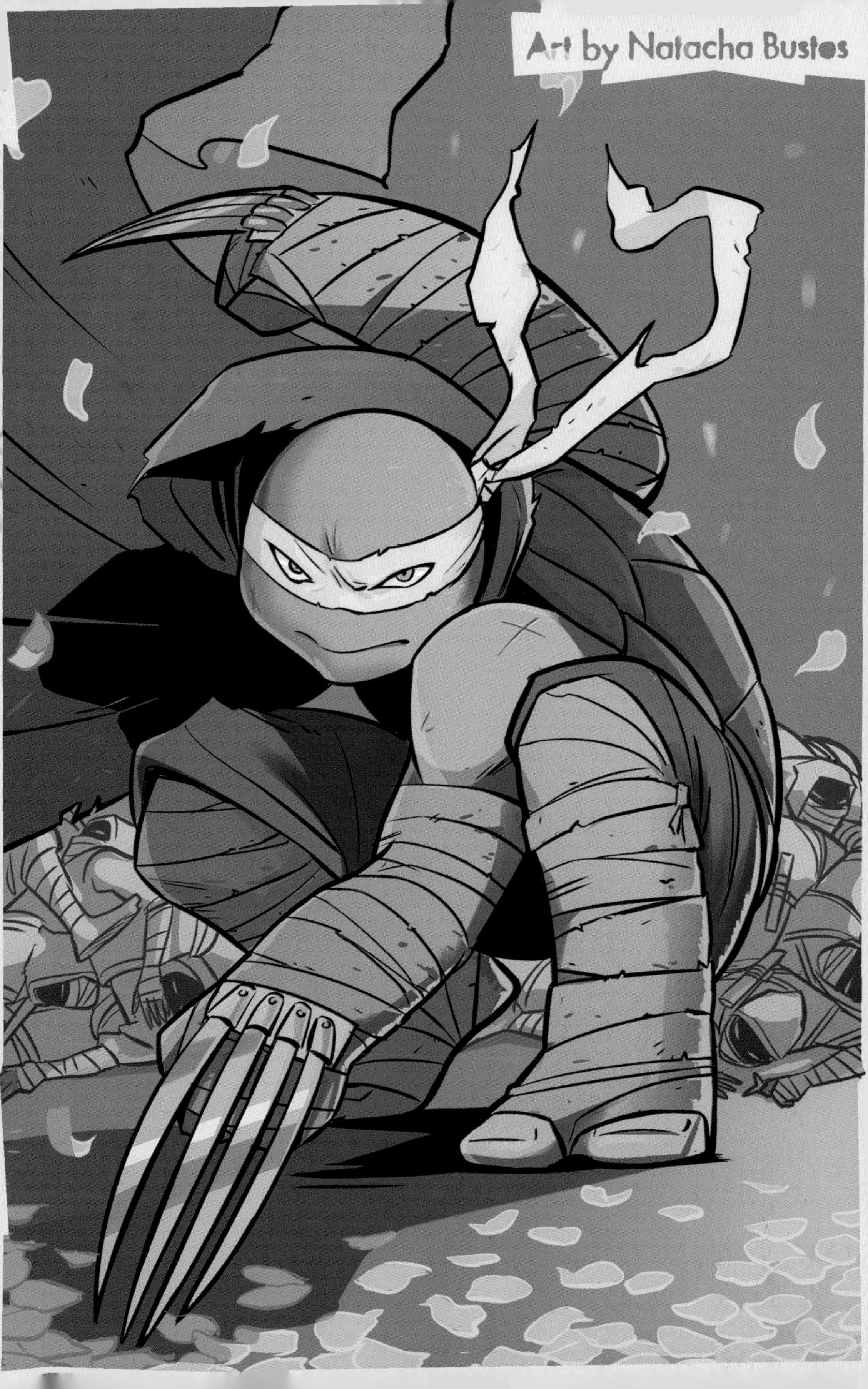
Art by Natacha Bustos

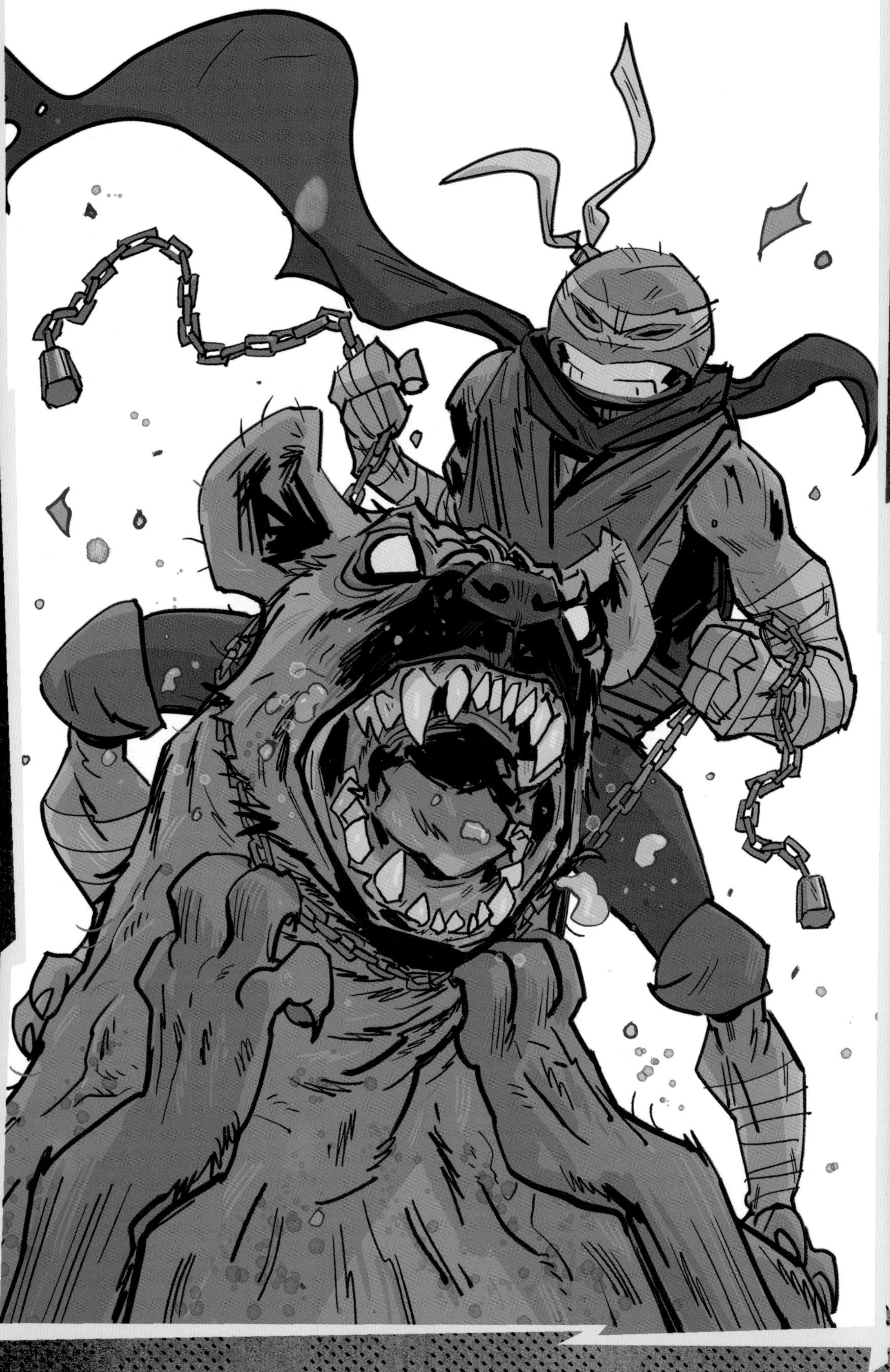

Art by Brahm Revel

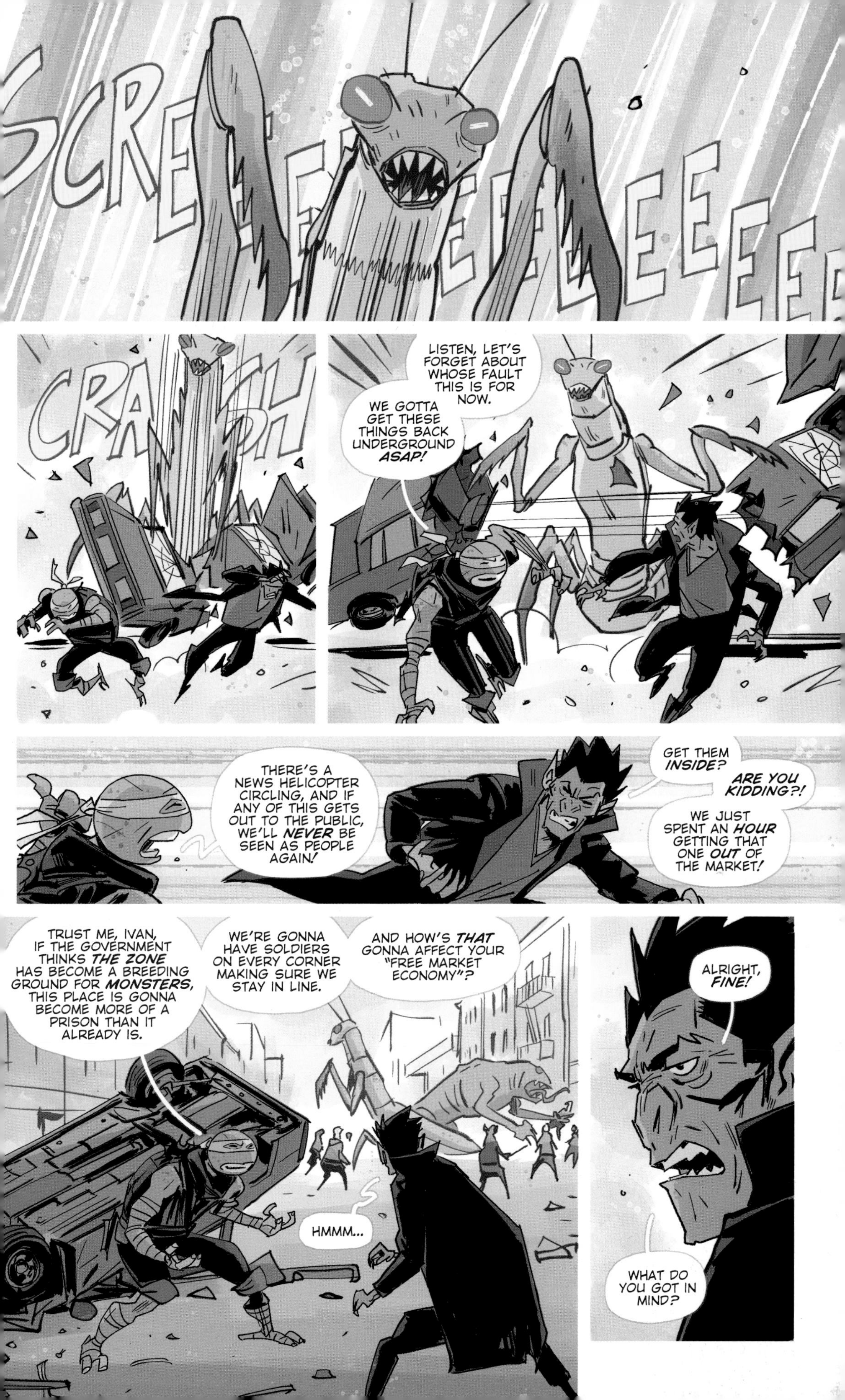
SCREEEEEEEEE
CRASH
LISTEN, LET'S FORGET ABOUT WHOSE FAULT THIS IS FOR NOW.
WE GOTTA GET THESE THINGS BACK UNDERGROUND ASAP!
THERE'S A NEWS HELICOPTER CIRCLING, AND IF ANY OF THIS GETS OUT TO THE PUBLIC, WE'LL NEVER BE SEEN AS PEOPLE AGAIN!
GET THEM INSIDE?
ARE YOU KIDDING?!
WE JUST SPENT AN HOUR GETTING THAT ONE OUT OF THE MARKET!
TRUST ME, IVAN, IF THE GOVERNMENT THINKS THE ZONE HAS BECOME A BREEDING GROUND FOR MONSTERS, THIS PLACE IS GONNA BECOME MORE OF A PRISON THAN IT ALREADY IS.
WE'RE GONNA HAVE SOLDIERS ON EVERY CORNER MAKING SURE WE STAY IN LINE.
AND HOW'S THAT GONNA AFFECT YOUR "FREE MARKET ECONOMY"?
HMMM...
ALRIGHT, FINE!
WHAT DO YOU GOT IN MIND?

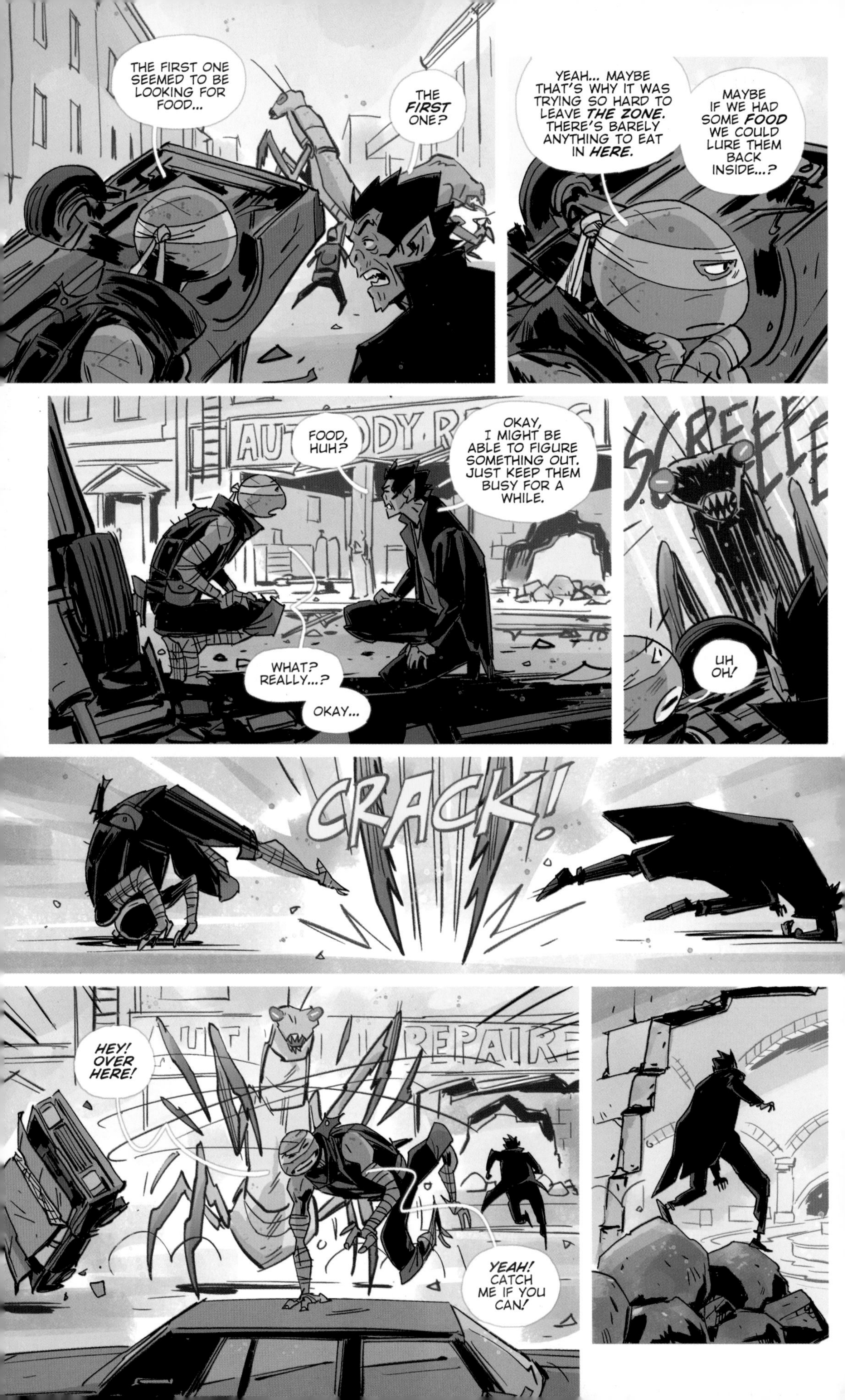
THE FIRST ONE SEEMED TO BE LOOKING FOR FOOD...
THE *FIRST* ONE?
YEAH... MAYBE THAT'S WHY IT WAS TRYING SO HARD TO LEAVE *THE ZONE.* THERE'S BARELY ANYTHING TO EAT IN *HERE.*
MAYBE IF WE HAD SOME *FOOD* WE COULD LURE THEM BACK INSIDE...?
FOOD, HUH?
OKAY, I MIGHT BE ABLE TO FIGURE SOMETHING OUT. JUST KEEP THEM BUSY FOR A WHILE.
WHAT? REALLY...?
OKAY...
SCREEEE
UH OH!
CRACK!
HEY! OVER HERE!
YEAH! CATCH ME IF YOU CAN!

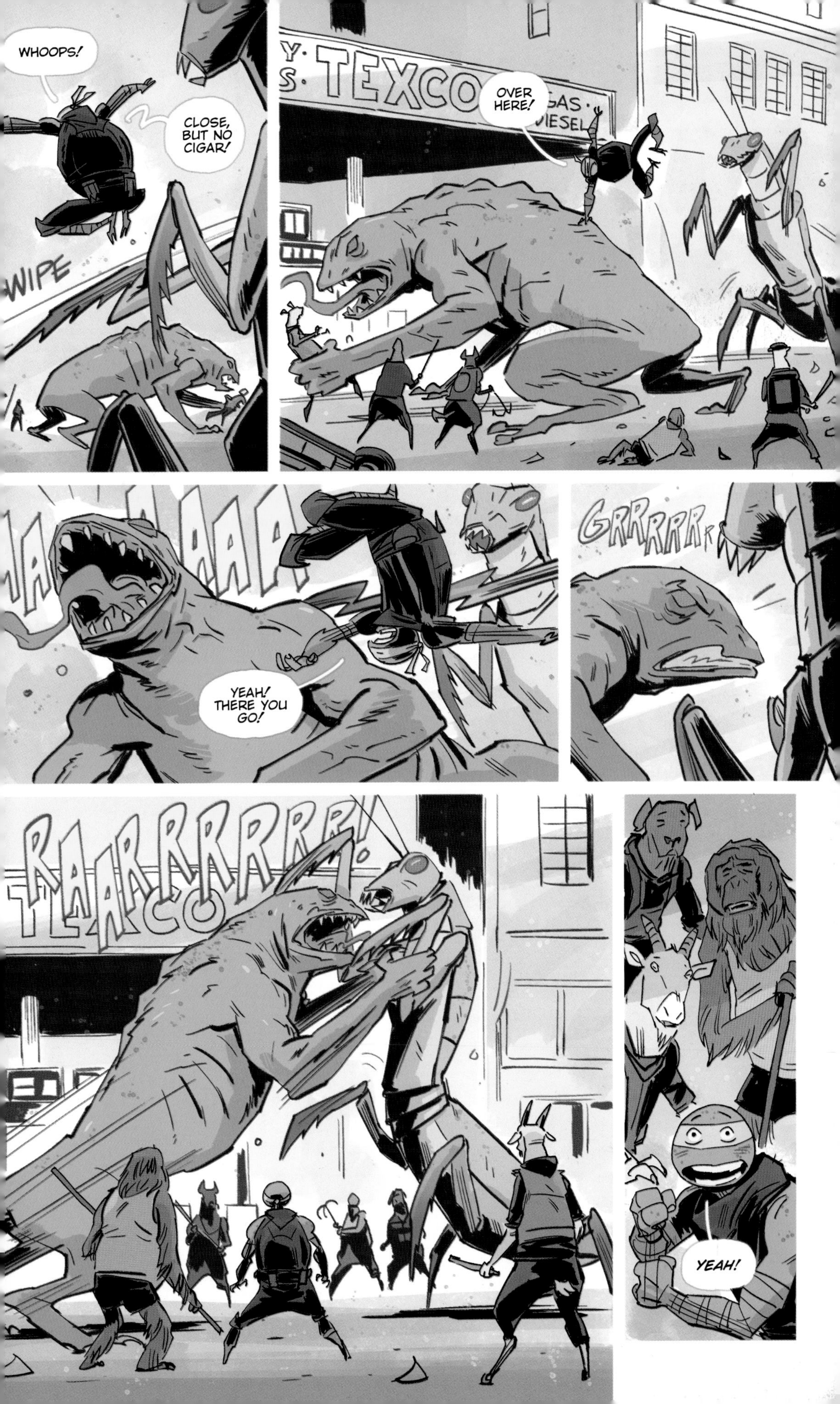
WHOOPS!
CLOSE, BUT NO CIGAR!
WIPE
TEXCO
GAS
DIESEL
OVER HERE!
YEAH! THERE YOU GO!
GRRRRRR
RAARRRRR!
YEAH!

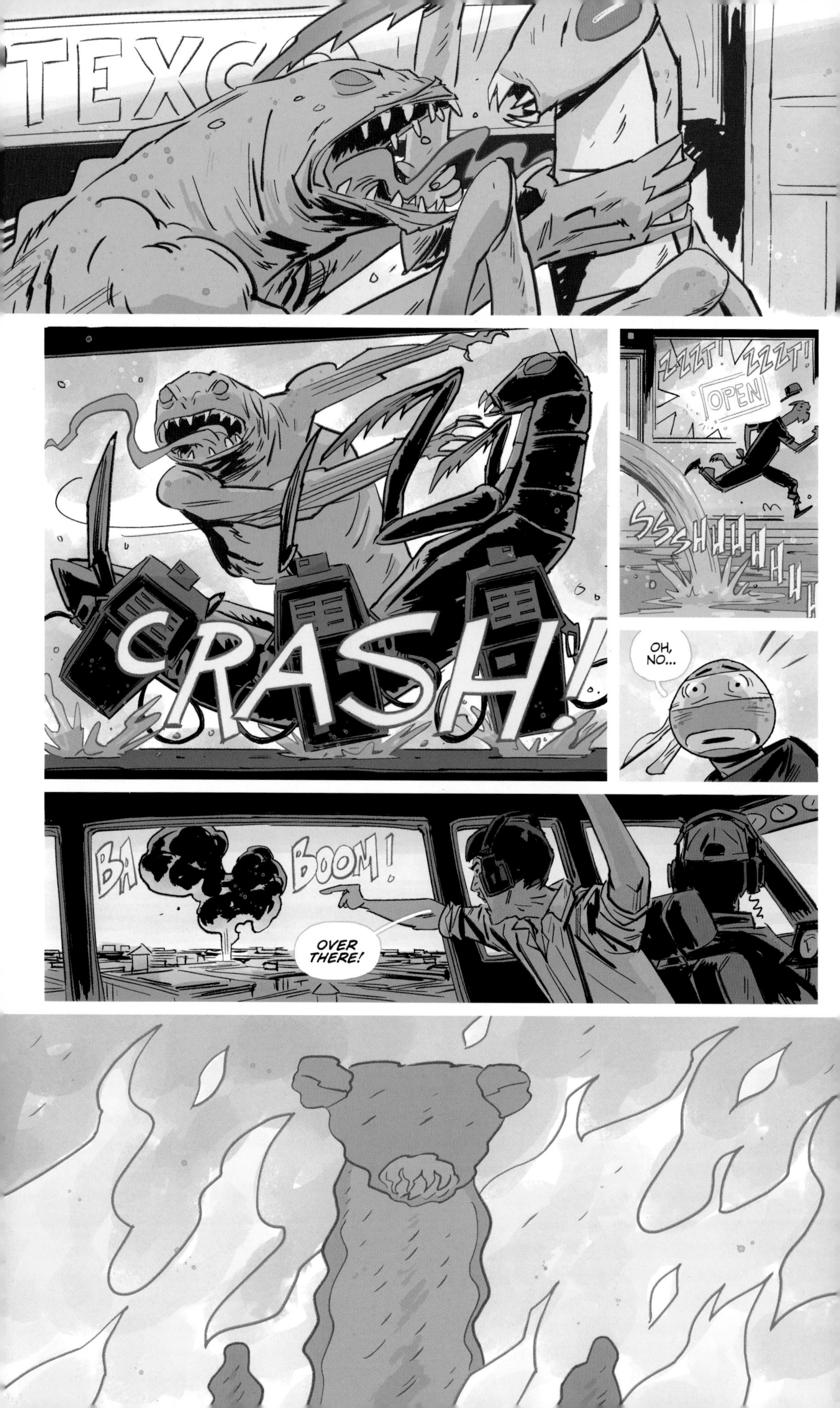
TEXC
CRASH!
ZZZT! ZZZT!
OPEN
SSSHHHHHHHHH
OH, NO...
BA BOOM!
OVER THERE!

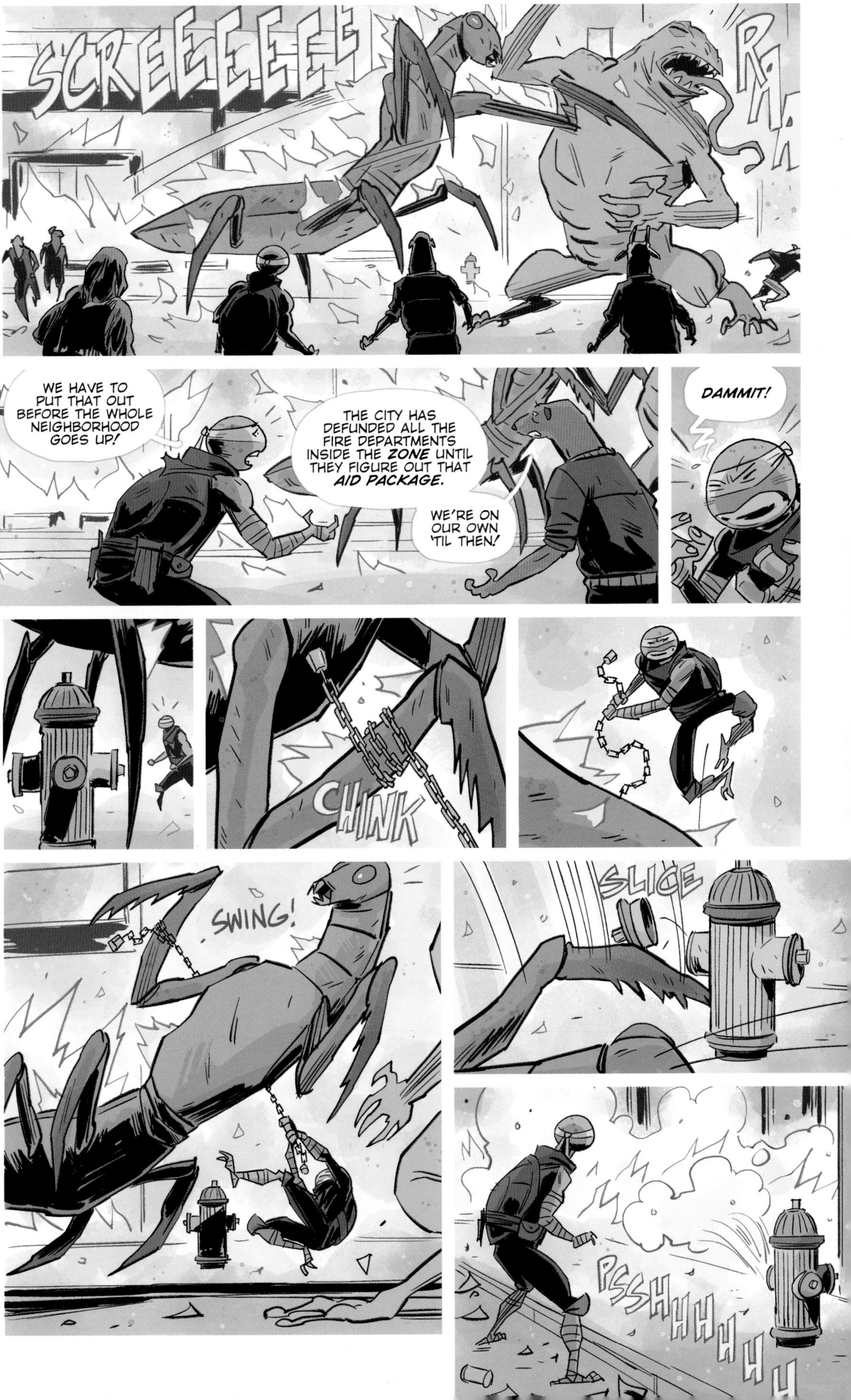
SCREEEEEE
RA
WE HAVE TO PUT THAT OUT BEFORE THE WHOLE NEIGHBORHOOD GOES UP!
THE CITY HAS DEFUNDED ALL THE FIRE DEPARTMENTS INSIDE THE ZONE UNTIL THEY FIGURE OUT THAT AID PACKAGE.
WE'RE ON OUR OWN 'TIL THEN!
DAMMIT!
CHINK
SWING!
SLICE
PSSHHHHHHH

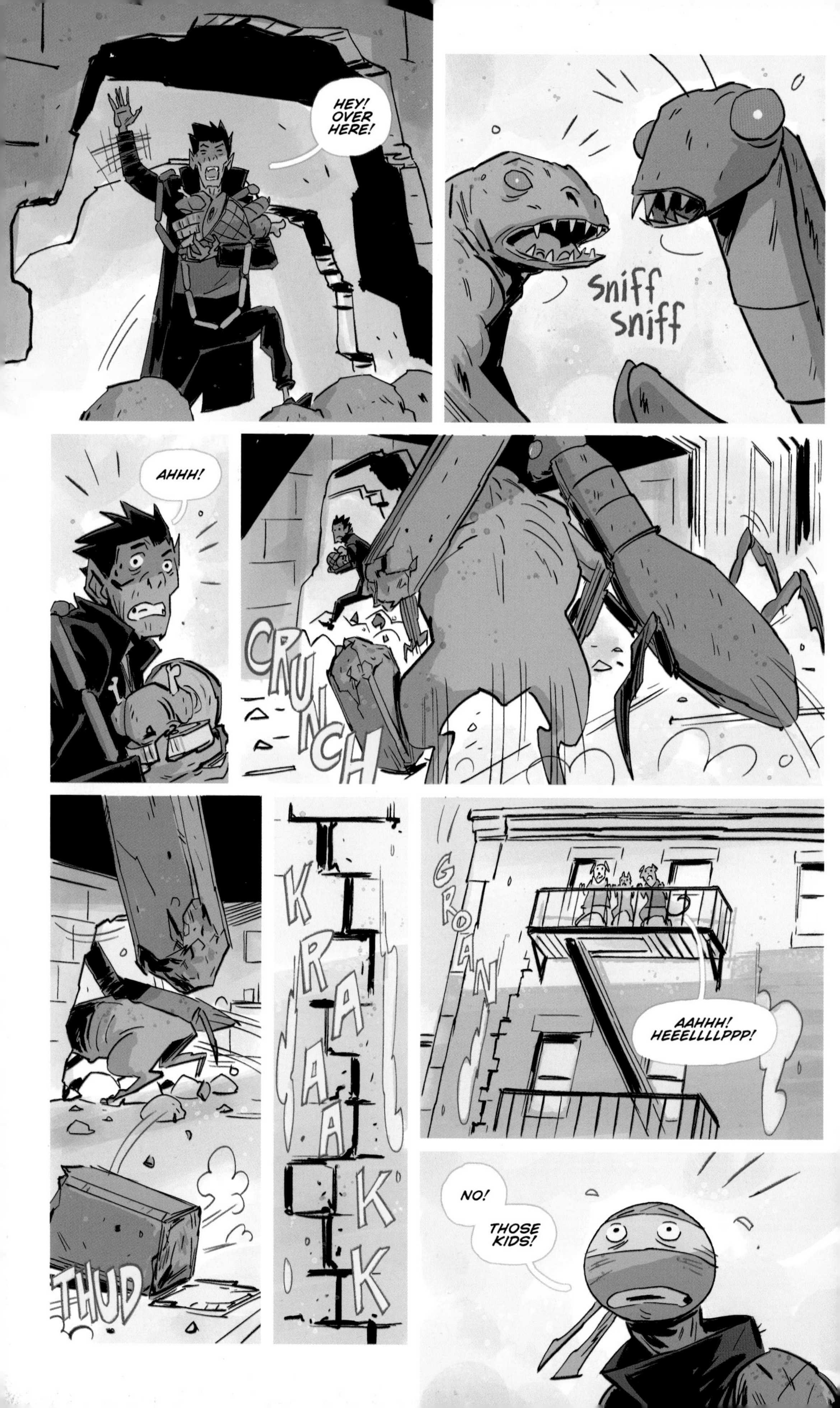
HEY! OVER HERE!
Sniff sniff
AHHH!
CRUNCH
THUD
KRAAAK
GROAN
AAHHH! HEEELLLLLPPP!
NO!
THOSE KIDS!

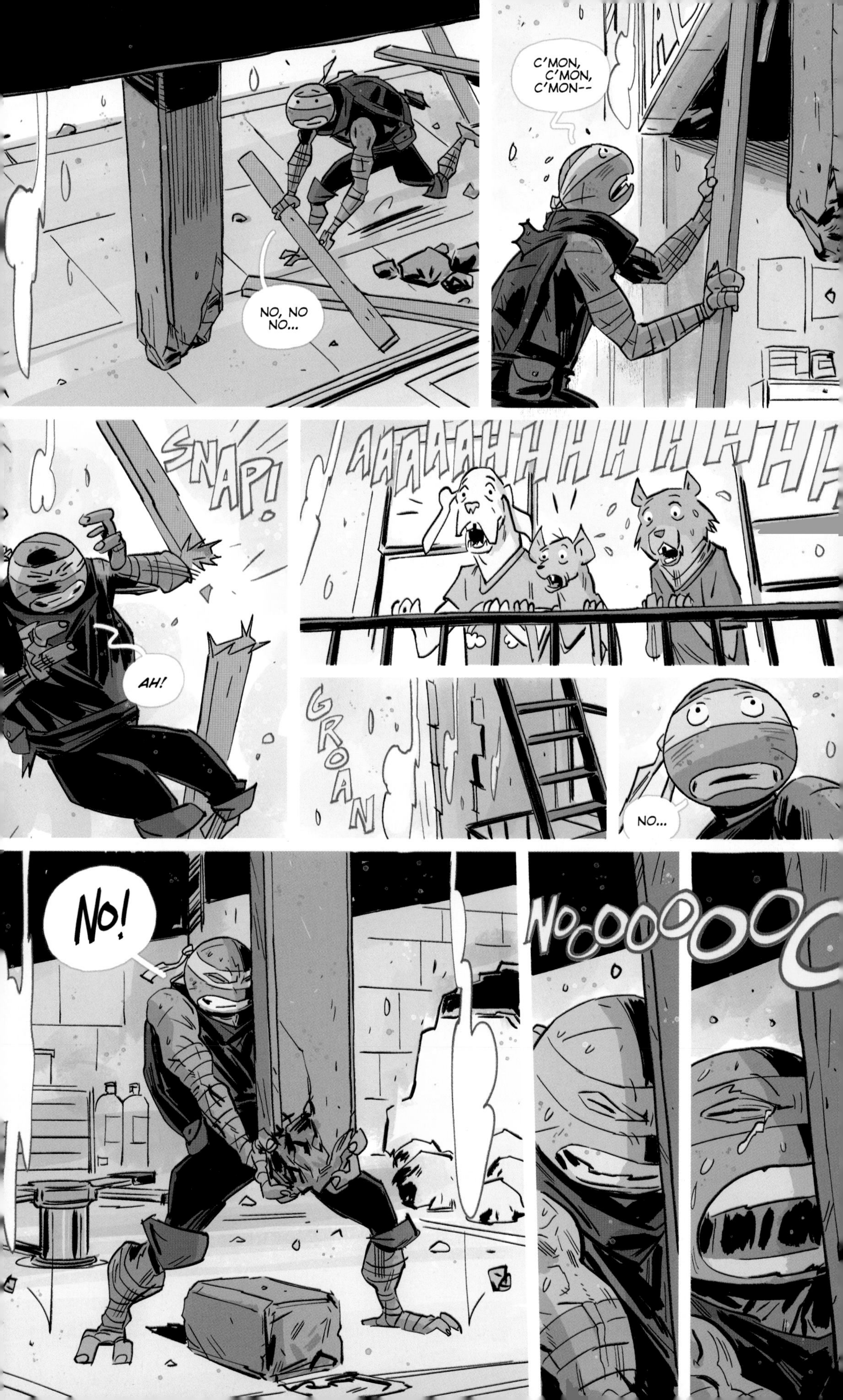

NO, NO
NO...
C'MON,
C'MON,
C'MON--
SNAP!
AH!
AAAAAHHHHHHHHHH
GROAN
NO...
NO!
NOOOOOOO

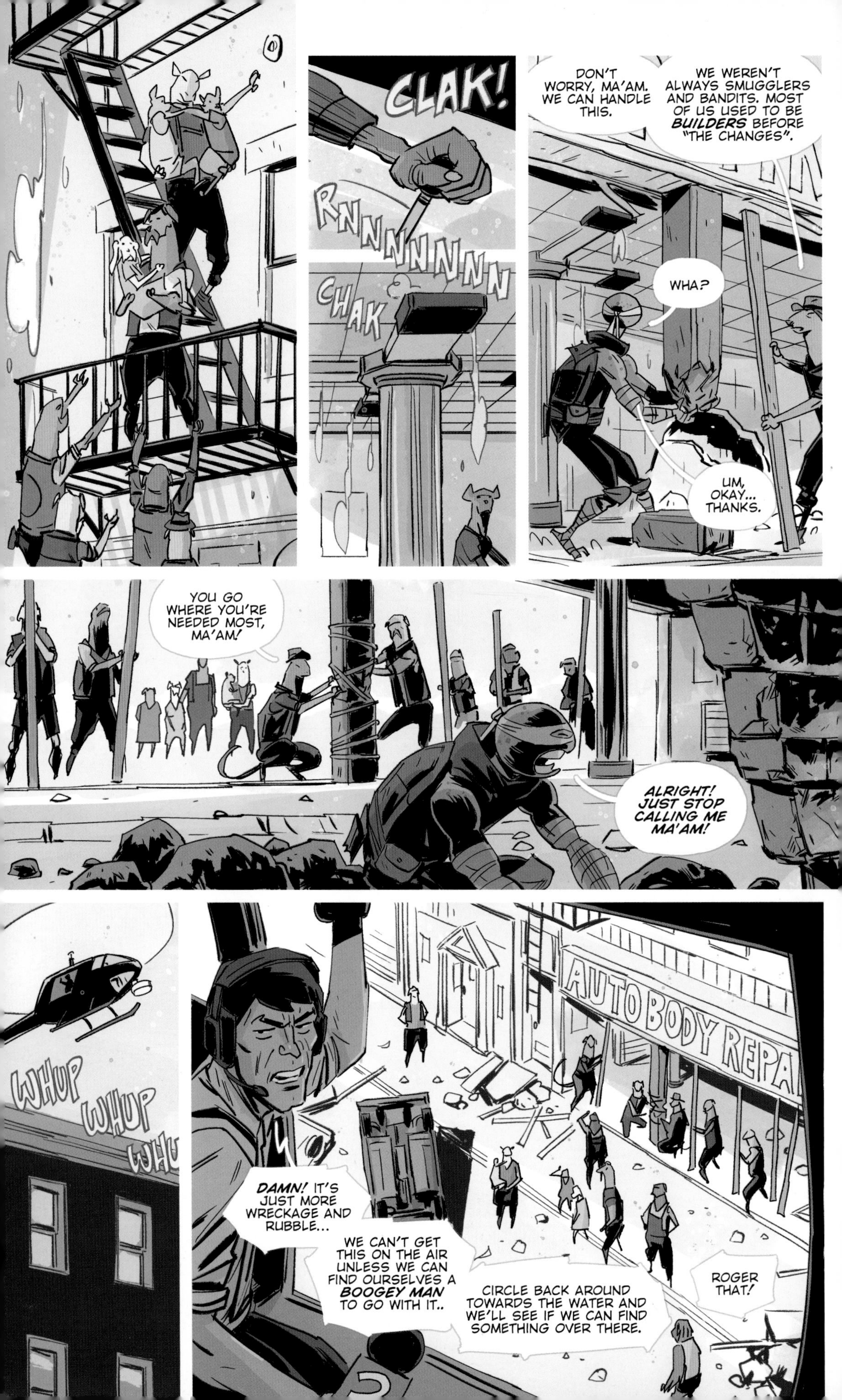
CLAK!
RNNNNNNNNN
CHAK
DON'T WORRY, MA'AM. WE CAN HANDLE THIS.
WE WEREN'T ALWAYS SMUGGLERS AND BANDITS. MOST OF US USED TO BE BUILDERS BEFORE "THE CHANGES".
WHA?
UM, OKAY... THANKS.
YOU GO WHERE YOU'RE NEEDED MOST, MA'AM!
ALRIGHT! JUST STOP CALLING ME MA'AM!
WHUP WHUP WHU
AUTO BODY REPA
DAMN! IT'S JUST MORE WRECKAGE AND RUBBLE...
WE CAN'T GET THIS ON THE AIR UNLESS WE CAN FIND OURSELVES A BOOGEY MAN TO GO WITH IT..
CIRCLE BACK AROUND TOWARDS THE WATER AND WE'LL SEE IF WE CAN FIND SOMETHING OVER THERE.
ROGER THAT!

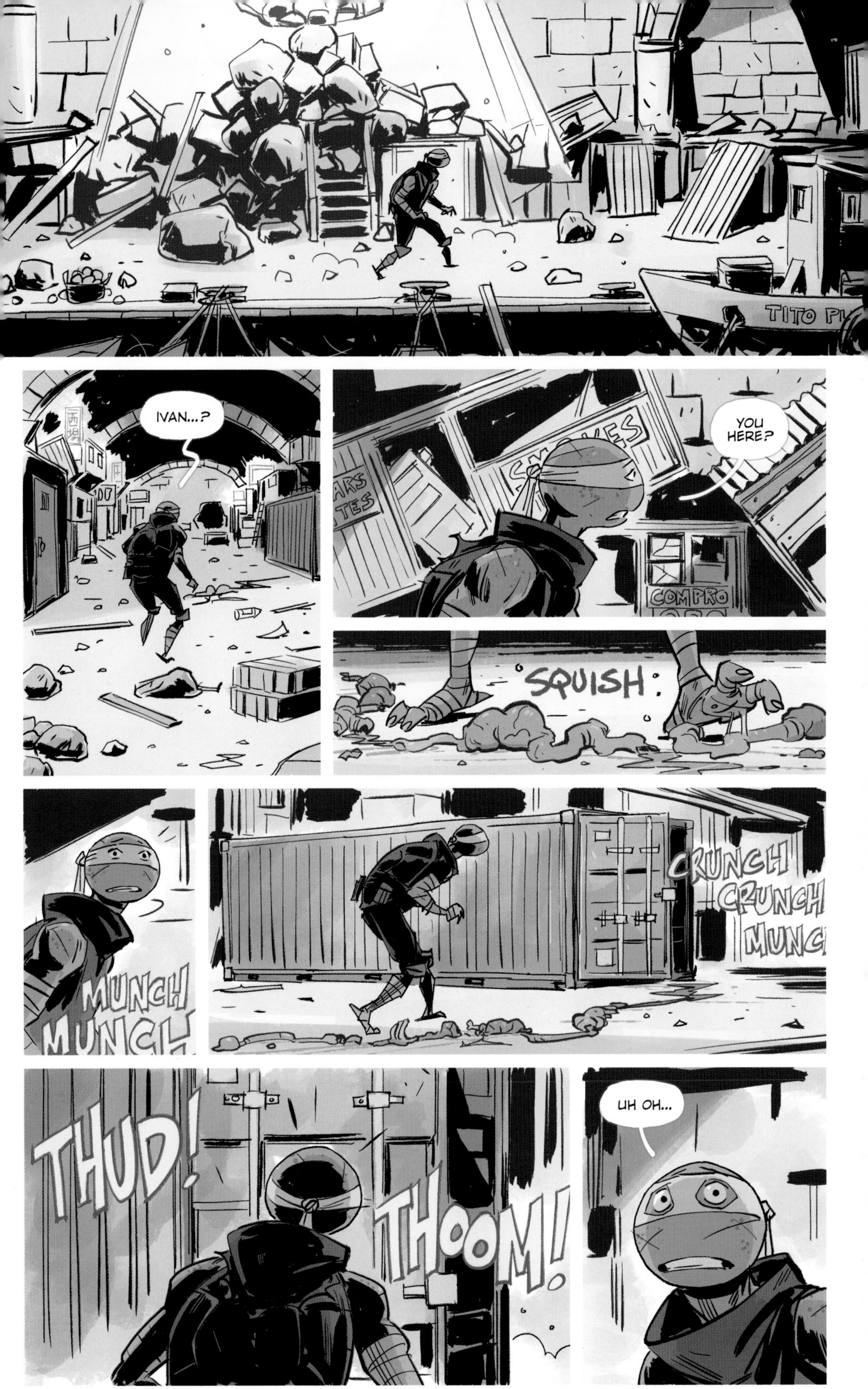
IVAN...?
YOU HERE?
COMPRO
SQUISH
MUNCH
MUNCH
CRUNCH
CRUNCH
THUD!
THOOM!
UH OH...

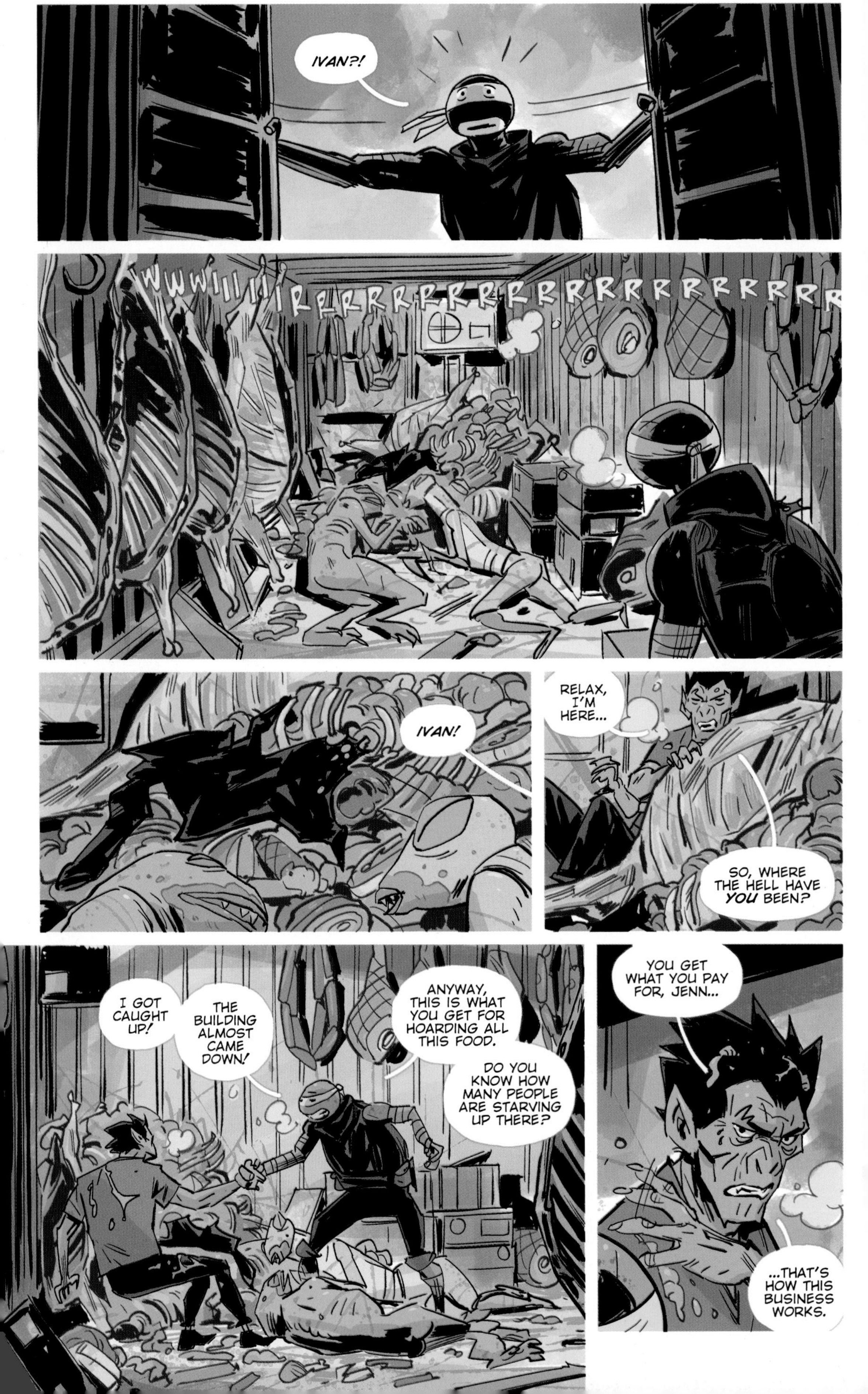
IVAN?!
WWWIIIIIRRRRRRRRRRRRRRRRRRRR
IVAN!
RELAX, I'M HERE...
SO, WHERE THE HELL HAVE YOU BEEN?
I GOT CAUGHT UP!
THE BUILDING ALMOST CAME DOWN!
ANYWAY, THIS IS WHAT YOU GET FOR HOARDING ALL THIS FOOD.
DO YOU KNOW HOW MANY PEOPLE ARE STARVING UP THERE?
YOU GET WHAT YOU PAY FOR, JENN...
...THAT'S HOW THIS BUSINESS WORKS.

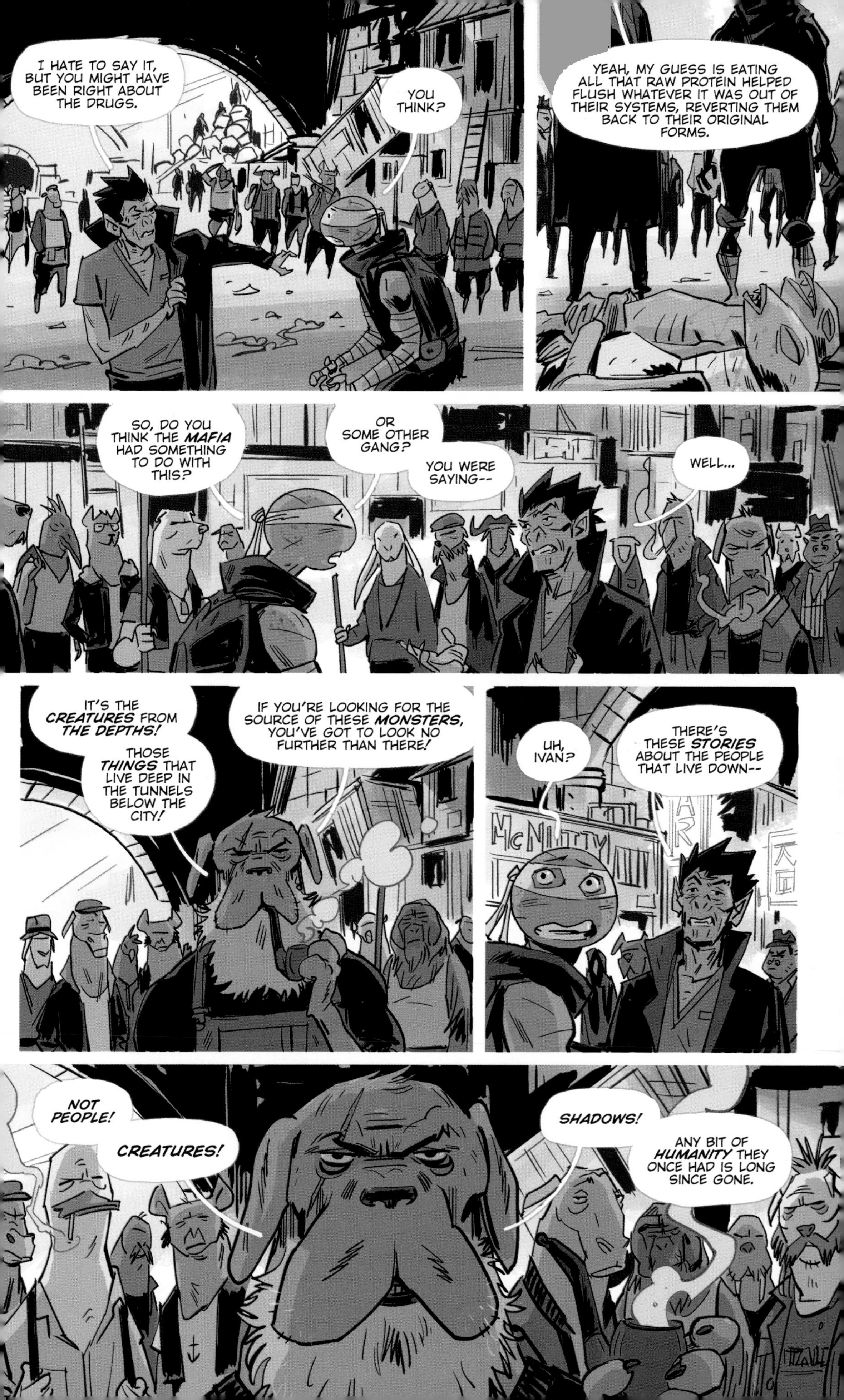
I HATE TO SAY IT, BUT YOU MIGHT HAVE BEEN RIGHT ABOUT THE DRUGS.
YOU THINK?
YEAH, MY GUESS IS EATING ALL THAT RAW PROTEIN HELPED FLUSH WHATEVER IT WAS OUT OF THEIR SYSTEMS, REVERTING THEM BACK TO THEIR ORIGINAL FORMS.
SO, DO YOU THINK THE MAFIA HAD SOMETHING TO DO WITH THIS?
OR SOME OTHER GANG?
YOU WERE SAYING--
WELL...
IT'S THE CREATURES FROM THE DEPTHS!
THOSE THINGS THAT LIVE DEEP IN THE TUNNELS BELOW THE CITY!
IF YOU'RE LOOKING FOR THE SOURCE OF THESE MONSTERS, YOU'VE GOT TO LOOK NO FURTHER THAN THERE!
UH, IVAN?
THERE'S THESE STORIES ABOUT THE PEOPLE THAT LIVE DOWN--
NOT PEOPLE!
CREATURES!
SHADOWS!
ANY BIT OF HUMANITY THEY ONCE HAD IS LONG SINCE GONE.

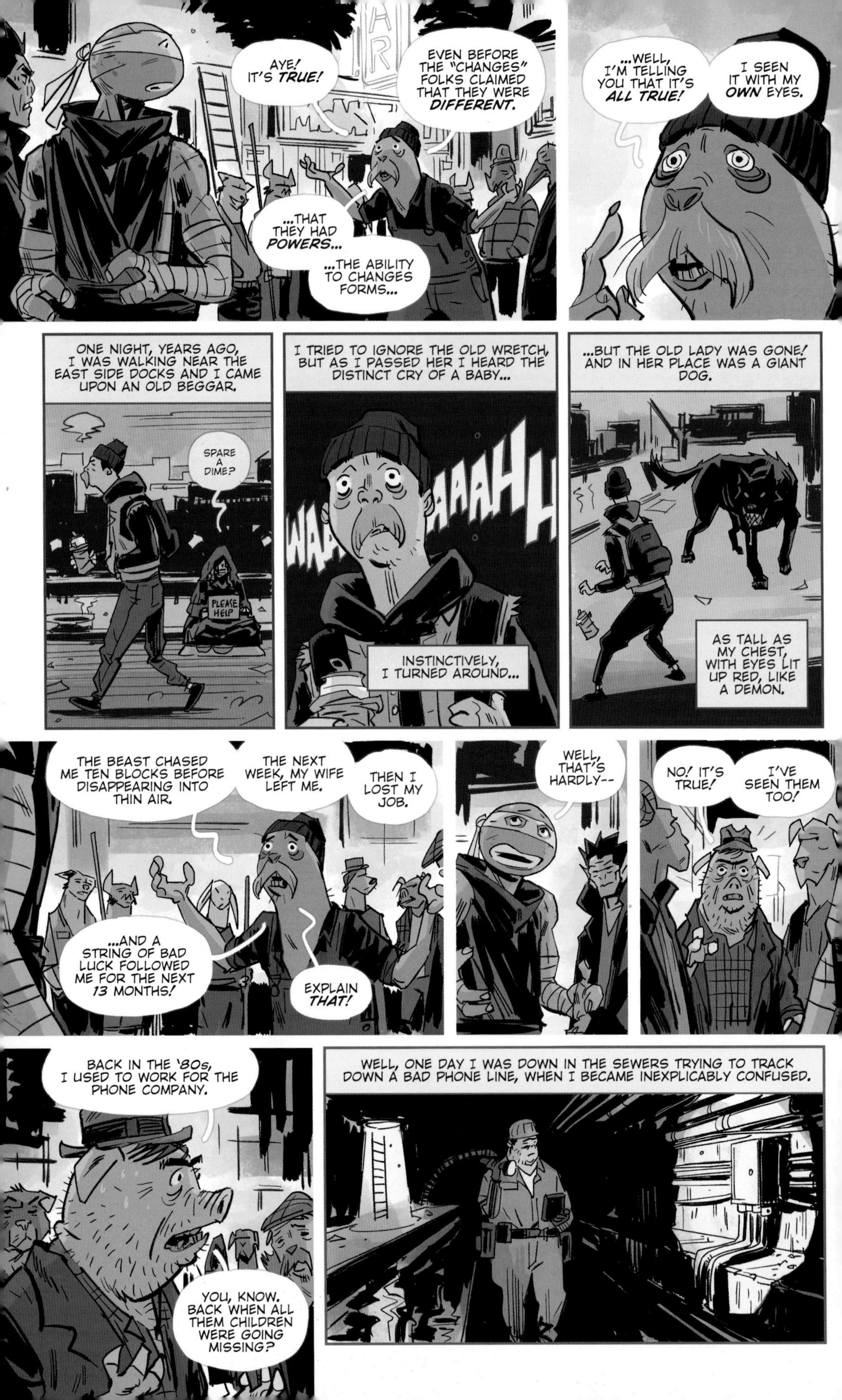

AYE! IT'S TRUE!
EVEN BEFORE THE "CHANGES" FOLKS CLAIMED THAT THEY WERE DIFFERENT.
...THAT THEY HAD POWERS...
...THE ABILITY TO CHANGES FORMS...
...WELL, I'M TELLING YOU THAT IT'S ALL TRUE!
I SEEN IT WITH MY OWN EYES.
ONE NIGHT, YEARS AGO, I WAS WALKING NEAR THE EAST SIDE DOCKS AND I CAME UPON AN OLD BEGGAR.
SPARE A DIME?
PLEASE HELP
I TRIED TO IGNORE THE OLD WRETCH, BUT AS I PASSED HER I HEARD THE DISTINCT CRY OF A BABY...
WAAAAAHH
INSTINCTIVELY, I TURNED AROUND...
...BUT THE OLD LADY WAS GONE! AND IN HER PLACE WAS A GIANT DOG.
AS TALL AS MY CHEST, WITH EYES LIT UP RED, LIKE A DEMON.
THE BEAST CHASED ME TEN BLOCKS BEFORE DISAPPEARING INTO THIN AIR.
THE NEXT WEEK, MY WIFE LEFT ME.
THEN I LOST MY JOB.
...AND A STRING OF BAD LUCK FOLLOWED ME FOR THE NEXT 13 MONTHS!
EXPLAIN THAT!
WELL, THAT'S HARDLY--
NO! IT'S TRUE!
I'VE SEEN THEM TOO!
BACK IN THE '80s, I USED TO WORK FOR THE PHONE COMPANY.
YOU, KNOW. BACK WHEN ALL THEM CHILDREN WERE GOING MISSING?
WELL, ONE DAY I WAS DOWN IN THE SEWERS TRYING TO TRACK DOWN A BAD PHONE LINE, WHEN I BECAME INEXPLICABLY CONFUSED.

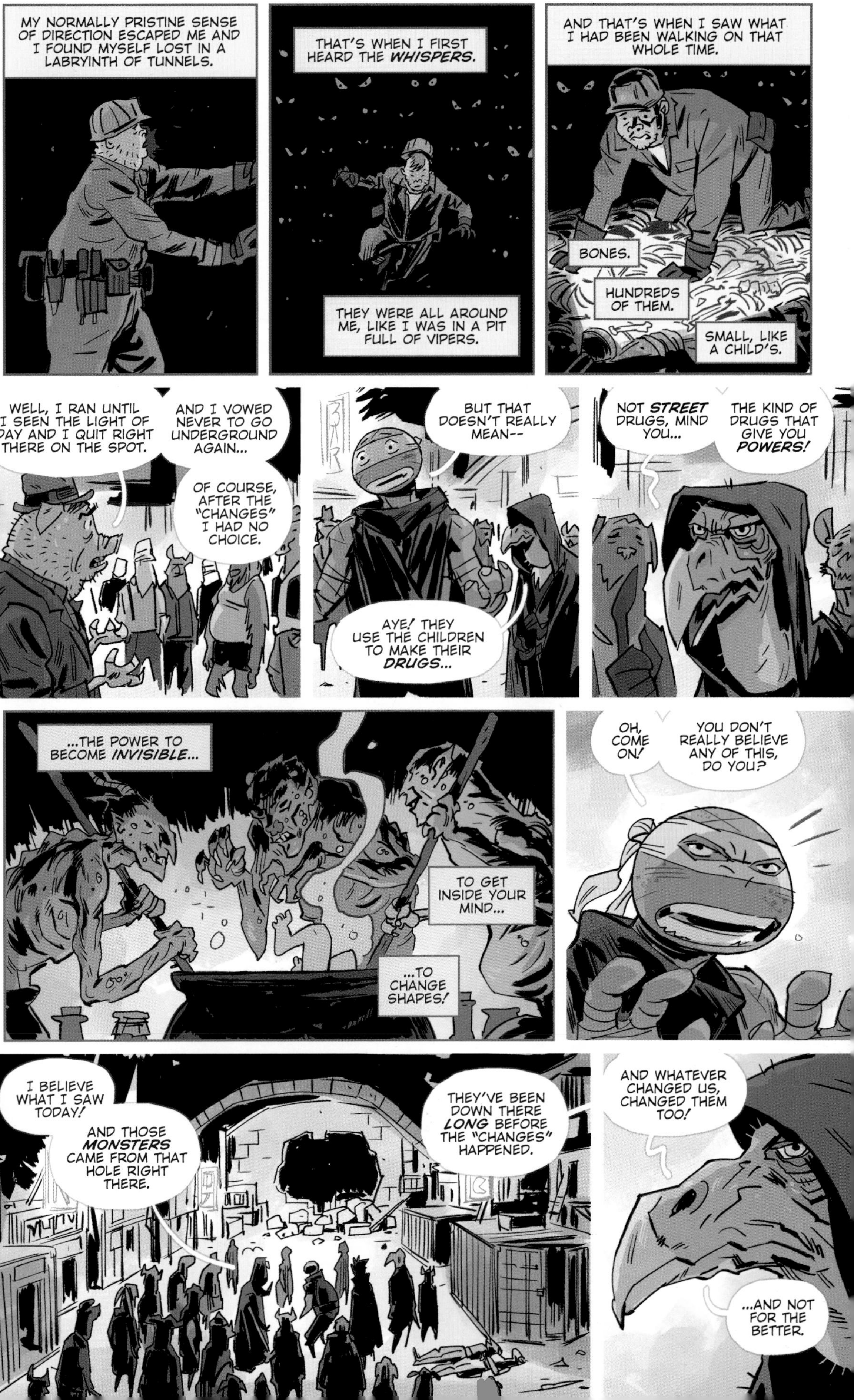
MY NORMALLY PRISTINE SENSE OF DIRECTION ESCAPED ME AND I FOUND MYSELF LOST IN A LABRYINTH OF TUNNELS.
THAT'S WHEN I FIRST HEARD THE *WHISPERS.*
THEY WERE ALL AROUND ME, LIKE I WAS IN A PIT FULL OF VIPERS.
AND THAT'S WHEN I SAW WHAT I HAD BEEN WALKING ON THAT WHOLE TIME.
BONES.
HUNDREDS OF THEM.
SMALL, LIKE A CHILD'S.
WELL, I RAN UNTIL I SEEN THE LIGHT OF DAY AND I QUIT RIGHT THERE ON THE SPOT.
AND I VOWED NEVER TO GO UNDERGROUND AGAIN...
OF COURSE, AFTER THE "CHANGES" I HAD NO CHOICE.
BUT THAT DOESN'T REALLY MEAN--
AYE! THEY USE THE CHILDREN TO MAKE THEIR *DRUGS*...
NOT *STREET* DRUGS, MIND YOU...
THE KIND OF DRUGS THAT GIVE YOU *POWERS!*
...THE POWER TO BECOME *INVISIBLE*...
TO GET INSIDE YOUR MIND...
...TO CHANGE SHAPES!
OH, COME ON!
YOU DON'T REALLY BELIEVE ANY OF THIS, DO YOU?
I BELIEVE WHAT I SAW TODAY!
AND THOSE *MONSTERS* CAME FROM THAT HOLE RIGHT THERE.
THEY'VE BEEN DOWN THERE *LONG* BEFORE THE "CHANGES" HAPPENED.
AND WHATEVER CHANGED US, CHANGED THEM TOO!
...AND NOT FOR THE BETTER.

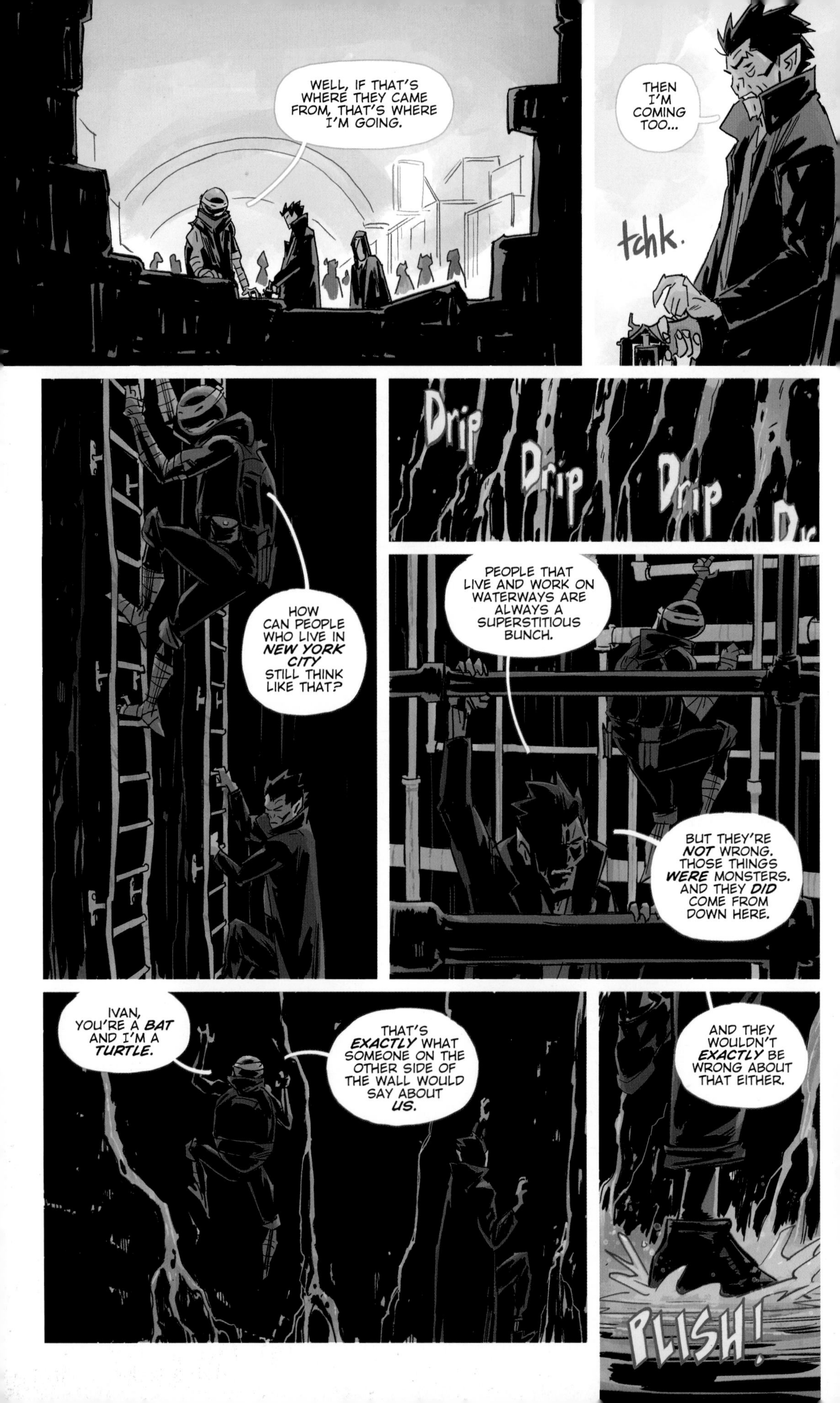
WELL, IF THAT'S WHERE THEY CAME FROM, THAT'S WHERE I'M GOING.
THEN I'M COMING TOO...
tchk.
HOW CAN PEOPLE WHO LIVE IN NEW YORK CITY STILL THINK LIKE THAT?
Drip Drip Drip
PEOPLE THAT LIVE AND WORK ON WATERWAYS ARE ALWAYS A SUPERSTITIOUS BUNCH.
BUT THEY'RE NOT WRONG. THOSE THINGS WERE MONSTERS. AND THEY DID COME FROM DOWN HERE.
IVAN, YOU'RE A BAT AND I'M A TURTLE.
THAT'S EXACTLY WHAT SOMEONE ON THE OTHER SIDE OF THE WALL WOULD SAY ABOUT US.
AND THEY WOULDN'T EXACTLY BE WRONG ABOUT THAT EITHER.
PLISH!

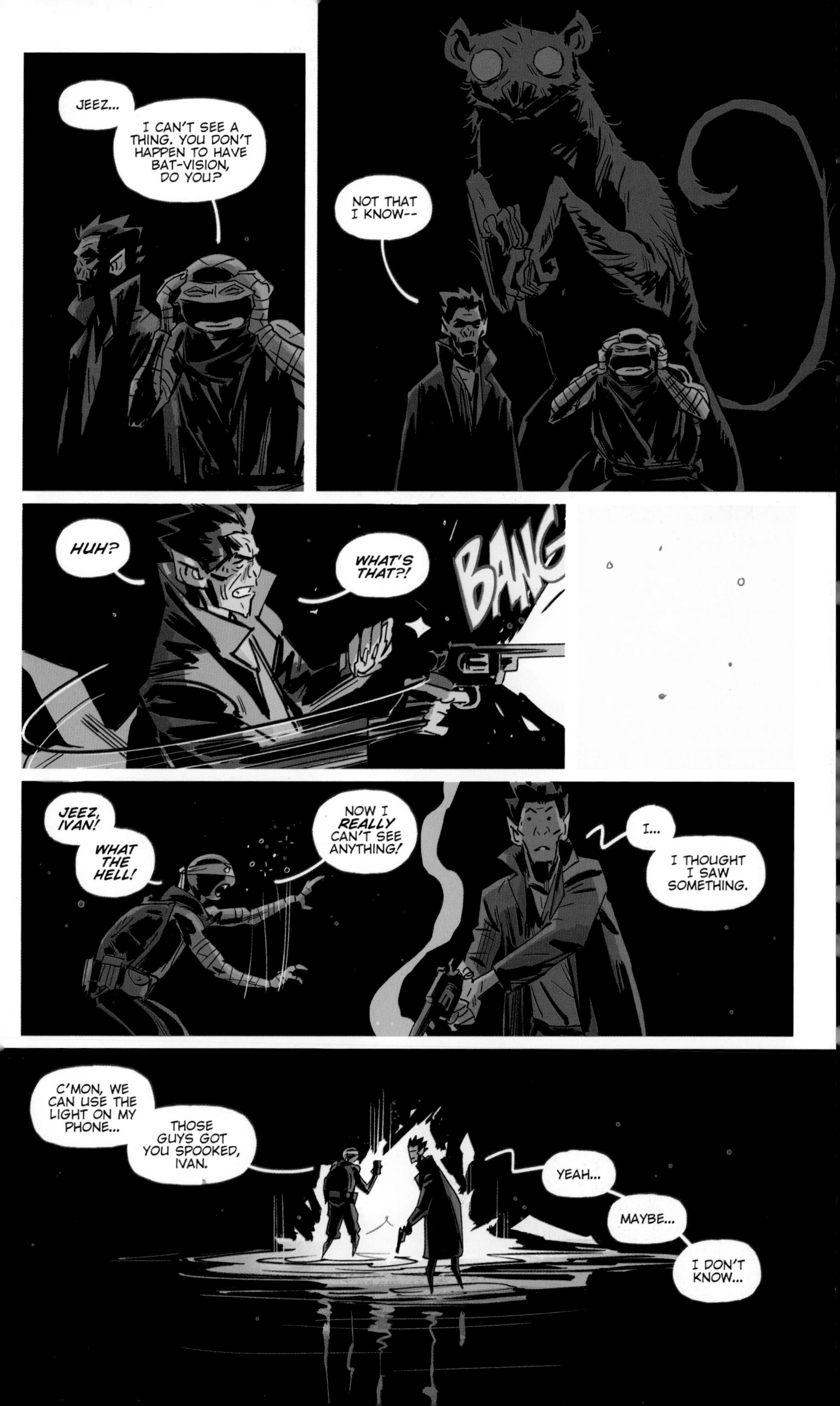
JEEZ...
I CAN'T SEE A THING. YOU DON'T HAPPEN TO HAVE BAT-VISION, DO YOU?
NOT THAT I KNOW--
HUH?
WHAT'S THAT?!
BANG
JEEZ, IVAN!
WHAT THE HELL!
NOW I REALLY CAN'T SEE ANYTHING!
I...
I THOUGHT I SAW SOMETHING.
C'MON, WE CAN USE THE LIGHT ON MY PHONE...
THOSE GUYS GOT YOU SPOOKED, IVAN.
YEAH...
MAYBE...
I DON'T KNOW...

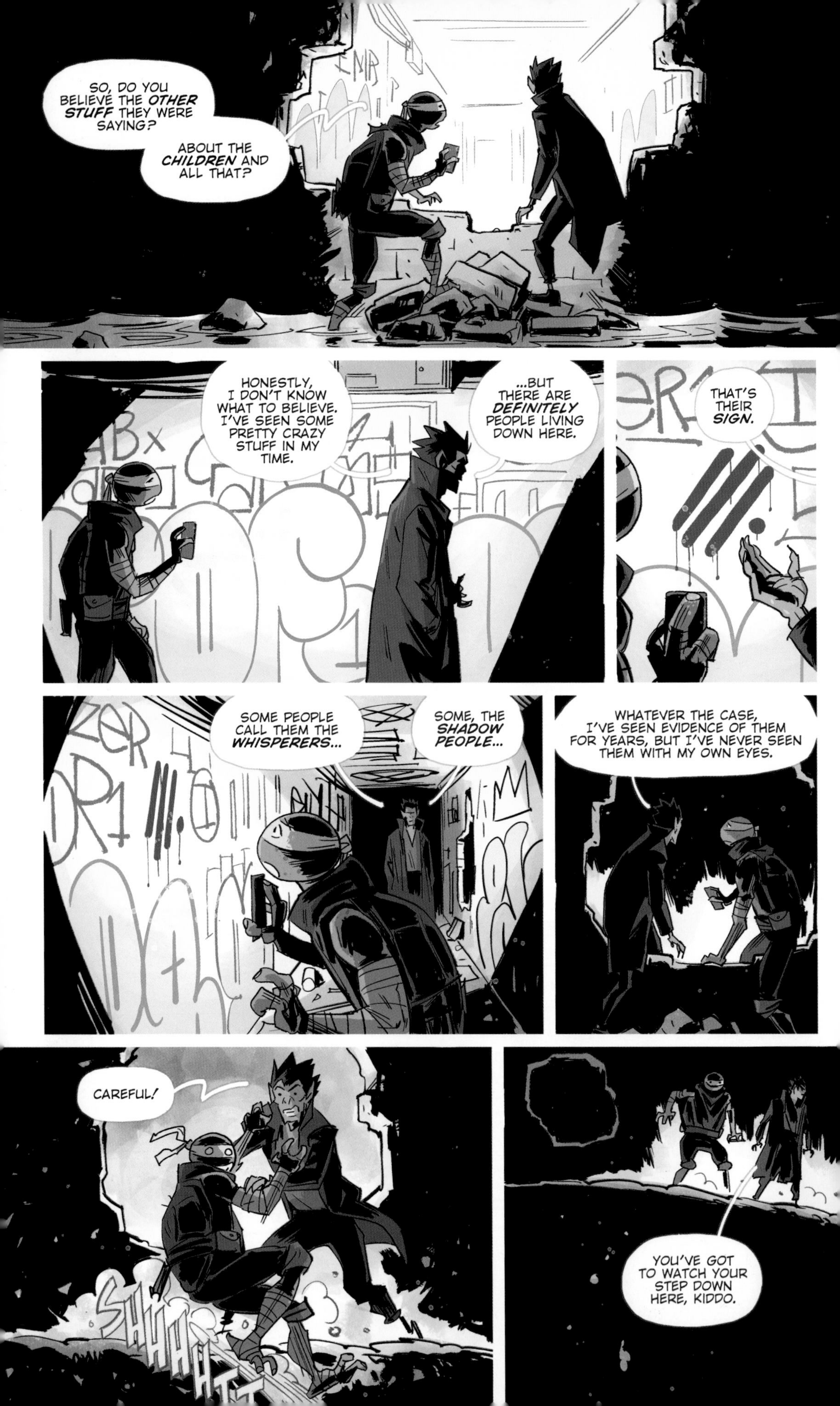

SO, DO YOU BELIEVE THE OTHER STUFF THEY WERE SAYING?
ABOUT THE CHILDREN AND ALL THAT?
HONESTLY, I DON'T KNOW WHAT TO BELIEVE. I'VE SEEN SOME PRETTY CRAZY STUFF IN MY TIME.
...BUT THERE ARE DEFINITELY PEOPLE LIVING DOWN HERE.
THAT'S THEIR SIGN.
SOME PEOPLE CALL THEM THE WHISPERERS...
SOME, THE SHADOW PEOPLE...
WHATEVER THE CASE, I'VE SEEN EVIDENCE OF THEM FOR YEARS, BUT I'VE NEVER SEEN THEM WITH MY OWN EYES.
CAREFUL!
SHHHHTT
YOU'VE GOT TO WATCH YOUR STEP DOWN HERE, KIDDO.

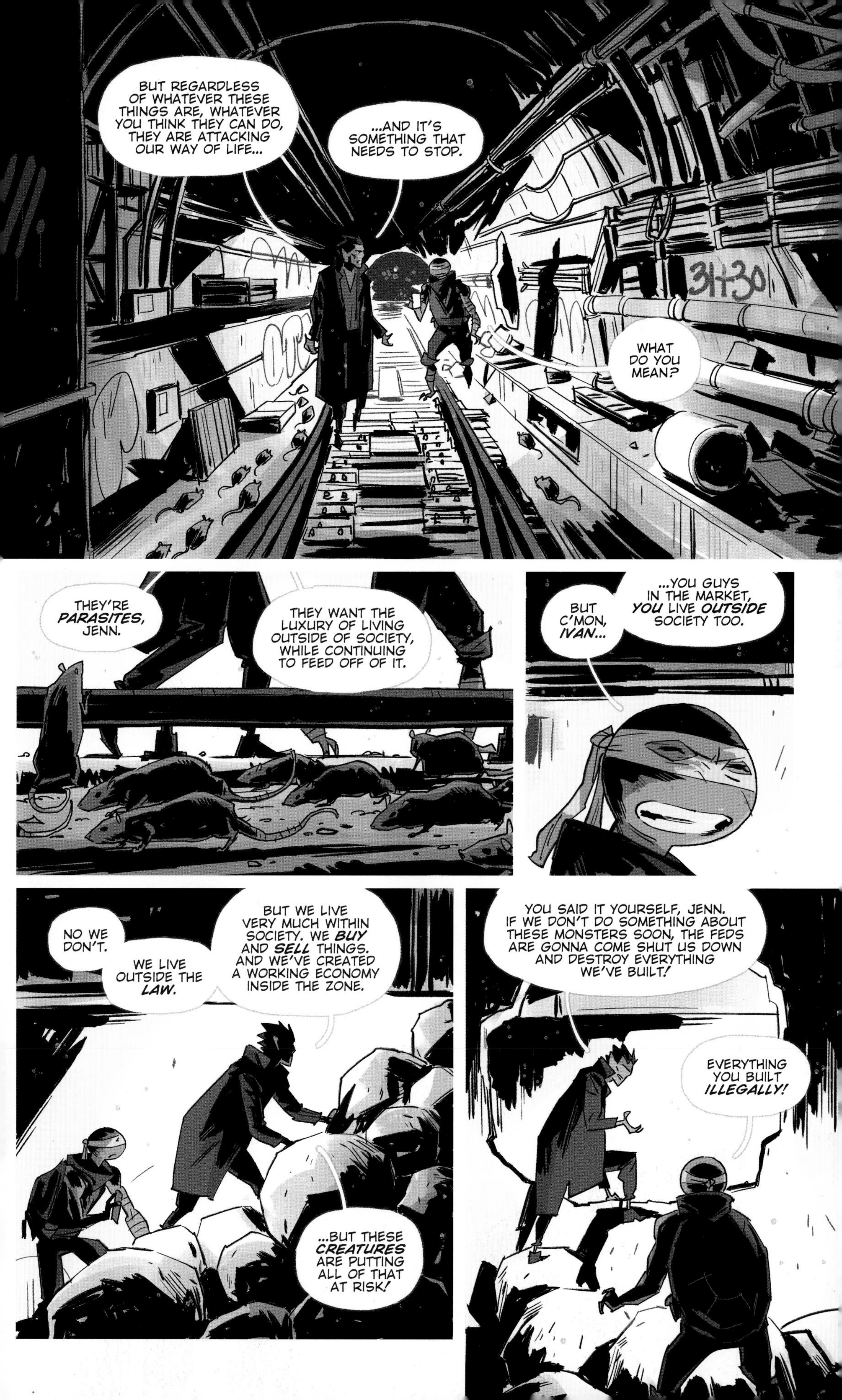

BUT REGARDLESS OF WHATEVER THESE THINGS ARE, WHATEVER YOU THINK THEY CAN DO, THEY ARE ATTACKING OUR WAY OF LIFE...
...AND IT'S SOMETHING THAT NEEDS TO STOP.
3H30
WHAT DO YOU MEAN?
THEY'RE *PARASITES,* JENN.
THEY WANT THE LUXURY OF LIVING OUTSIDE OF SOCIETY, WHILE CONTINUING TO FEED OFF OF IT.
BUT C'MON, *IVAN...*
...YOU GUYS IN THE MARKET, *YOU* LIVE *OUTSIDE* SOCIETY TOO.
NO WE DON'T.
WE LIVE OUTSIDE THE *LAW.*
BUT WE LIVE VERY MUCH WITHIN SOCIETY. WE *BUY* AND *SELL* THINGS. AND WE'VE CREATED A WORKING ECONOMY INSIDE THE ZONE.
...BUT THESE *CREATURES* ARE PUTTING ALL OF THAT AT RISK!
YOU SAID IT YOURSELF, JENN. IF WE DON'T DO SOMETHING ABOUT THESE MONSTERS SOON, THE FEDS ARE GONNA COME SHUT US DOWN AND DESTROY EVERYTHING WE'VE BUILT!
EVERYTHING YOU BUILT *ILLEGALLY!*

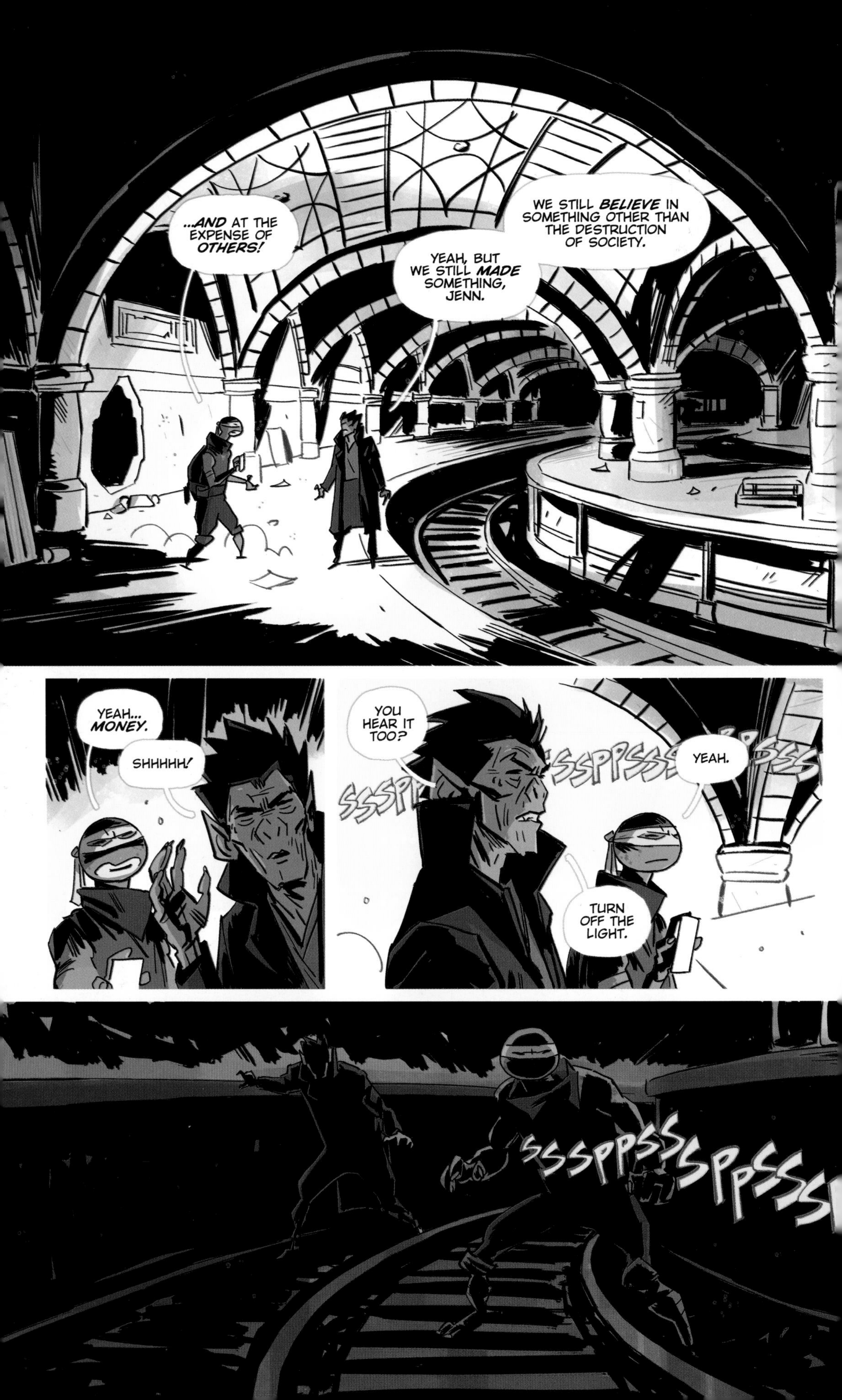
...AND AT THE EXPENSE OF OTHERS!
YEAH, BUT WE STILL MADE SOMETHING, JENN.
WE STILL BELIEVE IN SOMETHING OTHER THAN THE DESTRUCTION OF SOCIETY.
YEAH... MONEY.
SHHHHH!
YOU HEAR IT TOO?
SSSPP
SSSPPSSS
YEAH.
TURN OFF THE LIGHT.
SSSPPSSSPPSSS

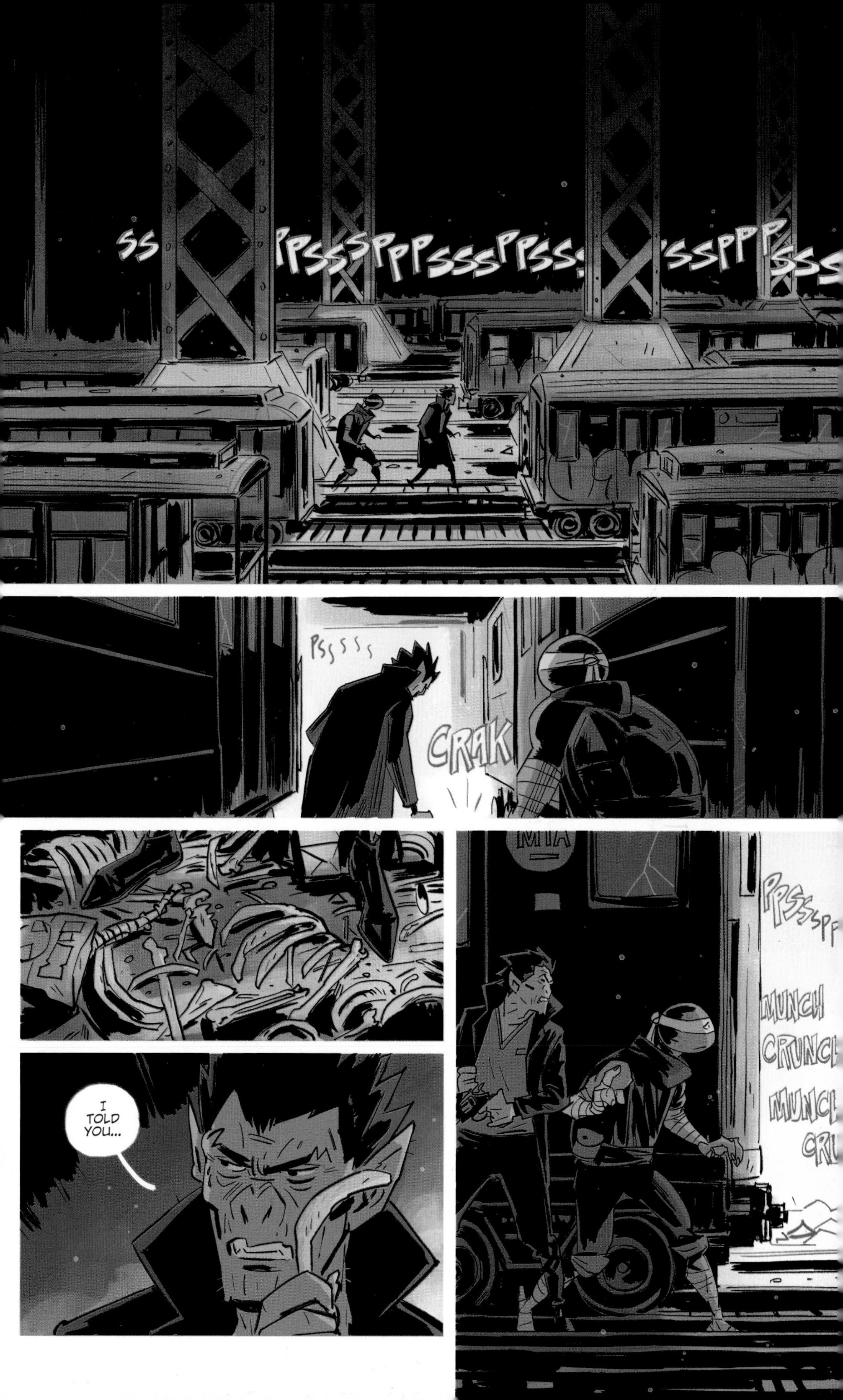

SSPPSSSPPPSSSPPSSS
SSSPPPSSS
PSSSSS
CRAK
PPSSSSPP
MUNCH
CRUNCH
MUNCH
CRU
I TOLD YOU...

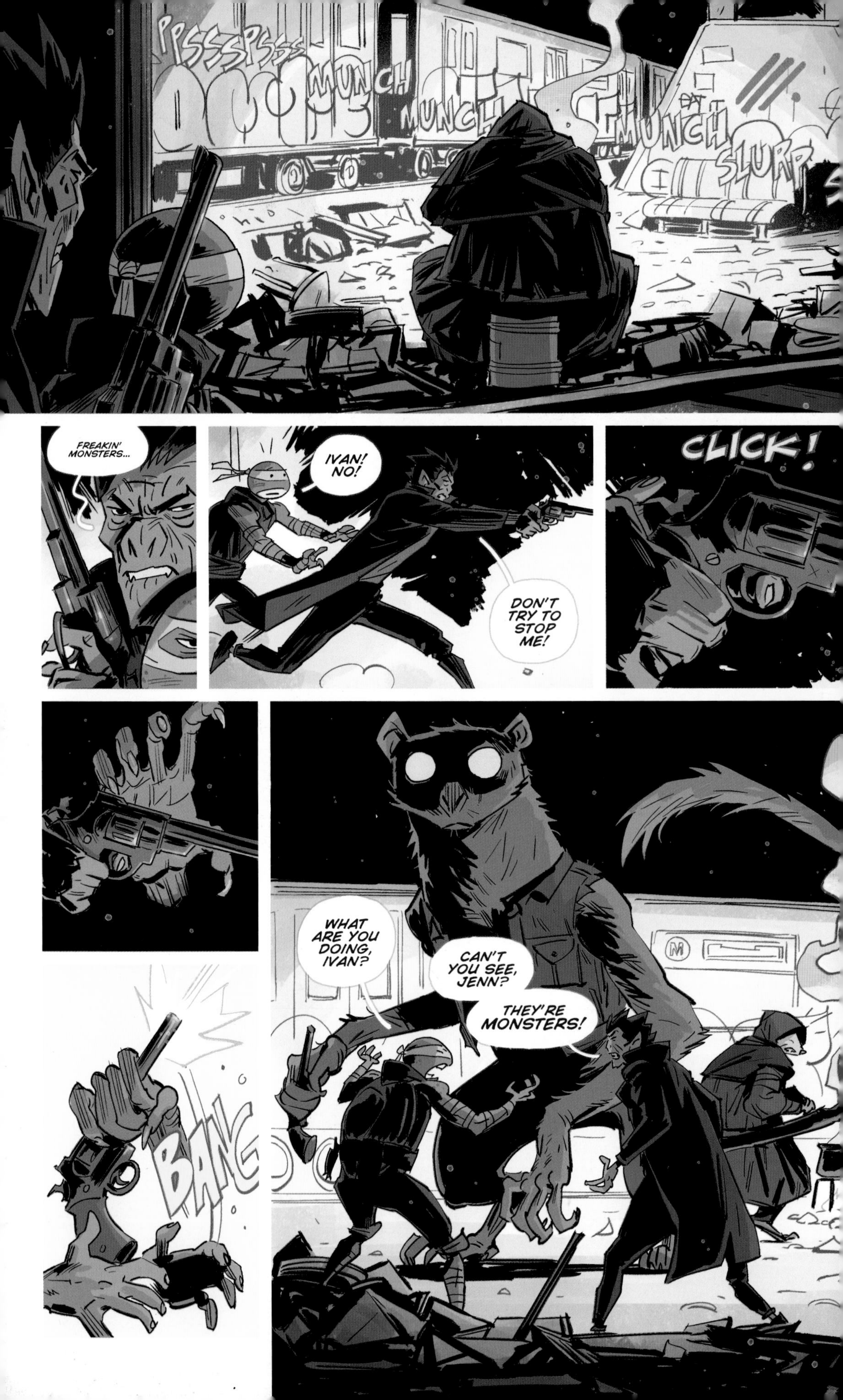
PSSSPSSS
MUNCH
MUNCH
MUNCH
SLURP
FREAKIN' MONSTERS...
IVAN! NO!
DON'T TRY TO STOP ME!
CLICK!
BANG
WHAT ARE YOU DOING, IVAN?
CAN'T YOU SEE, JENN?
THEY'RE MONSTERS!

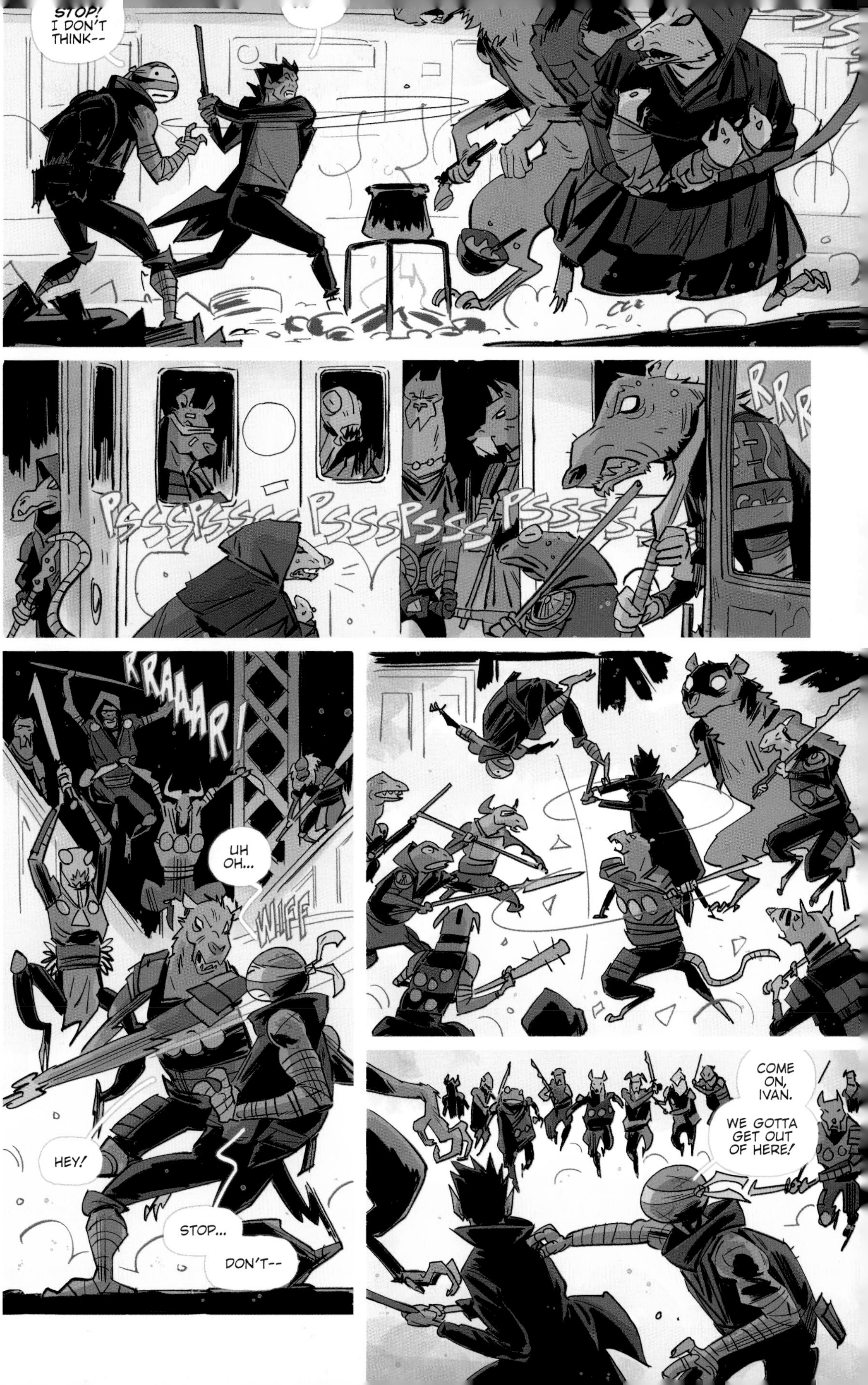
STOP! I DON'T THINK--
PSSSPSSSSS PSSSPSSSS PSSSSSS
RRR
RRAAAAR!
UH OH...
WHFF
HEY!
STOP...
DON'T--
COME ON, IVAN.
WE GOTTA GET OUT OF HERE!

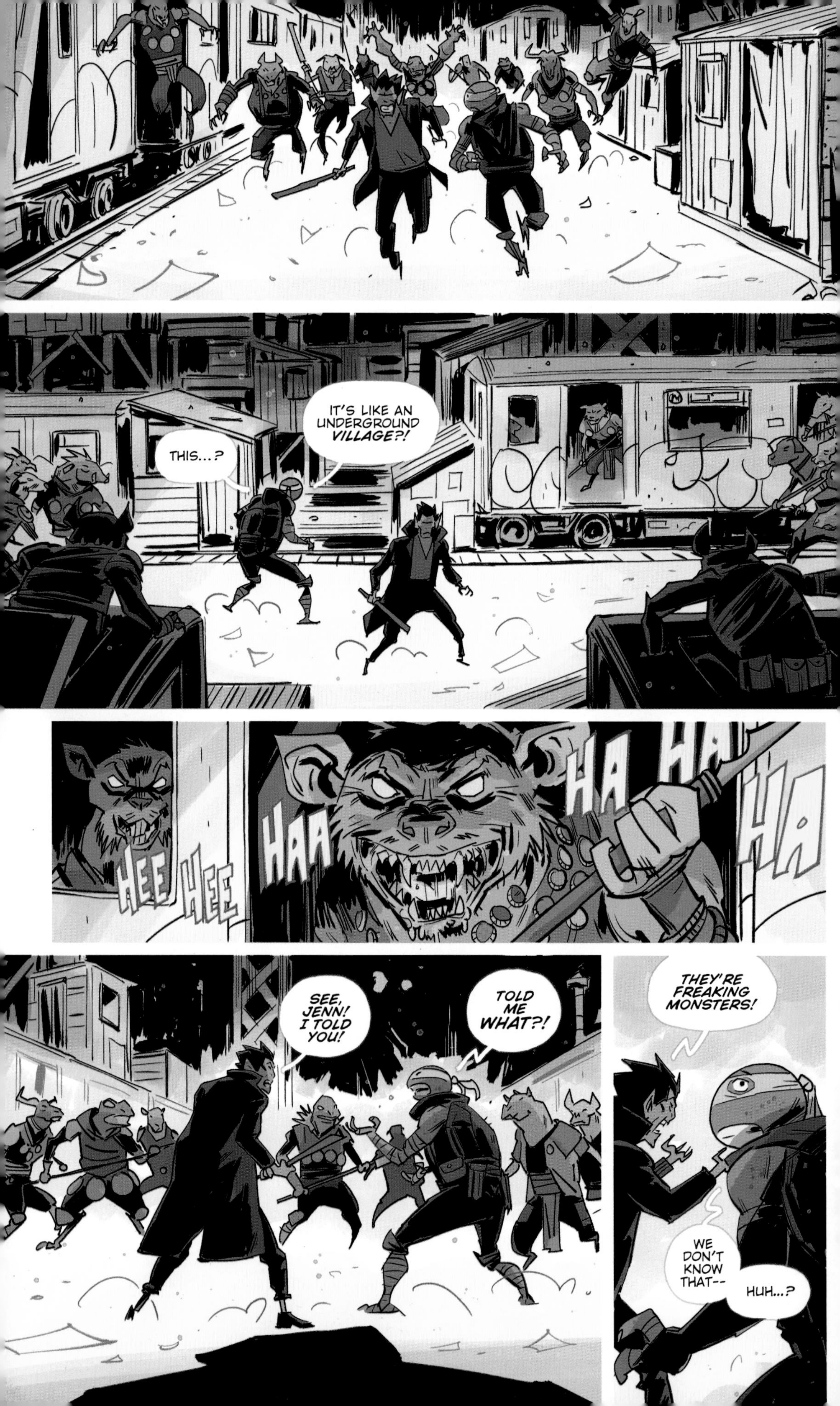
THIS...?
IT'S LIKE AN UNDERGROUND VILLAGE?!
HEE HEE
HAA
HA HA
HA
SEE, JENN! I TOLD YOU!
TOLD ME WHAT?!
THEY'RE FREAKING MONSTERS!
WE DON'T KNOW THAT--
HUH...?

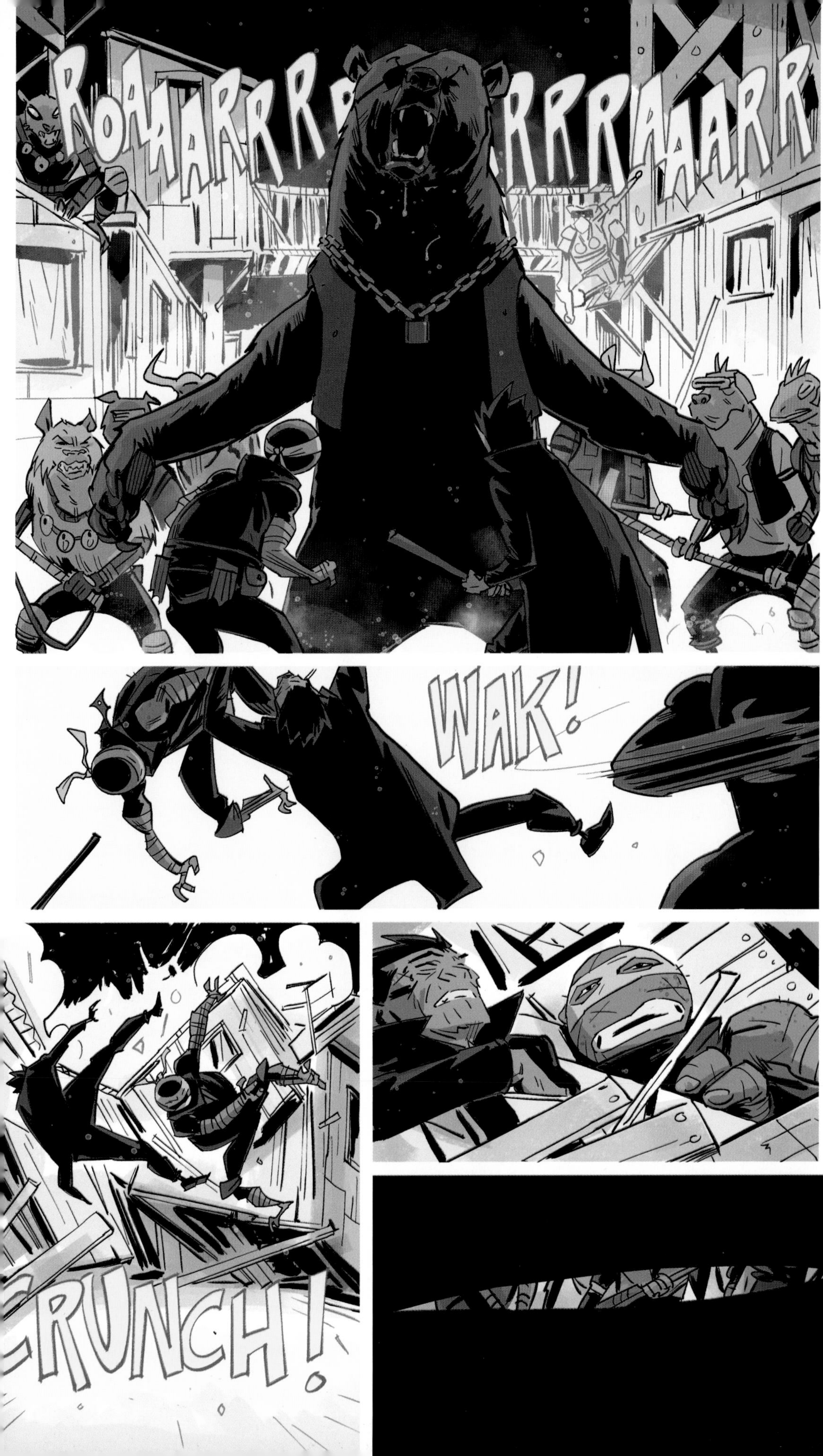

ROAAARRR
RRRAAARR
WAK!
CRUNCH!

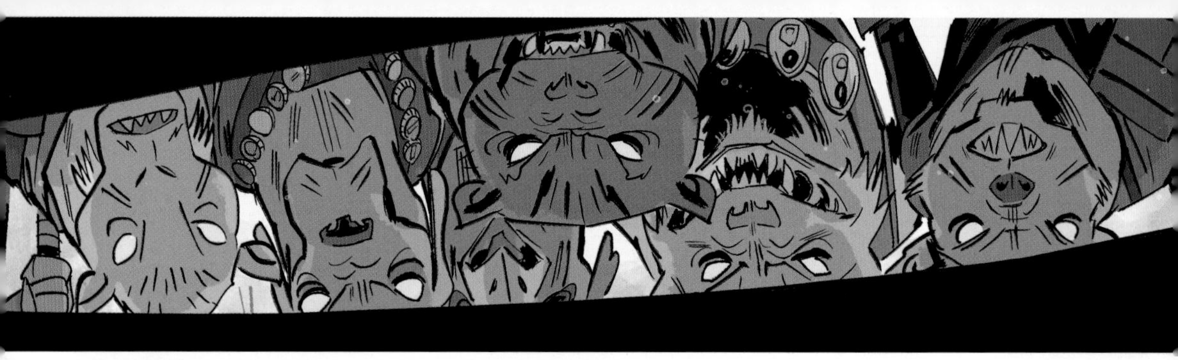

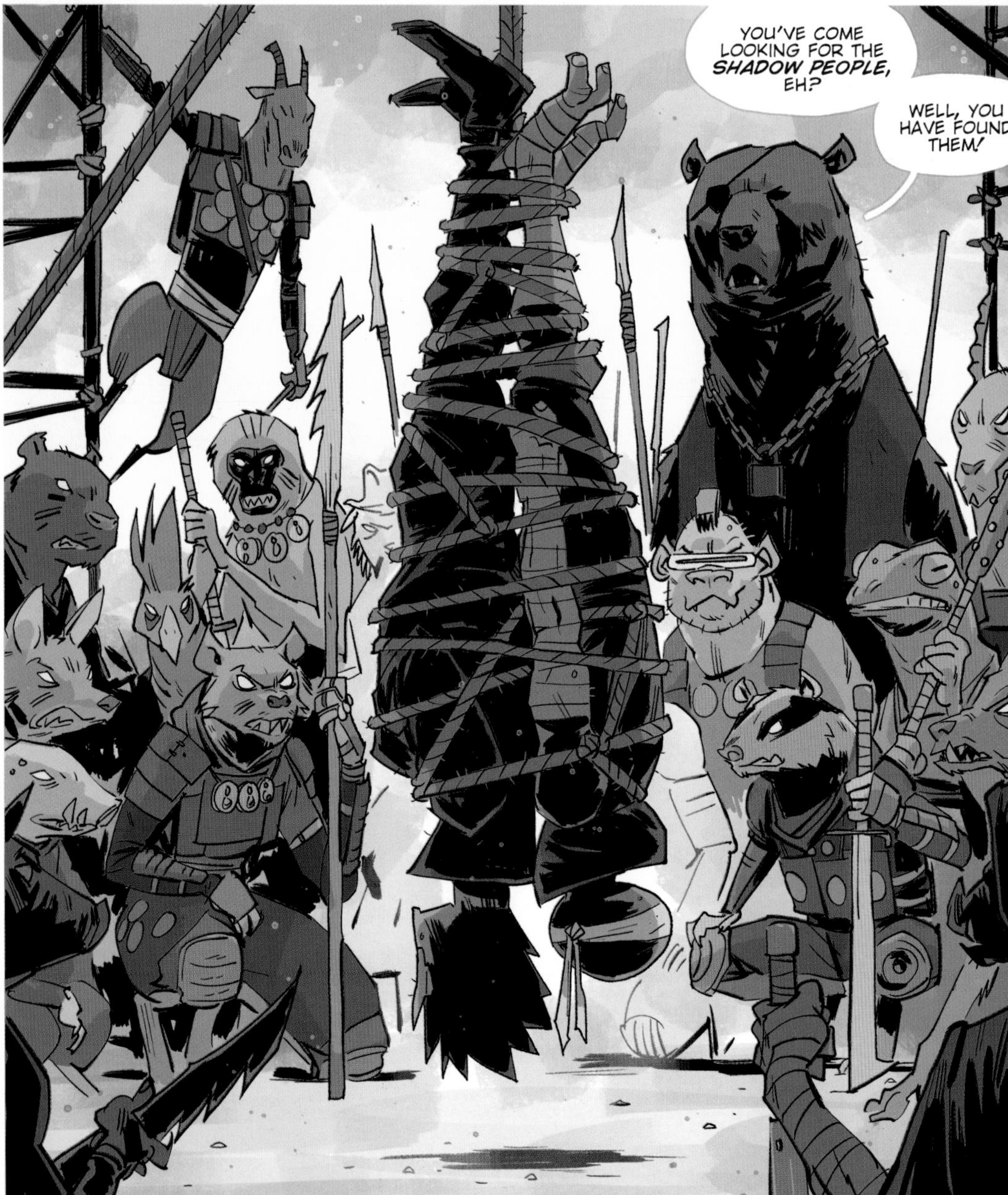

YOU'VE COME LOOKING FOR THE *SHADOW PEOPLE,* EH?
WELL, YOU HAVE FOUND THEM!

Art by Juni Ba

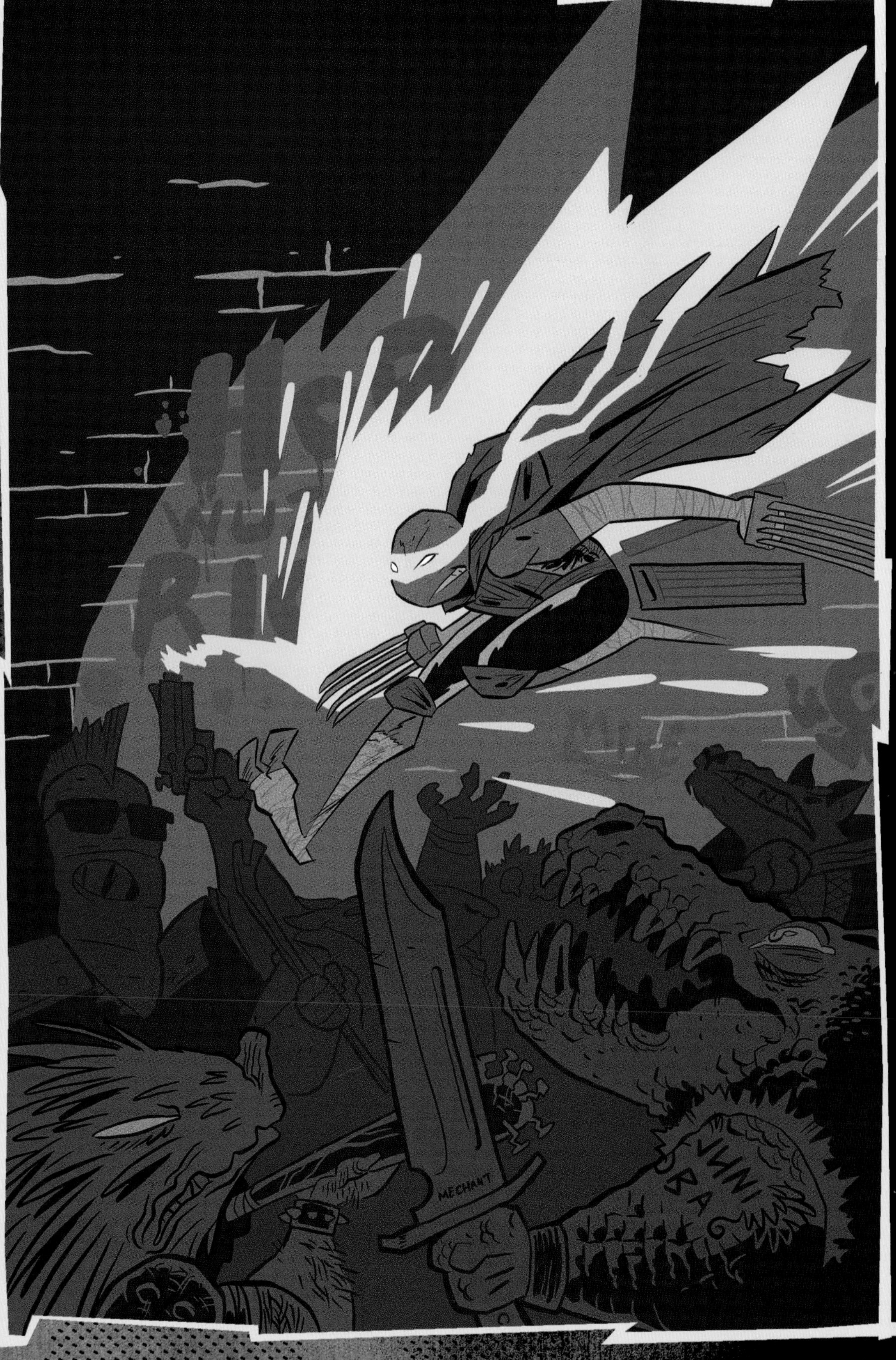
MECHANT

Art by Brahm Revel

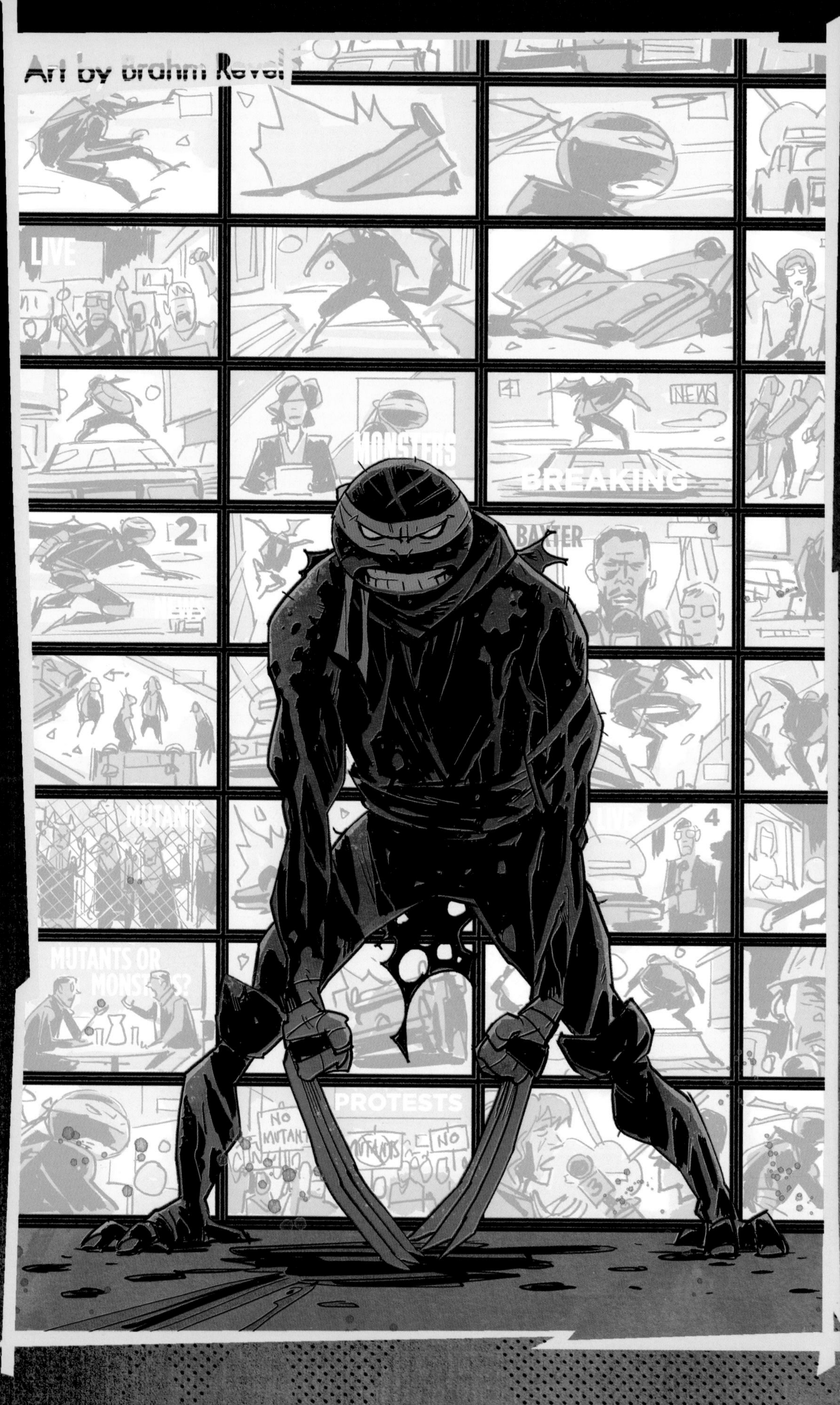
LIVE
NEWS
MONSTERS
BREAKING
2
BAXTER
MUTANTS
4
PROTESTS
NO
MUTANTS
NO

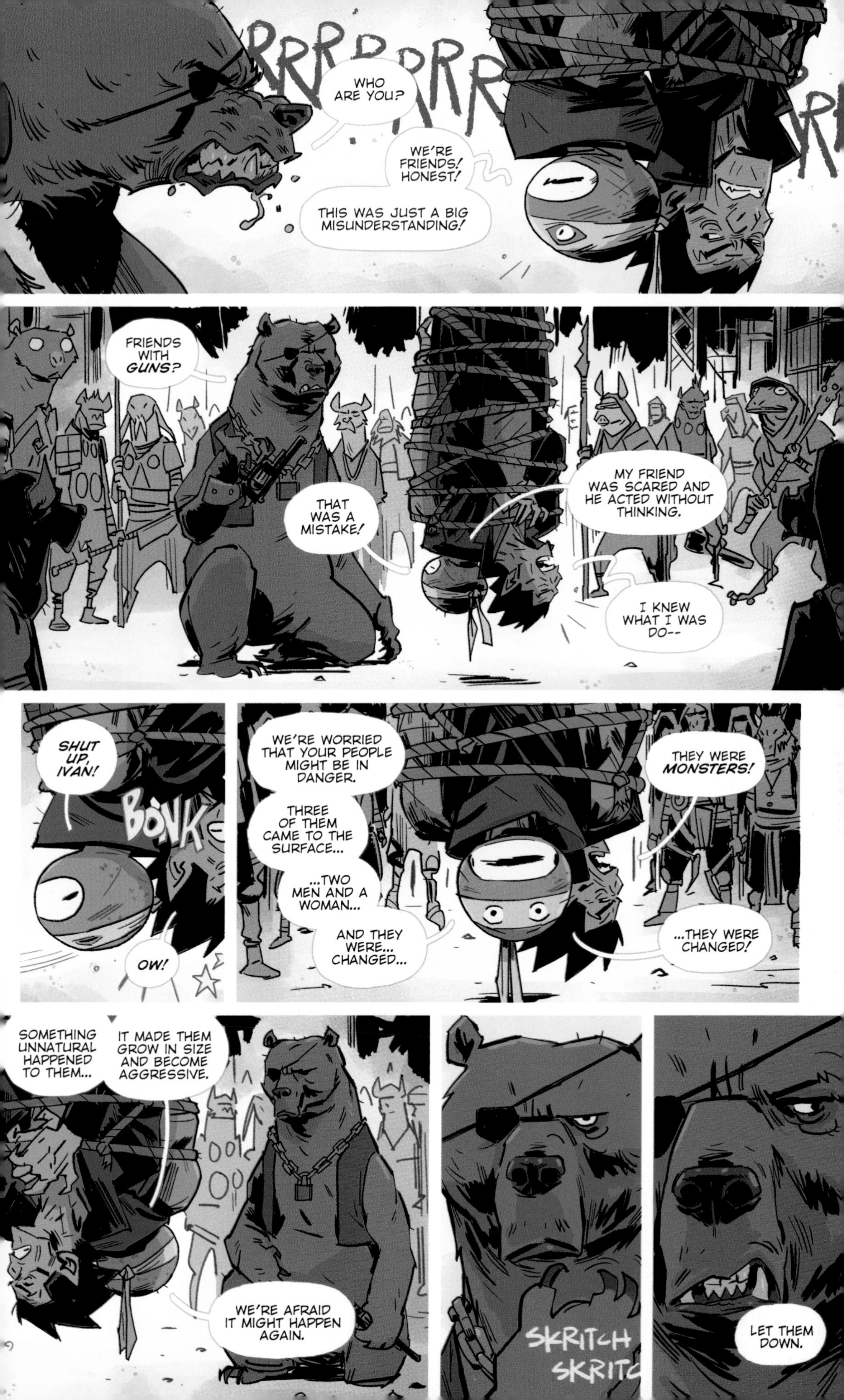
RRRRRRRR
WHO ARE YOU?
WE'RE FRIENDS! HONEST!
THIS WAS JUST A BIG MISUNDERSTANDING!
FRIENDS WITH GUNS?
THAT WAS A MISTAKE!
MY FRIEND WAS SCARED AND HE ACTED WITHOUT THINKING.
I KNEW WHAT I WAS DO--
SHUT UP, IVAN!
BONK
OW!
WE'RE WORRIED THAT YOUR PEOPLE MIGHT BE IN DANGER.
THREE OF THEM CAME TO THE SURFACE...
...TWO MEN AND A WOMAN...
AND THEY WERE... CHANGED...
THEY WERE MONSTERS!
...THEY WERE CHANGED!
SOMETHING UNNATURAL HAPPENED TO THEM...
IT MADE THEM GROW IN SIZE AND BECOME AGGRESSIVE.
WE'RE AFRAID IT MIGHT HAPPEN AGAIN.
SKRITCH
LET THEM DOWN.

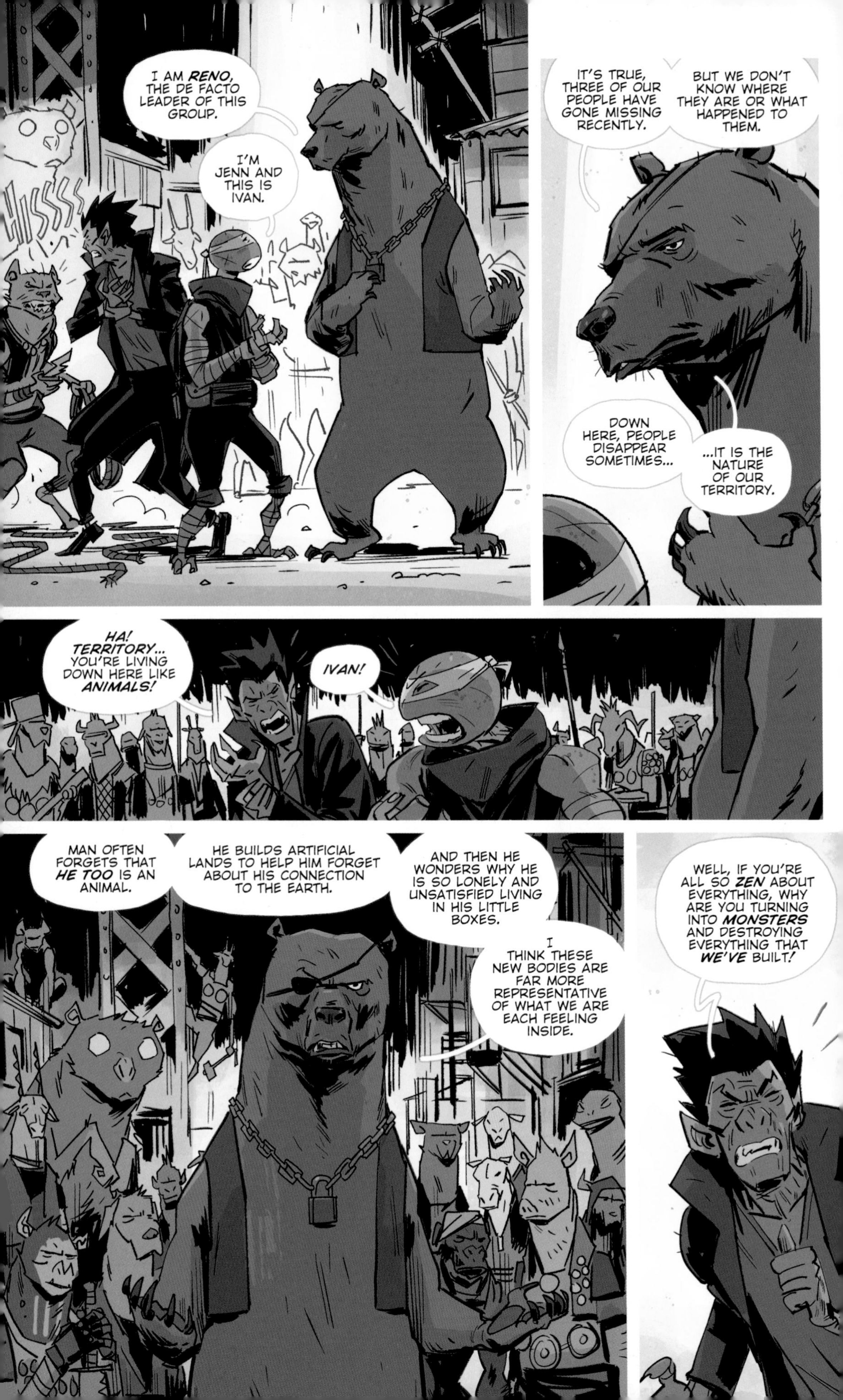
HISSSSS
I AM RENO, THE DE FACTO LEADER OF THIS GROUP.
I'M JENN AND THIS IS IVAN.
IT'S TRUE, THREE OF OUR PEOPLE HAVE GONE MISSING RECENTLY.
BUT WE DON'T KNOW WHERE THEY ARE OR WHAT HAPPENED TO THEM.
DOWN HERE, PEOPLE DISAPPEAR SOMETIMES...
...IT IS THE NATURE OF OUR TERRITORY.
HA! TERRITORY... YOU'RE LIVING DOWN HERE LIKE ANIMALS!
IVAN!
MAN OFTEN FORGETS THAT HE TOO IS AN ANIMAL.
HE BUILDS ARTIFICIAL LANDS TO HELP HIM FORGET ABOUT HIS CONNECTION TO THE EARTH.
AND THEN HE WONDERS WHY HE IS SO LONELY AND UNSATISFIED LIVING IN HIS LITTLE BOXES.
I THINK THESE NEW BODIES ARE FAR MORE REPRESENTATIVE OF WHAT WE ARE EACH FEELING INSIDE.
WELL, IF YOU'RE ALL SO ZEN ABOUT EVERYTHING, WHY ARE YOU TURNING INTO MONSTERS AND DESTROYING EVERYTHING THAT WE'VE BUILT!

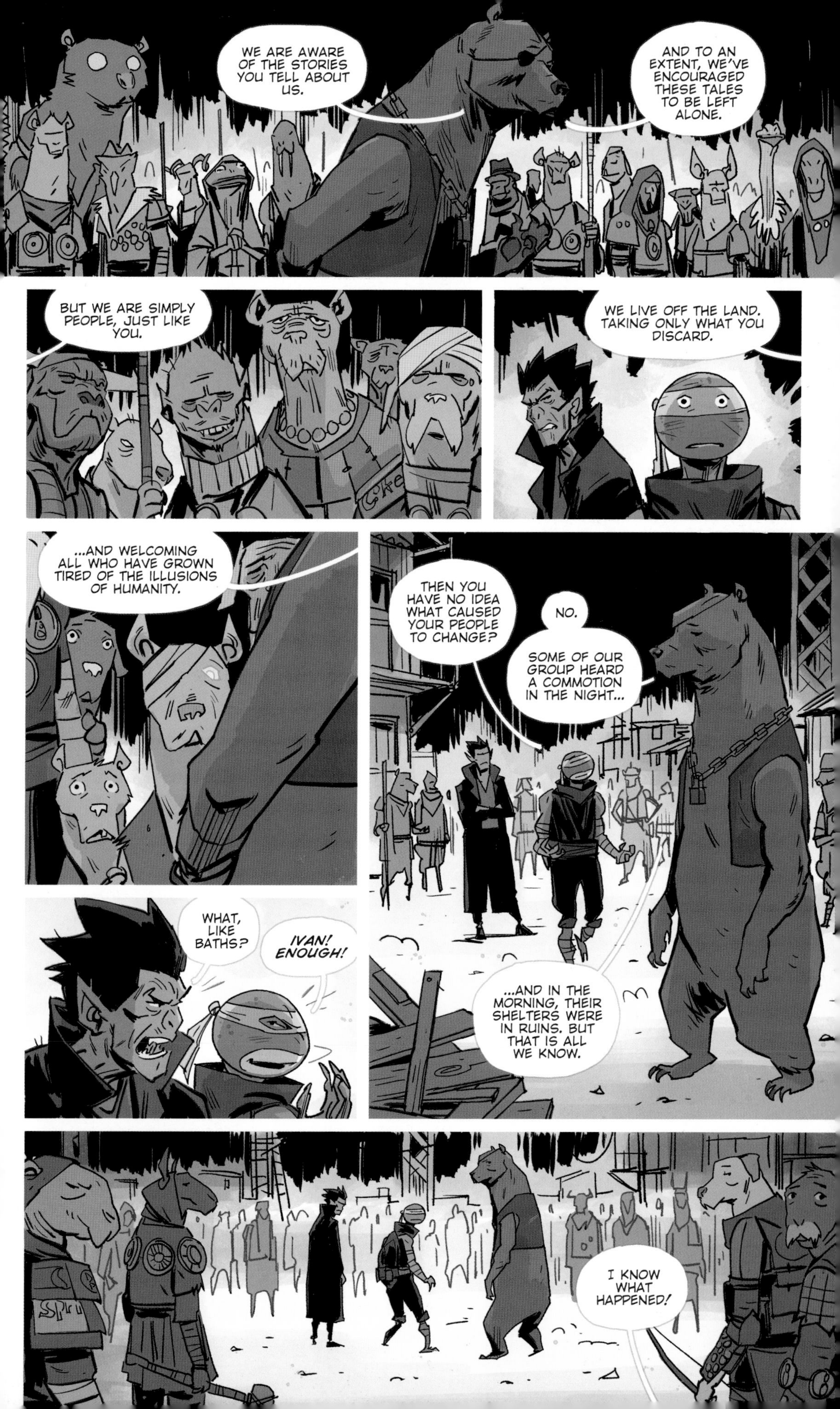
WE ARE AWARE OF THE STORIES YOU TELL ABOUT US.
AND TO AN EXTENT, WE'VE ENCOURAGED THESE TALES TO BE LEFT ALONE.
BUT WE ARE SIMPLY PEOPLE, JUST LIKE YOU.
WE LIVE OFF THE LAND. TAKING ONLY WHAT YOU DISCARD.
...AND WELCOMING ALL WHO HAVE GROWN TIRED OF THE ILLUSIONS OF HUMANITY.
THEN YOU HAVE NO IDEA WHAT CAUSED YOUR PEOPLE TO CHANGE?
NO.
SOME OF OUR GROUP HEARD A COMMOTION IN THE NIGHT...
...AND IN THE MORNING, THEIR SHELTERS WERE IN RUINS. BUT THAT IS ALL WE KNOW.
WHAT, LIKE BATHS?
IVAN! ENOUGH!
I KNOW WHAT HAPPENED!

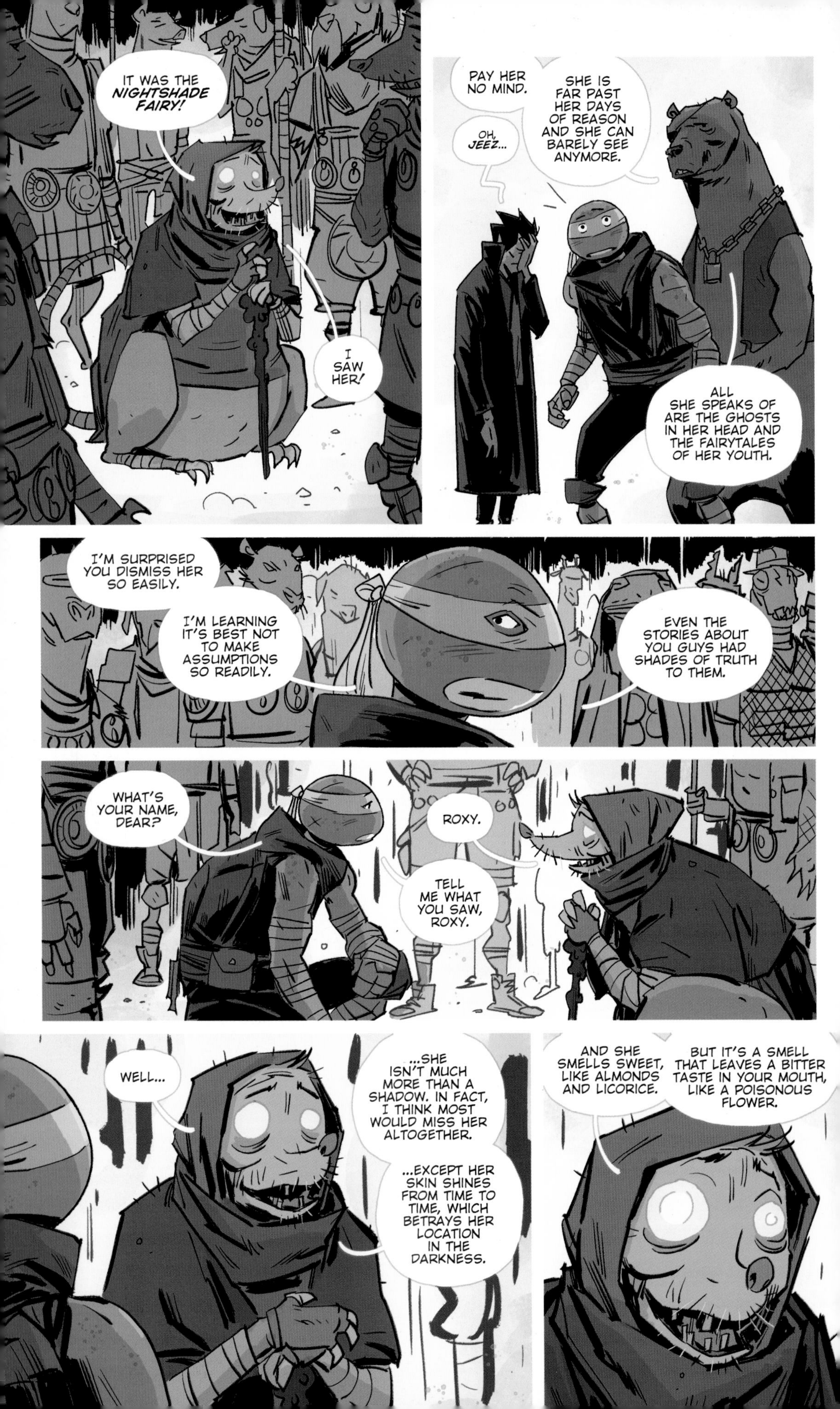
IT WAS THE *NIGHTSHADE FAIRY!*
I SAW HER!
PAY HER NO MIND.
SHE IS FAR PAST HER DAYS OF REASON AND SHE CAN BARELY SEE ANYMORE.
OH, *JEEZ...*
ALL SHE SPEAKS OF ARE THE GHOSTS IN HER HEAD AND THE FAIRYTALES OF HER YOUTH.
I'M SURPRISED YOU DISMISS HER SO EASILY.
I'M LEARNING IT'S BEST NOT TO MAKE ASSUMPTIONS SO READILY.
EVEN THE STORIES ABOUT YOU GUYS HAD SHADES OF TRUTH TO THEM.
WHAT'S YOUR NAME, DEAR?
ROXY.
TELL ME WHAT YOU SAW, ROXY.
WELL...
...SHE ISN'T MUCH MORE THAN A SHADOW. IN FACT, I THINK MOST WOULD MISS HER ALTOGETHER.
...EXCEPT HER SKIN SHINES FROM TIME TO TIME, WHICH BETRAYS HER LOCATION IN THE DARKNESS.
AND SHE SMELLS SWEET, LIKE ALMONDS AND LICORICE.
BUT IT'S A SMELL THAT LEAVES A BITTER TASTE IN YOUR MOUTH, LIKE A POISONOUS FLOWER.

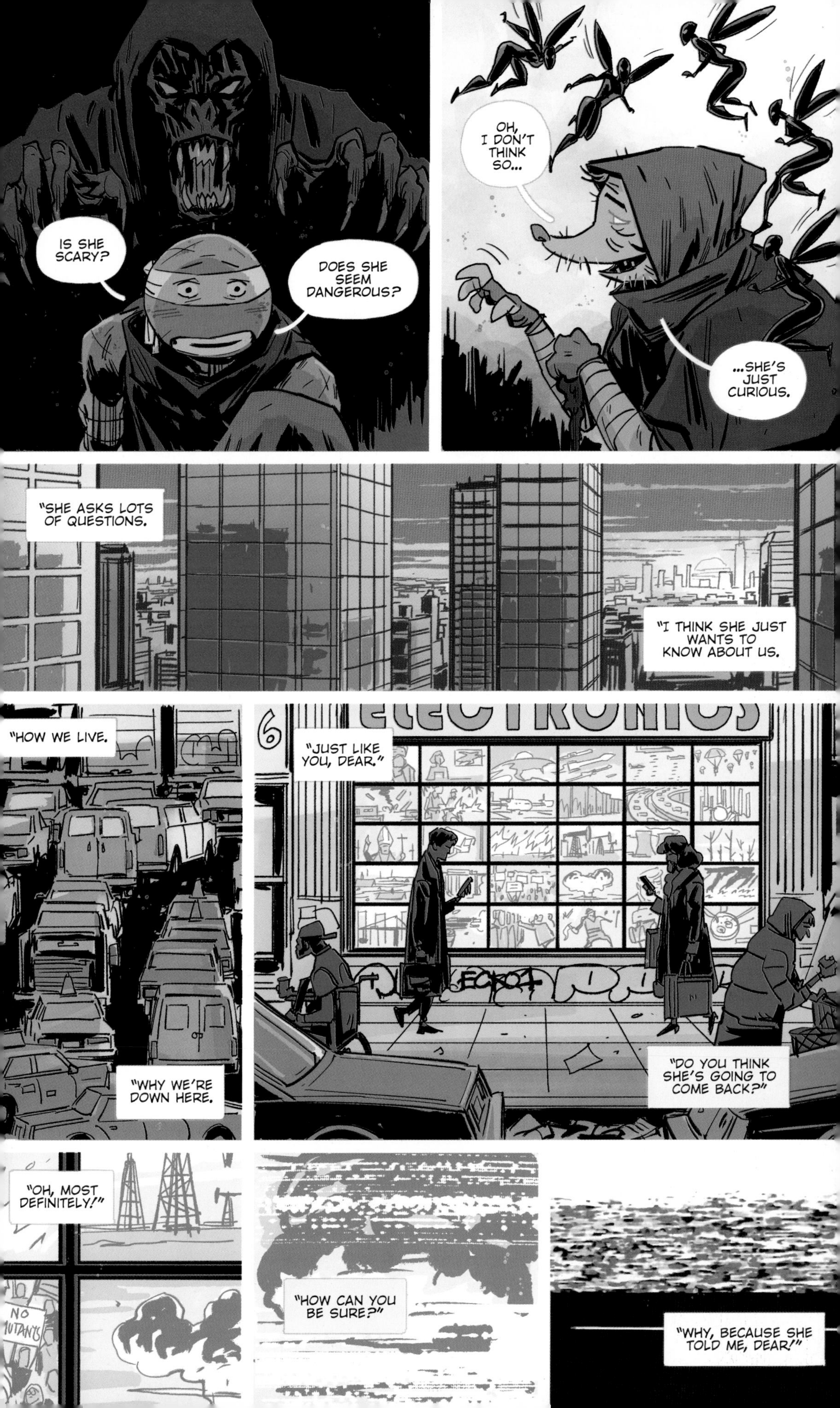

IS SHE SCARY?
DOES SHE SEEM DANGEROUS?
OH, I DON'T THINK SO...
...SHE'S JUST CURIOUS.
"SHE ASKS LOTS OF QUESTIONS.
"I THINK SHE JUST WANTS TO KNOW ABOUT US.
"HOW WE LIVE.
"WHY WE'RE DOWN HERE.
ELECTRONICS
"JUST LIKE YOU, DEAR."
"DO YOU THINK SHE'S GOING TO COME BACK?"
"OH, MOST DEFINITELY!"
NO MUTANTS
"HOW CAN YOU BE SURE?"
"WHY, BECAUSE SHE TOLD ME, DEAR!"

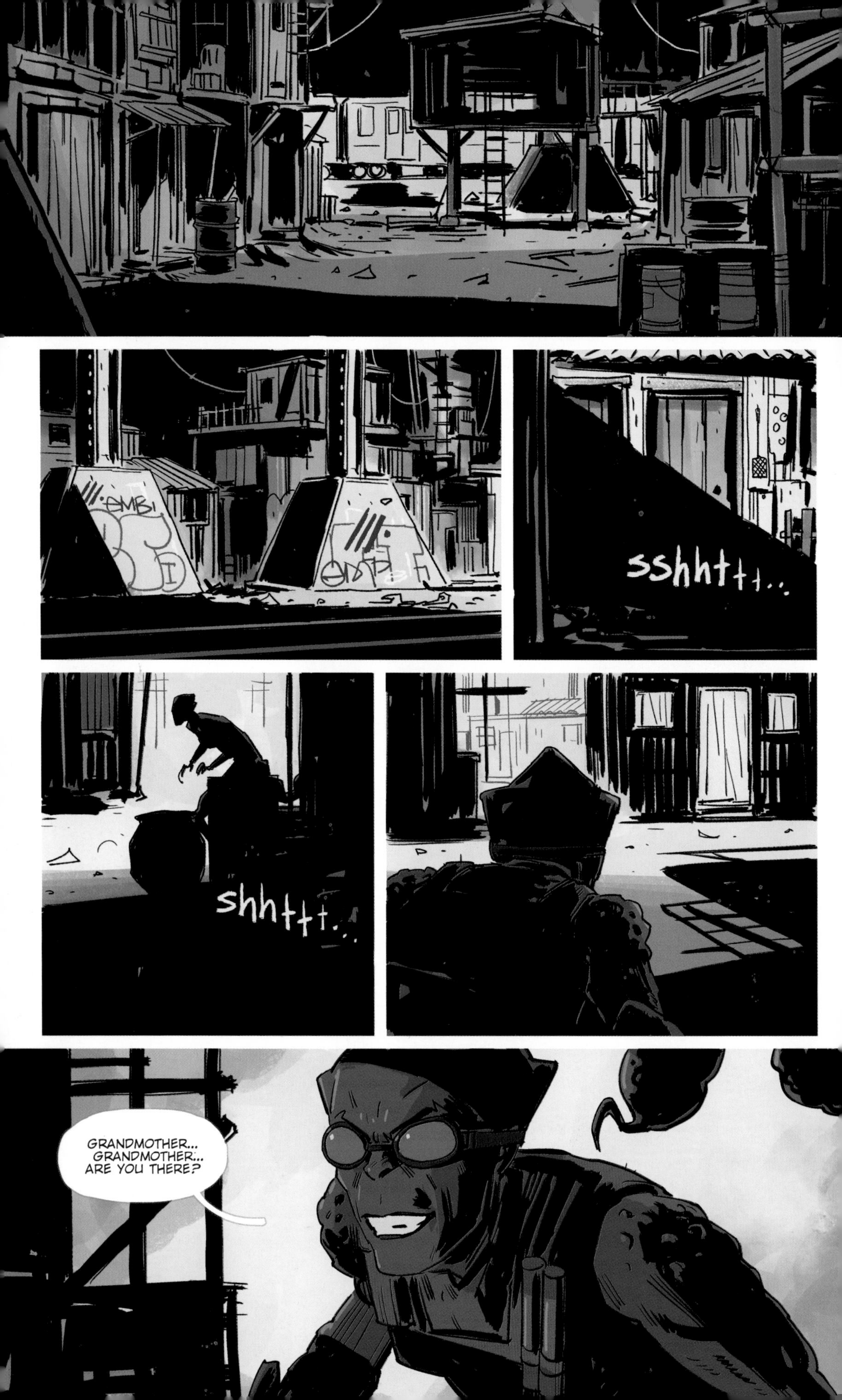
sshttt...
shhttt...
GRANDMOTHER... GRANDMOTHER... ARE YOU THERE?

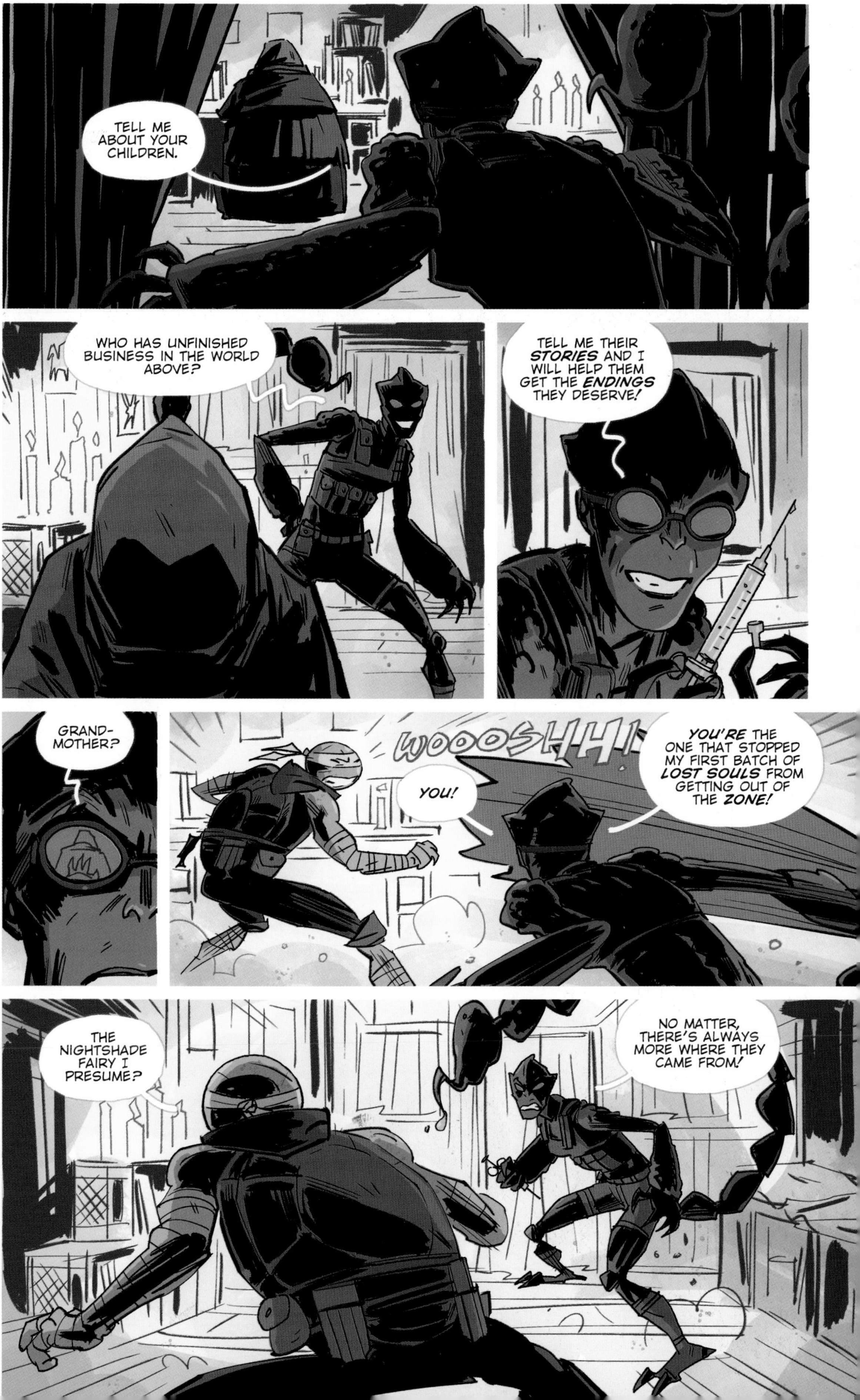
TELL ME ABOUT YOUR CHILDREN.
WHO HAS UNFINISHED BUSINESS IN THE WORLD ABOVE?
TELL ME THEIR STORIES AND I WILL HELP THEM GET THE ENDINGS THEY DESERVE!
GRAND-MOTHER?
WOOOSHH!
YOU!
YOU'RE THE ONE THAT STOPPED MY FIRST BATCH OF LOST SOULS FROM GETTING OUT OF THE ZONE!
THE NIGHTSHADE FAIRY I PRESUME?
NO MATTER, THERE'S ALWAYS MORE WHERE THEY CAME FROM!

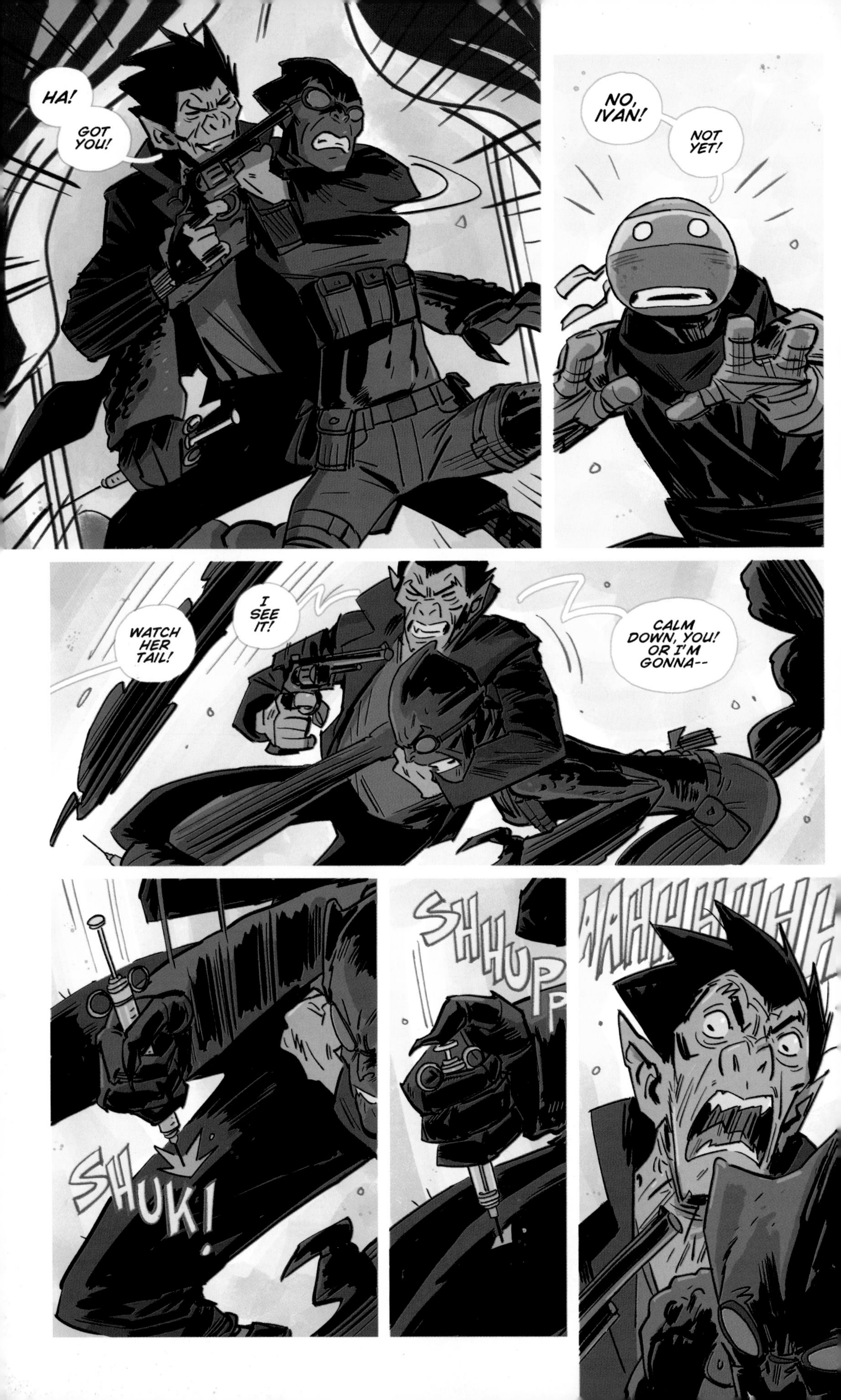
HA!
GOT YOU!
NO, IVAN!
NOT YET!
WATCH HER TAIL!
I SEE IT!
CALM DOWN, YOU! OR I'M GONNA--
SHUK!
SHHUPP
AAHHHHHHH

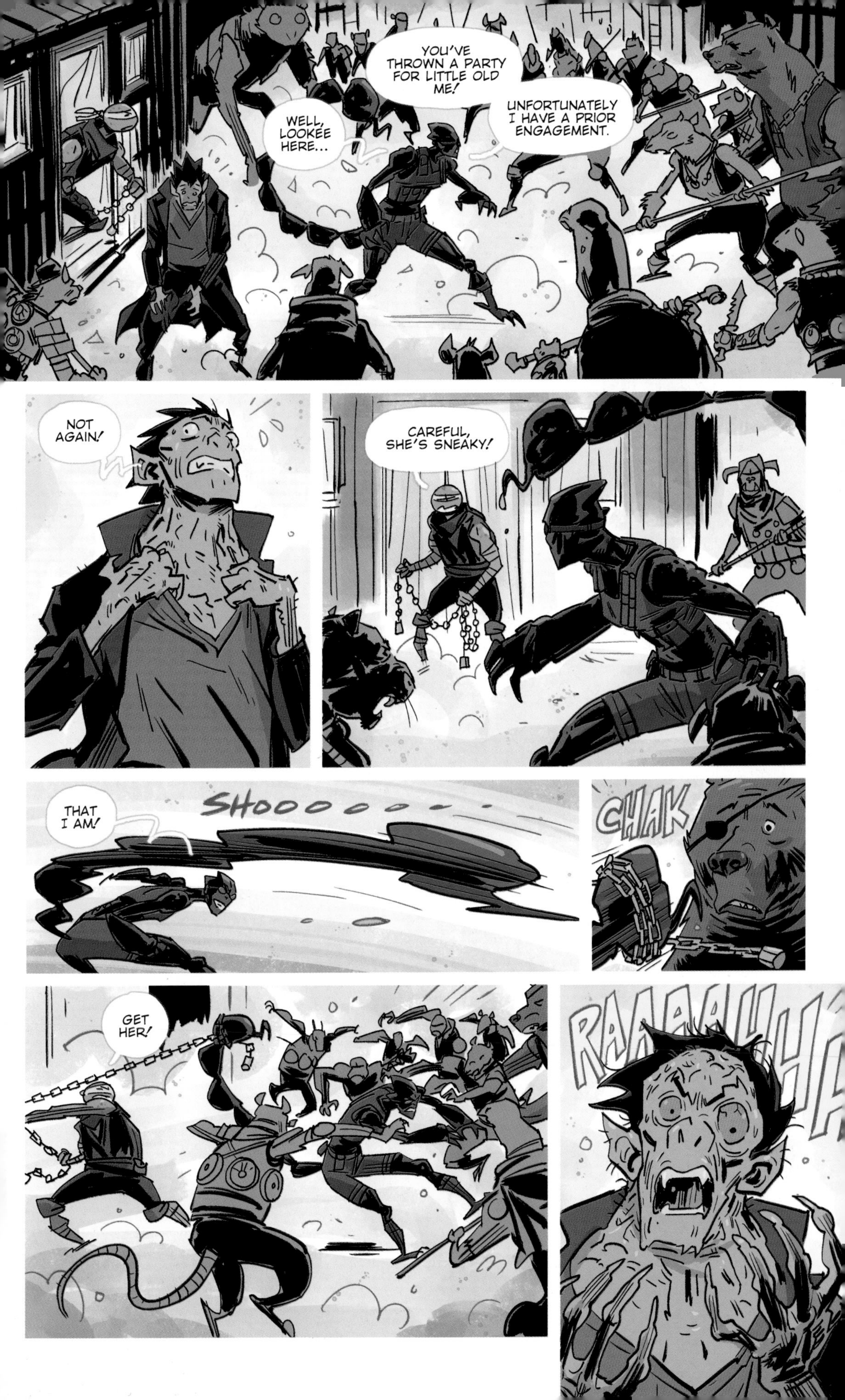
WELL, LOOKEE HERE...
YOU'VE THROWN A PARTY FOR LITTLE OLD ME!
UNFORTUNATELY I HAVE A PRIOR ENGAGEMENT.
NOT AGAIN!
CAREFUL, SHE'S SNEAKY!
THAT I AM!
SHOOOOOO--
CHAK
GET HER!
RAAAAHH

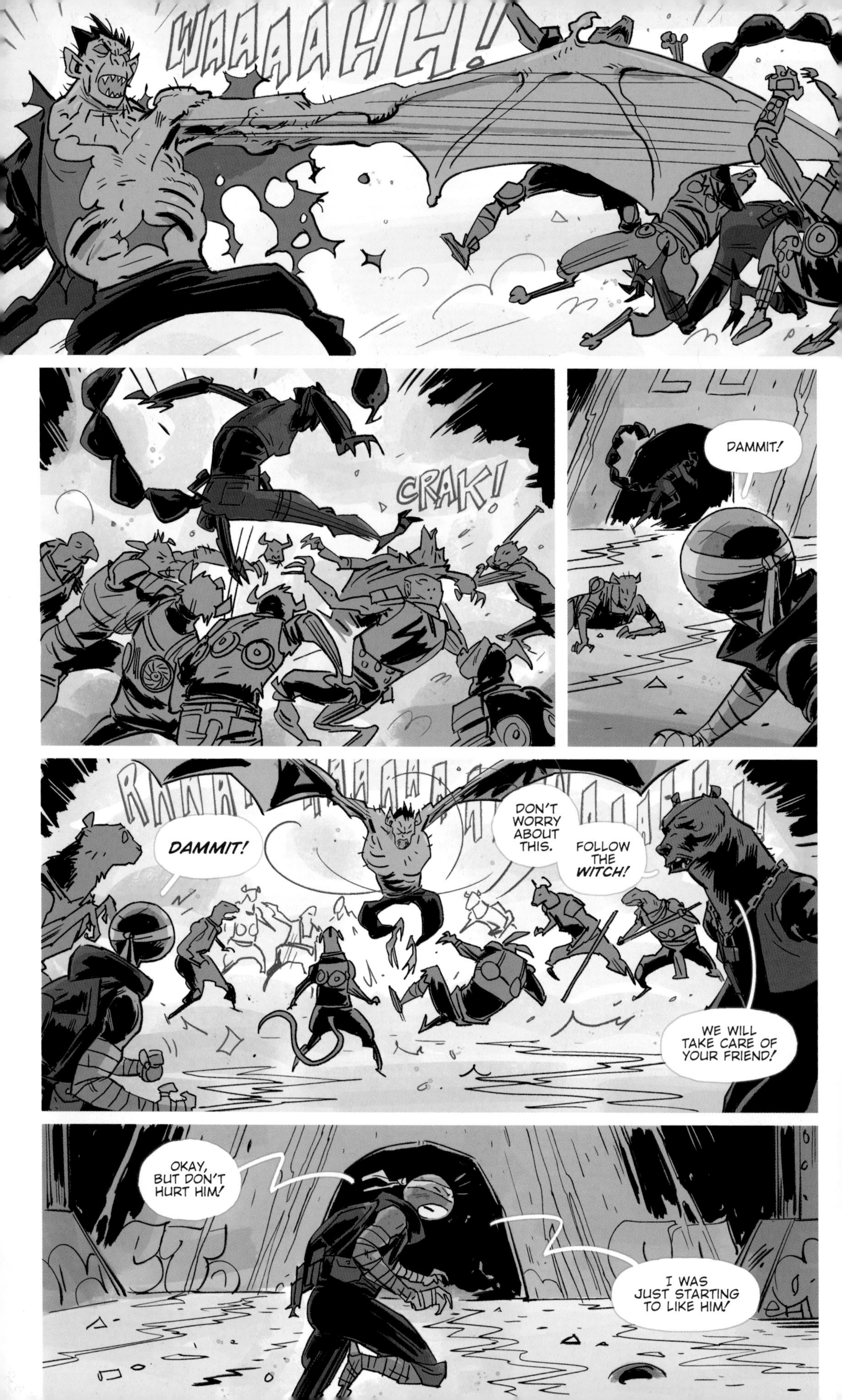

WAAAAAHH!
CRAK!
DAMMIT!
RAAAAAAAAAAAAAAAAAAAAAA!
DAMMIT!
DON'T WORRY ABOUT THIS.
FOLLOW THE WITCH!
WE WILL TAKE CARE OF YOUR FRIEND!
OKAY, BUT DON'T HURT HIM!
I WAS JUST STARTING TO LIKE HIM!

SHOOOO TAK!

SUCKER PUNCH...

...REAL CLASSY!

BLOK!

NATURALLY...

A GIRL HAS TO KEEP HER SUITORS ON THEIR TOES.

SPEAKING OF... YOU'RE *NEW* AREN'T YOU?

I DON'T SEEM TO REMEMBER A SISTER IN THE TURTLE FAMILY CHRISTMAS CARD.

CRAK!

I'M *ZODI*, BY THE WAY.

YEAH, I HEARD OF YOU...

JENNIKA...

WHAT? NO FEMALE RENAISSANCE PAINTERS?

...SHAME.

WELL, IT'S BEEN A PLEASURE...

REALLY, IT HAS...

...BUT UNFORTUNATELY I REALLY HAVE TO BE GOING.

CHAK CHAK CH CHAK CHAK CH

GRAB!

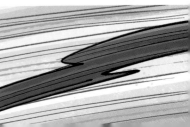

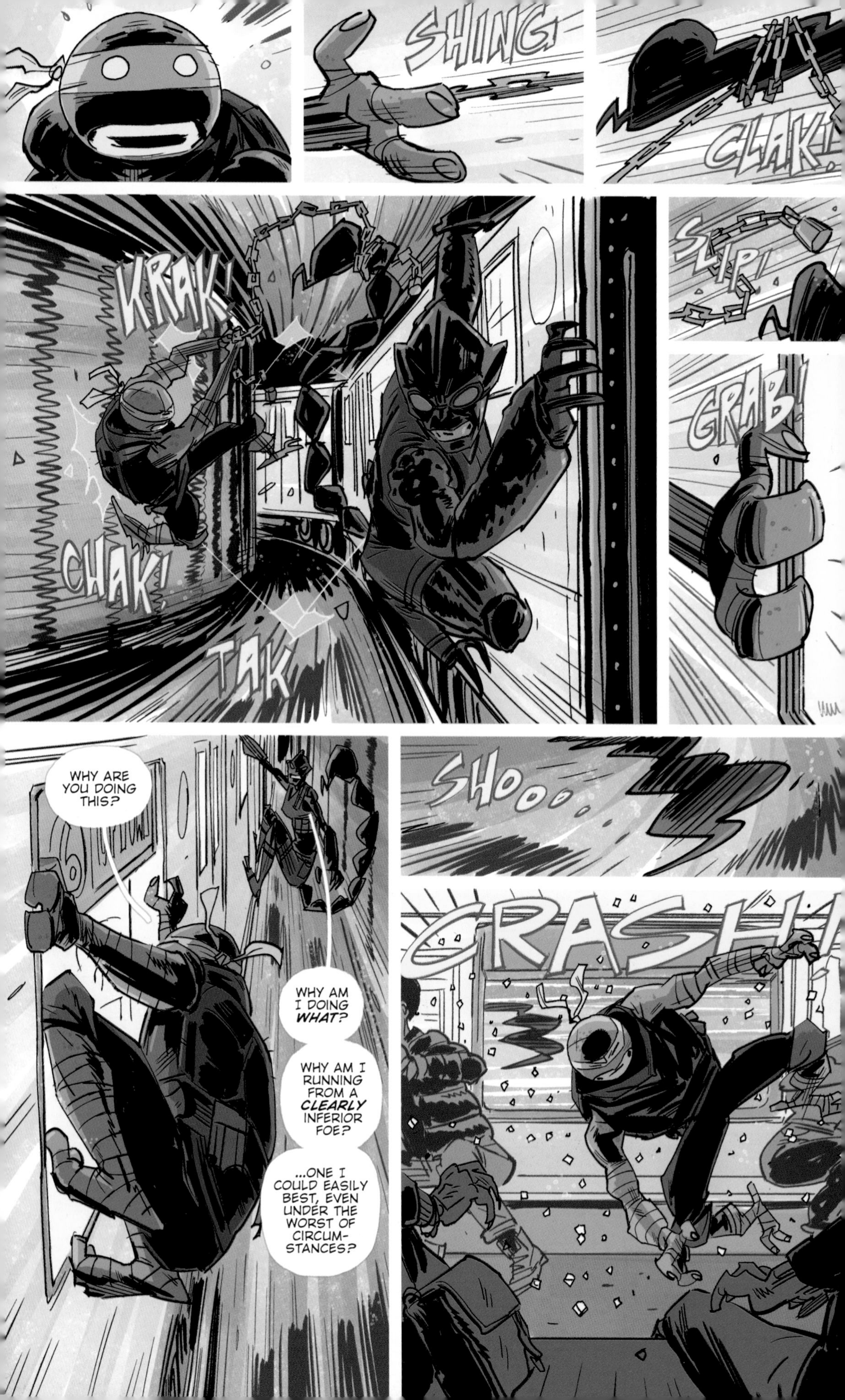
SHING
CLAK!
KRAK!
CHAK!
TAK
SLIP!
GRAB!
WHY ARE YOU DOING THIS?
WHY AM I DOING *WHAT*?
WHY AM I RUNNING FROM A *CLEARLY* INFERIOR FOE?
...ONE I COULD EASILY BEST, EVEN UNDER THE WORST OF CIRCUM-STANCES?
SHOOOO...
CRASH!

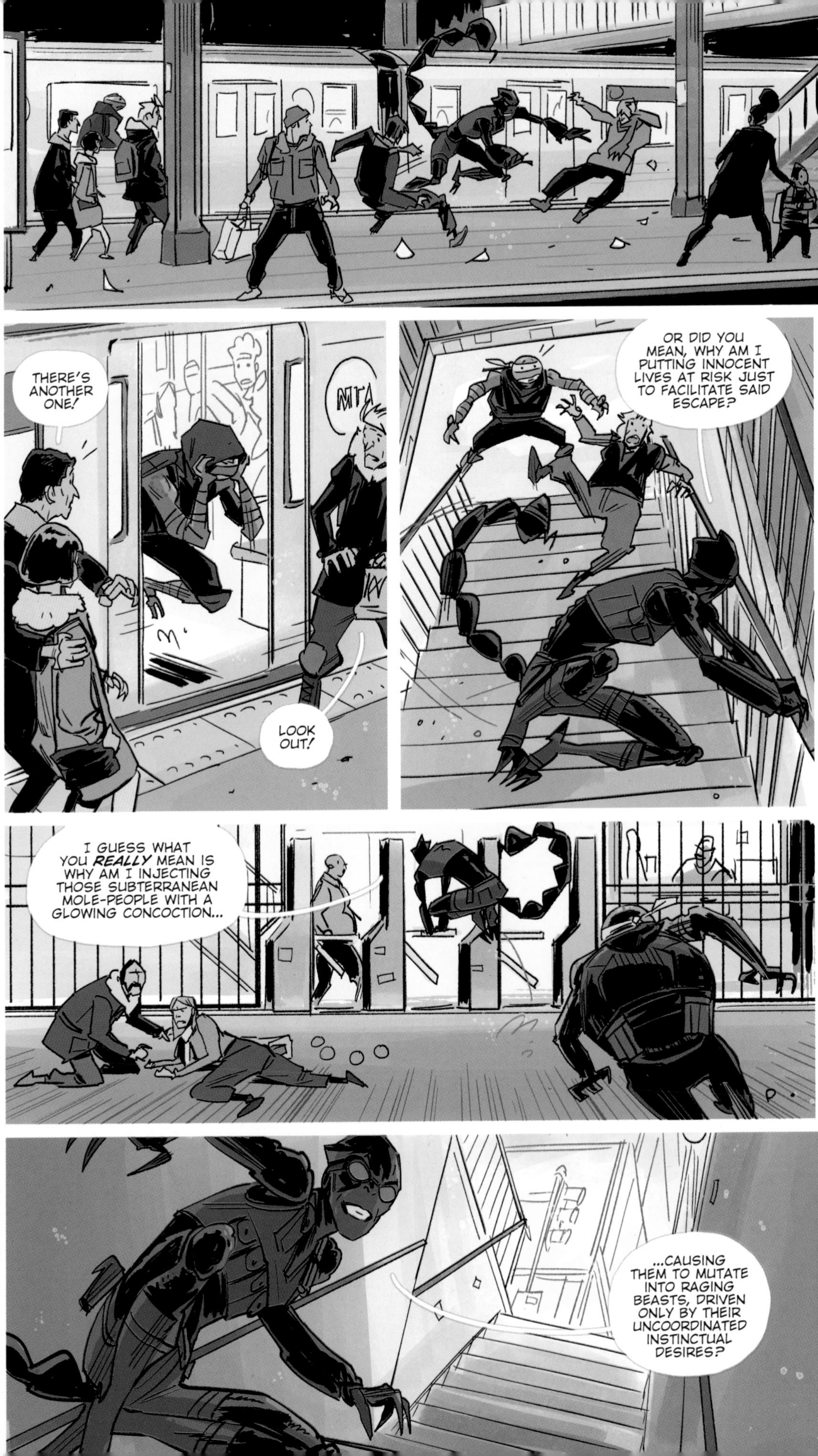
THERE'S ANOTHER ONE!
LOOK OUT!
OR DID YOU MEAN, WHY AM I PUTTING INNOCENT LIVES AT RISK JUST TO FACILITATE SAID ESCAPE?
I GUESS WHAT YOU *REALLY* MEAN IS WHY AM I INJECTING THOSE SUBTERRANEAN MOLE-PEOPLE WITH A GLOWING CONCOCTION...
...CAUSING THEM TO MUTATE INTO RAGING BEASTS, DRIVEN ONLY BY THEIR UNCOORDINATED INSTINCTUAL DESIRES?

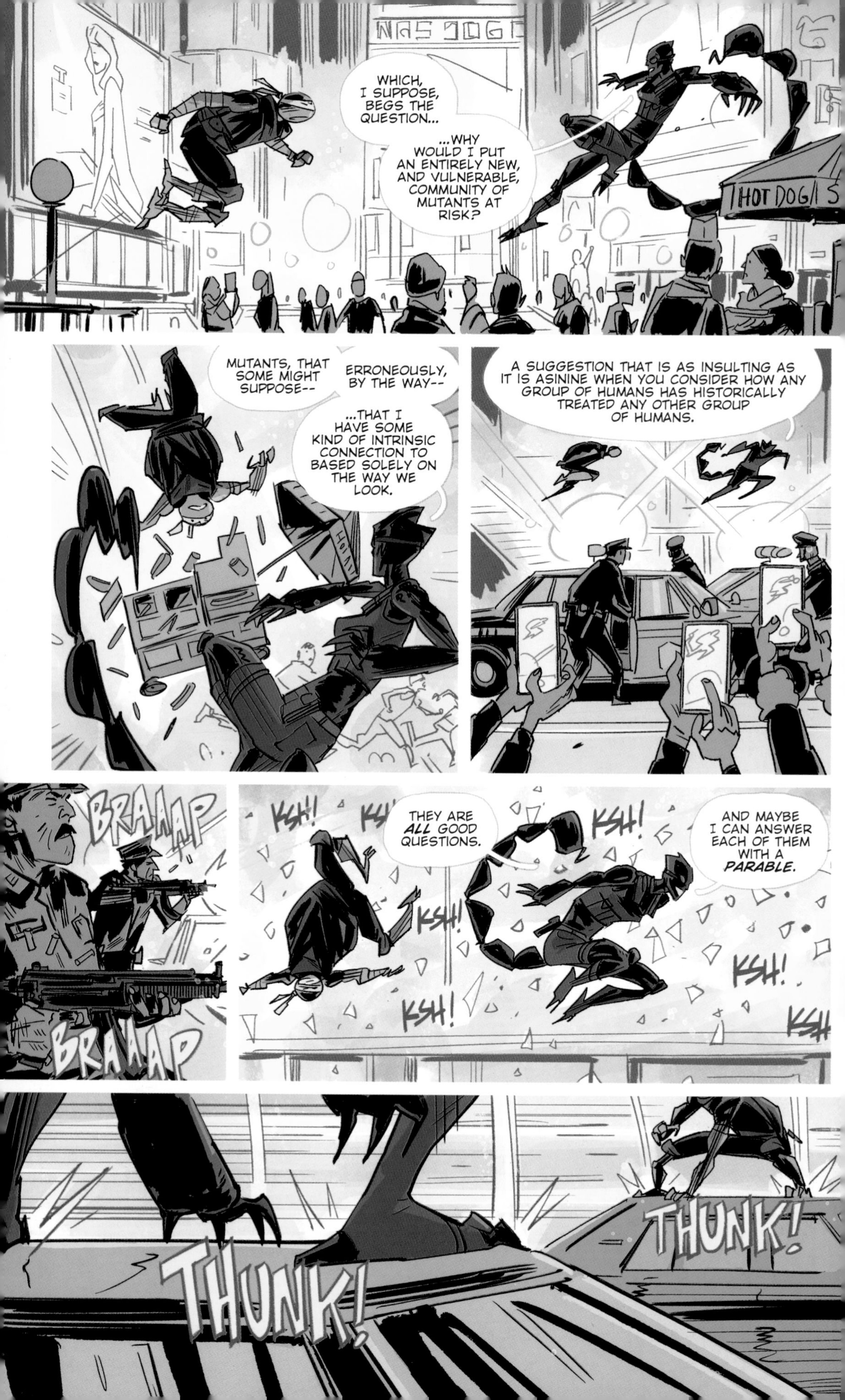

WHICH, I SUPPOSE, BEGS THE QUESTION...
...WHY WOULD I PUT AN ENTIRELY NEW, AND VULNERABLE, COMMUNITY OF MUTANTS AT RISK?
HOT DOGS
MUTANTS, THAT SOME MIGHT SUPPOSE--
ERRONEOUSLY, BY THE WAY--
...THAT I HAVE SOME KIND OF INTRINSIC CONNECTION TO BASED SOLELY ON THE WAY WE LOOK.
A SUGGESTION THAT IS AS INSULTING AS IT IS ASININE WHEN YOU CONSIDER HOW ANY GROUP OF HUMANS HAS HISTORICALLY TREATED ANY OTHER GROUP OF HUMANS.
BRAAAP
BRAAAP
KSH!
KSH!
THEY ARE ALL GOOD QUESTIONS.
KSH!
AND MAYBE I CAN ANSWER EACH OF THEM WITH A PARABLE.
KSH!
KSH!
KSH!
KSH
THUNK!
THUNK!

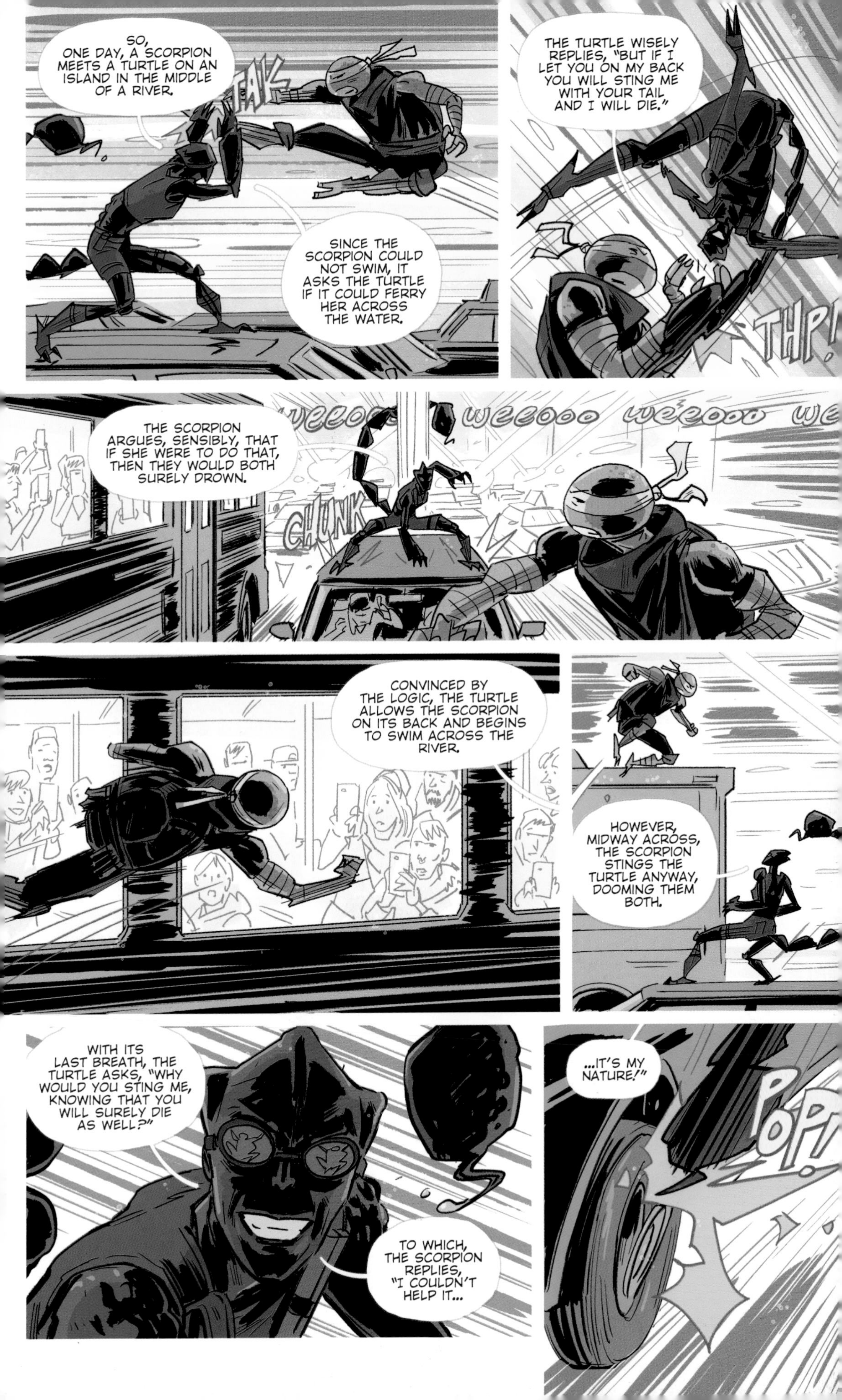
SO, ONE DAY, A SCORPION MEETS A TURTLE ON AN ISLAND IN THE MIDDLE OF A RIVER.
SINCE THE SCORPION COULD NOT SWIM, IT ASKS THE TURTLE IF IT COULD FERRY HER ACROSS THE WATER.
THE TURTLE WISELY REPLIES, "BUT IF I LET YOU ON MY BACK YOU WILL STING ME WITH YOUR TAIL AND I WILL DIE."
THP!
THE SCORPION ARGUES, SENSIBLY, THAT IF SHE WERE TO DO THAT, THEN THEY WOULD BOTH SURELY DROWN.
WEEOOO WEEOOO
CHUNK
CONVINCED BY THE LOGIC, THE TURTLE ALLOWS THE SCORPION ON ITS BACK AND BEGINS TO SWIM ACROSS THE RIVER.
HOWEVER, MIDWAY ACROSS, THE SCORPION STINGS THE TURTLE ANYWAY, DOOMING THEM BOTH.
WITH ITS LAST BREATH, THE TURTLE ASKS, "WHY WOULD YOU STING ME, KNOWING THAT YOU WILL SURELY DIE AS WELL?"
TO WHICH, THE SCORPION REPLIES, "I COULDN'T HELP IT...
...IT'S MY NATURE!"
POP!

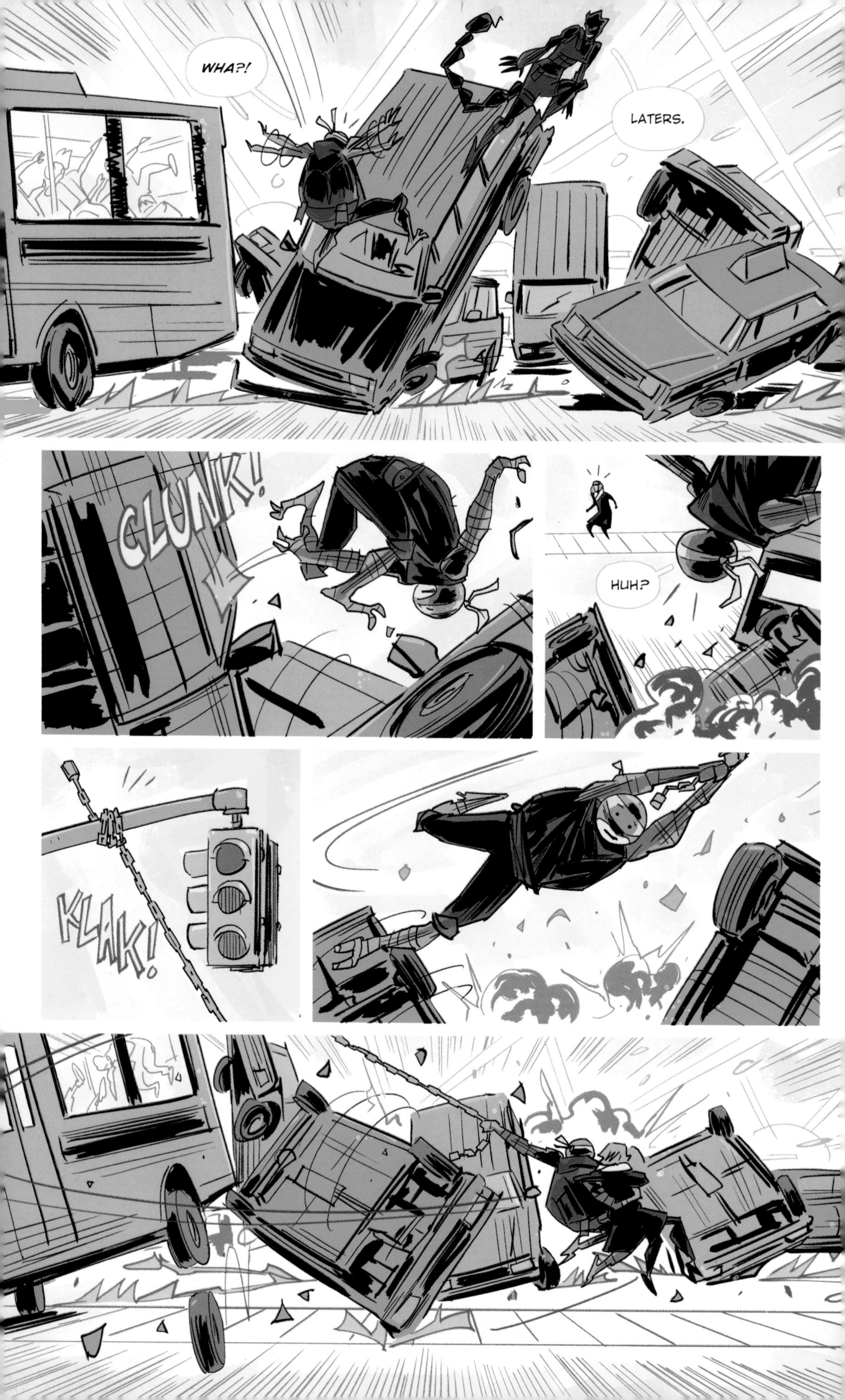
WHA?!
LATERS.
CLUNK!
HUH?
KLAK!

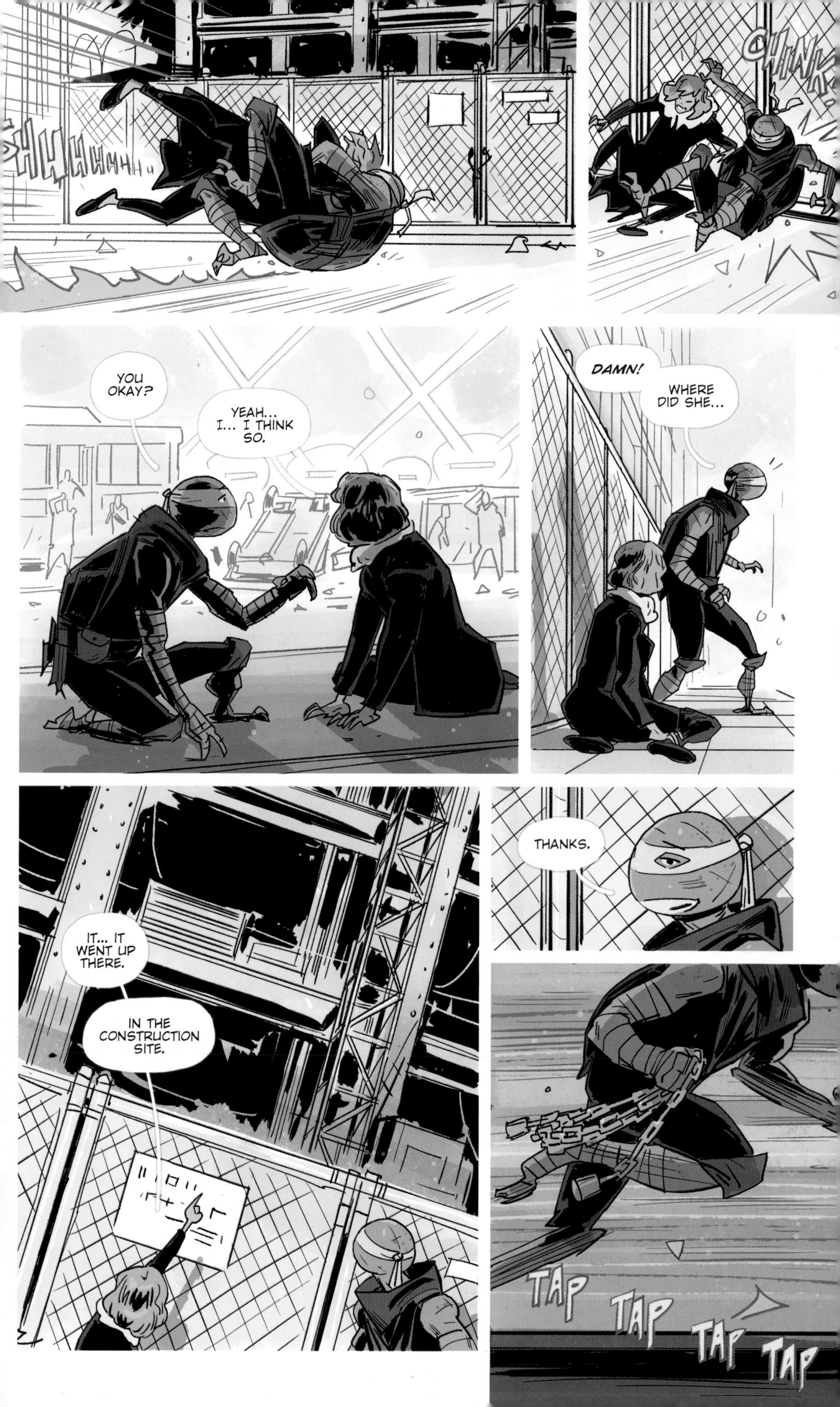

HHHHHHH
CHINK
YOU OKAY?
YEAH... I... I THINK SO.
DAMN!
WHERE DID SHE...
THANKS.
IT... IT WENT UP THERE.
IN THE CONSTRUCTION SITE.
TAP
TAP
TAP
TAP

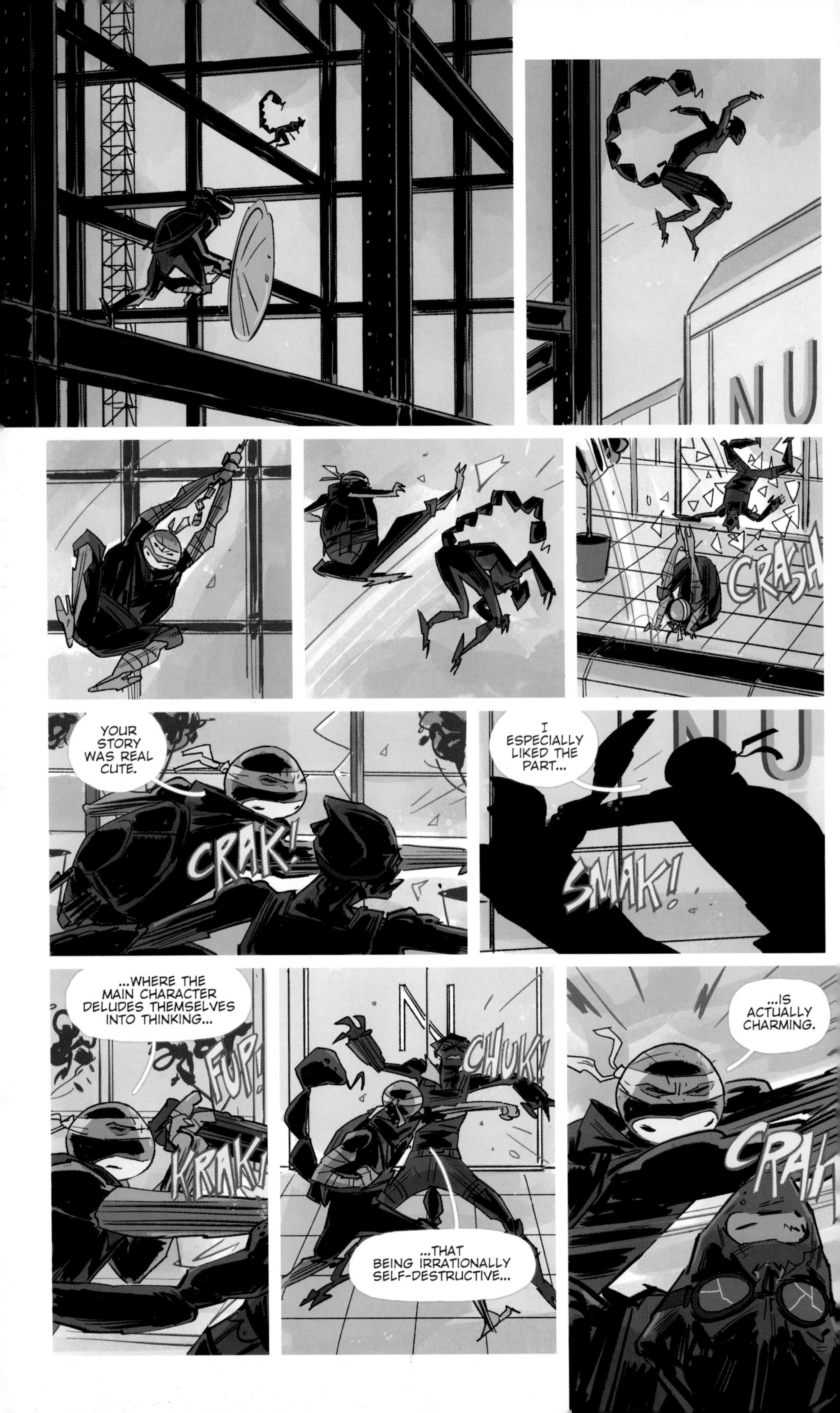

NU
CRASH
YOUR STORY WAS REAL CUTE.
CRAK!
I ESPECIALLY LIKED THE PART...
SMAK!
...WHERE THE MAIN CHARACTER DELUDES THEMSELVES INTO THINKING...
FUP!
KRAK!
CHUK!
...THAT BEING IRRATIONALLY SELF-DESTRUCTIVE...
...IS ACTUALLY CHARMING.
CRAK

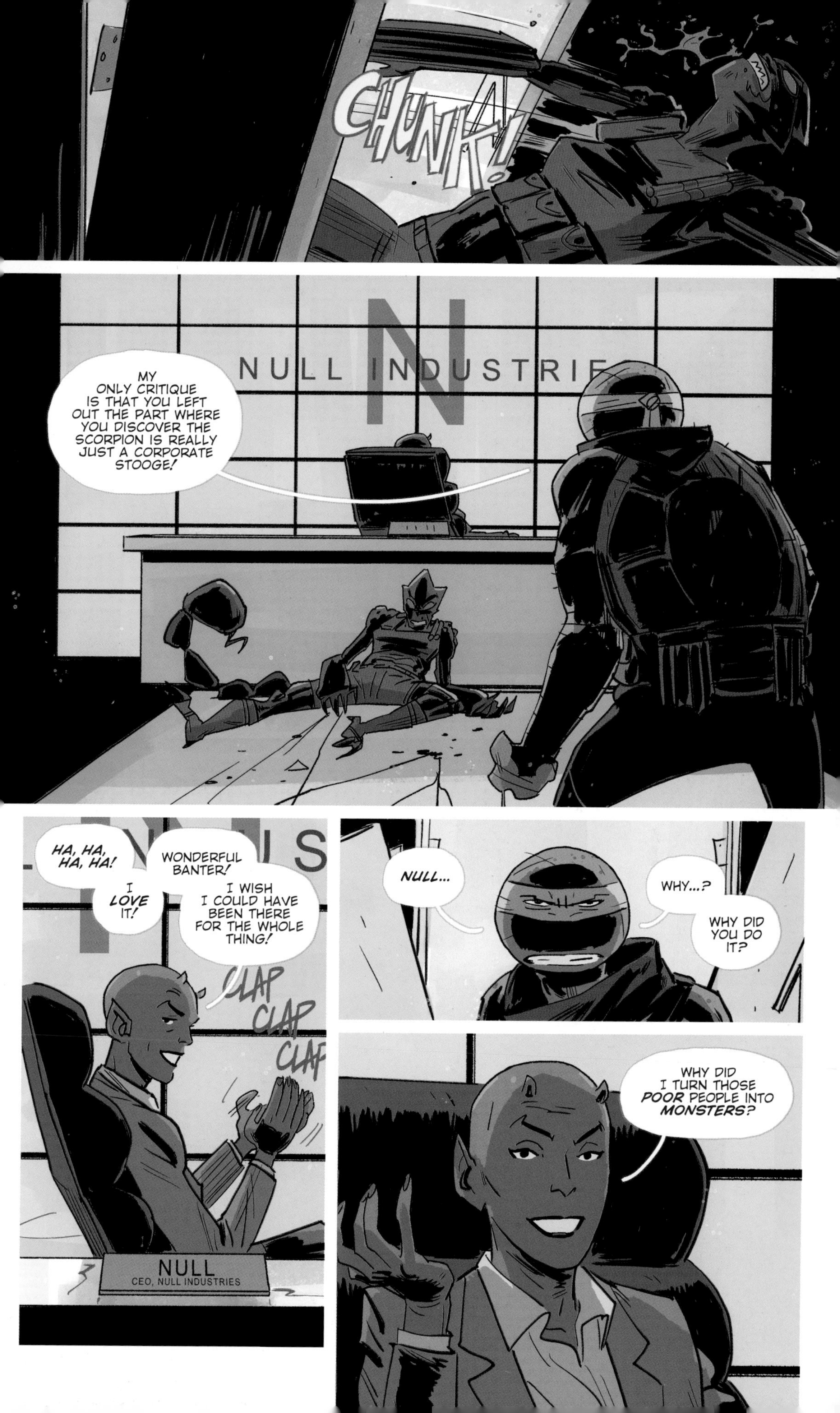
CHUNK!
MY ONLY CRITIQUE IS THAT YOU LEFT OUT THE PART WHERE YOU DISCOVER THE SCORPION IS REALLY JUST A CORPORATE STOOGE!
NULL INDUSTRIE
HA, HA, HA, HA!
I LOVE IT!
WONDERFUL BANTER!
I WISH I COULD HAVE BEEN THERE FOR THE WHOLE THING!
CLAP CLAP CLAP
NULL
CEO, NULL INDUSTRIES
NULL...
WHY...?
WHY DID YOU DO IT?
WHY DID I TURN THOSE POOR PEOPLE INTO MONSTERS?

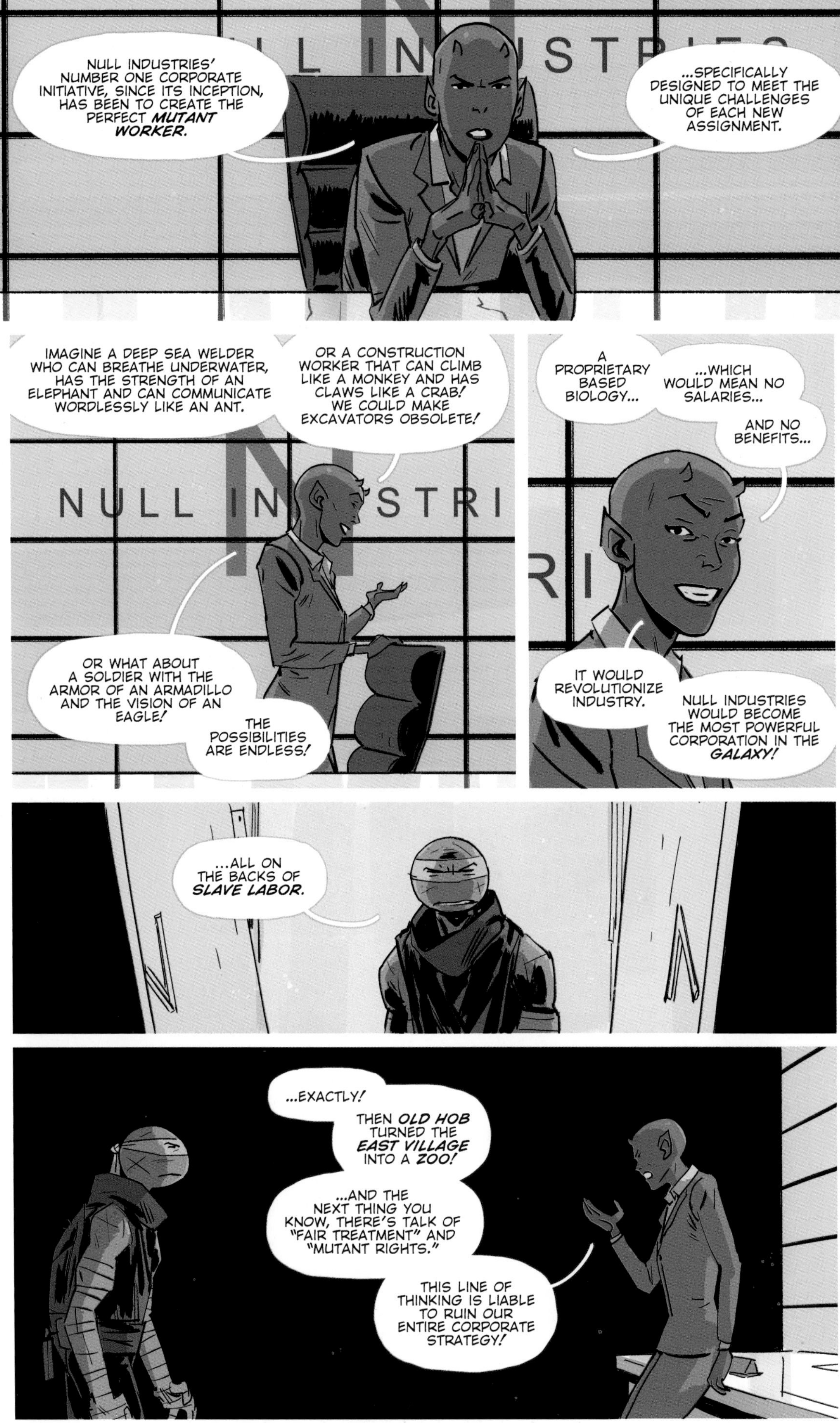
NULL INDUSTRIES
NULL INDUSTRIES' NUMBER ONE CORPORATE INITIATIVE, SINCE ITS INCEPTION, HAS BEEN TO CREATE THE PERFECT *MUTANT WORKER.*
...SPECIFICALLY DESIGNED TO MEET THE UNIQUE CHALLENGES OF EACH NEW ASSIGNMENT.
IMAGINE A DEEP SEA WELDER WHO CAN BREATHE UNDERWATER, HAS THE STRENGTH OF AN ELEPHANT AND CAN COMMUNICATE WORDLESSLY LIKE AN ANT.
OR A CONSTRUCTION WORKER THAT CAN CLIMB LIKE A MONKEY AND HAS CLAWS LIKE A CRAB! WE COULD MAKE EXCAVATORS OBSOLETE!
OR WHAT ABOUT A SOLDIER WITH THE ARMOR OF AN ARMADILLO AND THE VISION OF AN EAGLE!
THE POSSIBILITIES ARE ENDLESS!
A PROPRIETARY BASED BIOLOGY...
...WHICH WOULD MEAN NO SALARIES...
AND NO BENEFITS...
IT WOULD REVOLUTIONIZE INDUSTRY.
NULL INDUSTRIES WOULD BECOME THE MOST POWERFUL CORPORATION IN THE *GALAXY!*
...ALL ON THE BACKS OF *SLAVE LABOR.*
...EXACTLY!
THEN *OLD HOB* TURNED THE *EAST VILLAGE* INTO A *ZOO!*
...AND THE NEXT THING YOU KNOW, THERE'S TALK OF "FAIR TREATMENT" AND "MUTANT RIGHTS."
THIS LINE OF THINKING IS LIABLE TO RUIN OUR ENTIRE CORPORATE STRATEGY!

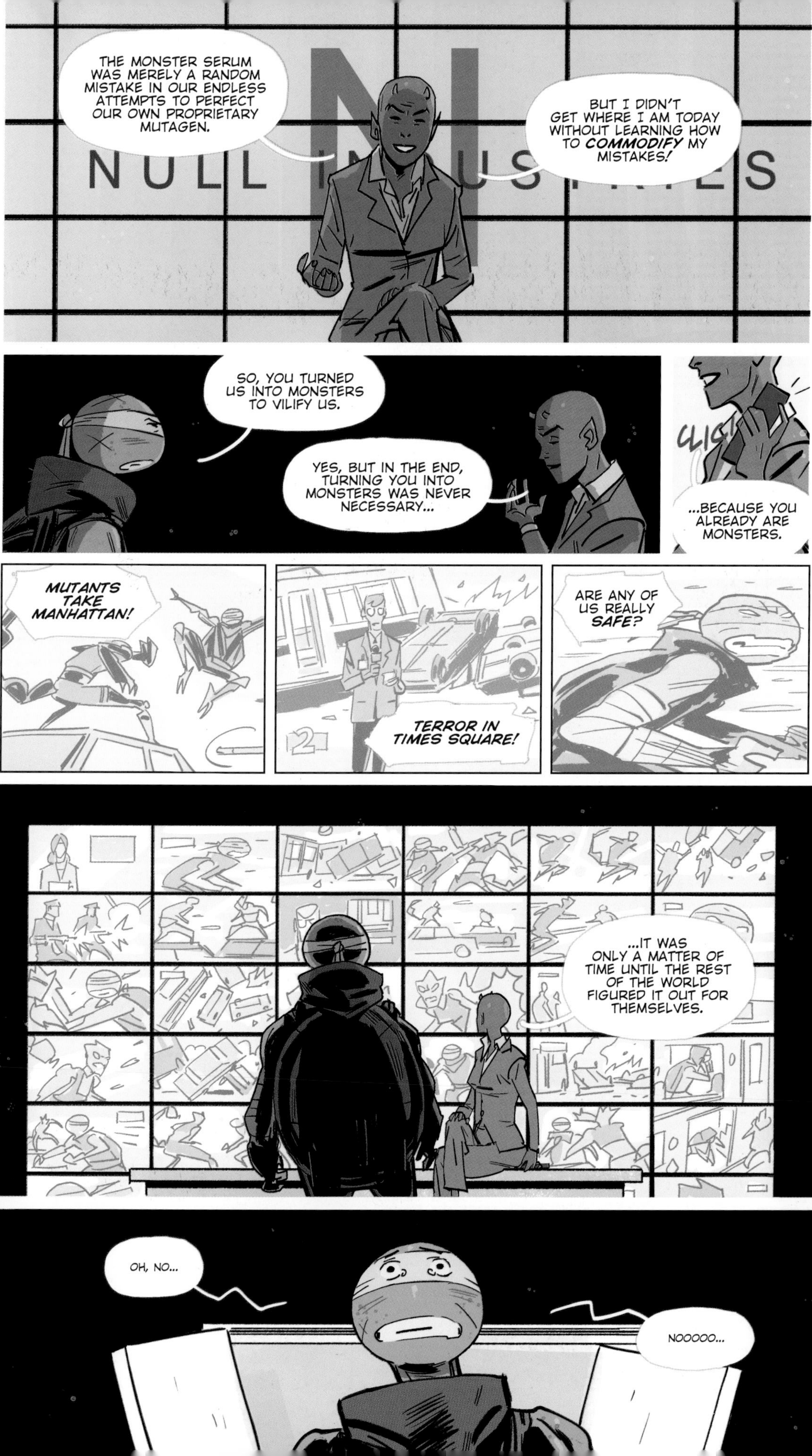
NULL INDUSTRIES
THE MONSTER SERUM WAS MERELY A RANDOM MISTAKE IN OUR ENDLESS ATTEMPTS TO PERFECT OUR OWN PROPRIETARY MUTAGEN.
BUT I DIDN'T GET WHERE I AM TODAY WITHOUT LEARNING HOW TO COMMODIFY MY MISTAKES!
SO, YOU TURNED US INTO MONSTERS TO VILIFY US.
YES, BUT IN THE END, TURNING YOU INTO MONSTERS WAS NEVER NECESSARY...
...BECAUSE YOU ALREADY ARE MONSTERS.
MUTANTS TAKE MANHATTAN!
TERROR IN TIMES SQUARE!
ARE ANY OF US REALLY SAFE?
...IT WAS ONLY A MATTER OF TIME UNTIL THE REST OF THE WORLD FIGURED IT OUT FOR THEMSELVES.
OH, NO...
NOOOOO...

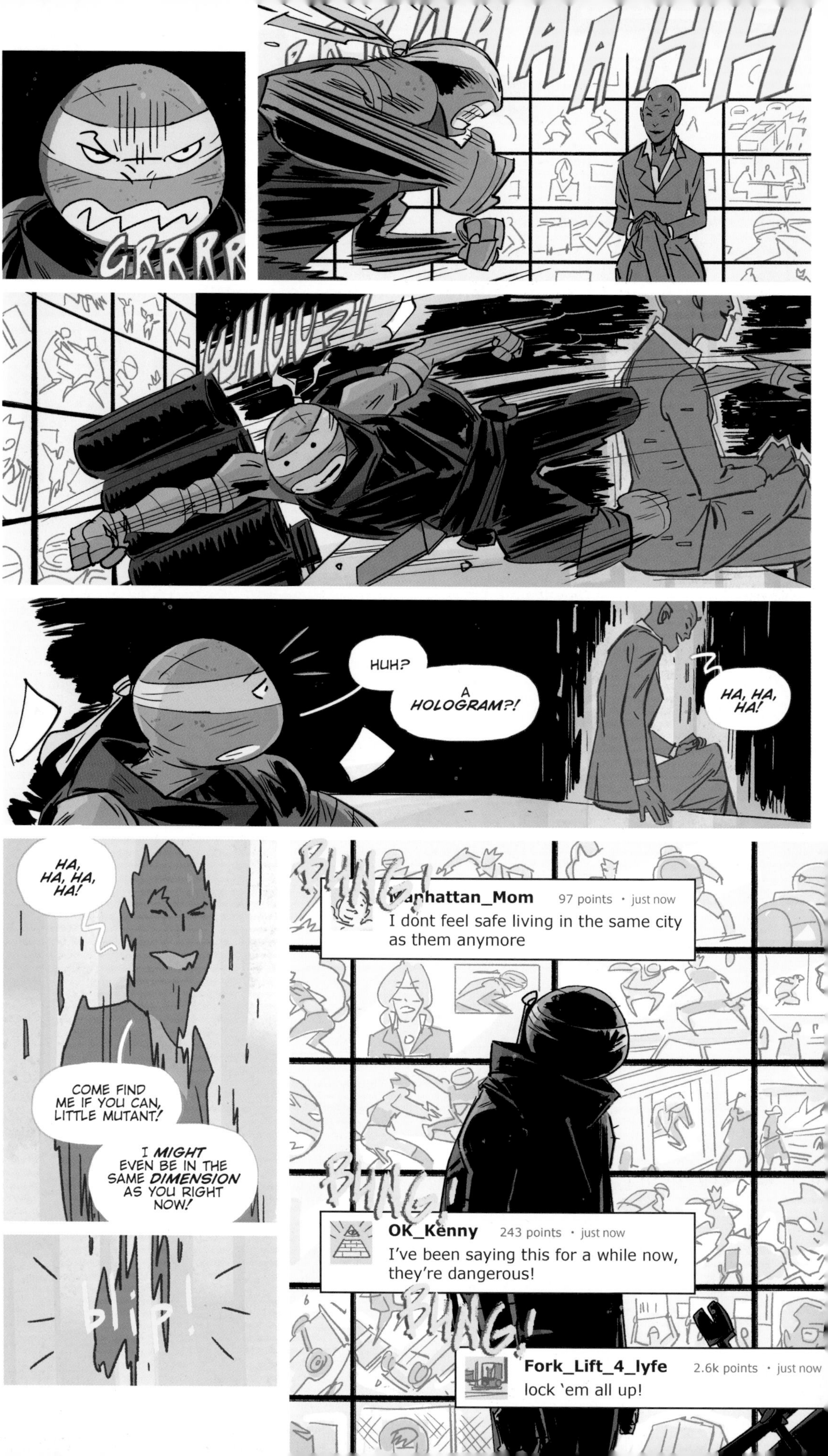
GRRRR
AAAAHH
WHUU?!
HUH?
A HOLOGRAM?!
HA, HA, HA!
HA, HA, HA, HA!
COME FIND ME IF YOU CAN, LITTLE MUTANT!
I MIGHT EVEN BE IN THE SAME DIMENSION AS YOU RIGHT NOW!
blip!
BUNG!
Manhattan_Mom 97 points • just now
I dont feel safe living in the same city as them anymore
BUNG!
OK_Kenny 243 points • just now
I've been saying this for a while now, they're dangerous!
BUNG!
Fork_Lift_4_lyfe 2.6k points • just now
lock 'em all up!

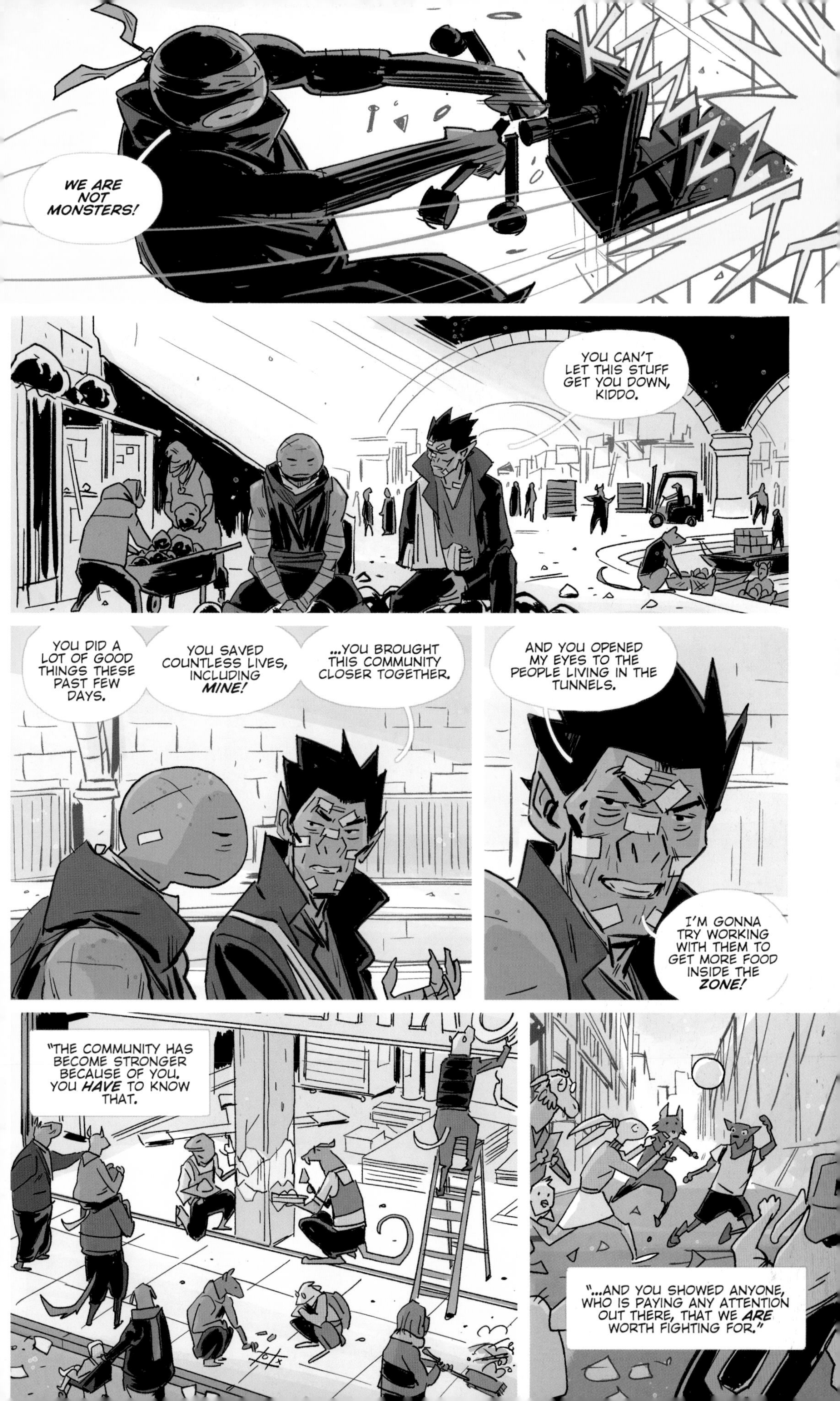
WE ARE NOT MONSTERS!
KZZZZZZT
YOU CAN'T LET THIS STUFF GET YOU DOWN, KIDDO.
YOU DID A LOT OF GOOD THINGS THESE PAST FEW DAYS.
YOU SAVED COUNTLESS LIVES, INCLUDING MINE!
...YOU BROUGHT THIS COMMUNITY CLOSER TOGETHER.
AND YOU OPENED MY EYES TO THE PEOPLE LIVING IN THE TUNNELS.
I'M GONNA TRY WORKING WITH THEM TO GET MORE FOOD INSIDE THE ZONE!
"THE COMMUNITY HAS BECOME STRONGER BECAUSE OF YOU. YOU HAVE TO KNOW THAT.
"...AND YOU SHOWED ANYONE, WHO IS PAYING ANY ATTENTION OUT THERE, THAT WE ARE WORTH FIGHTING FOR."

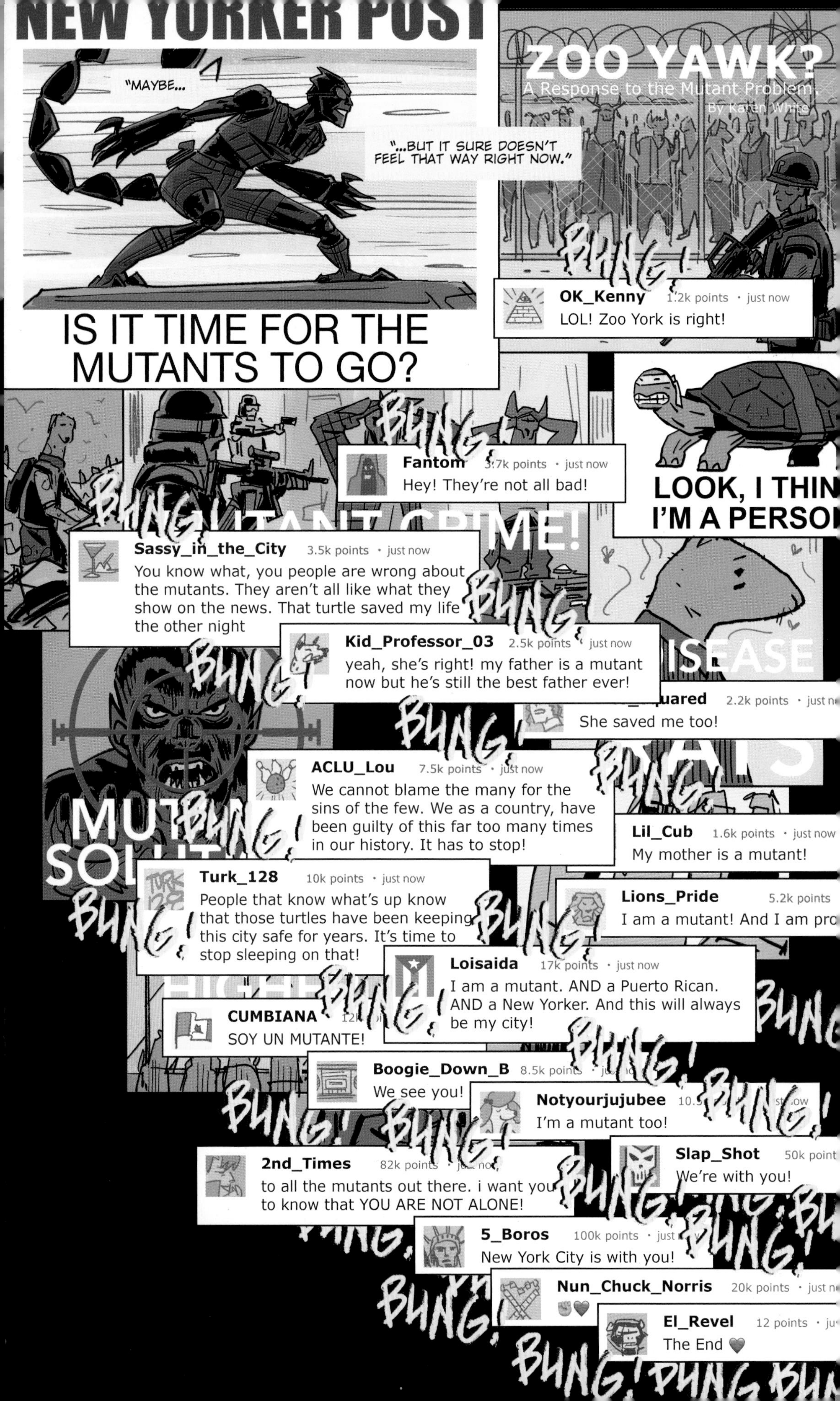
NEW YORKER POST
"MAYBE...
"...BUT IT SURE DOESN'T FEEL THAT WAY RIGHT NOW."
IS IT TIME FOR THE MUTANTS TO GO?
ZOO YAWK?
A Response to the Mutant Problem.
By Karen White
BUNG!
OK_Kenny 1.2k points • just now
LOL! Zoo York is right!
BUNG!
Fantom 3.7k points • just now
Hey! They're not all bad!
LOOK, I THIN
I'M A PERSO
BUNG!
Sassy_in_the_City 3.5k points • just now
You know what, you people are wrong about the mutants. They aren't all like what they show on the news. That turtle saved my life the other night
BUNG!
Kid_Professor_03 2.5k points • just now
yeah, she's right! my father is a mutant now but he's still the best father ever!
BUNG!
She saved me too!
BUNG!
ACLU_Lou 7.5k points • just now
We cannot blame the many for the sins of the few. We as a country, have been guilty of this far too many times in our history. It has to stop!
BUNG!
Lil_Cub 1.6k points • just now
My mother is a mutant!
BUNG!
Turk_128 10k points • just now
People that know what's up know that those turtles have been keeping this city safe for years. It's time to stop sleeping on that!
BUNG!
Lions_Pride 5.2k points
I am a mutant! And I am pro
BUNG!
Loisaida 17k points • just now
I am a mutant. AND a Puerto Rican. AND a New Yorker. And this will always be my city!
BUNG!
CUMBIANA
SOY UN MUTANTE!
Boogie_Down_B 8.5k points
We see you!
BUNG!
Notyourjujubee
I'm a mutant too!
BUNG!
Slap_Shot 50k points
We're with you!
2nd_Times 82k points
to all the mutants out there. i want you to know that YOU ARE NOT ALONE!
BUNG!
5_Boros 100k points
New York City is with you!
BUNG!
Nun_Chuck_Norris 20k points
El_Revel 12 points
The End
BUNG!

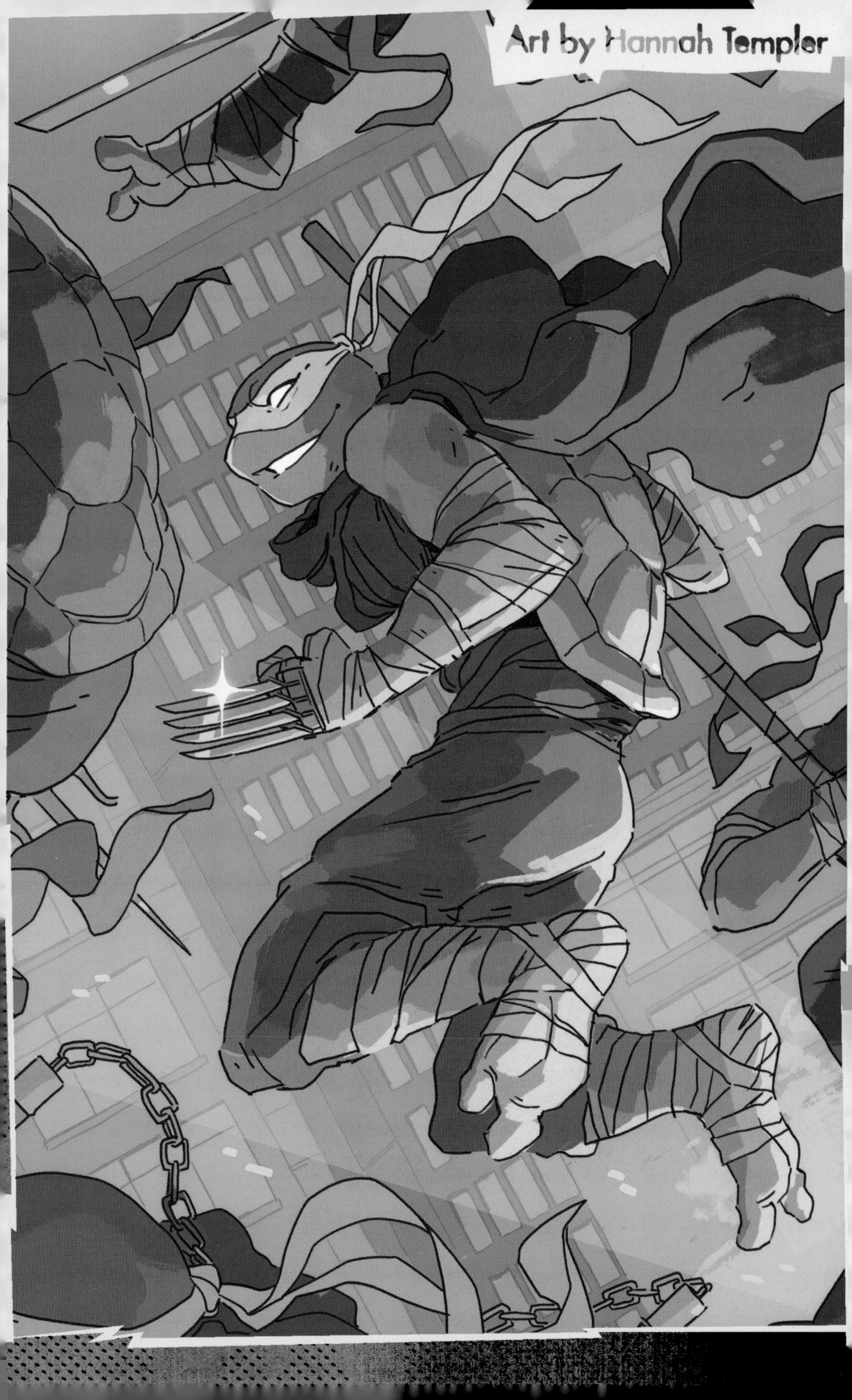
Art by Hannah Templer

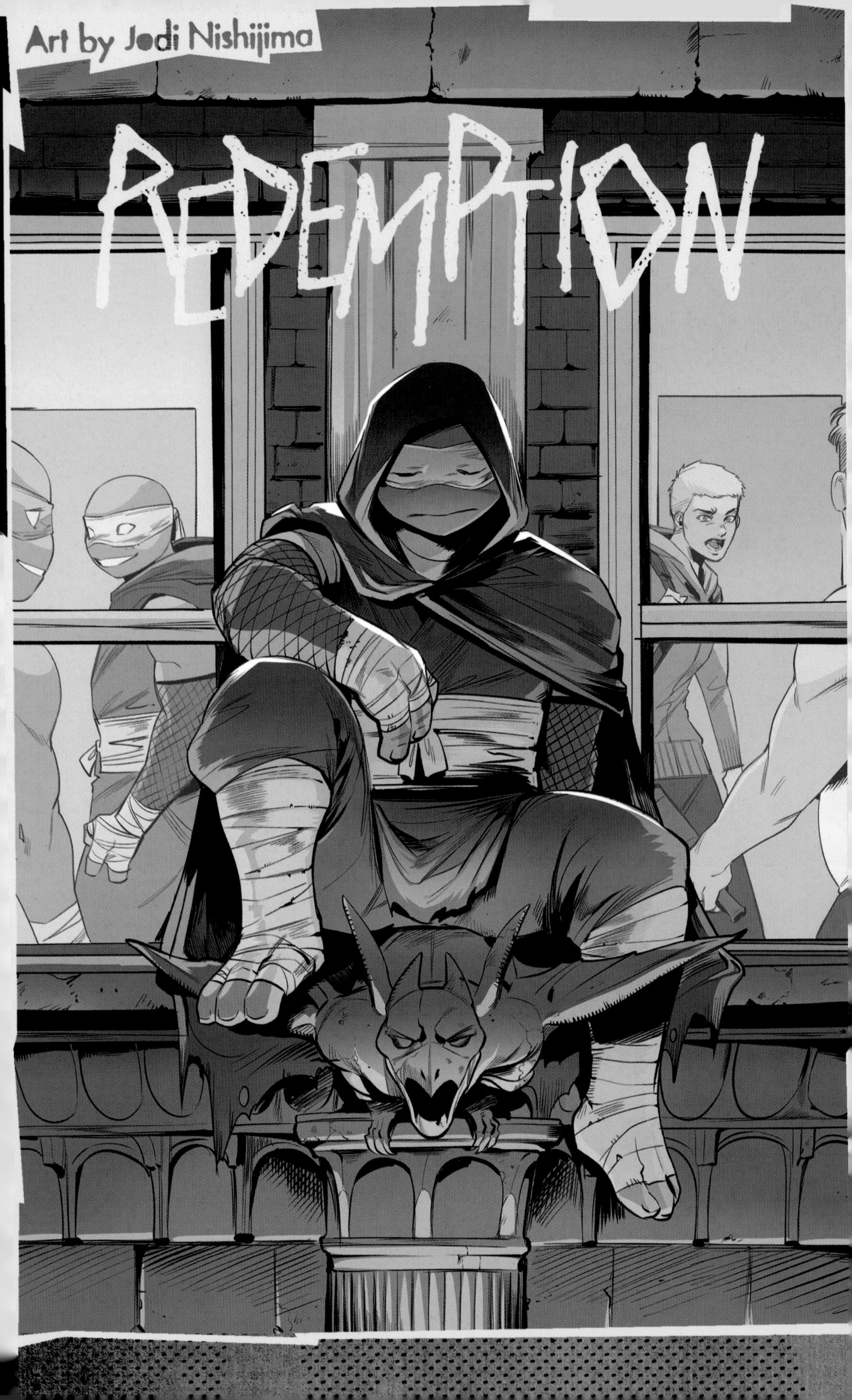
Art by Jodi Nishijima
REDEMPTION

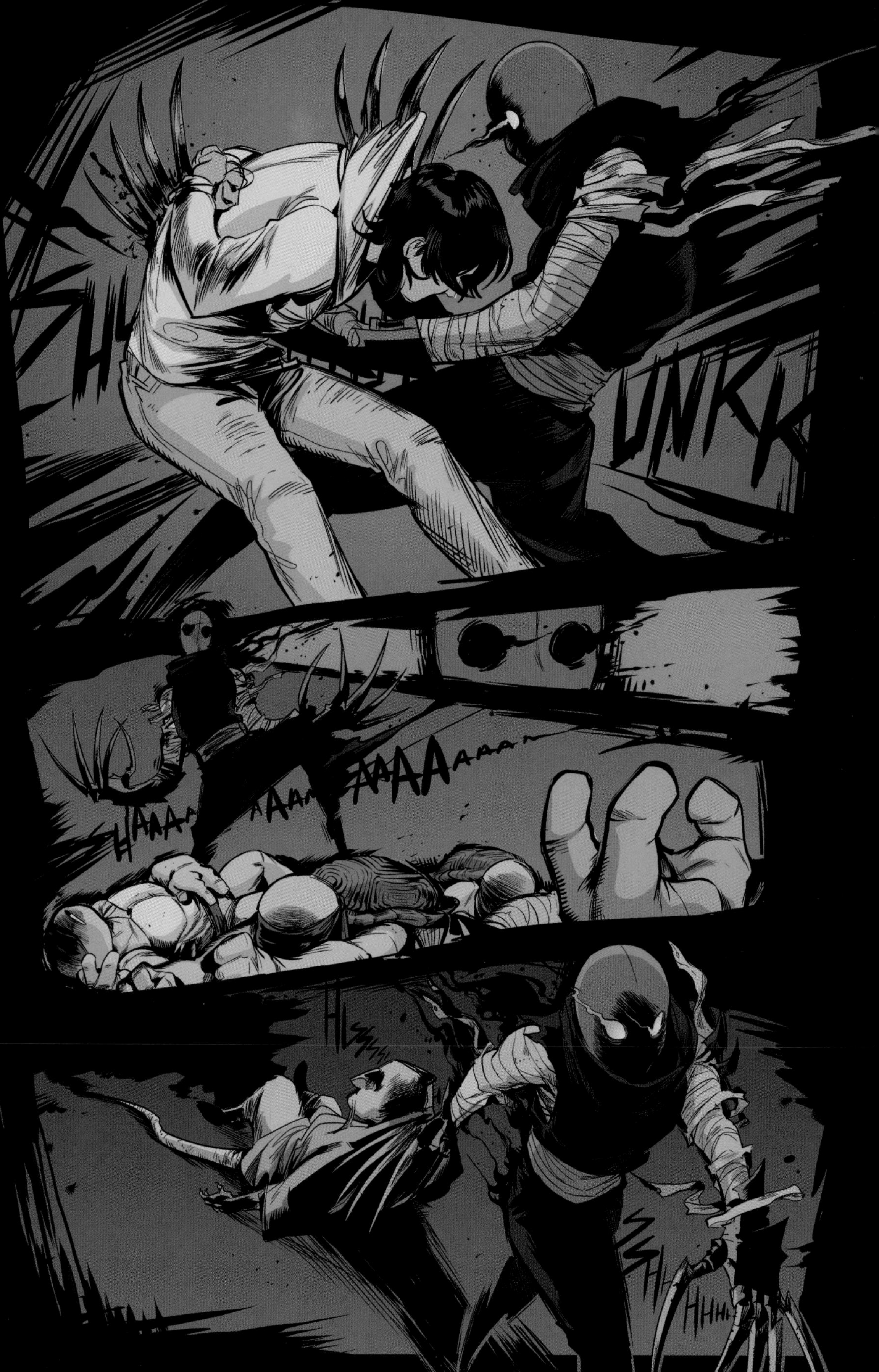
UNKK
HAAAA AAAAAAAAaaaa
HISSSS
SHHH HHH

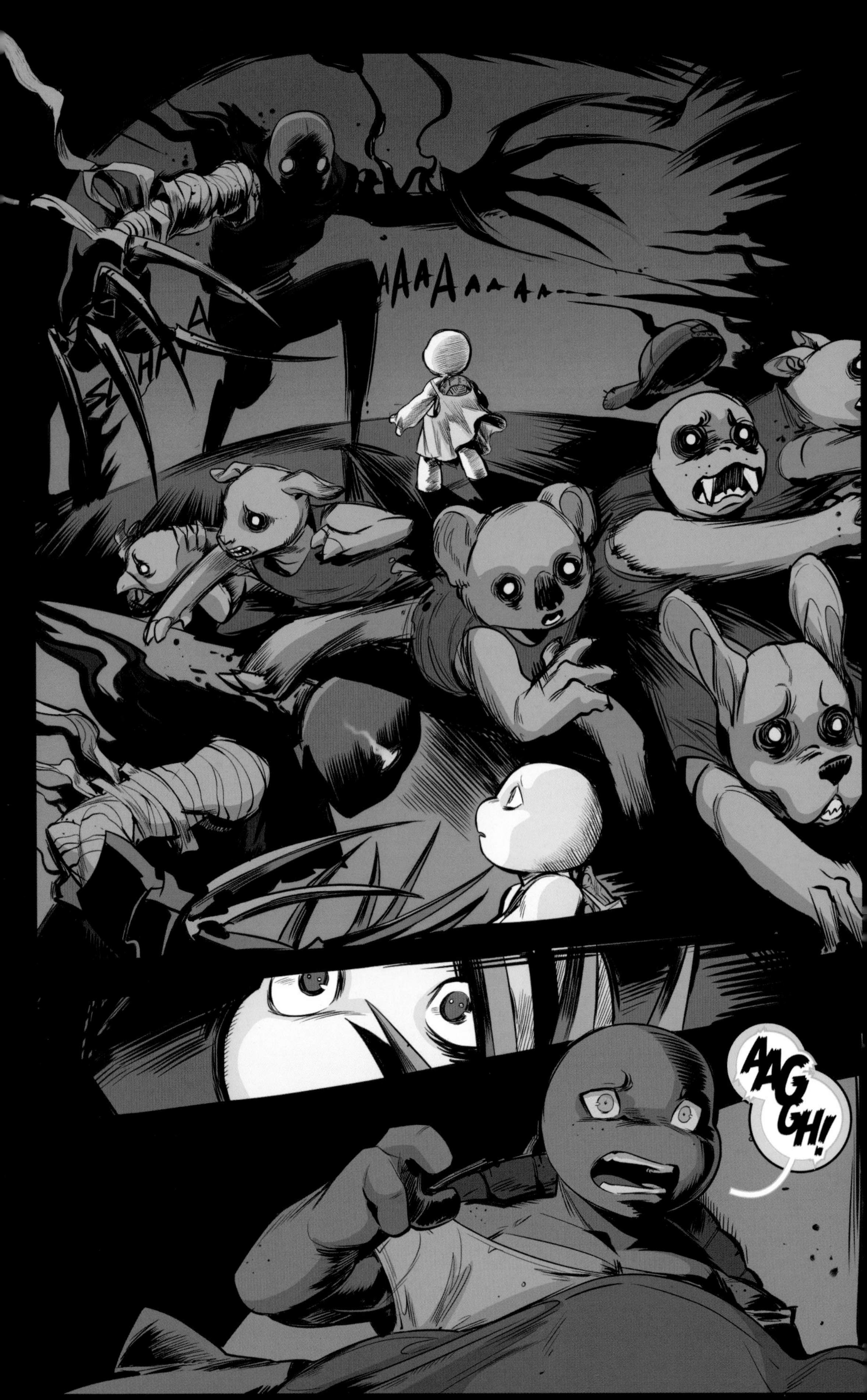
AAAAaaaa...
AAGGH!

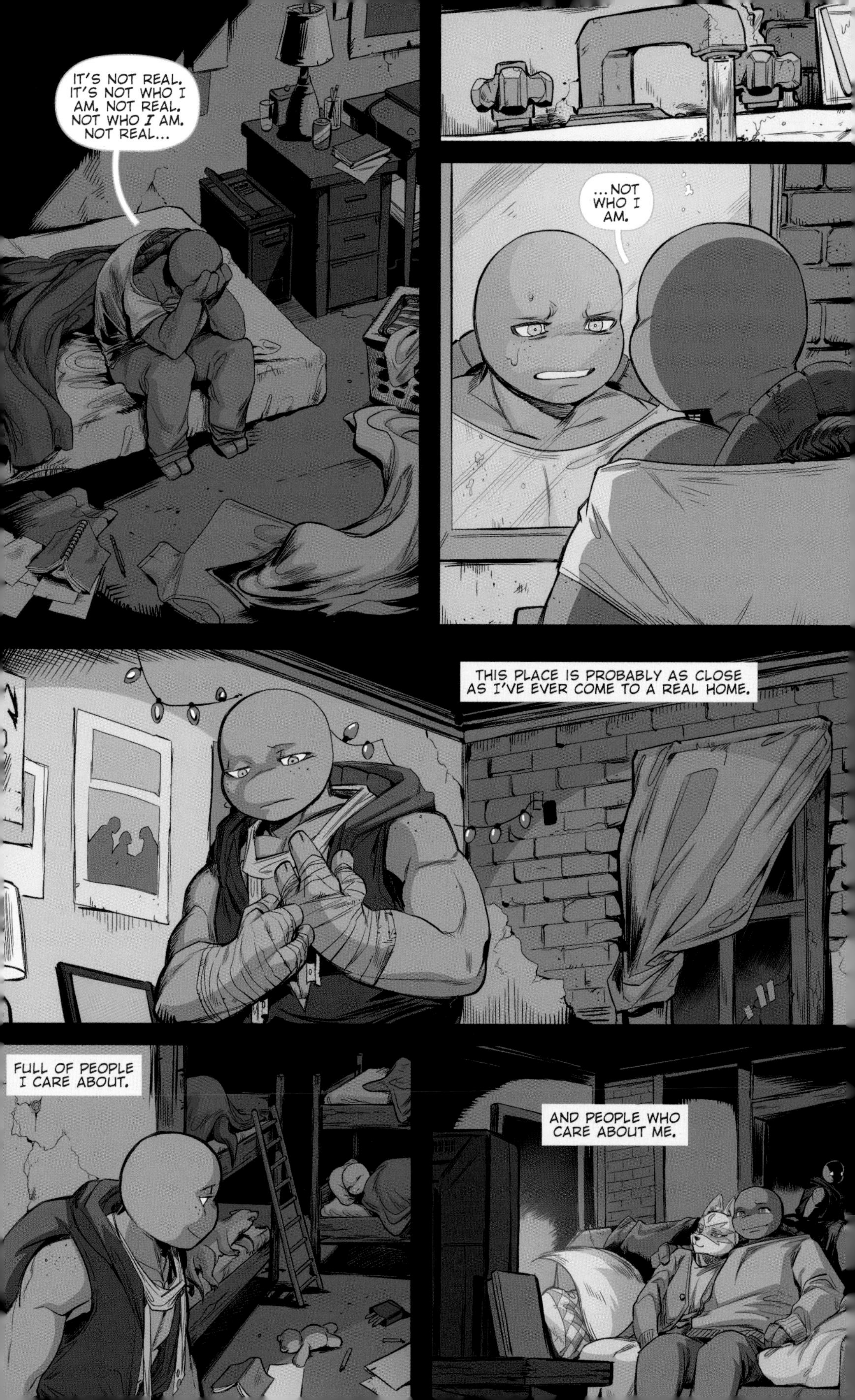
IT'S NOT REAL. IT'S NOT WHO I AM. NOT REAL. NOT WHO *I* AM. NOT REAL...
...NOT WHO I AM.
THIS PLACE IS PROBABLY AS CLOSE AS I'VE EVER COME TO A REAL HOME.
FULL OF PEOPLE I CARE ABOUT.
AND PEOPLE WHO CARE ABOUT ME.

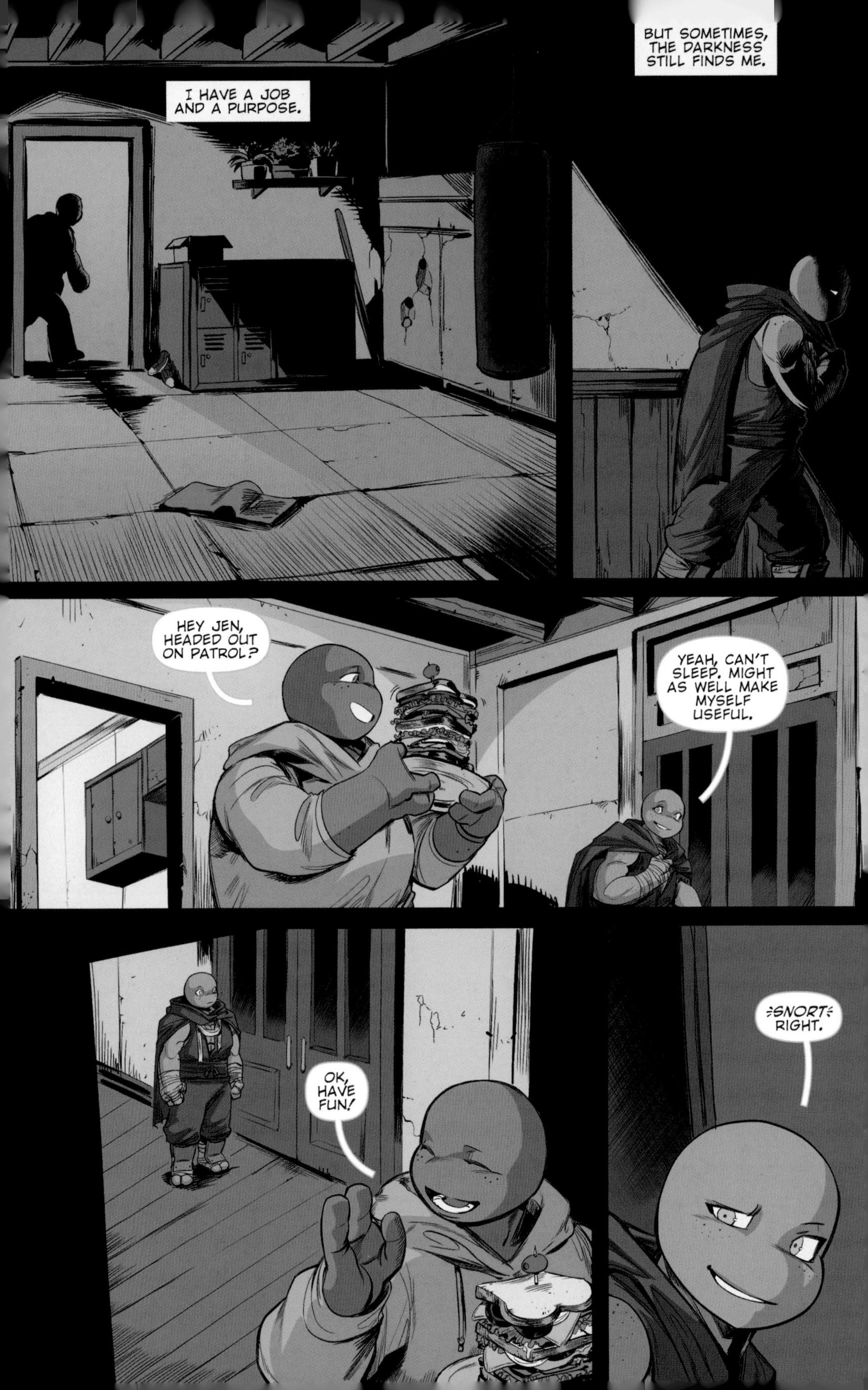
I HAVE A JOB AND A PURPOSE.
BUT SOMETIMES, THE DARKNESS STILL FINDS ME.
HEY JEN, HEADED OUT ON PATROL?
YEAH, CAN'T SLEEP. MIGHT AS WELL MAKE MYSELF USEFUL.
OK, HAVE FUN!
SNORT RIGHT.

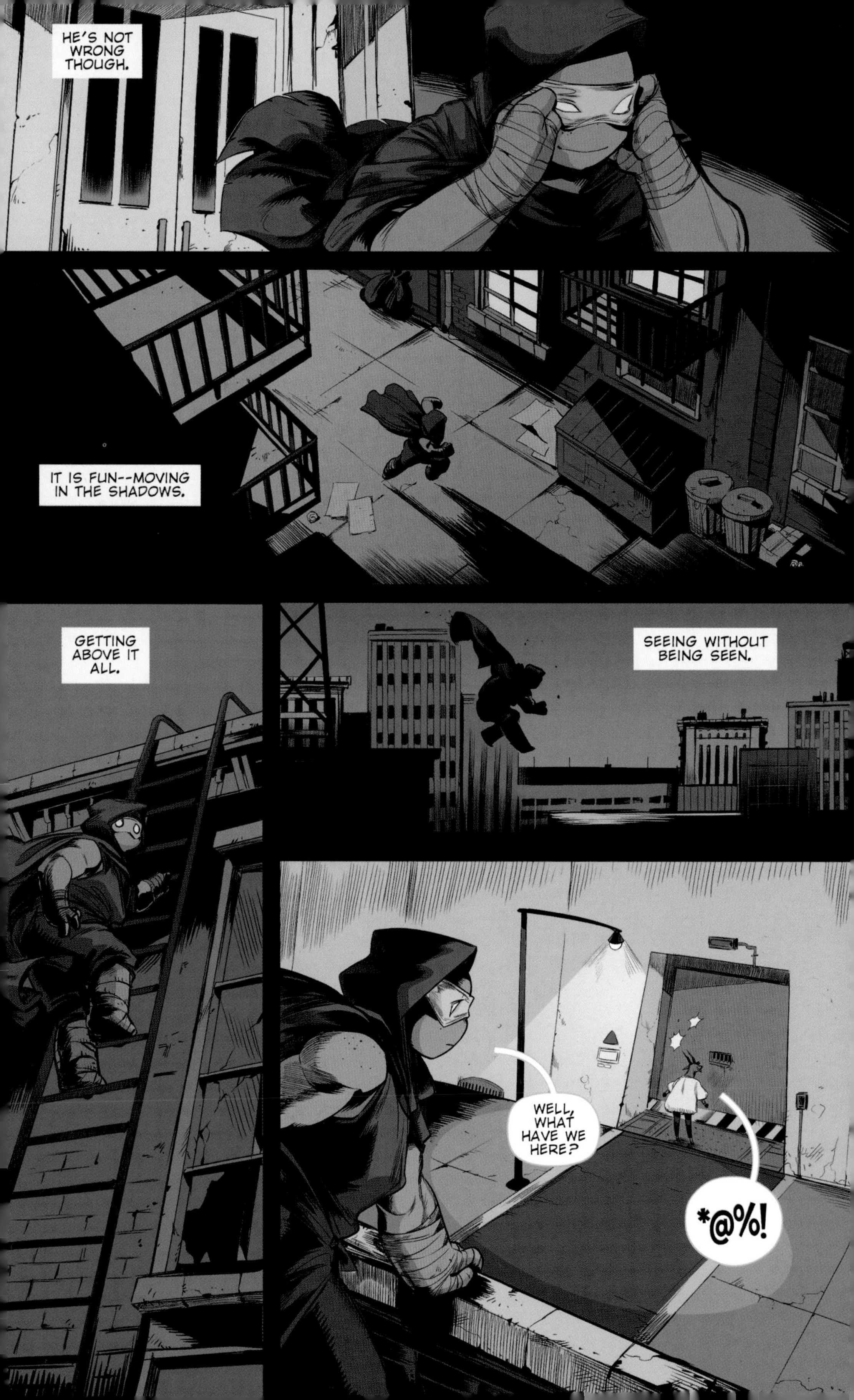
HE'S NOT WRONG THOUGH.
IT IS FUN--MOVING IN THE SHADOWS.
GETTING ABOVE IT ALL.
SEEING WITHOUT BEING SEEN.
WELL, WHAT HAVE WE HERE?
*@%!

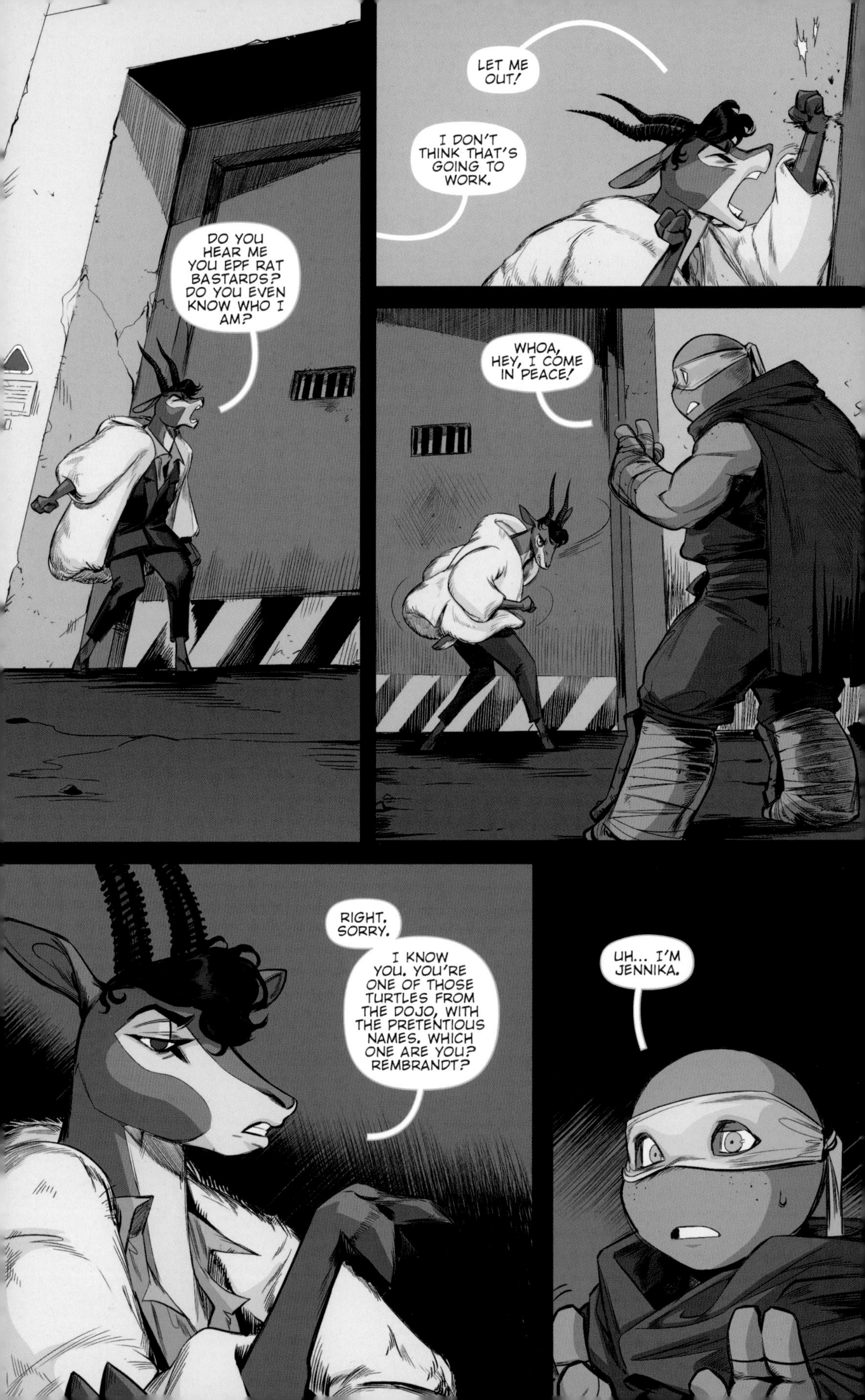
DO YOU HEAR ME YOU EPF RAT BASTARDS? DO YOU EVEN KNOW WHO I AM?
LET ME OUT!
I DON'T THINK THAT'S GOING TO WORK.
WHOA, HEY, I COME IN PEACE!
RIGHT. SORRY.
I KNOW YOU. YOU'RE ONE OF THOSE TURTLES FROM THE DOJO, WITH THE PRETENTIOUS NAMES. WHICH ONE ARE YOU? REMBRANDT?
UH... I'M JENNIKA.

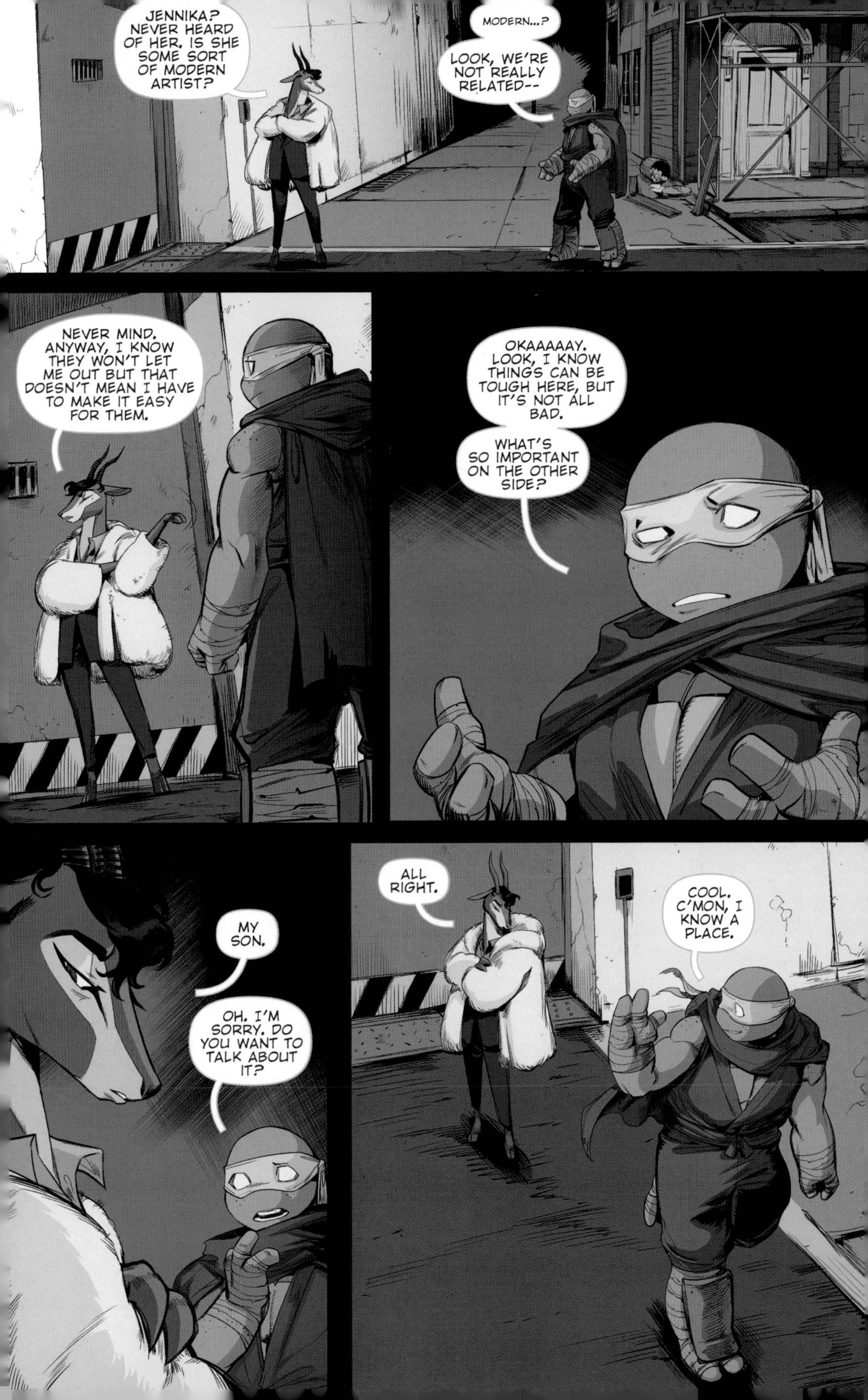
JENNIKA? NEVER HEARD OF HER. IS SHE SOME SORT OF MODERN ARTIST?
MODERN...?
LOOK, WE'RE NOT REALLY RELATED--
NEVER MIND. ANYWAY, I KNOW THEY WON'T LET ME OUT BUT THAT DOESN'T MEAN I HAVE TO MAKE IT EASY FOR THEM.
OKAAAAAY. LOOK, I KNOW THINGS CAN BE TOUGH HERE, BUT IT'S NOT ALL BAD.
WHAT'S SO IMPORTANT ON THE OTHER SIDE?
MY SON.
OH. I'M SORRY. DO YOU WANT TO TALK ABOUT IT?
ALL RIGHT.
COOL. C'MON, I KNOW A PLACE.

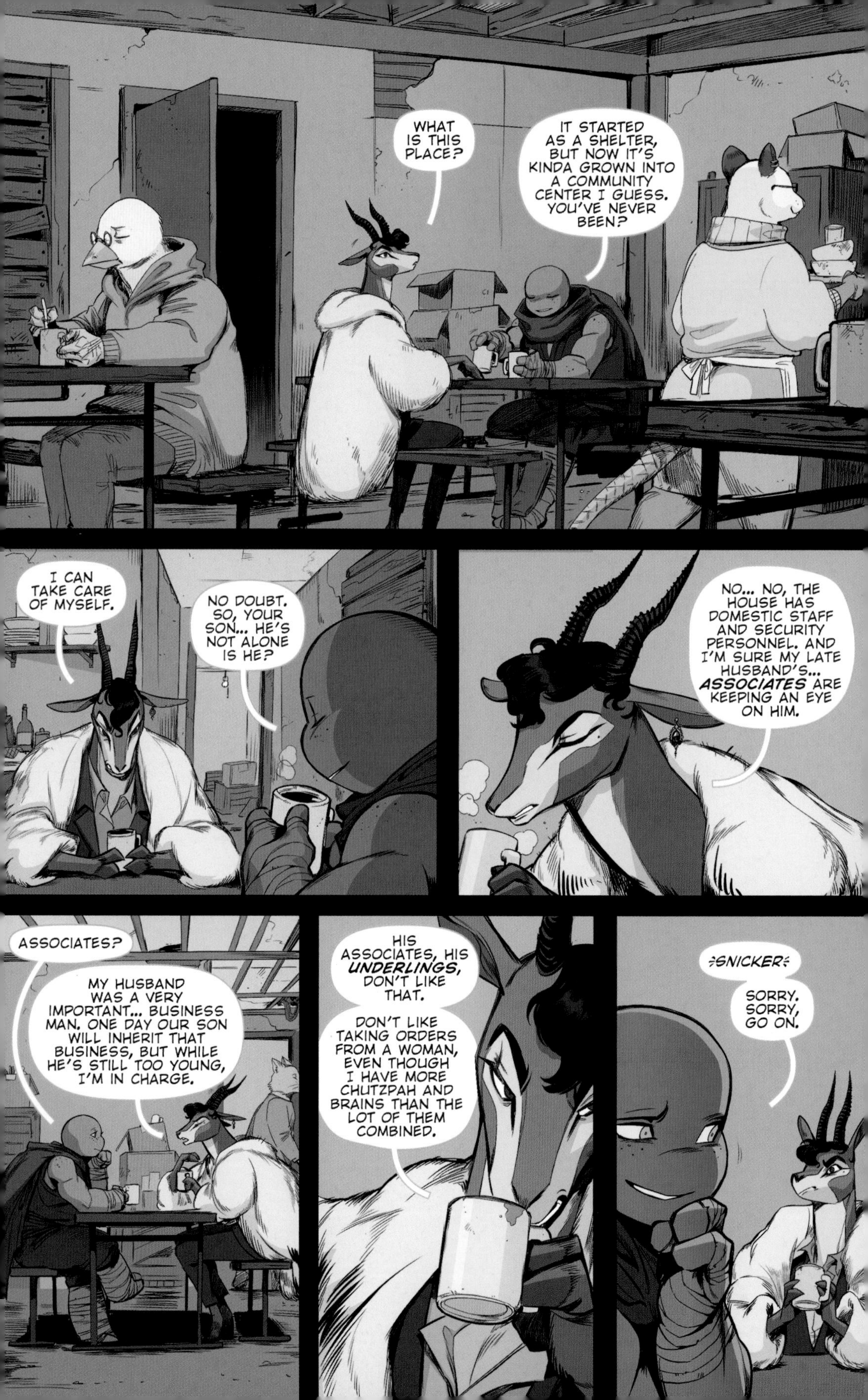
WHAT IS THIS PLACE?
IT STARTED AS A SHELTER, BUT NOW IT'S KINDA GROWN INTO A COMMUNITY CENTER I GUESS. YOU'VE NEVER BEEN?
I CAN TAKE CARE OF MYSELF.
NO DOUBT. SO, YOUR SON... HE'S NOT ALONE IS HE?
NO... NO, THE HOUSE HAS DOMESTIC STAFF AND SECURITY PERSONNEL. AND I'M SURE MY LATE HUSBAND'S... ASSOCIATES ARE KEEPING AN EYE ON HIM.
ASSOCIATES?
MY HUSBAND WAS A VERY IMPORTANT... BUSINESS MAN. ONE DAY OUR SON WILL INHERIT THAT BUSINESS, BUT WHILE HE'S STILL TOO YOUNG, I'M IN CHARGE.
HIS ASSOCIATES, HIS UNDERLINGS, DON'T LIKE THAT.
DON'T LIKE TAKING ORDERS FROM A WOMAN, EVEN THOUGH I HAVE MORE CHUTZPAH AND BRAINS THAN THE LOT OF THEM COMBINED.
≠SNICKER≠
SORRY. SORRY, GO ON.

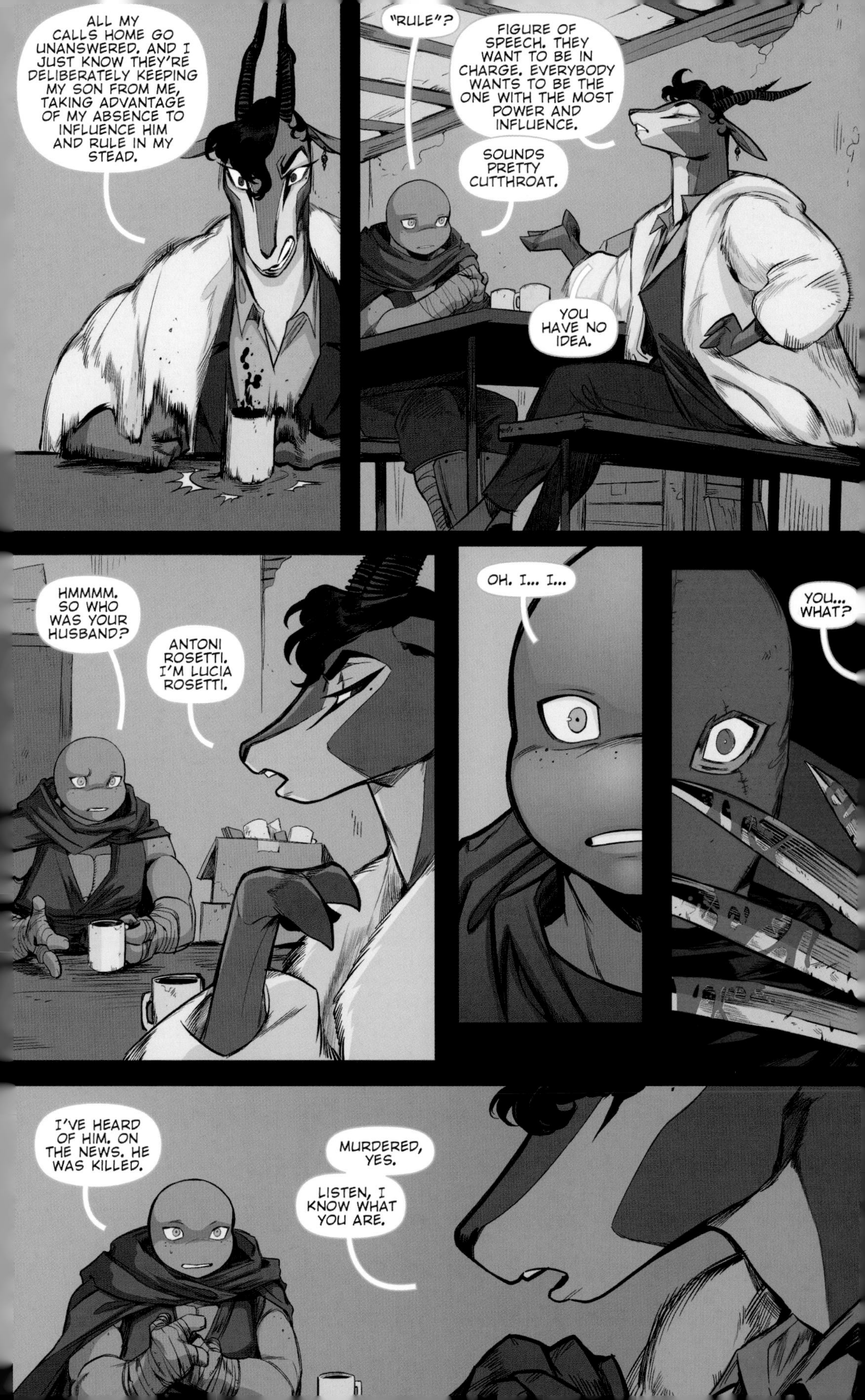
ALL MY CALLS HOME GO UNANSWERED. AND I JUST KNOW THEY'RE DELIBERATELY KEEPING MY SON FROM ME, TAKING ADVANTAGE OF MY ABSENCE TO INFLUENCE HIM AND RULE IN MY STEAD.
"RULE"?
FIGURE OF SPEECH. THEY WANT TO BE IN CHARGE. EVERYBODY WANTS TO BE THE ONE WITH THE MOST POWER AND INFLUENCE.
SOUNDS PRETTY CUTTHROAT.
YOU HAVE NO IDEA.
HMMMM. SO WHO WAS YOUR HUSBAND?
ANTONI ROSETTI. I'M LUCIA ROSETTI.
OH. I... I...
YOU... WHAT?
I'VE HEARD OF HIM. ON THE NEWS. HE WAS KILLED.
MURDERED, YES.
LISTEN, I KNOW WHAT YOU ARE.

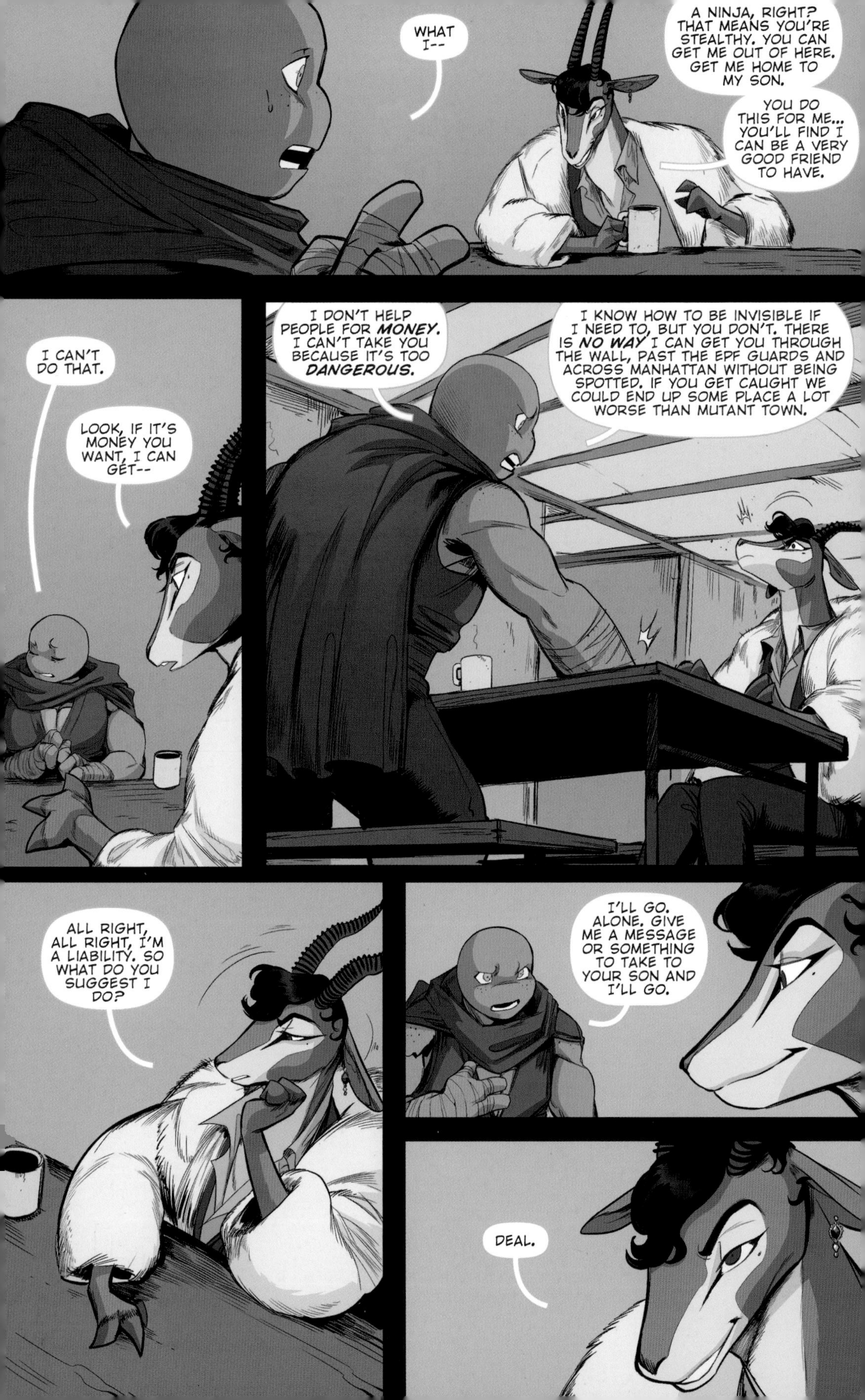
WHAT I--
A NINJA, RIGHT? THAT MEANS YOU'RE STEALTHY. YOU CAN GET ME OUT OF HERE. GET ME HOME TO MY SON.
YOU DO THIS FOR ME... YOU'LL FIND I CAN BE A VERY GOOD FRIEND TO HAVE.
I CAN'T DO THAT.
LOOK, IF IT'S MONEY YOU WANT, I CAN GET--
I DON'T HELP PEOPLE FOR **MONEY.** I CAN'T TAKE YOU BECAUSE IT'S TOO **DANGEROUS.**
I KNOW HOW TO BE INVISIBLE IF I NEED TO, BUT YOU DON'T. THERE IS **NO WAY** I CAN GET YOU THROUGH THE WALL, PAST THE EPF GUARDS AND ACROSS MANHATTAN WITHOUT BEING SPOTTED. IF YOU GET CAUGHT WE COULD END UP SOME PLACE A LOT WORSE THAN MUTANT TOWN.
ALL RIGHT, ALL RIGHT, I'M A LIABILITY. SO WHAT DO YOU SUGGEST I DO?
I'LL GO. ALONE. GIVE ME A MESSAGE OR SOMETHING TO TAKE TO YOUR SON AND I'LL GO.
DEAL.

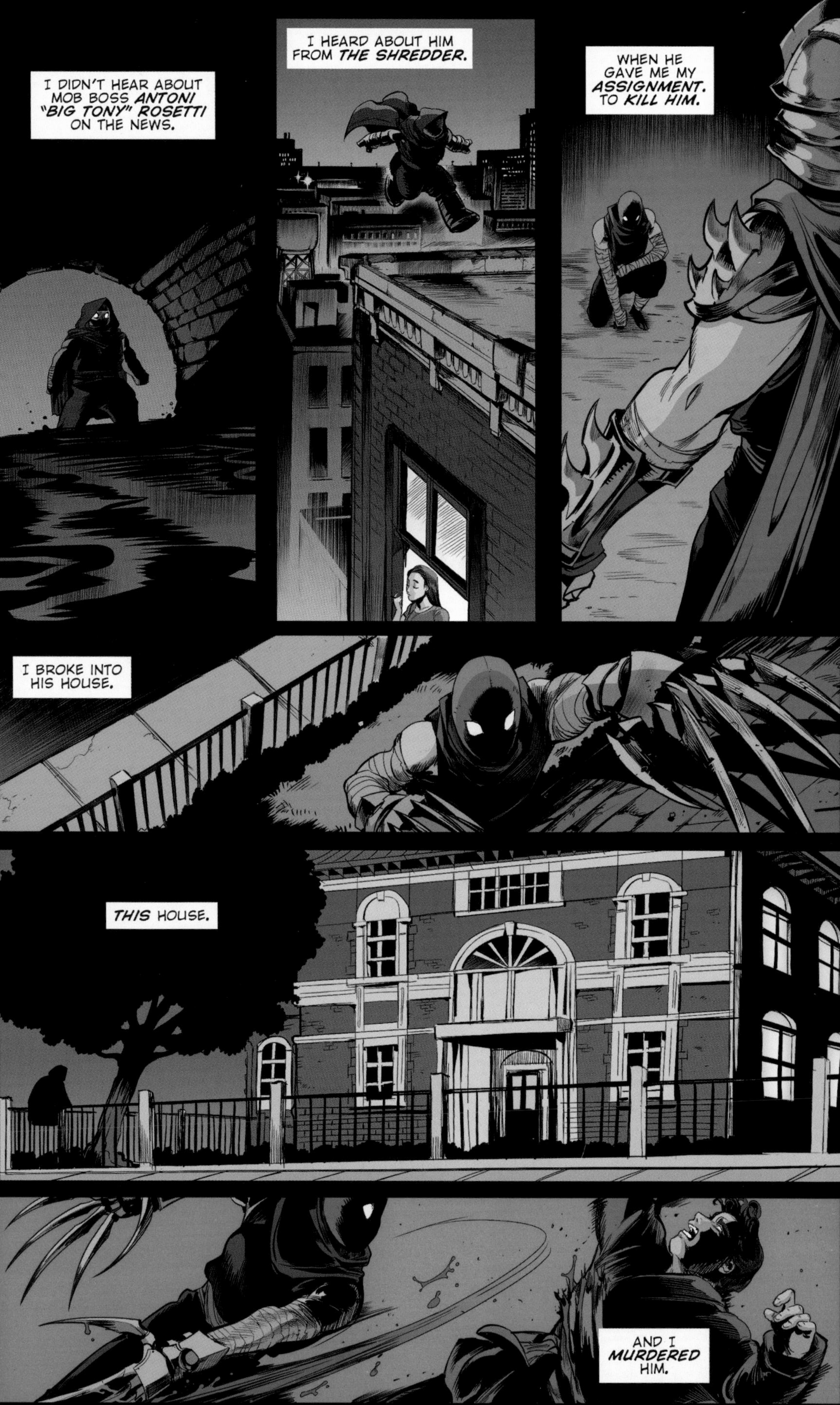
I DIDN'T HEAR ABOUT MOB BOSS ANTONI "BIG TONY" ROSETTI ON THE NEWS.
I HEARD ABOUT HIM FROM THE SHREDDER.
WHEN HE GAVE ME MY ASSIGNMENT. TO KILL HIM.
I BROKE INTO HIS HOUSE.
THIS HOUSE.
AND I MURDERED HIM.

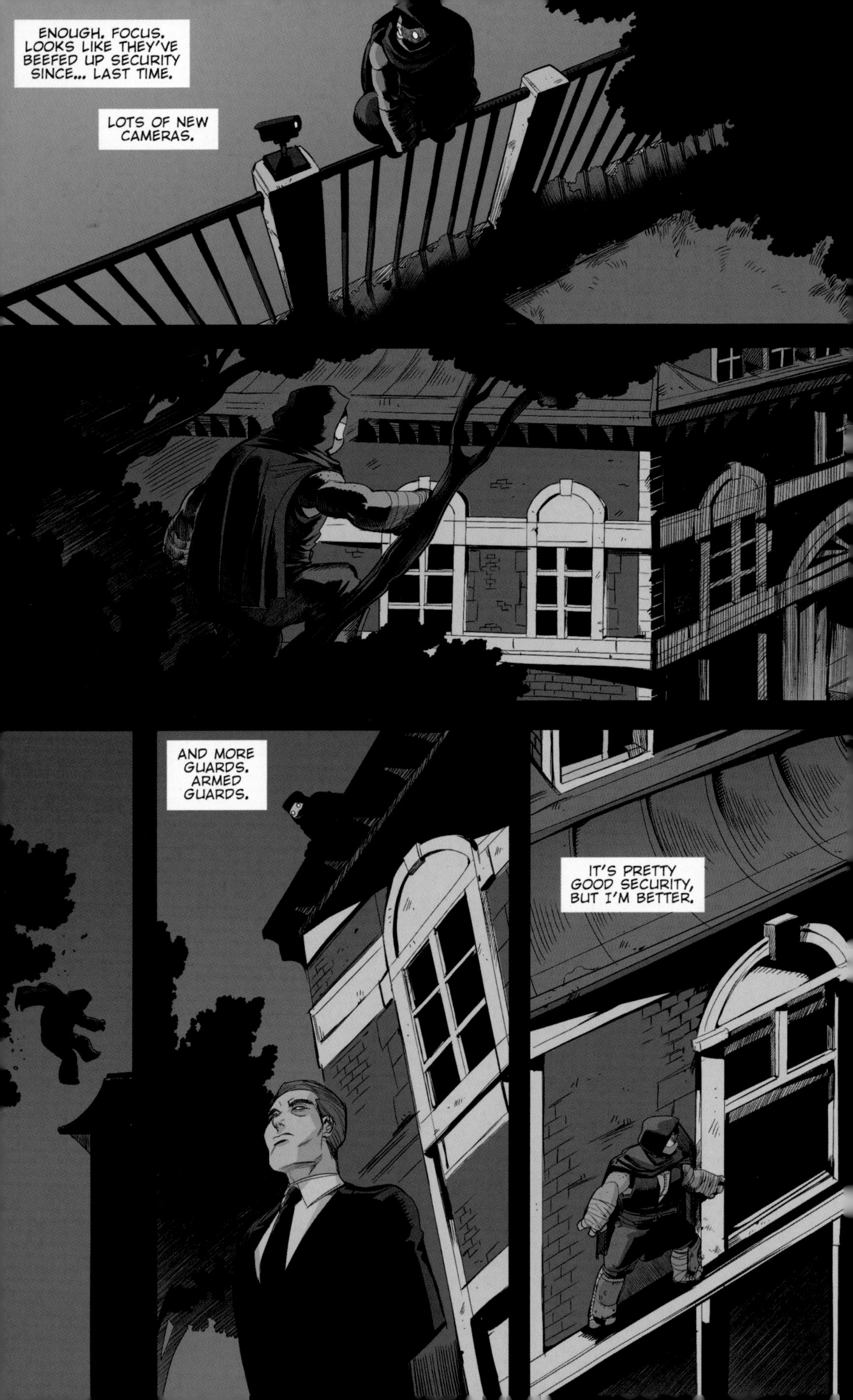
ENOUGH. FOCUS. LOOKS LIKE THEY'VE BEEFED UP SECURITY SINCE... LAST TIME.
LOTS OF NEW CAMERAS.
AND MORE GUARDS. ARMED GUARDS.
IT'S PRETTY GOOD SECURITY, BUT I'M BETTER.

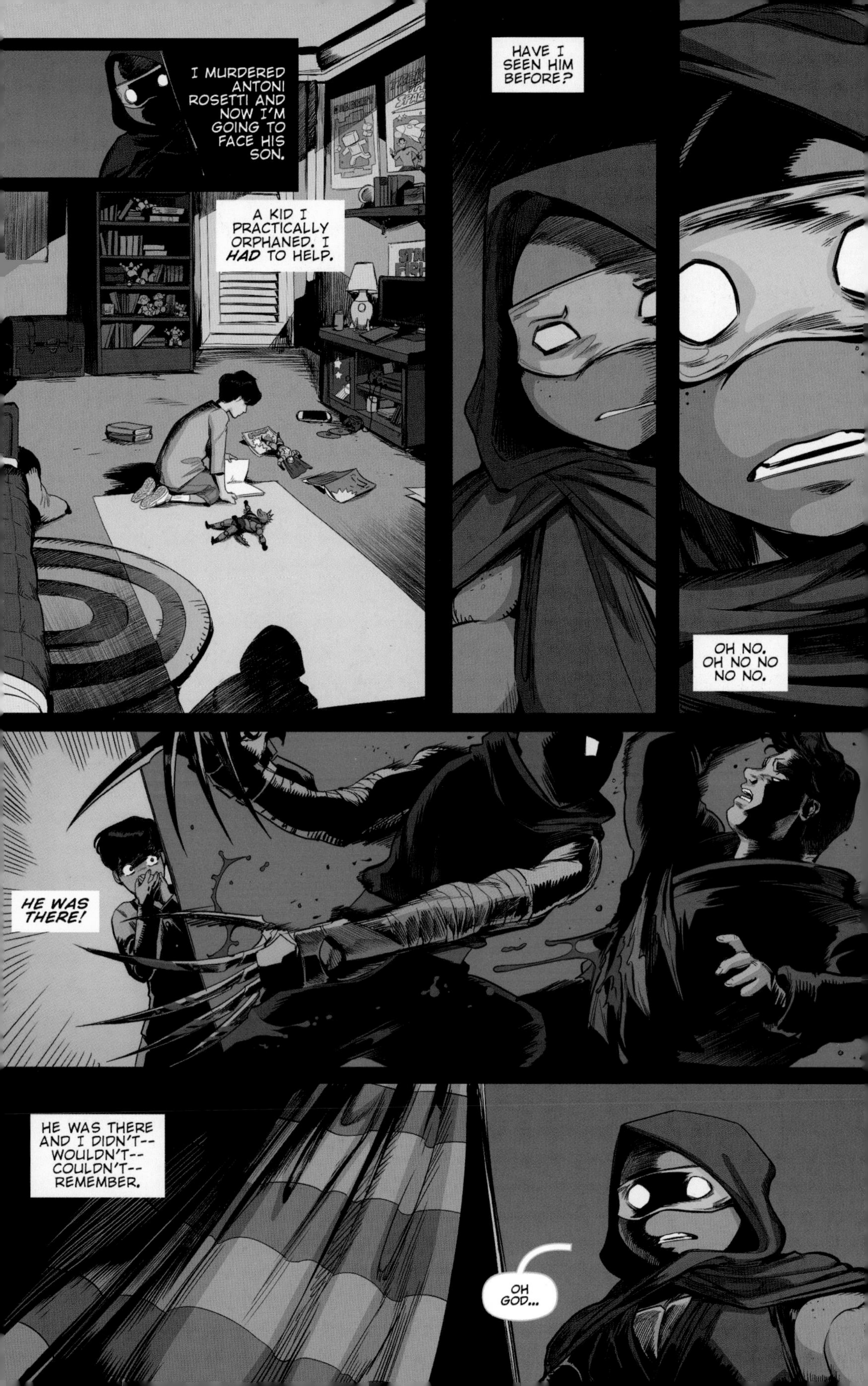

I MURDERED ANTONI ROSETTI AND NOW I'M GOING TO FACE HIS SON.
A KID I PRACTICALLY ORPHANED. I *HAD* TO HELP.
HAVE I SEEN HIM BEFORE?
OH NO. OH NO NO NO NO.
*HE WAS THERE!*
HE WAS THERE AND I DIDN'T-- WOULDN'T-- COULDN'T-- REMEMBER.
OH GOD...

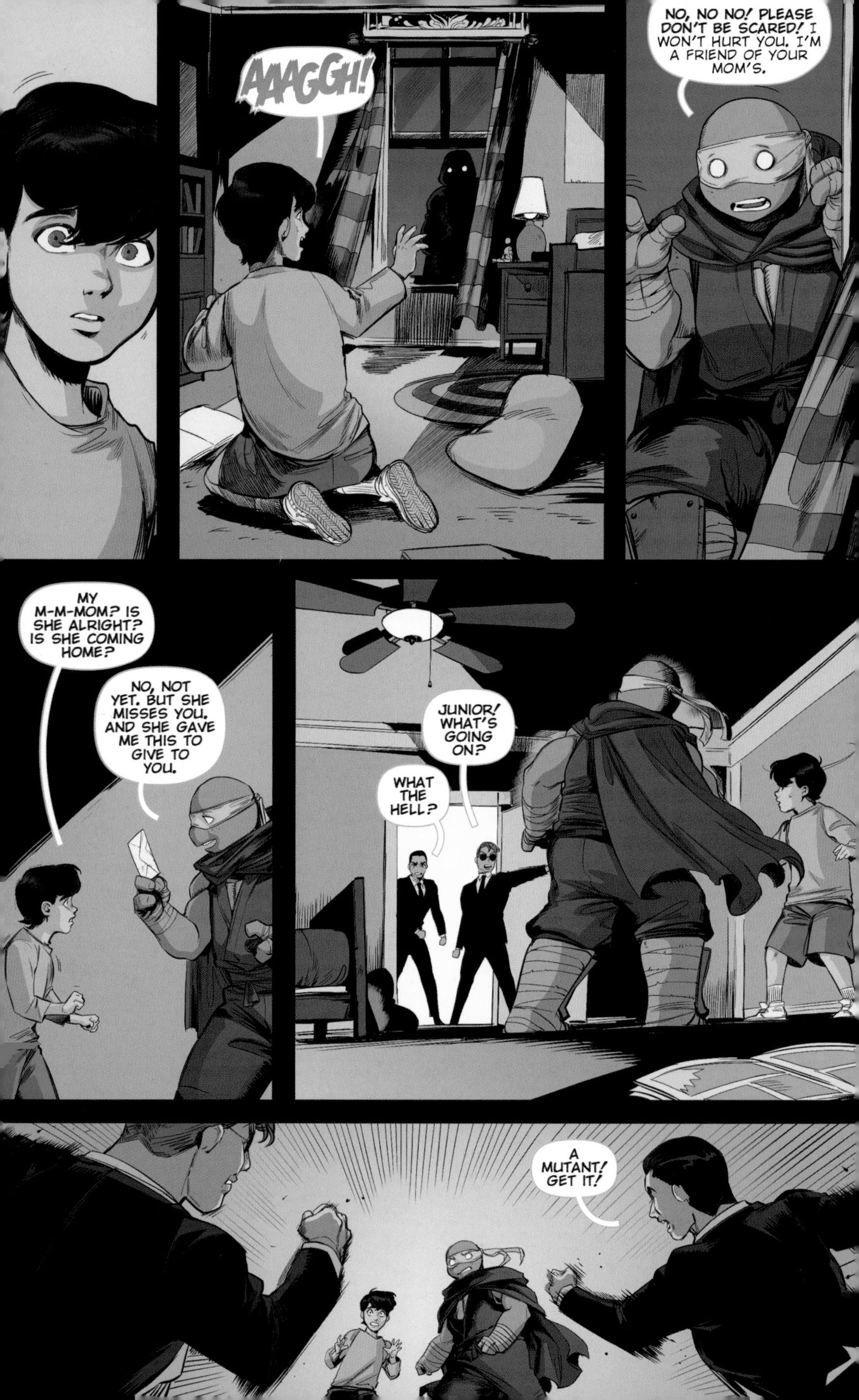
AAAGGH!
NO, NO NO! PLEASE DON'T BE SCARED! I WON'T HURT YOU. I'M A FRIEND OF YOUR MOM'S.
MY M-M-MOM? IS SHE ALRIGHT? IS SHE COMING HOME?
NO, NOT YET. BUT SHE MISSES YOU. AND SHE GAVE ME THIS TO GIVE TO YOU.
JUNIOR! WHAT'S GOING ON?
WHAT THE HELL?
A MUTANT! GET IT!

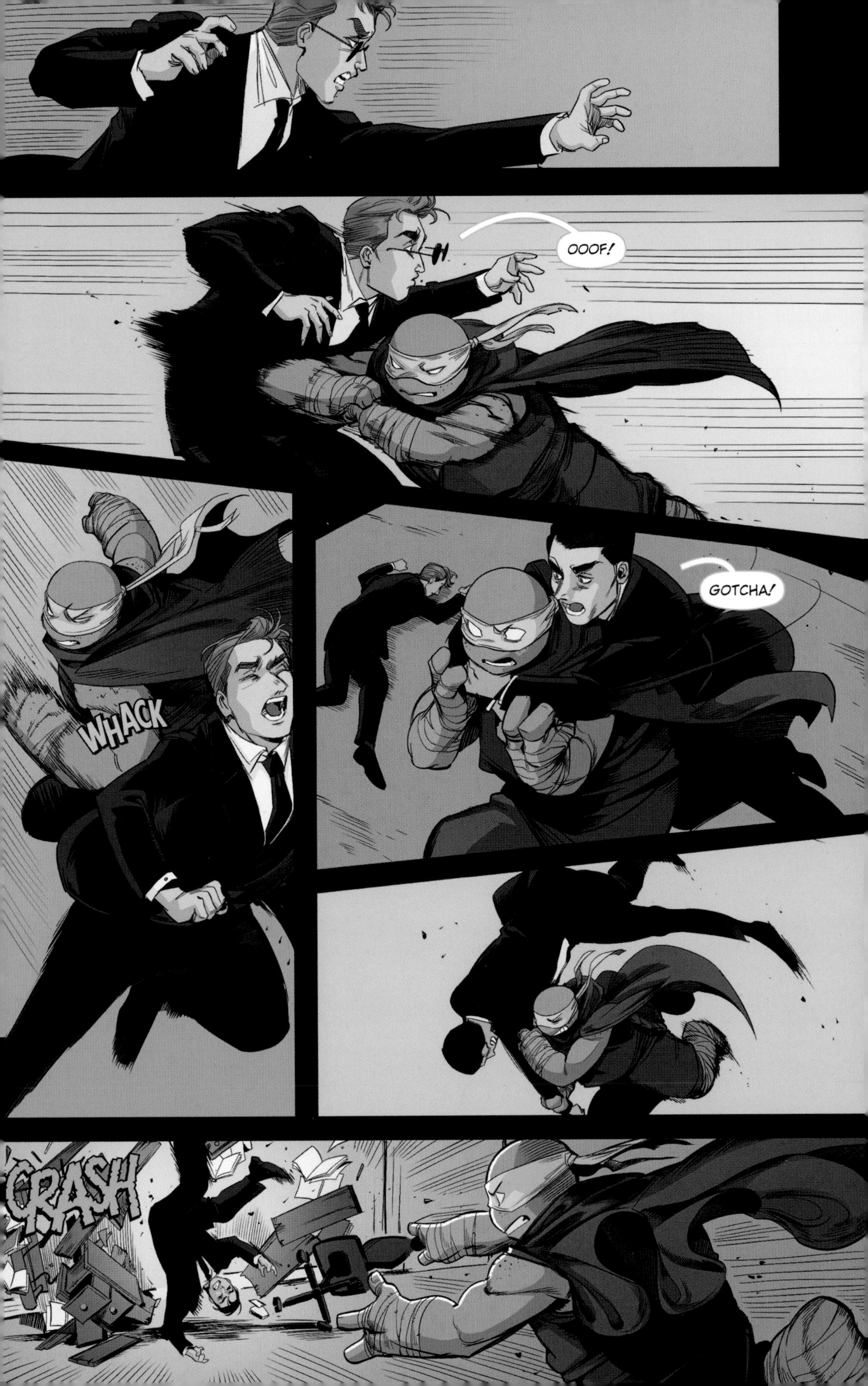
OOOF!
WHACK
GOTCHA!
CRASH

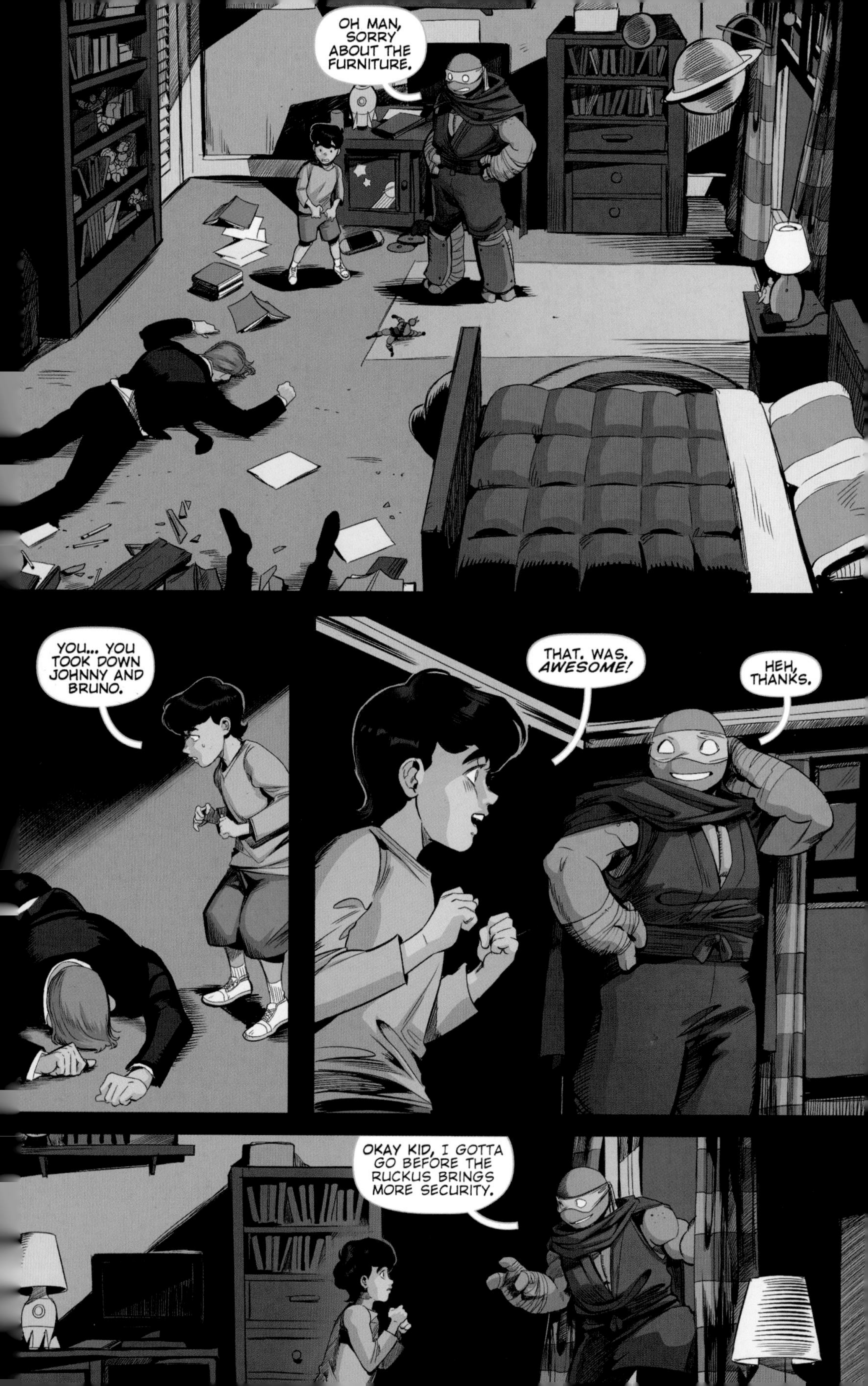
OH MAN, SORRY ABOUT THE FURNITURE.
YOU... YOU TOOK DOWN JOHNNY AND BRUNO.
THAT. WAS. *AWESOME!*
HEH, THANKS.
OKAY KID, I GOTTA GO BEFORE THE RUCKUS BRINGS MORE SECURITY.

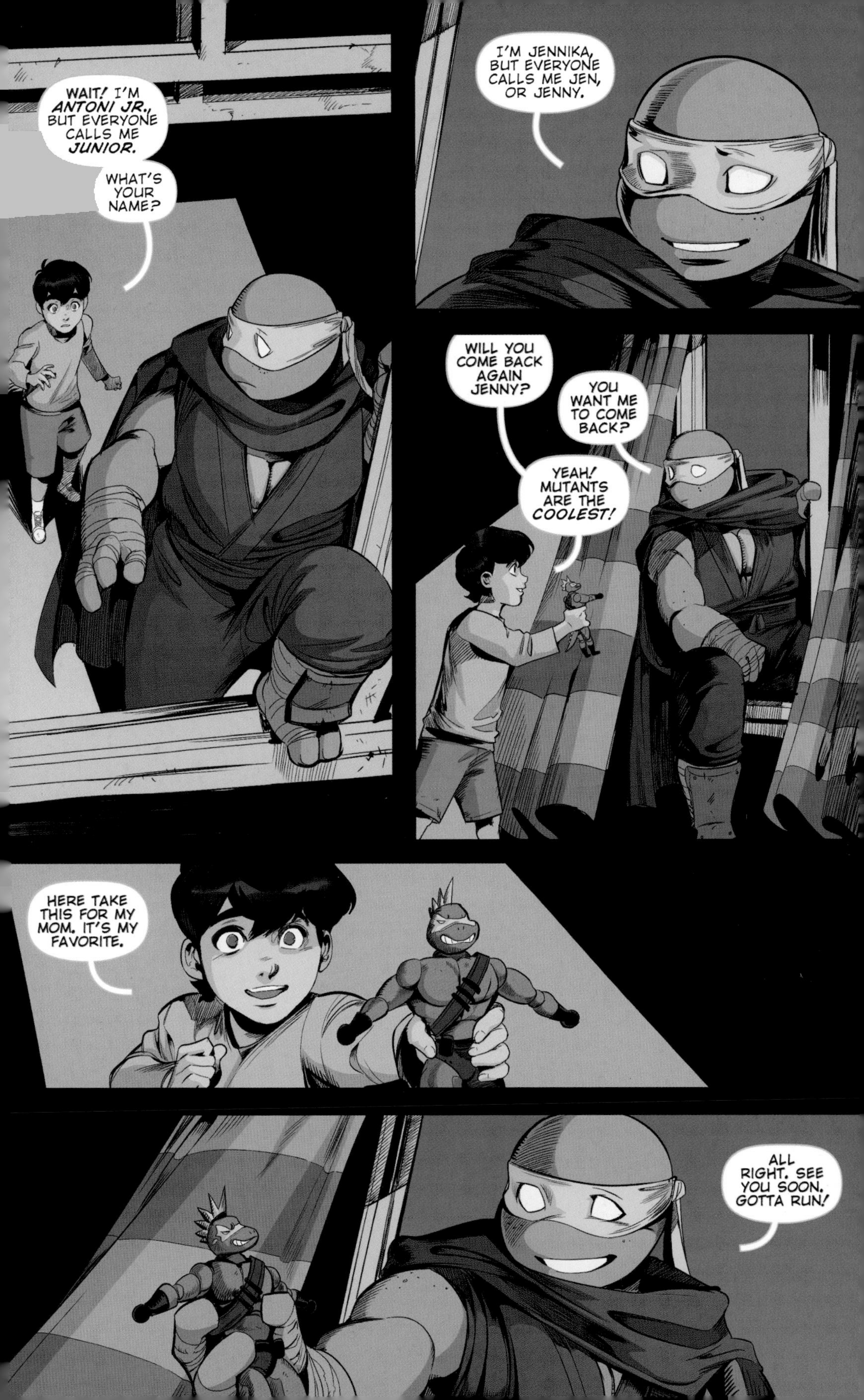
WAIT! I'M ANTONI JR., BUT EVERYONE CALLS ME JUNIOR.
WHAT'S YOUR NAME?
I'M JENNIKA, BUT EVERYONE CALLS ME JEN, OR JENNY.
WILL YOU COME BACK AGAIN JENNY?
YOU WANT ME TO COME BACK?
YEAH! MUTANTS ARE THE COOLEST!
HERE TAKE THIS FOR MY MOM. IT'S MY FAVORITE.
ALL RIGHT. SEE YOU SOON. GOTTA RUN!

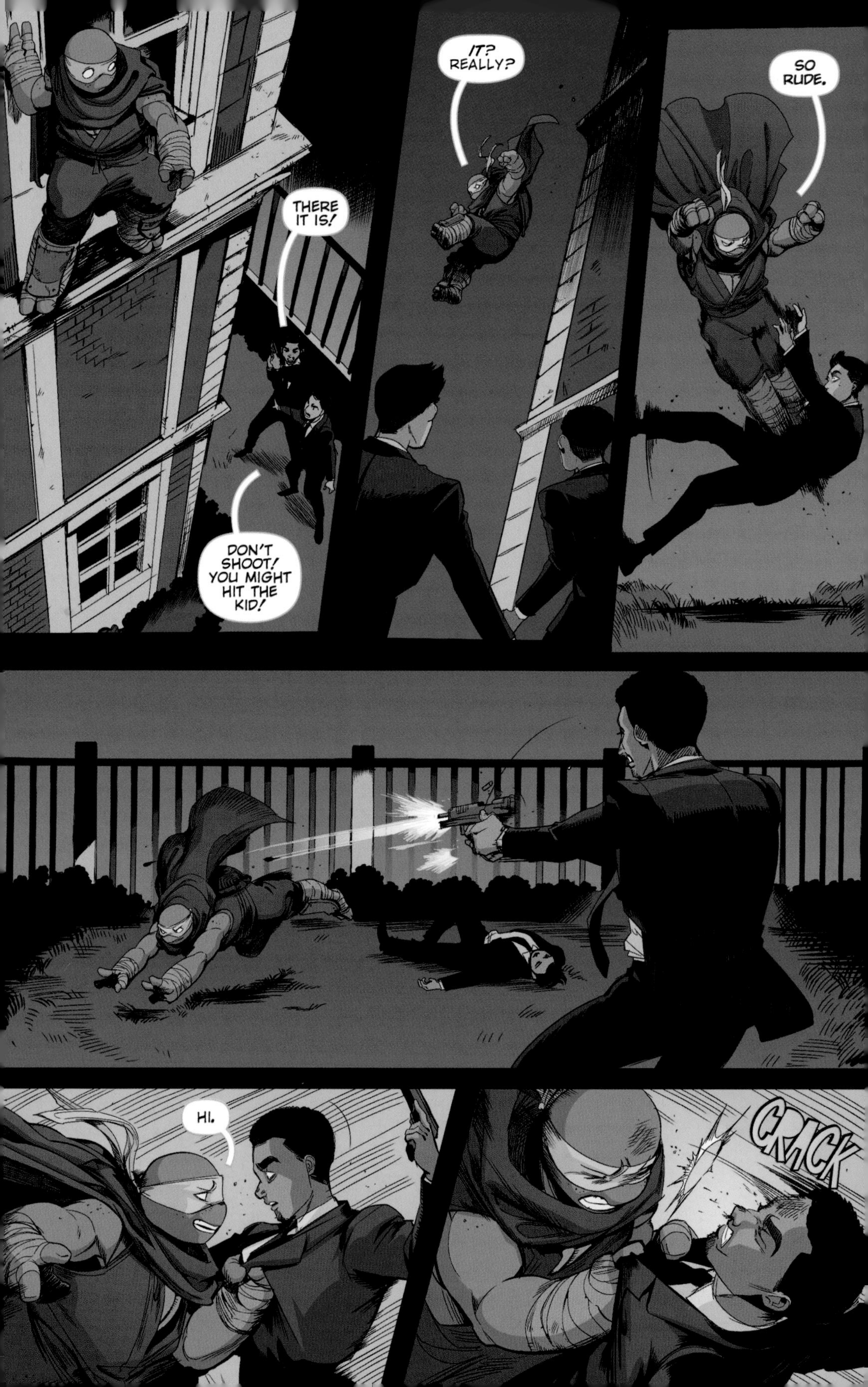
THERE IT IS!
DON'T SHOOT! YOU MIGHT HIT THE KID!
IT? REALLY?
SO RUDE.
HI.
CRACK

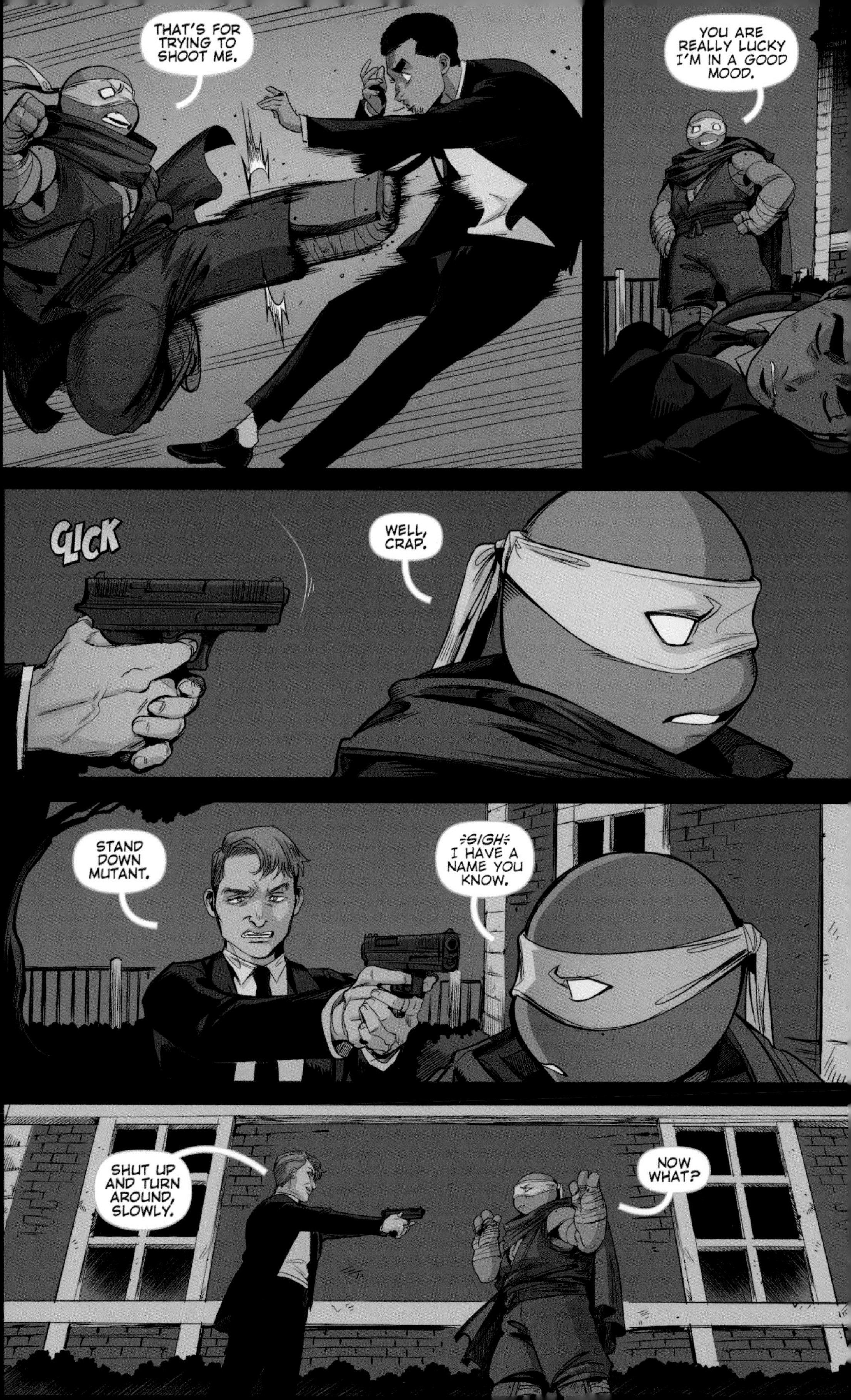
THAT'S FOR TRYING TO SHOOT ME.
YOU ARE REALLY LUCKY I'M IN A GOOD MOOD.
CLICK
WELL, CRAP.
STAND DOWN MUTANT.
*SIGH* I HAVE A NAME YOU KNOW.
SHUT UP AND TURN AROUND, SLOWLY.
NOW WHAT?

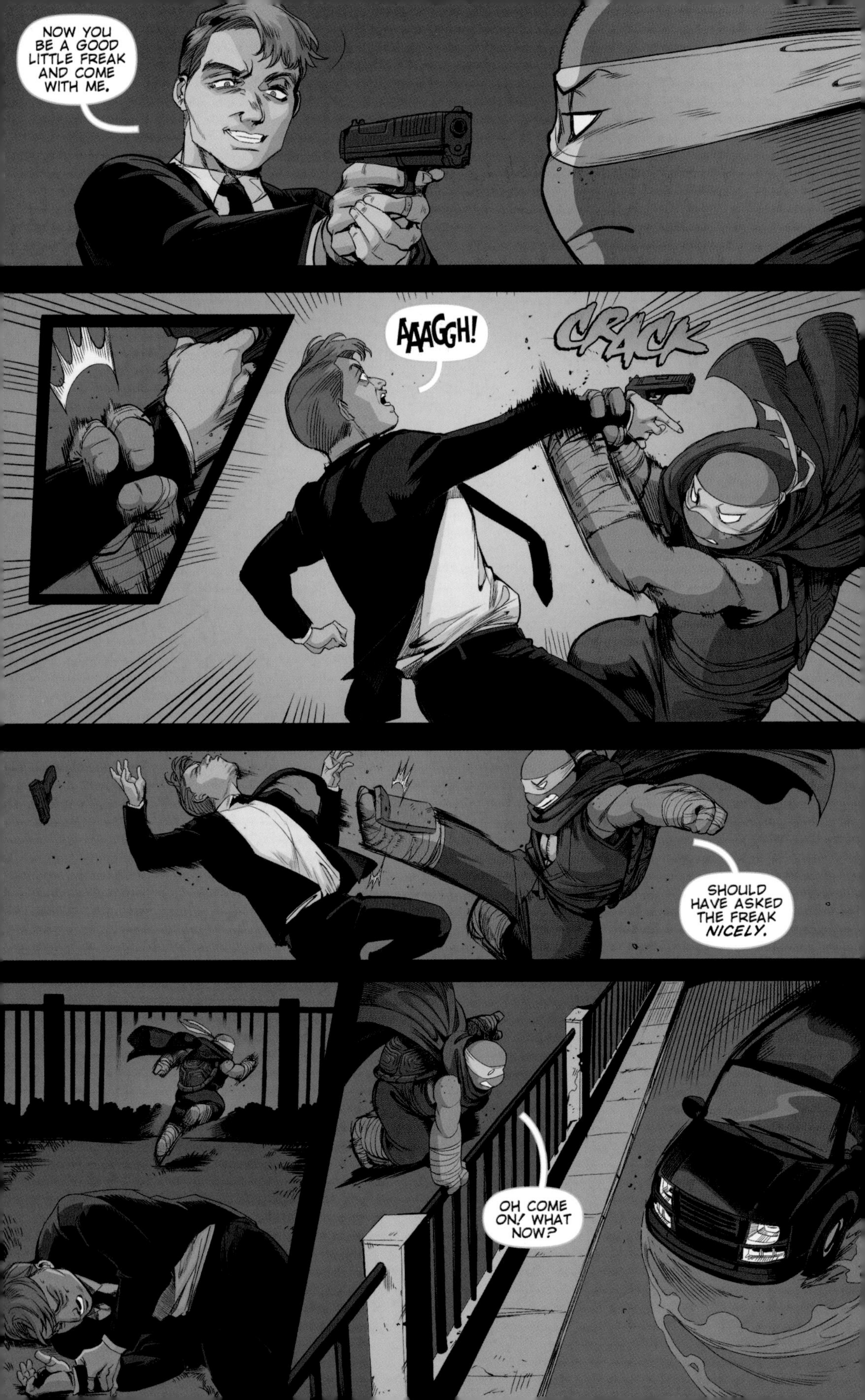
NOW YOU BE A GOOD LITTLE FREAK AND COME WITH ME.
AAAGGH!
CRACK
SHOULD HAVE ASKED THE FREAK *NICELY*.
OH COME ON! WHAT NOW?

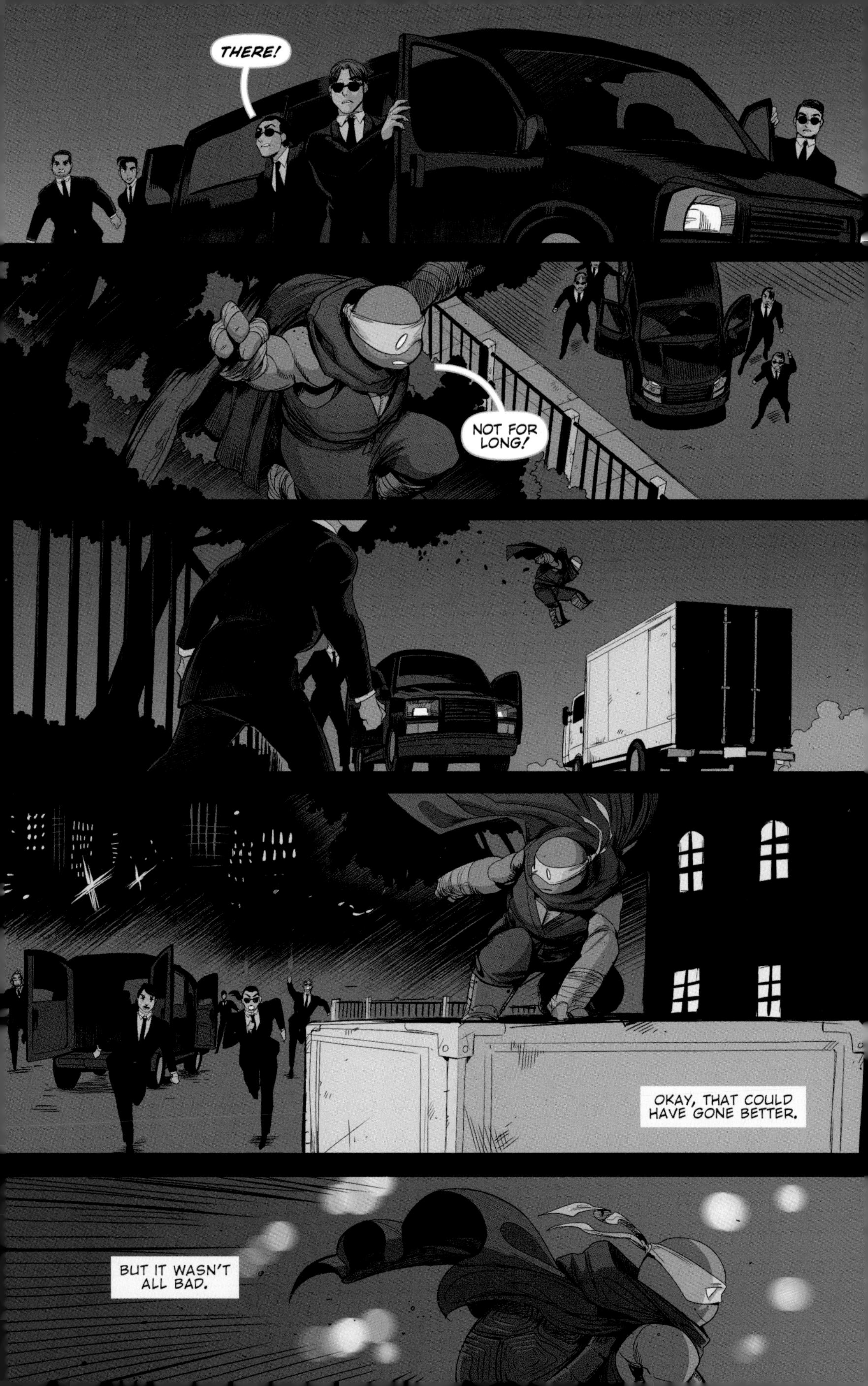
THERE!
NOT FOR LONG!
OKAY, THAT COULD HAVE GONE BETTER.
BUT IT WASN'T ALL BAD.

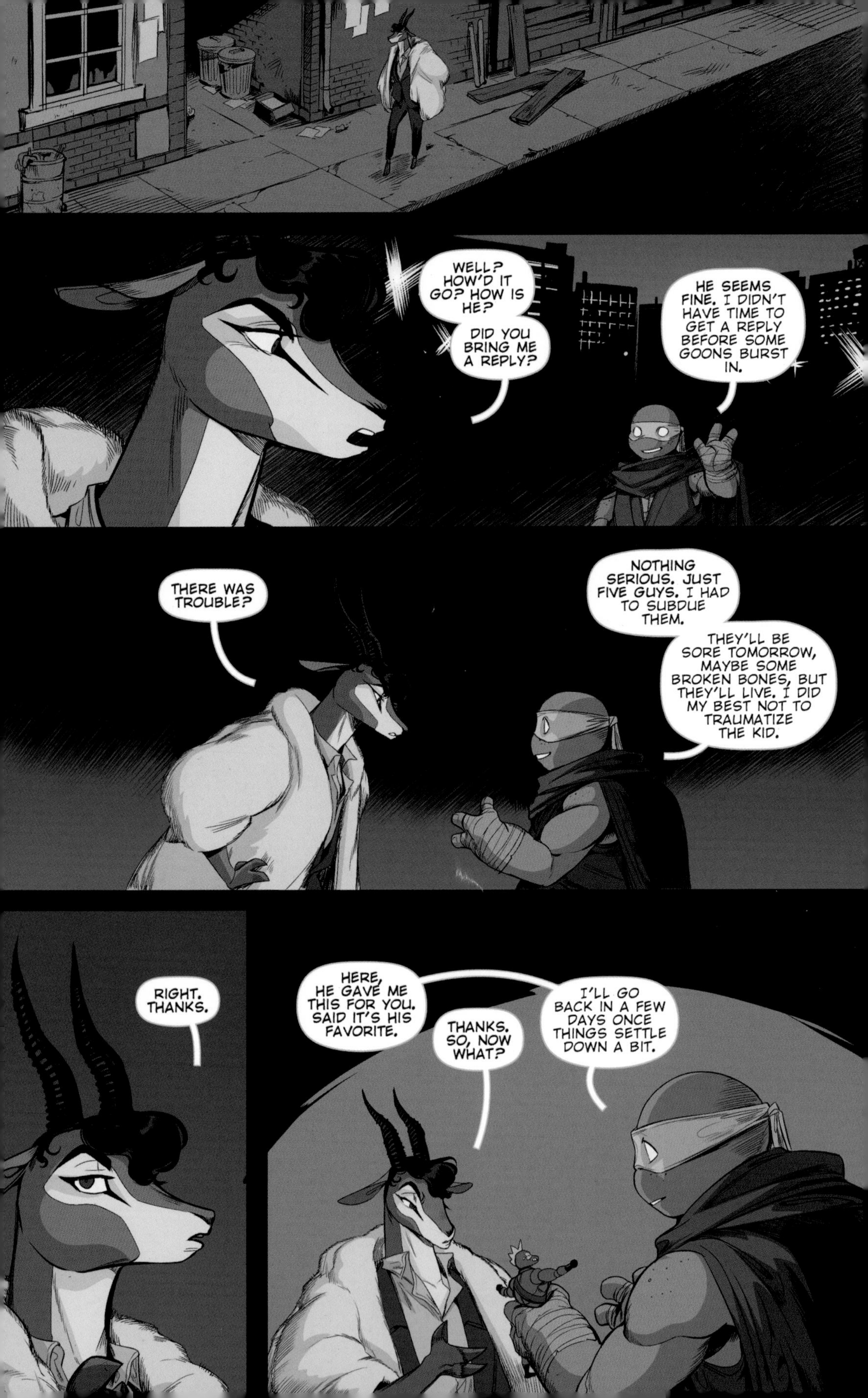
WELL? HOW'D IT GO? HOW IS HE?
DID YOU BRING ME A REPLY?
HE SEEMS FINE. I DIDN'T HAVE TIME TO GET A REPLY BEFORE SOME GOONS BURST IN.
THERE WAS TROUBLE?
NOTHING SERIOUS. JUST FIVE GUYS. I HAD TO SUBDUE THEM.
THEY'LL BE SORE TOMORROW, MAYBE SOME BROKEN BONES, BUT THEY'LL LIVE. I DID MY BEST NOT TO TRAUMATIZE THE KID.
RIGHT. THANKS.
HERE, HE GAVE ME THIS FOR YOU. SAID IT'S HIS FAVORITE.
I'LL GO BACK IN A FEW DAYS ONCE THINGS SETTLE DOWN A BIT.
THANKS. SO, NOW WHAT?

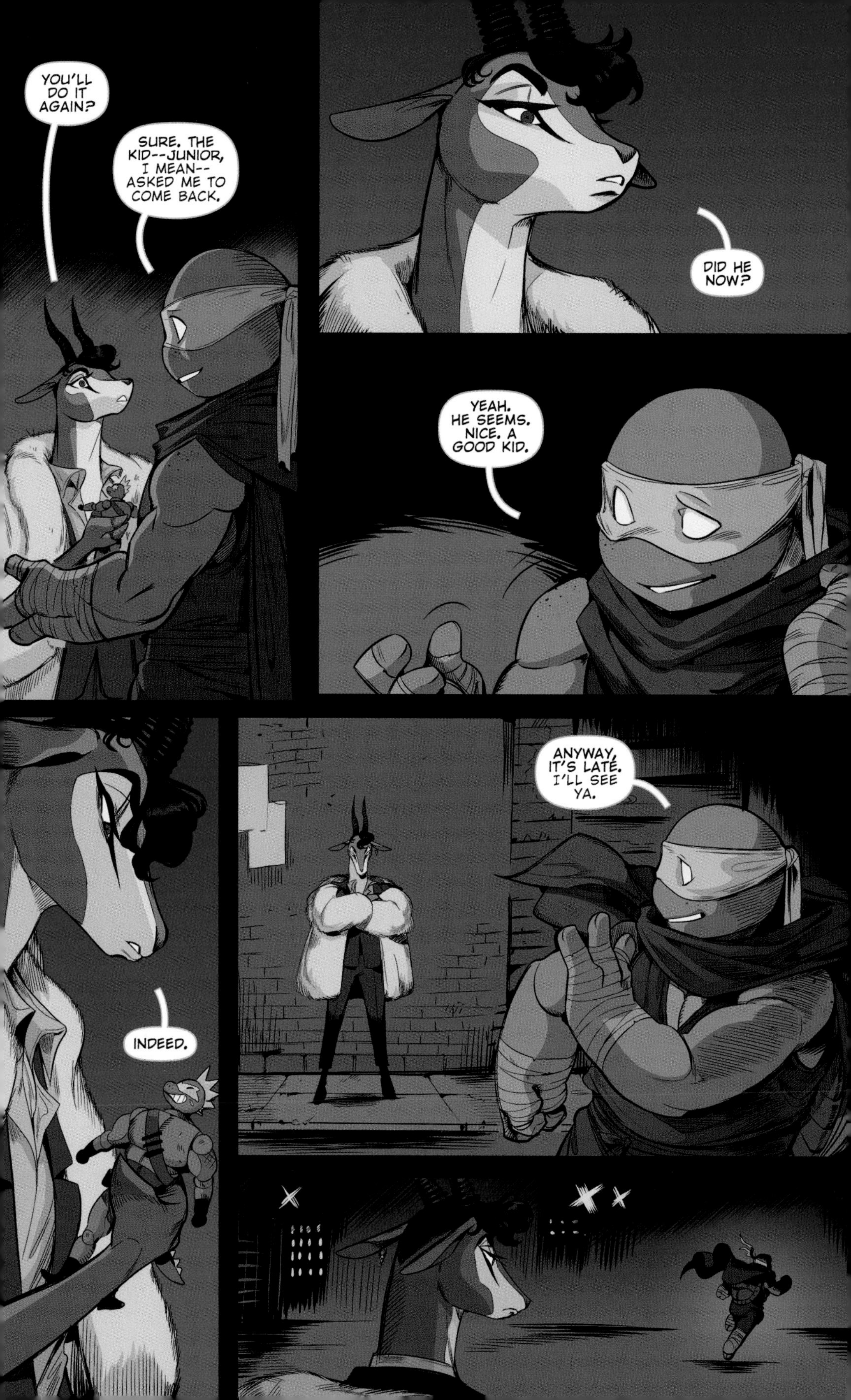
YOU'LL DO IT AGAIN?
SURE. THE KID--JUNIOR, I MEAN--ASKED ME TO COME BACK.
DID HE NOW?
YEAH. HE SEEMS. NICE. A GOOD KID.
INDEED.
ANYWAY, IT'S LATE. I'LL SEE YA.

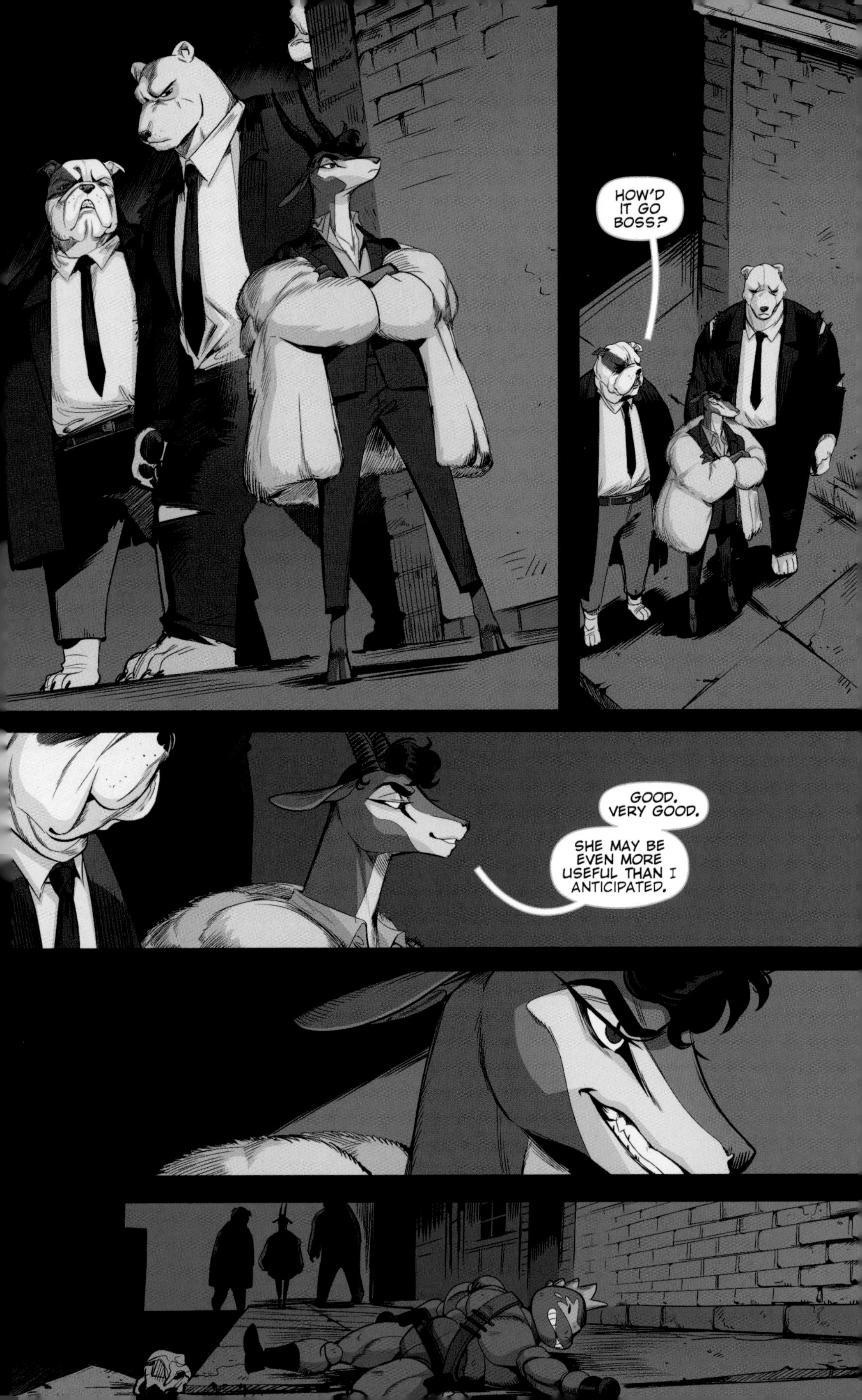
HOW'D IT GO BOSS?
GOOD. VERY GOOD.
SHE MAY BE EVEN MORE USEFUL THAN I ANTICIPATED.

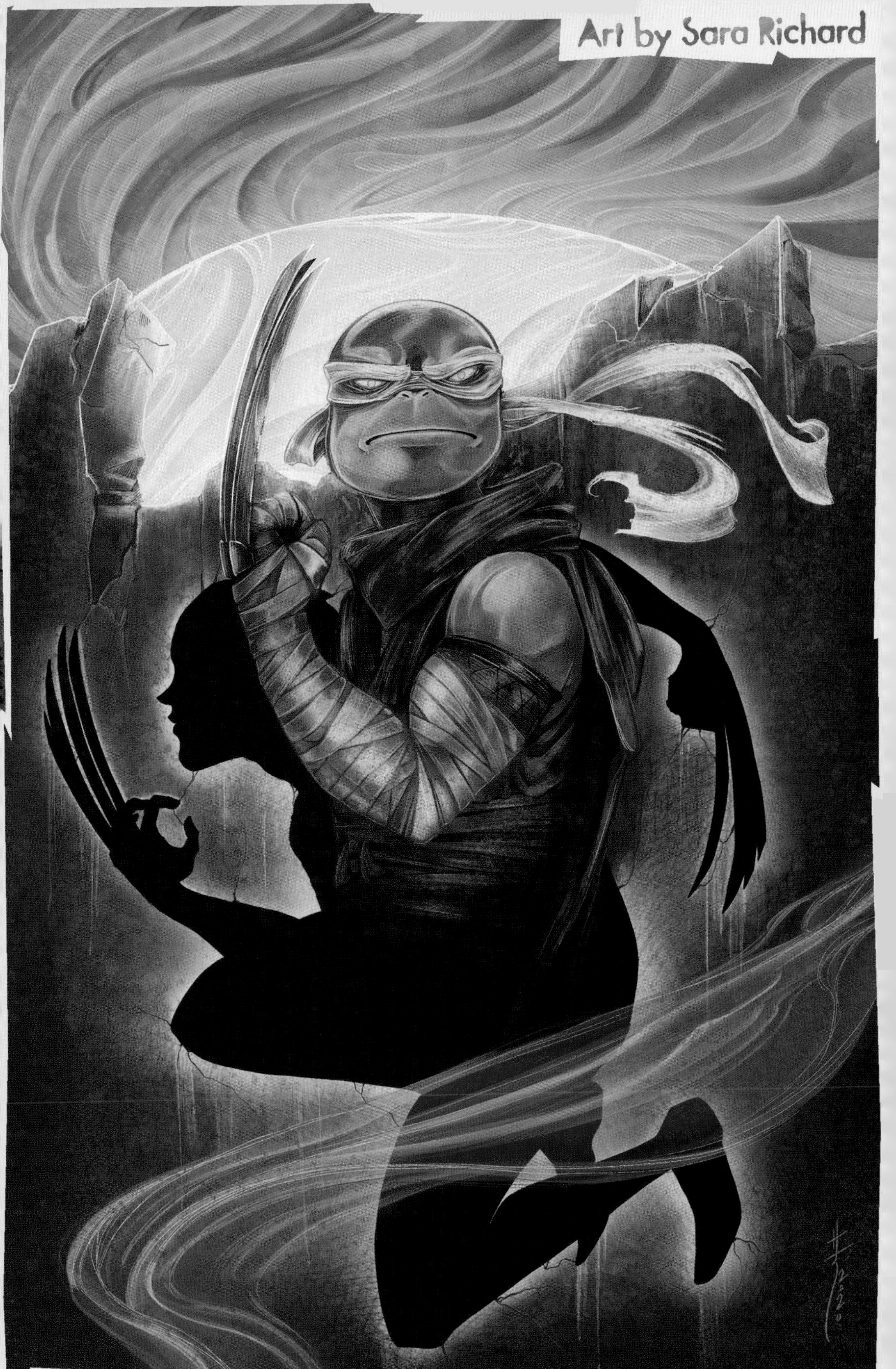

Art by Sara Richard

Art by Jodi Nishijima

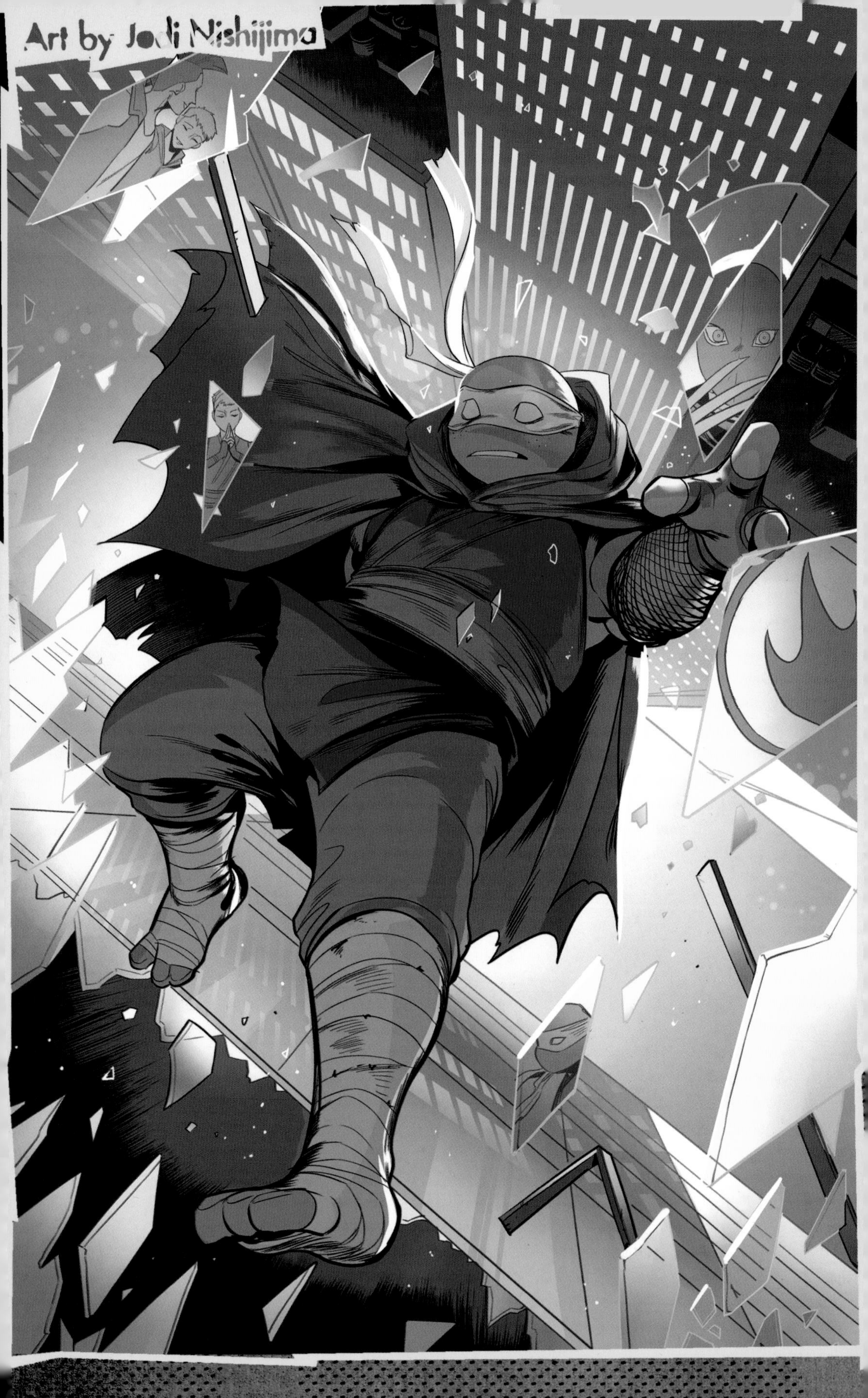

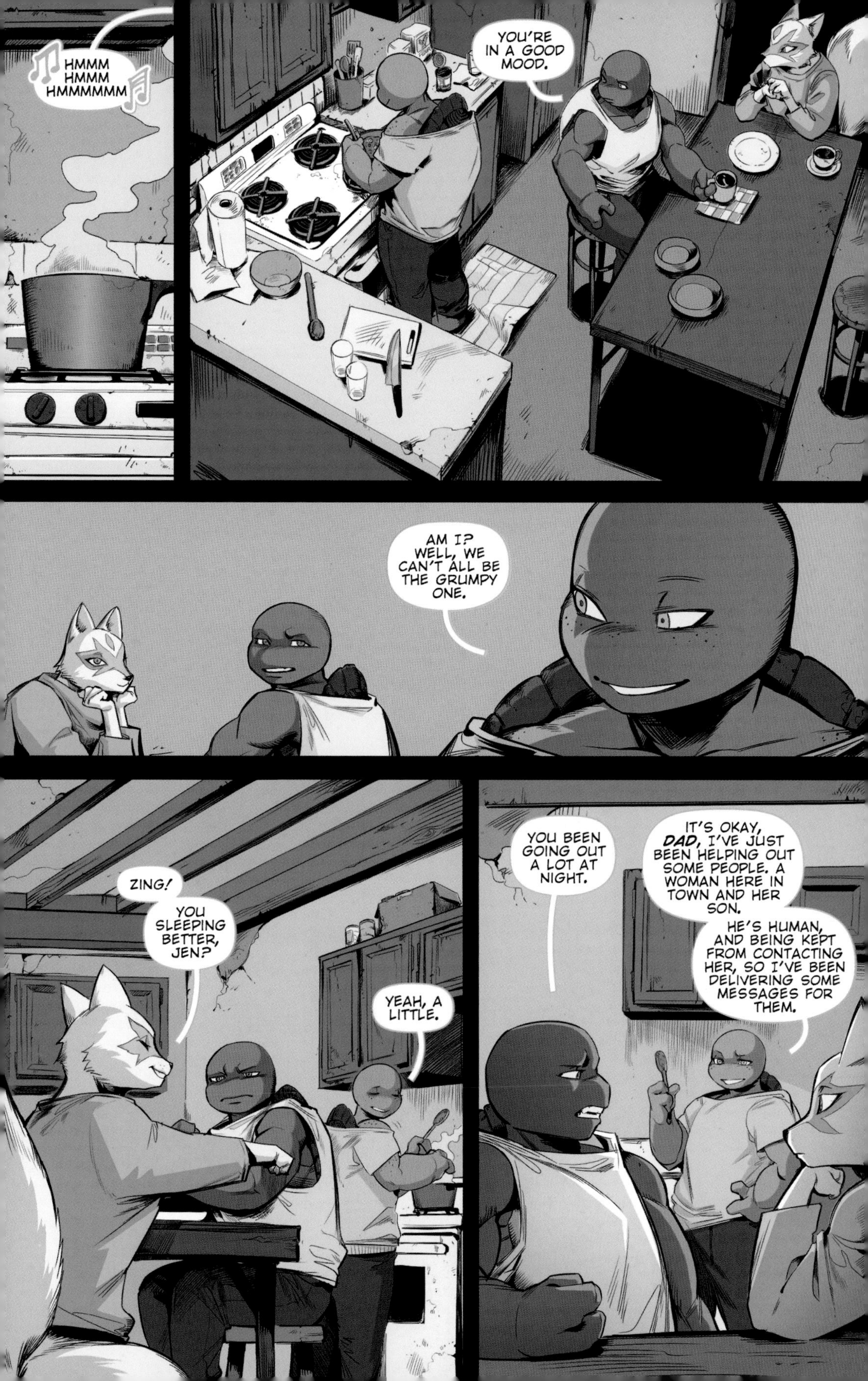

HMMM HMMM HMMMMMM
YOU'RE IN A GOOD MOOD.
AM I? WELL, WE CAN'T ALL BE THE GRUMPY ONE.
ZING!
YOU SLEEPING BETTER, JEN?
YEAH, A LITTLE.
YOU BEEN GOING OUT A LOT AT NIGHT.
IT'S OKAY, DAD, I'VE JUST BEEN HELPING OUT SOME PEOPLE. A WOMAN HERE IN TOWN AND HER SON.
HE'S HUMAN, AND BEING KEPT FROM CONTACTING HER, SO I'VE BEEN DELIVERING SOME MESSAGES FOR THEM.

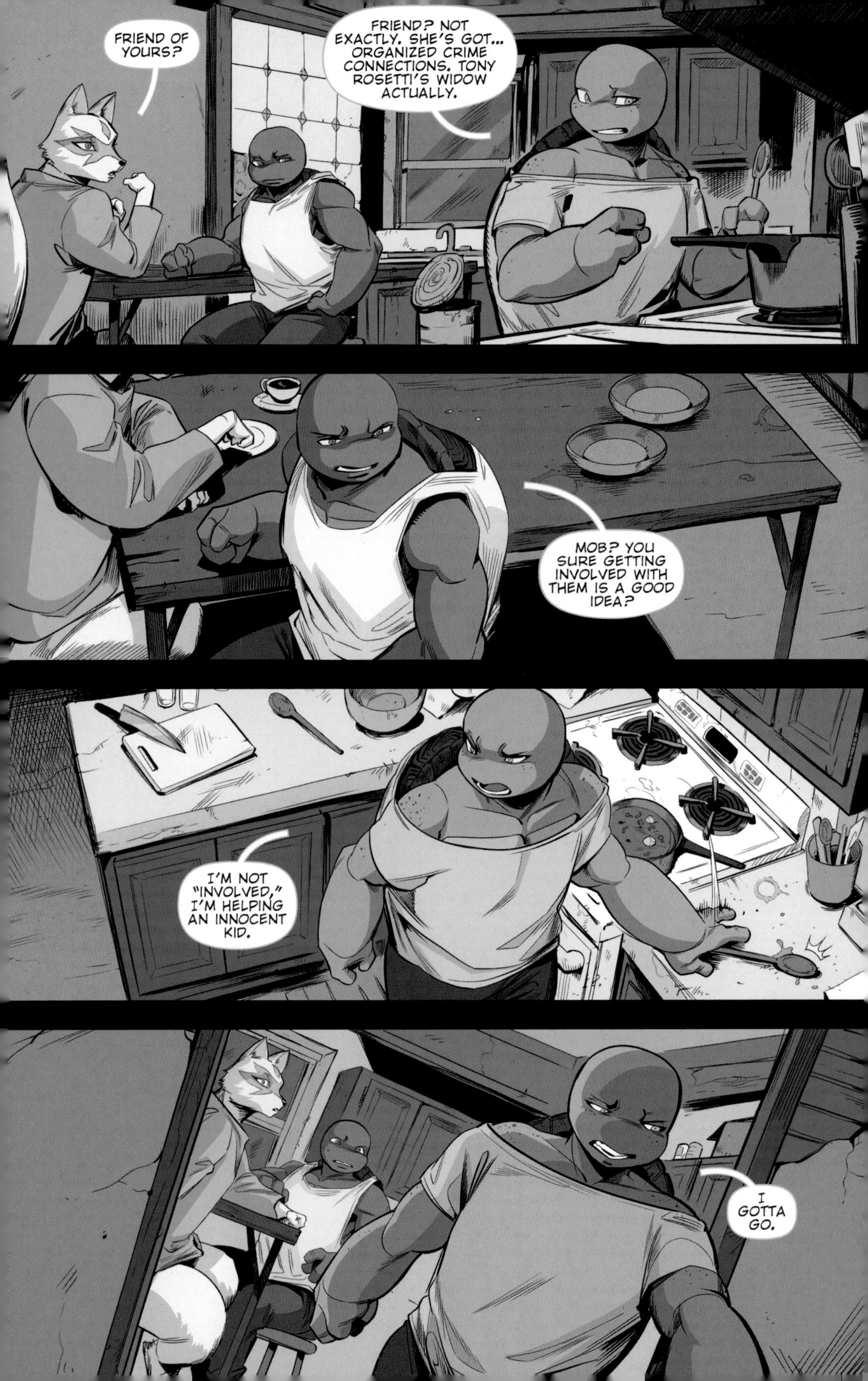
FRIEND OF YOURS?
FRIEND? NOT EXACTLY. SHE'S GOT... ORGANIZED CRIME CONNECTIONS. TONY ROSETTI'S WIDOW ACTUALLY.
MOB? YOU SURE GETTING INVOLVED WITH THEM IS A GOOD IDEA?
I'M NOT "INVOLVED," I'M HELPING AN INNOCENT KID.
I GOTTA GO.

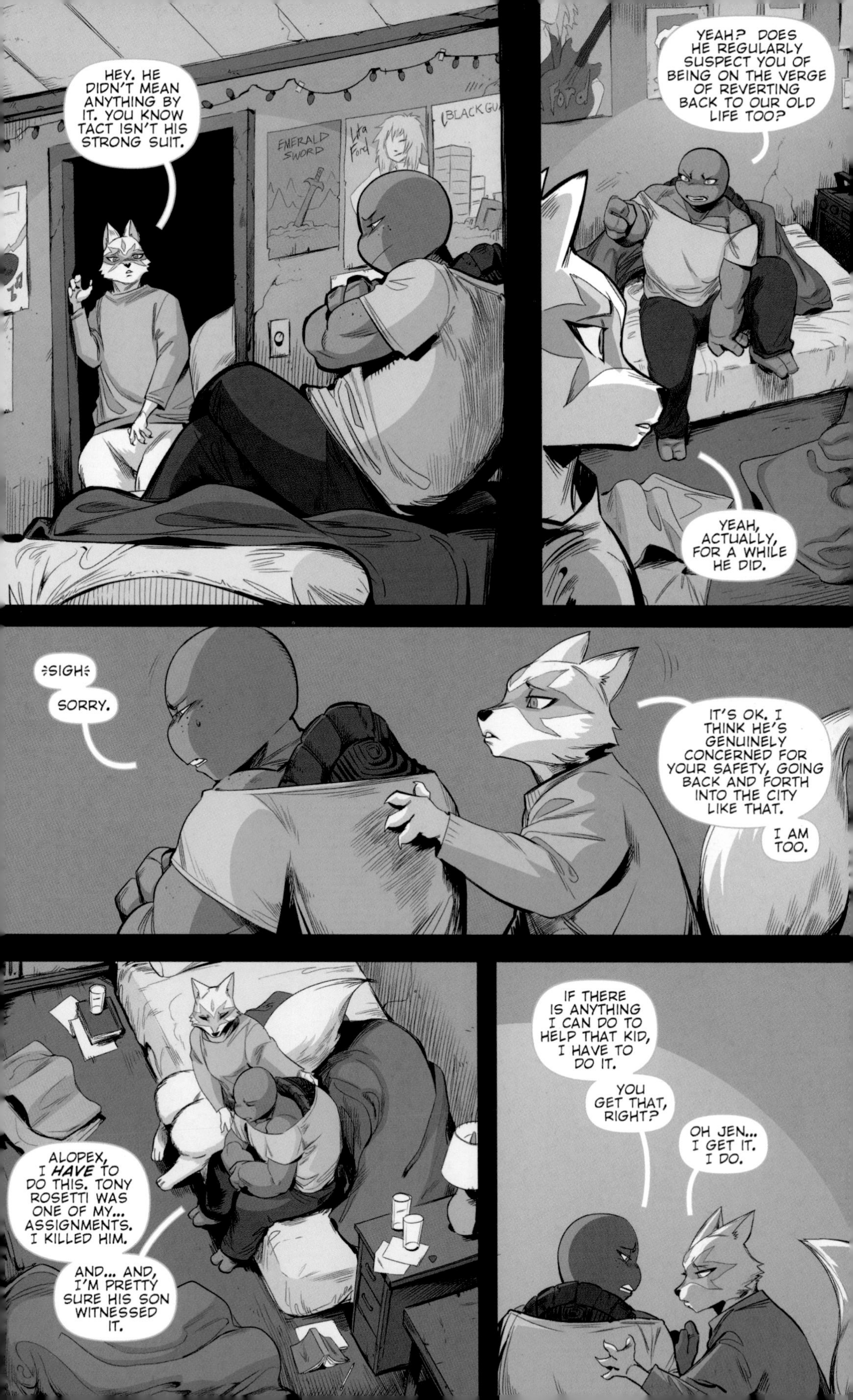
HEY. HE DIDN'T MEAN ANYTHING BY IT. YOU KNOW TACT ISN'T HIS STRONG SUIT.
EMERALD SWORD
Lita Ford
BLACK GU
YEAH? DOES HE REGULARLY SUSPECT YOU OF BEING ON THE VERGE OF REVERTING BACK TO OUR OLD LIFE TOO?
YEAH, ACTUALLY, FOR A WHILE HE DID.
⸗SIGH⸗
SORRY.
IT'S OK. I THINK HE'S GENUINELY CONCERNED FOR YOUR SAFETY, GOING BACK AND FORTH INTO THE CITY LIKE THAT.
I AM TOO.
ALOPEX, I ***HAVE*** TO DO THIS. TONY ROSETTI WAS ONE OF MY... ASSIGNMENTS. I KILLED HIM.
AND... AND, I'M PRETTY SURE HIS SON WITNESSED IT.
IF THERE IS ANYTHING I CAN DO TO HELP THAT KID, I HAVE TO DO IT.
YOU GET THAT, RIGHT?
OH JEN... I GET IT. I DO.

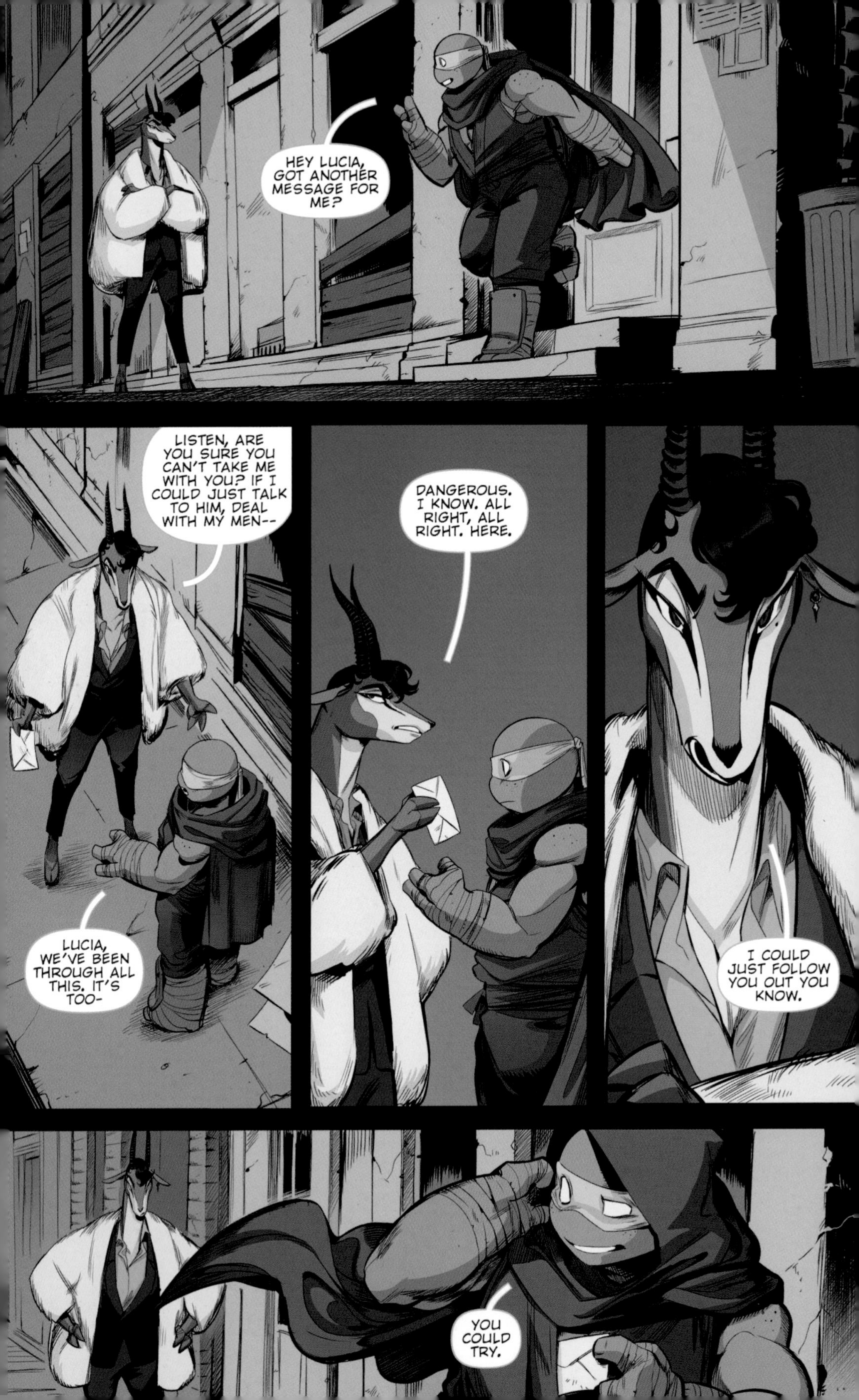
HEY LUCIA, GOT ANOTHER MESSAGE FOR ME?
LISTEN, ARE YOU SURE YOU CAN'T TAKE ME WITH YOU? IF I COULD JUST TALK TO HIM, DEAL WITH MY MEN--
LUCIA, WE'VE BEEN THROUGH ALL THIS. IT'S TOO-
DANGEROUS. I KNOW. ALL RIGHT, ALL RIGHT. HERE.
I COULD JUST FOLLOW YOU OUT YOU KNOW.
YOU COULD TRY.

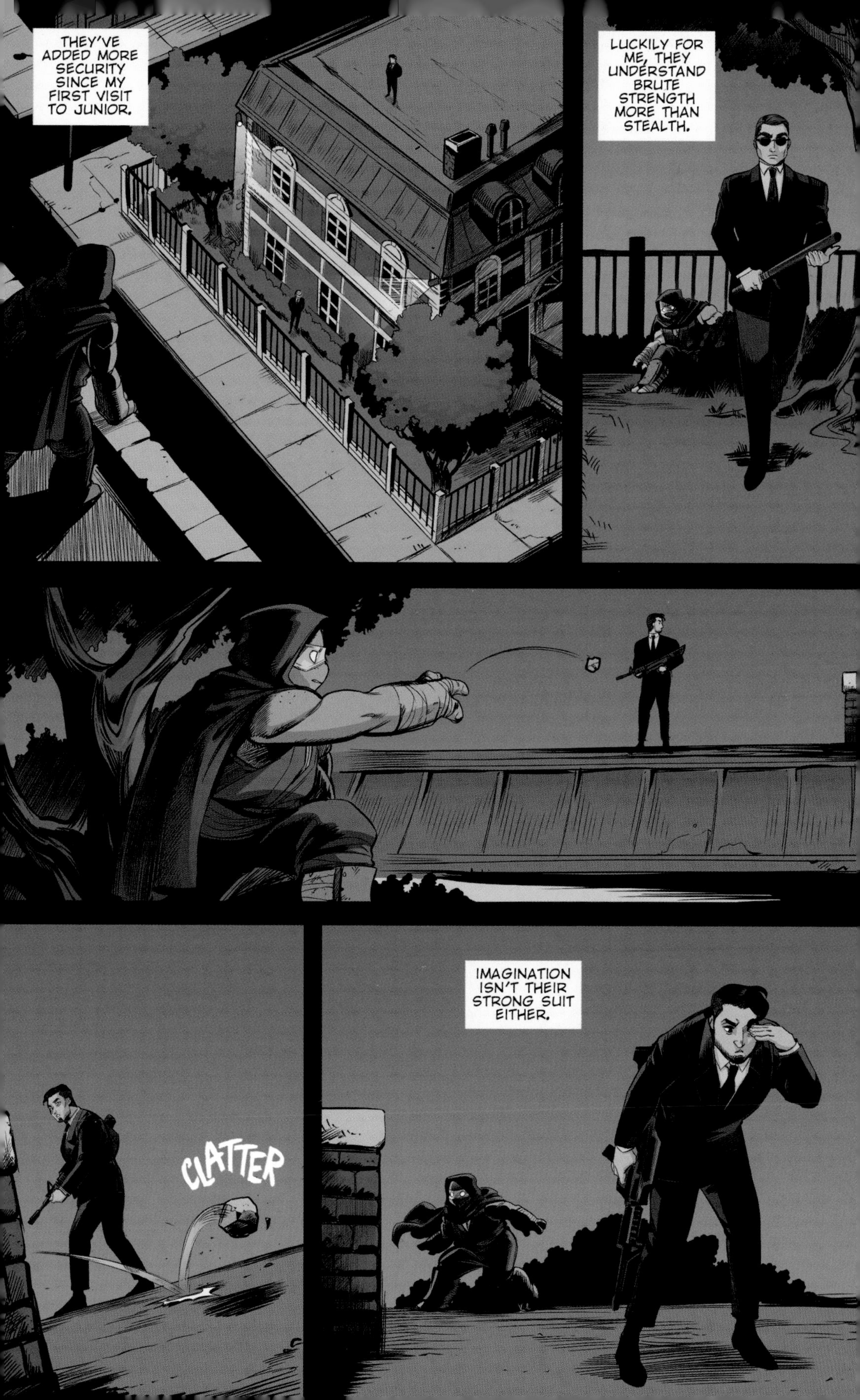
THEY'VE ADDED MORE SECURITY SINCE MY FIRST VISIT TO JUNIOR.
LUCKILY FOR ME, THEY UNDERSTAND BRUTE STRENGTH MORE THAN STEALTH.
CLATTER
IMAGINATION ISN'T THEIR STRONG SUIT EITHER.

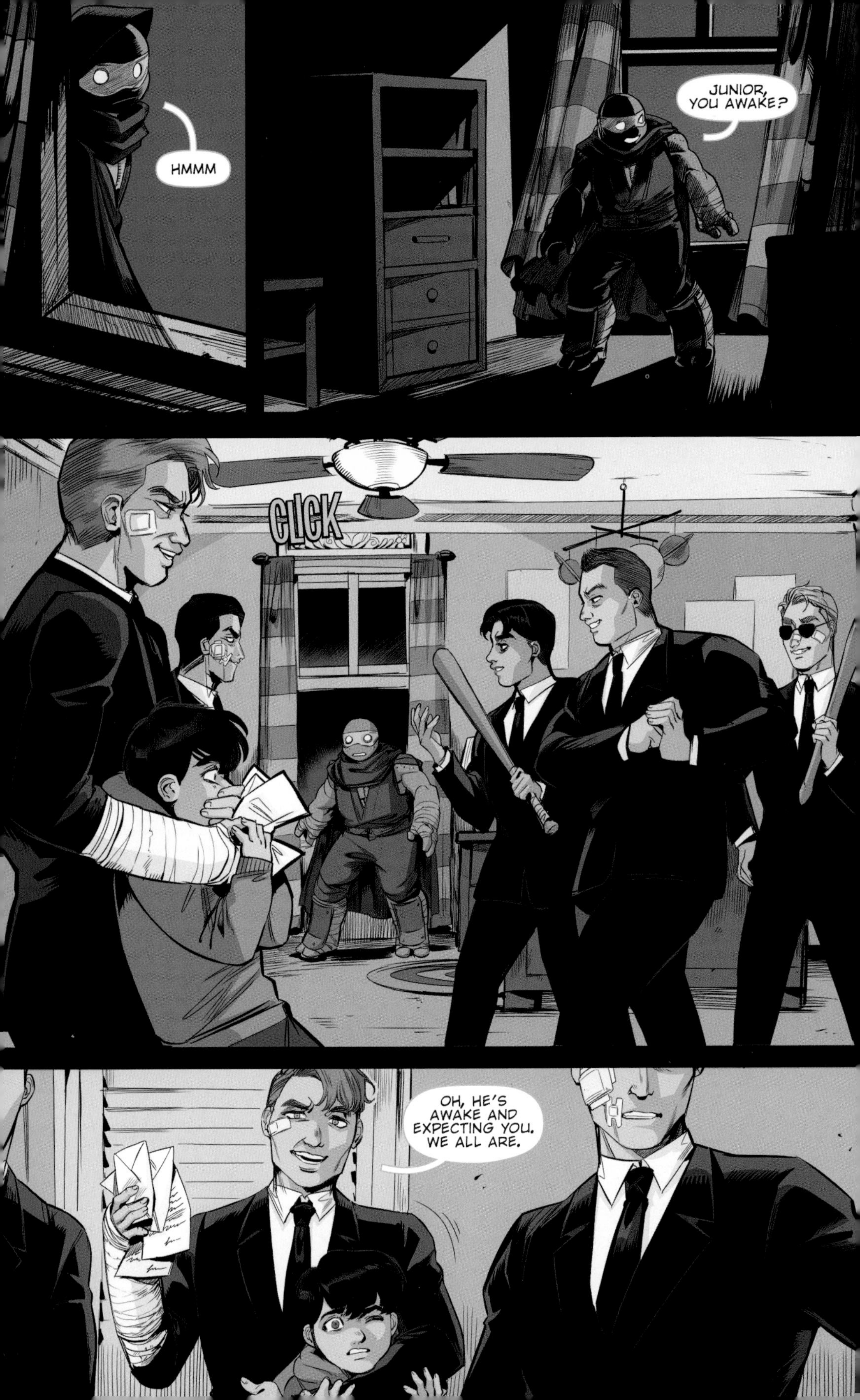
HMMM
JUNIOR, YOU AWAKE?
CLICK
OH, HE'S AWAKE AND EXPECTING YOU. WE ALL ARE.

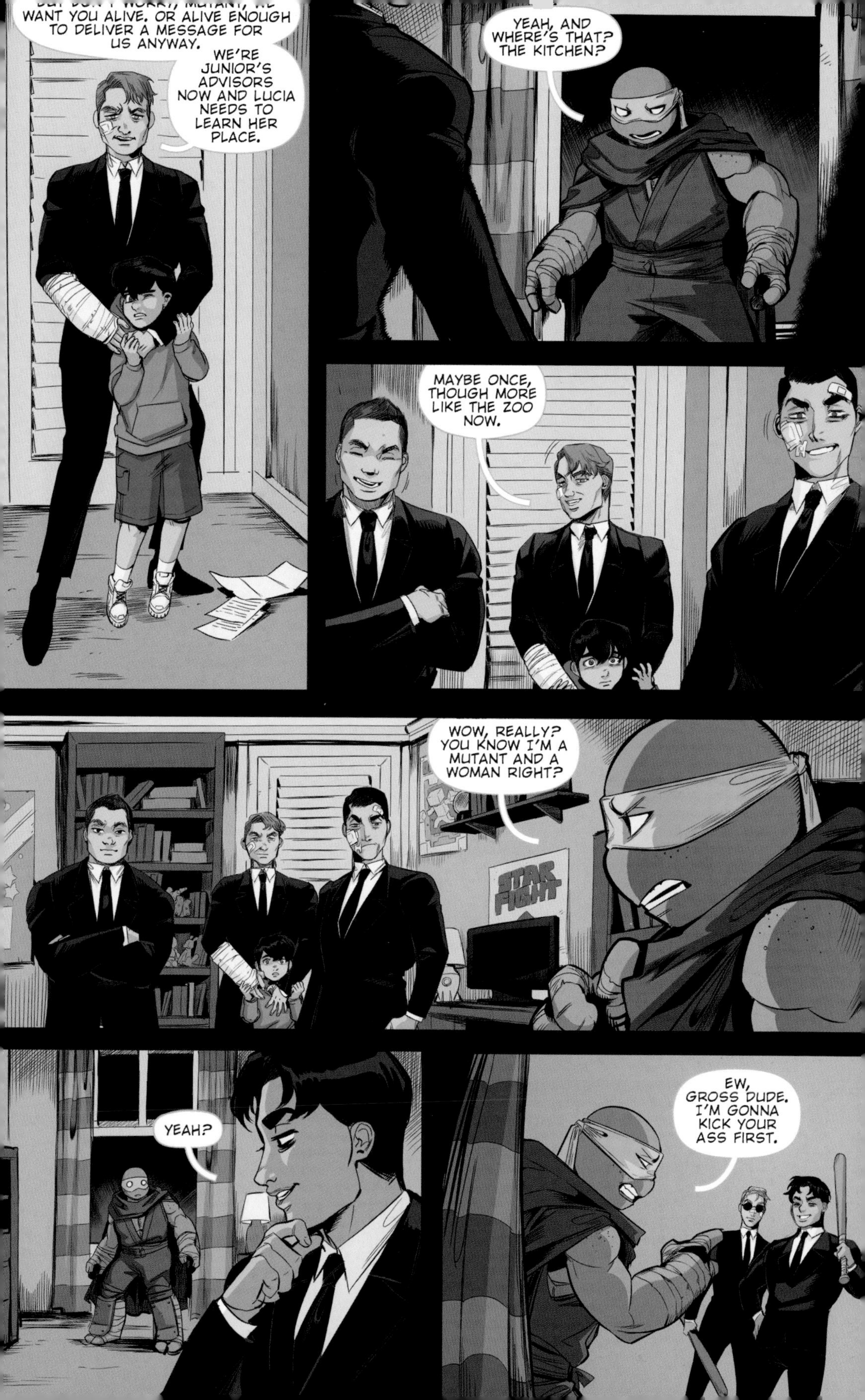
WANT YOU ALIVE. OR ALIVE ENOUGH TO DELIVER A MESSAGE FOR US ANYWAY.
WE'RE JUNIOR'S ADVISORS NOW AND LUCIA NEEDS TO LEARN HER PLACE.
YEAH, AND WHERE'S THAT? THE KITCHEN?
MAYBE ONCE, THOUGH MORE LIKE THE ZOO NOW.
WOW, REALLY? YOU KNOW I'M A MUTANT AND A WOMAN RIGHT?
STAR FIGHT
YEAH?
EW, GROSS DUDE. I'M GONNA KICK YOUR ASS FIRST.

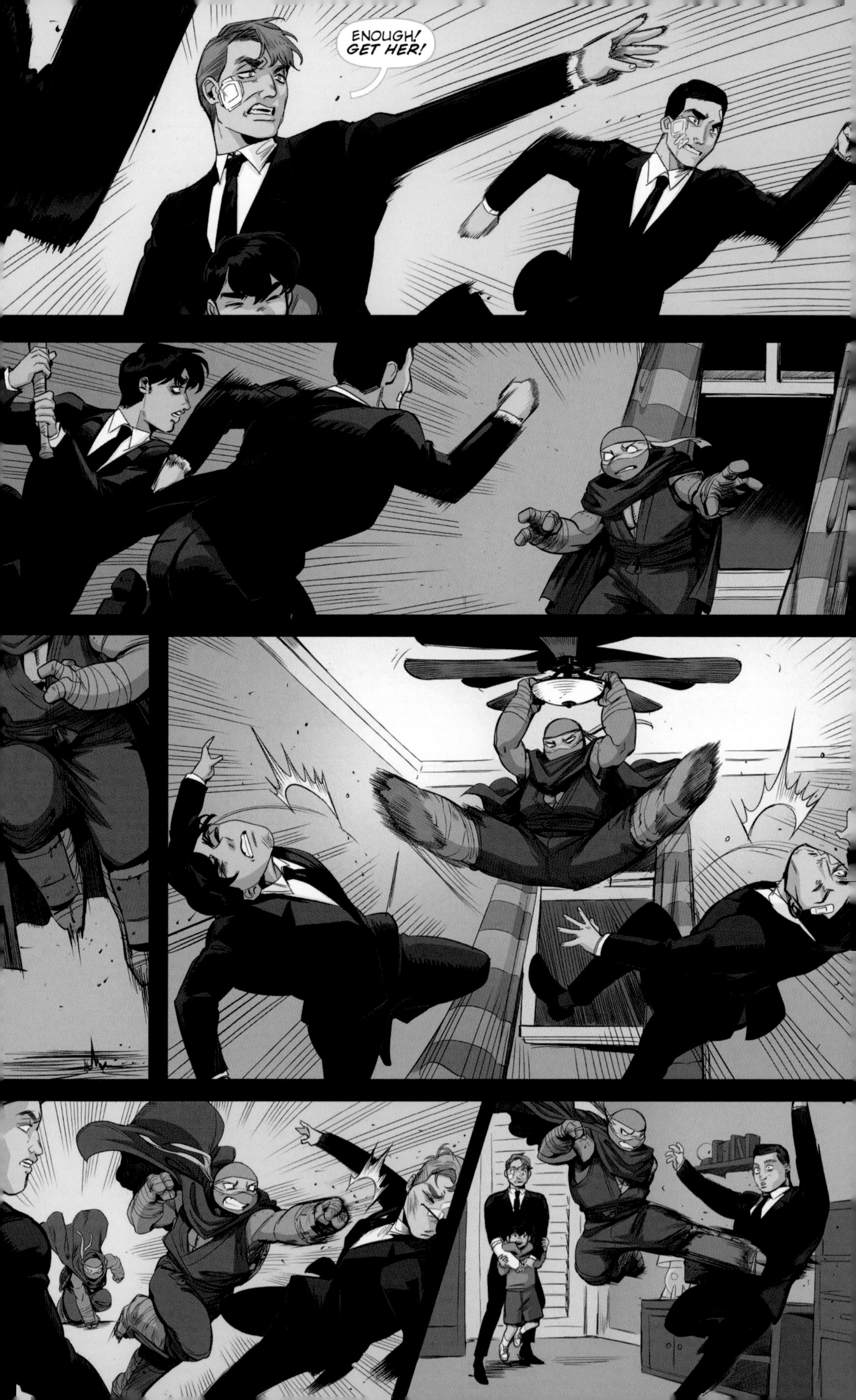
ENOUGH! GET HER!

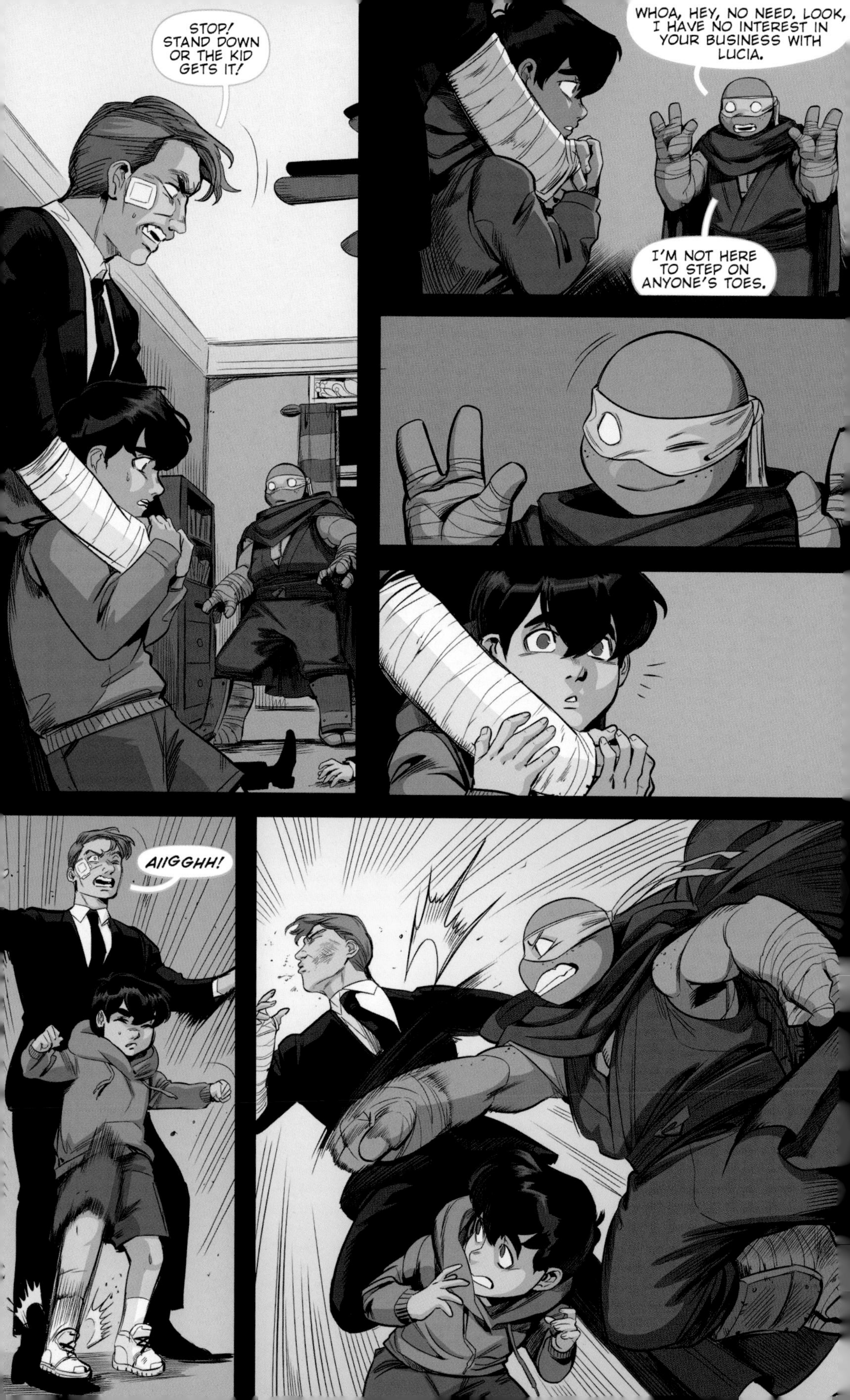
STOP! STAND DOWN OR THE KID GETS IT!
WHOA, HEY, NO NEED. LOOK, I HAVE NO INTEREST IN YOUR BUSINESS WITH LUCIA.
I'M NOT HERE TO STEP ON ANYONE'S TOES.
AIIGGHH!

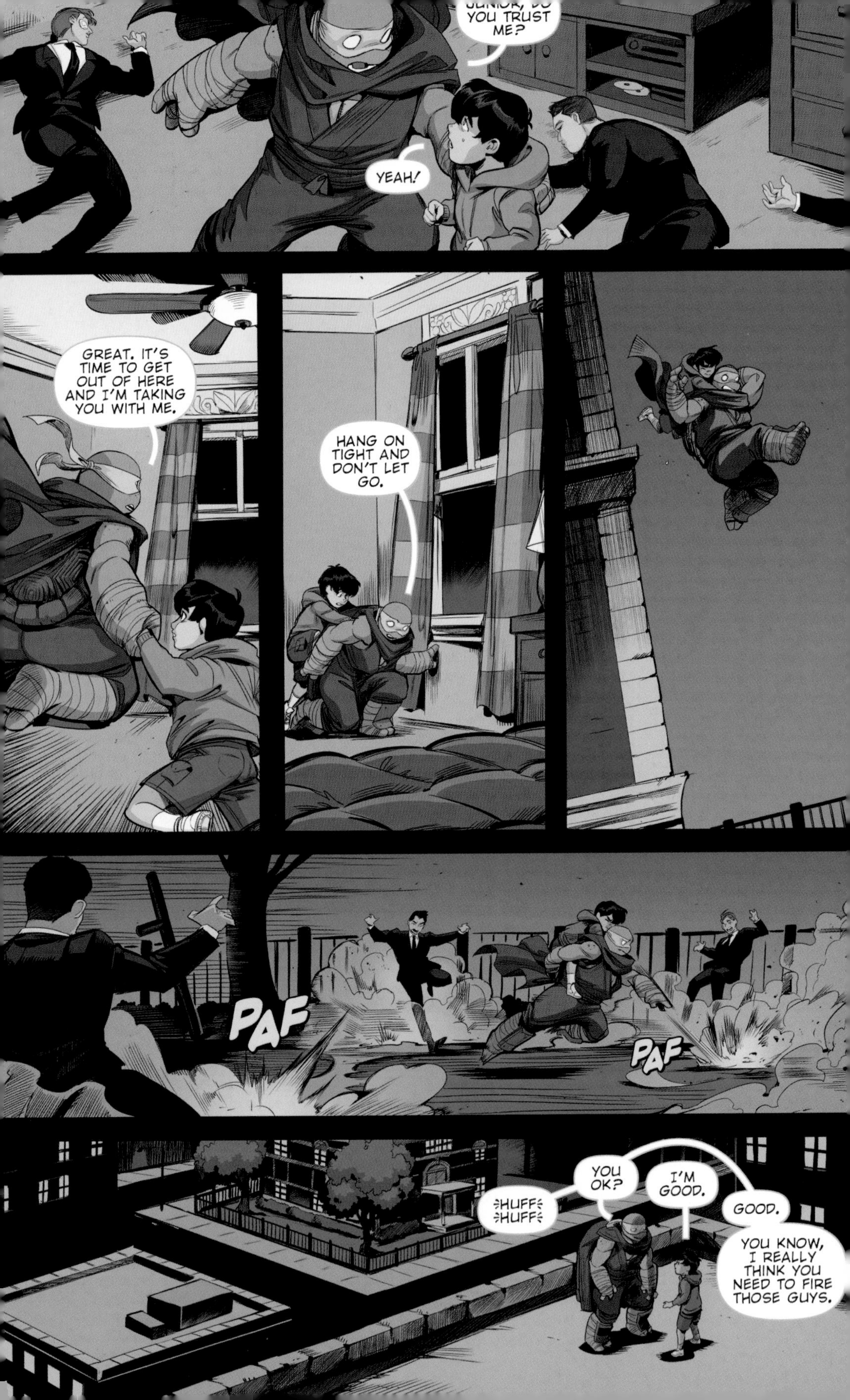
YOU TRUST ME?
YEAH!
GREAT. IT'S TIME TO GET OUT OF HERE AND I'M TAKING YOU WITH ME.
HANG ON TIGHT AND DON'T LET GO.
PAF
PAF
HUFF HUFF
YOU OK?
I'M GOOD.
GOOD.
YOU KNOW, I REALLY THINK YOU NEED TO FIRE THOSE GUYS.

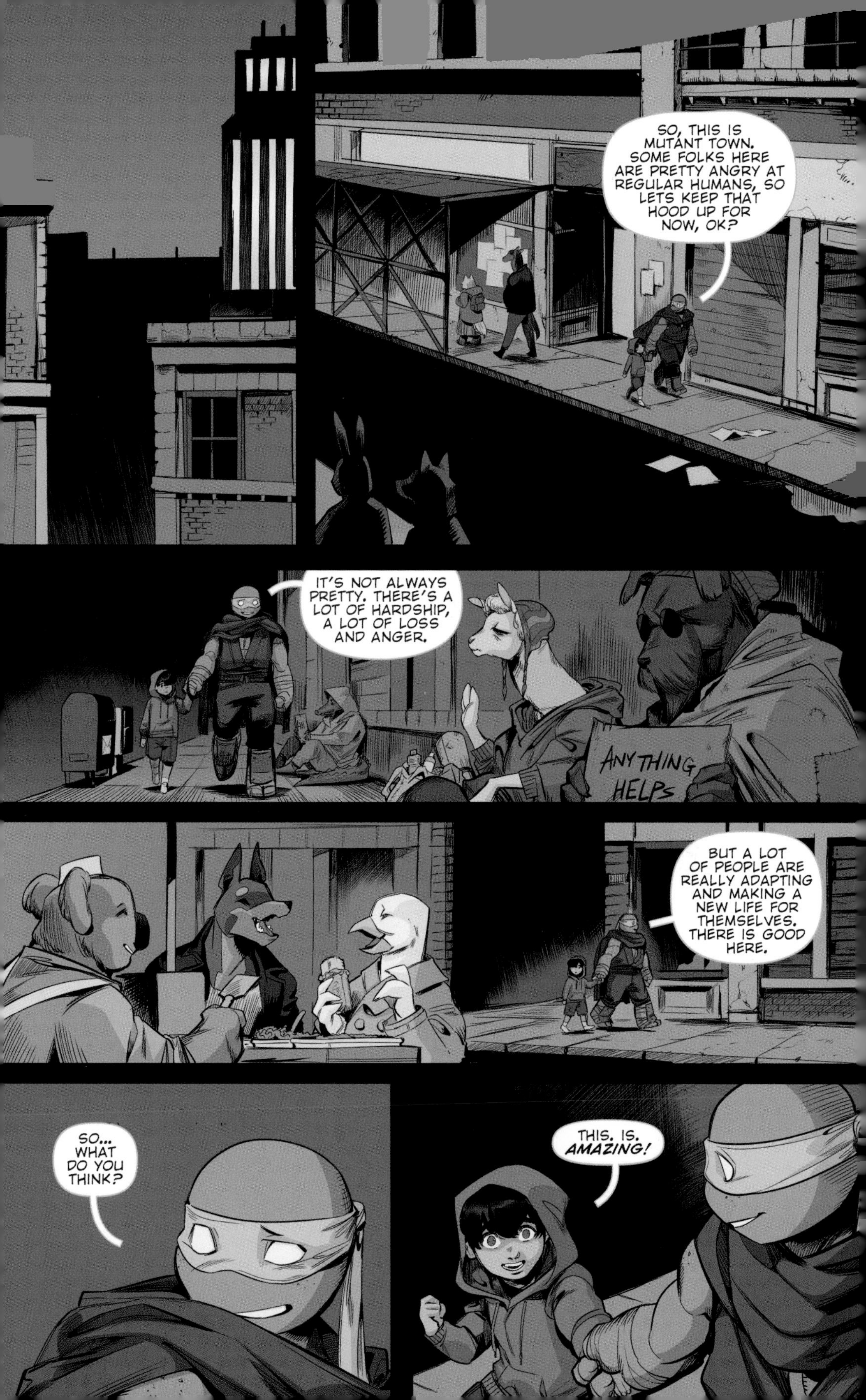
SO, THIS IS MUTANT TOWN. SOME FOLKS HERE ARE PRETTY ANGRY AT REGULAR HUMANS, SO LETS KEEP THAT HOOD UP FOR NOW, OK?
IT'S NOT ALWAYS PRETTY. THERE'S A LOT OF HARDSHIP, A LOT OF LOSS AND ANGER.
ANYTHING HELPS
BUT A LOT OF PEOPLE ARE REALLY ADAPTING AND MAKING A NEW LIFE FOR THEMSELVES. THERE IS GOOD HERE.
SO... WHAT DO YOU THINK?
THIS. IS. *AMAZING!*

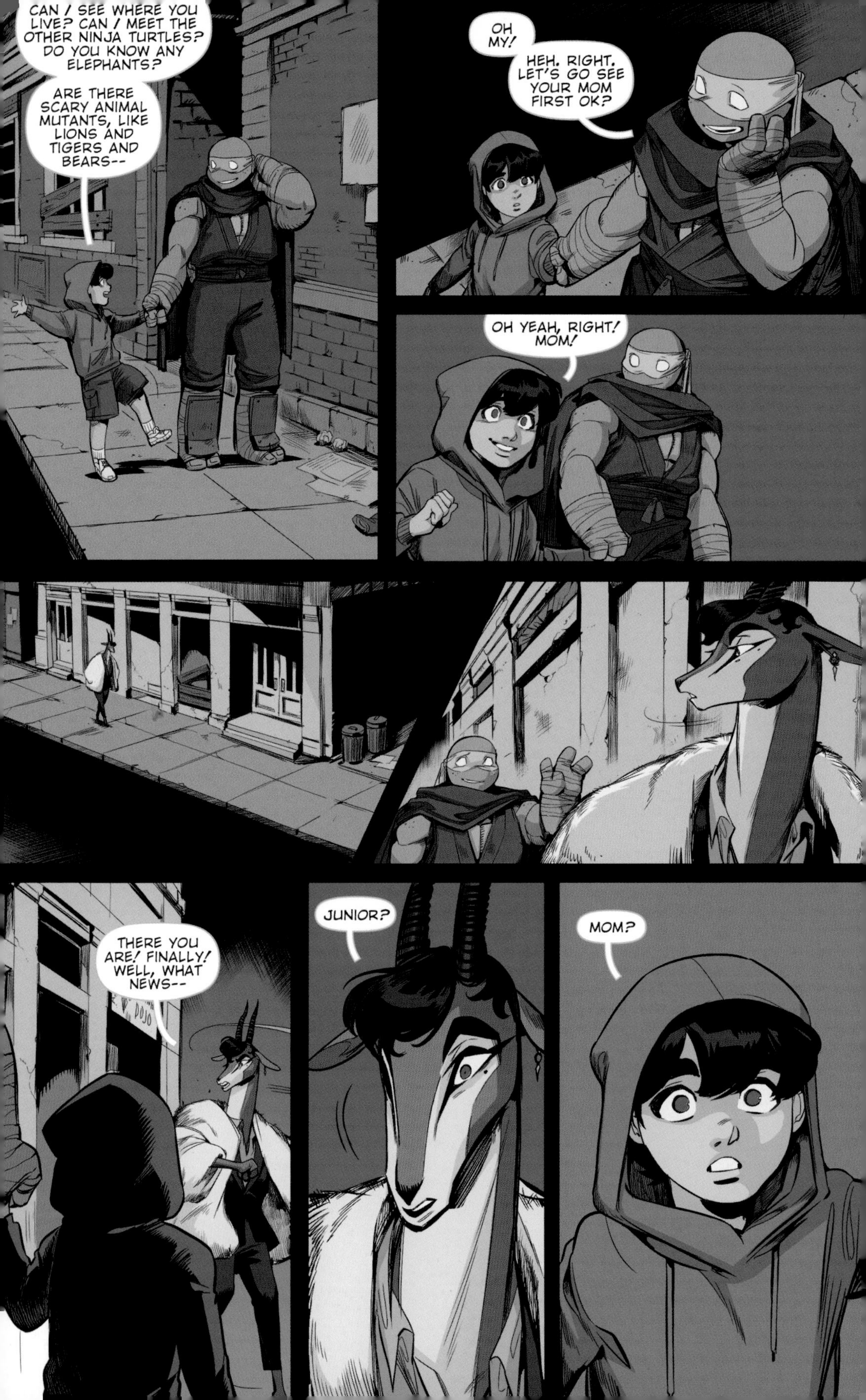
CAN I SEE WHERE YOU LIVE? CAN I MEET THE OTHER NINJA TURTLES? DO YOU KNOW ANY ELEPHANTS?
ARE THERE SCARY ANIMAL MUTANTS, LIKE LIONS AND TIGERS AND BEARS--
OH MY!
HEH. RIGHT. LET'S GO SEE YOUR MOM FIRST OK?
OH YEAH, RIGHT! MOM!
THERE YOU ARE! FINALLY! WELL, WHAT NEWS--
DOJO
JUNIOR?
MOM?

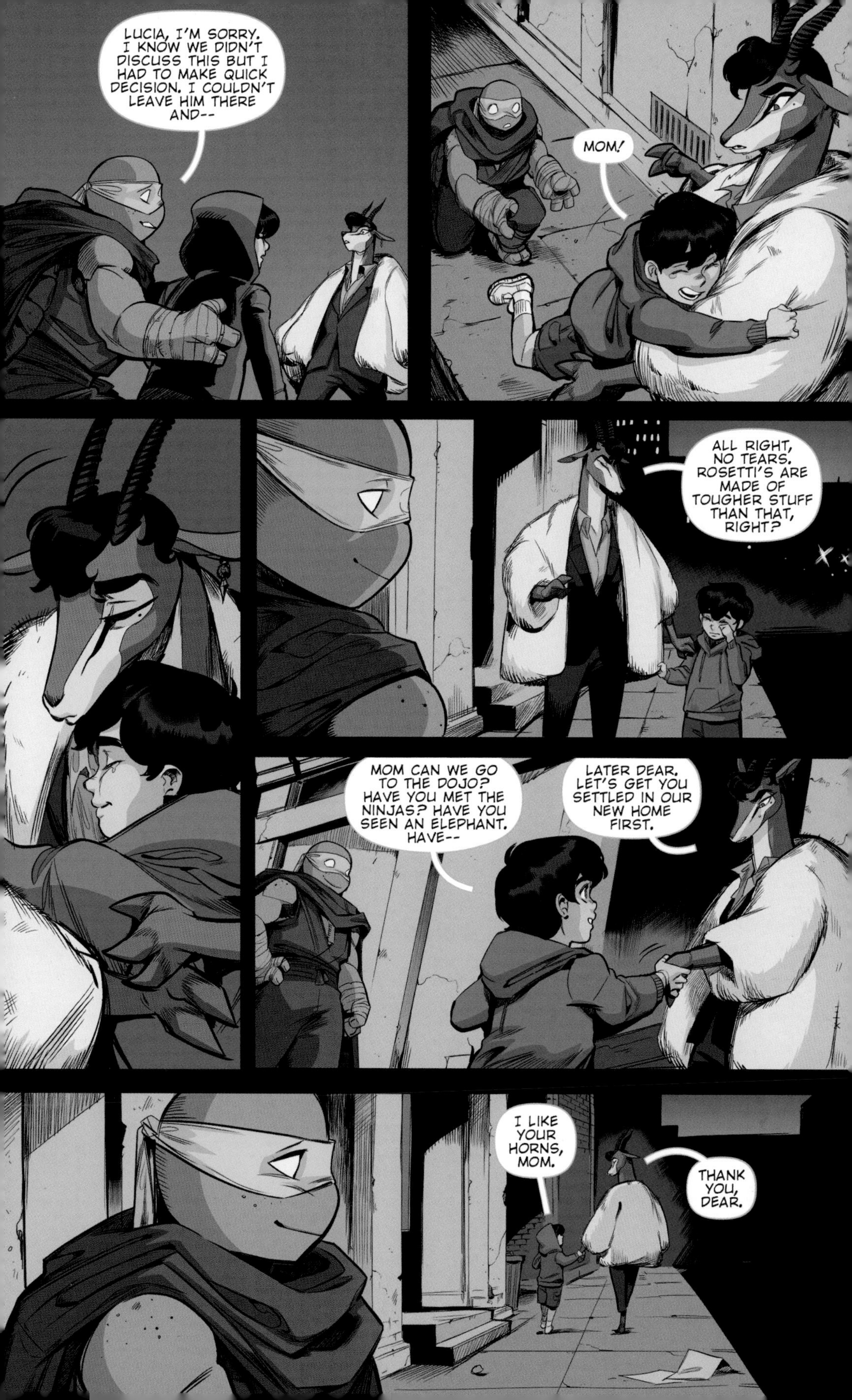
LUCIA, I'M SORRY. I KNOW WE DIDN'T DISCUSS THIS BUT I HAD TO MAKE QUICK DECISION. I COULDN'T LEAVE HIM THERE AND--
MOM!
ALL RIGHT, NO TEARS. ROSETTI'S ARE MADE OF TOUGHER STUFF THAN THAT, RIGHT?
MOM CAN WE GO TO THE DOJO? HAVE YOU MET THE NINJAS? HAVE YOU SEEN AN ELEPHANT. HAVE--
LATER DEAR. LET'S GET YOU SETTLED IN OUR NEW HOME FIRST.
I LIKE YOUR HORNS, MOM.
THANK YOU, DEAR.

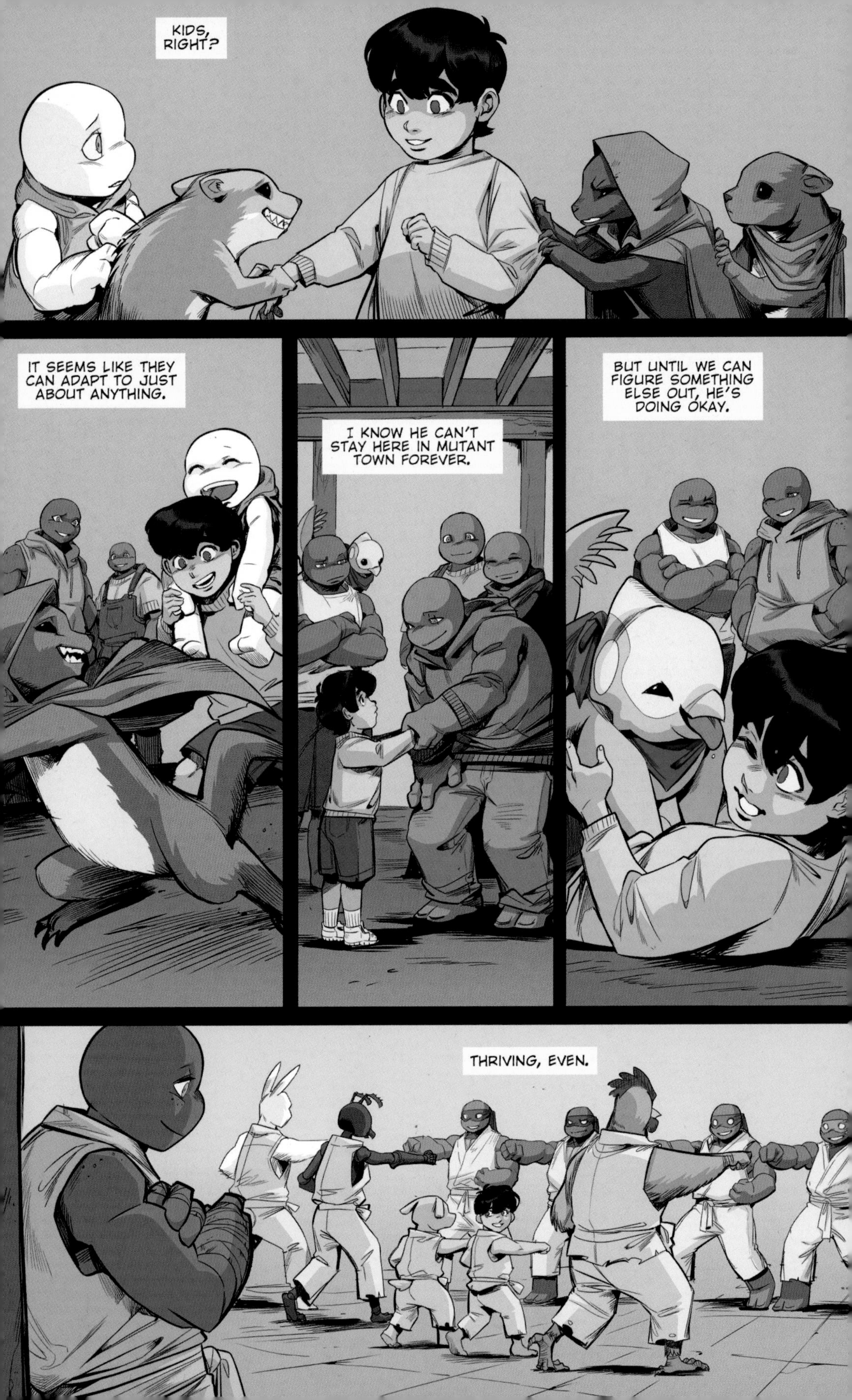
KIDS, RIGHT?
IT SEEMS LIKE THEY CAN ADAPT TO JUST ABOUT ANYTHING.
I KNOW HE CAN'T STAY HERE IN MUTANT TOWN FOREVER.
BUT UNTIL WE CAN FIGURE SOMETHING ELSE OUT, HE'S DOING OKAY.
THRIVING, EVEN.

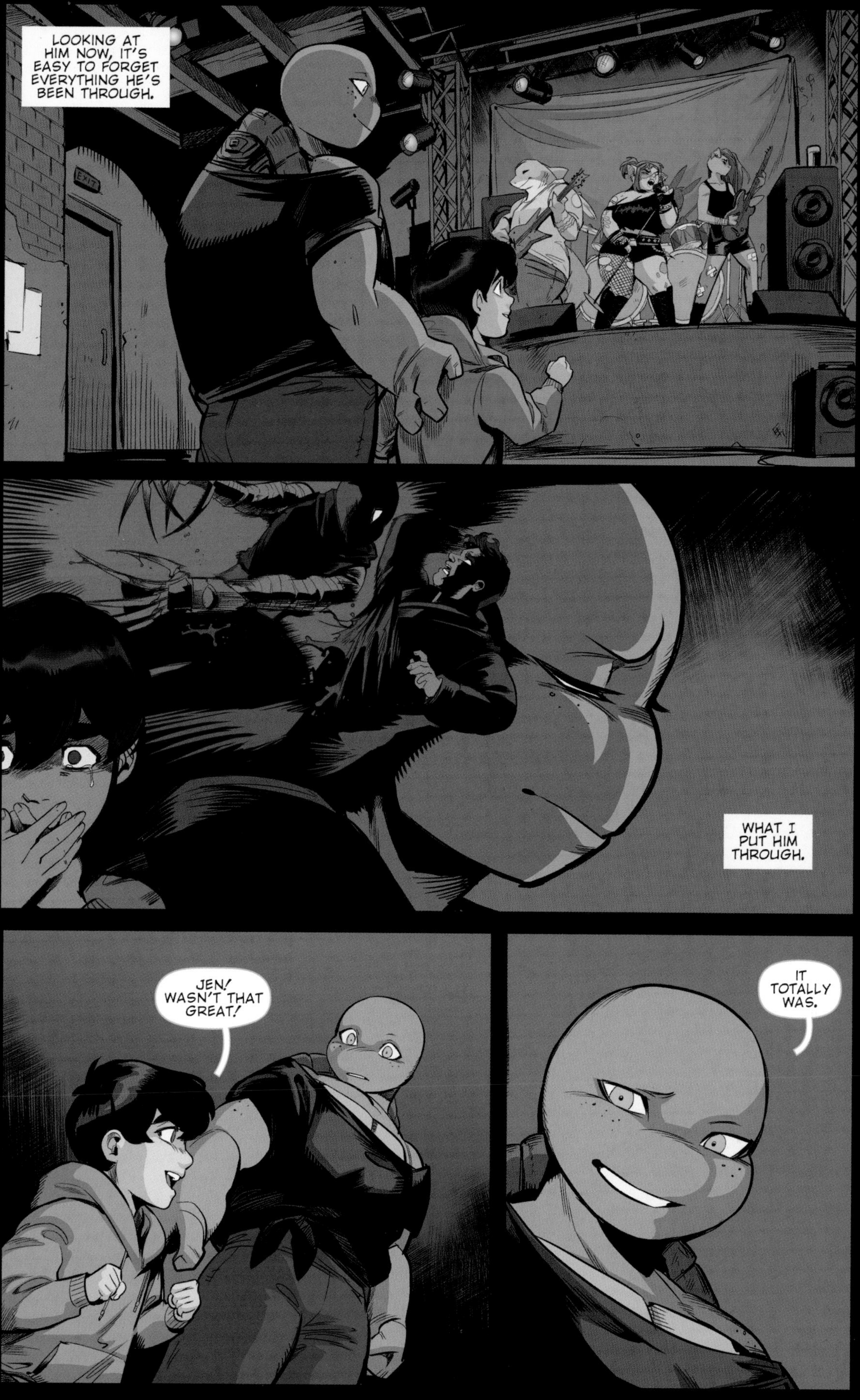

LOOKING AT HIM NOW, IT'S EASY TO FORGET EVERYTHING HE'S BEEN THROUGH.
EXIT
WHAT I PUT HIM THROUGH.
JEN! WASN'T THAT GREAT!
IT TOTALLY WAS.

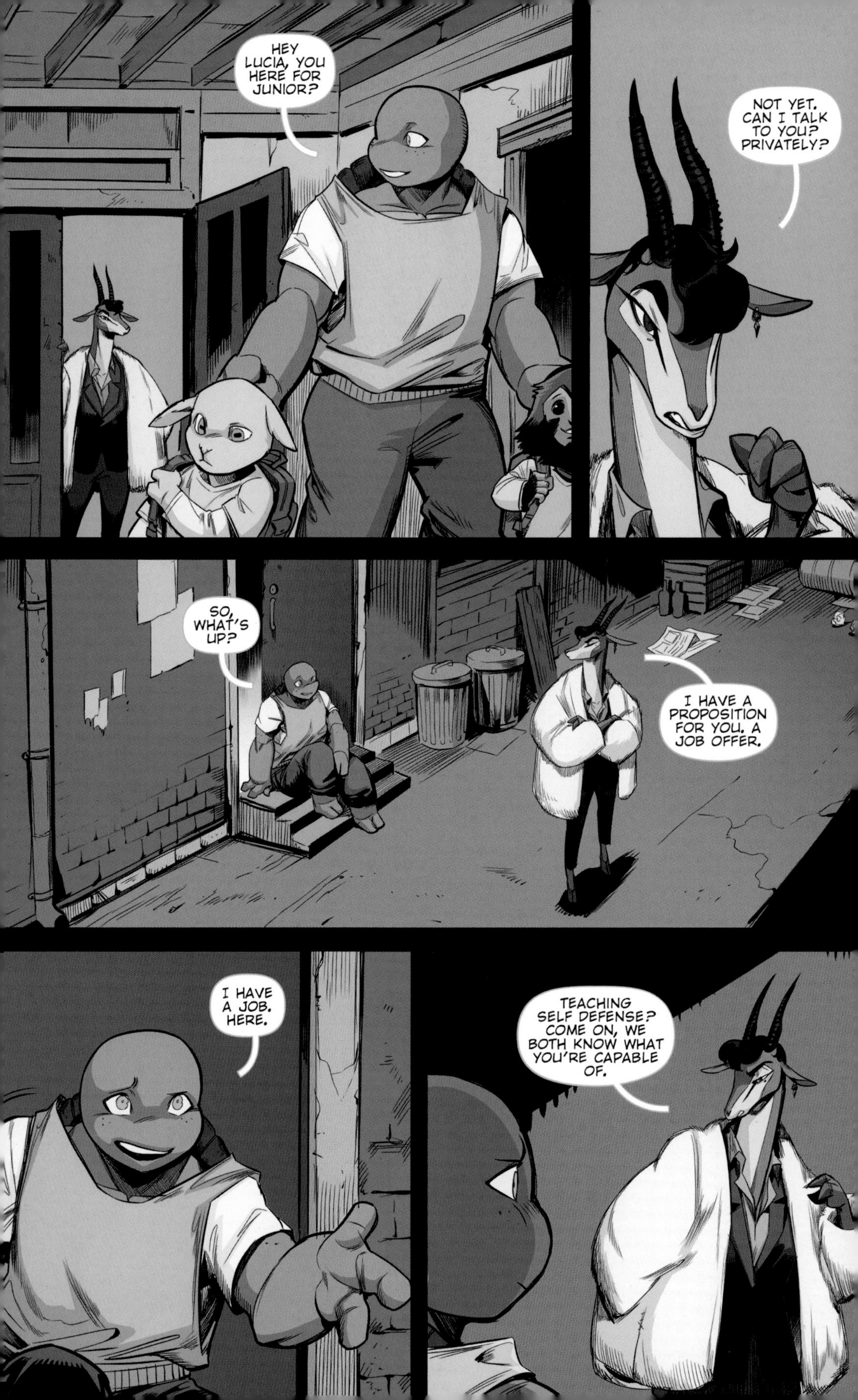
HEY LUCIA, YOU HERE FOR JUNIOR?
NOT YET. CAN I TALK TO YOU? PRIVATELY?
SO, WHAT'S UP?
I HAVE A PROPOSITION FOR YOU. A JOB OFFER.
I HAVE A JOB. HERE.
TEACHING SELF DEFENSE? COME ON, WE BOTH KNOW WHAT YOU'RE CAPABLE OF.

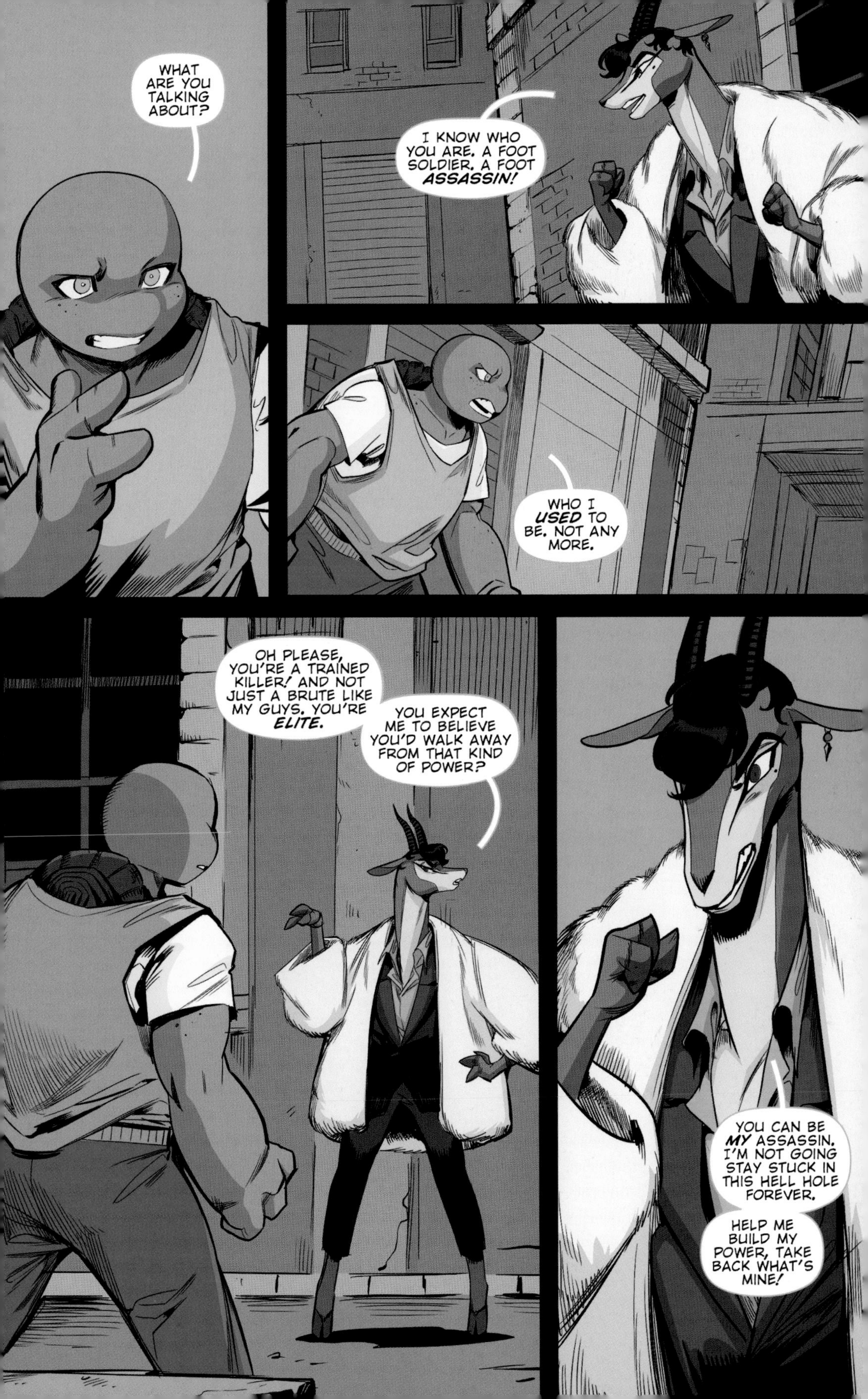
WHAT ARE YOU TALKING ABOUT?
I KNOW WHO YOU ARE. A FOOT SOLDIER. A FOOT ASSASSIN!
WHO I USED TO BE. NOT ANY MORE.
OH PLEASE, YOU'RE A TRAINED KILLER! AND NOT JUST A BRUTE LIKE MY GUYS. YOU'RE ELITE.
YOU EXPECT ME TO BELIEVE YOU'D WALK AWAY FROM THAT KIND OF POWER?
YOU CAN BE MY ASSASSIN. I'M NOT GOING STAY STUCK IN THIS HELL HOLE FOREVER.
HELP ME BUILD MY POWER, TAKE BACK WHAT'S MINE!

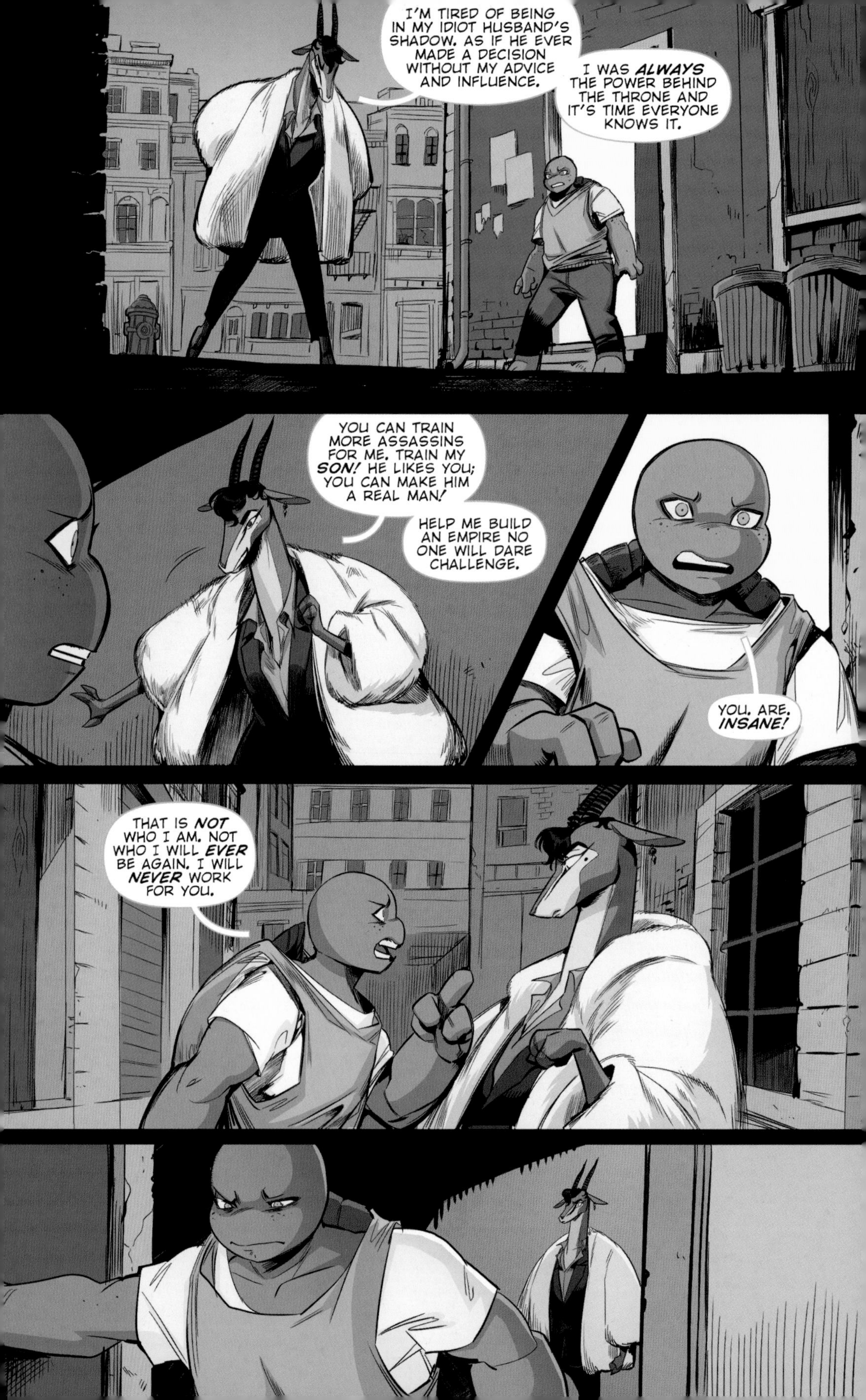

I'M TIRED OF BEING IN MY IDIOT HUSBAND'S SHADOW. AS IF HE EVER MADE A DECISION WITHOUT MY ADVICE AND INFLUENCE.
I WAS *ALWAYS* THE POWER BEHIND THE THRONE AND IT'S TIME EVERYONE KNOWS IT.
YOU CAN TRAIN MORE ASSASSINS FOR ME. TRAIN MY *SON!* HE LIKES YOU; YOU CAN MAKE HIM A REAL MAN!
HELP ME BUILD AN EMPIRE NO ONE WILL DARE CHALLENGE.
YOU. ARE. *INSANE!*
THAT IS *NOT* WHO I AM. NOT WHO I WILL *EVER* BE AGAIN. I WILL *NEVER* WORK FOR YOU.

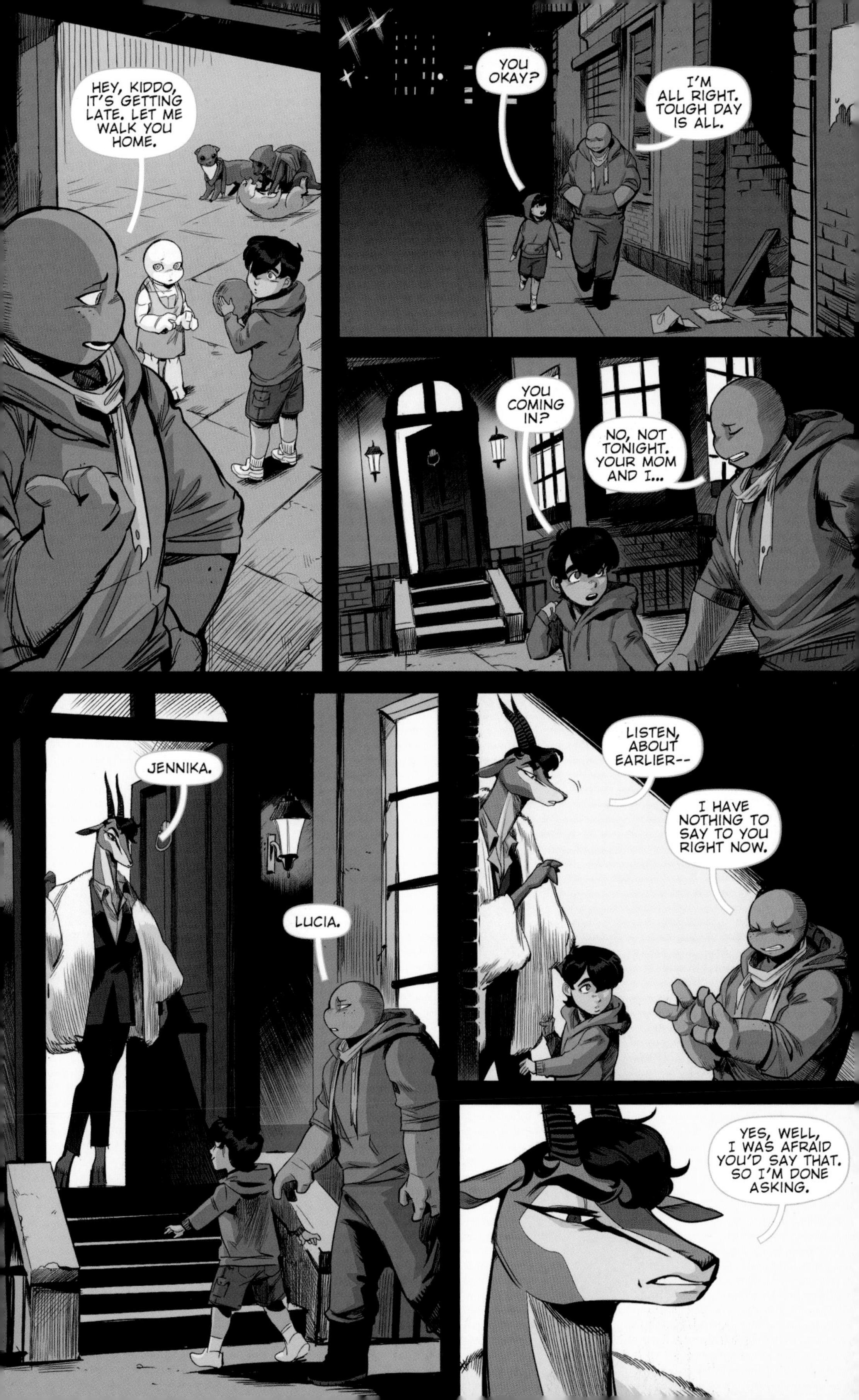
HEY, KIDDO, IT'S GETTING LATE. LET ME WALK YOU HOME.
YOU OKAY?
I'M ALL RIGHT. TOUGH DAY IS ALL.
YOU COMING IN?
NO, NOT TONIGHT. YOUR MOM AND I...
JENNIKA.
LUCIA.
LISTEN, ABOUT EARLIER--
I HAVE NOTHING TO SAY TO YOU RIGHT NOW.
YES, WELL, I WAS AFRAID YOU'D SAY THAT. SO I'M DONE ASKING.

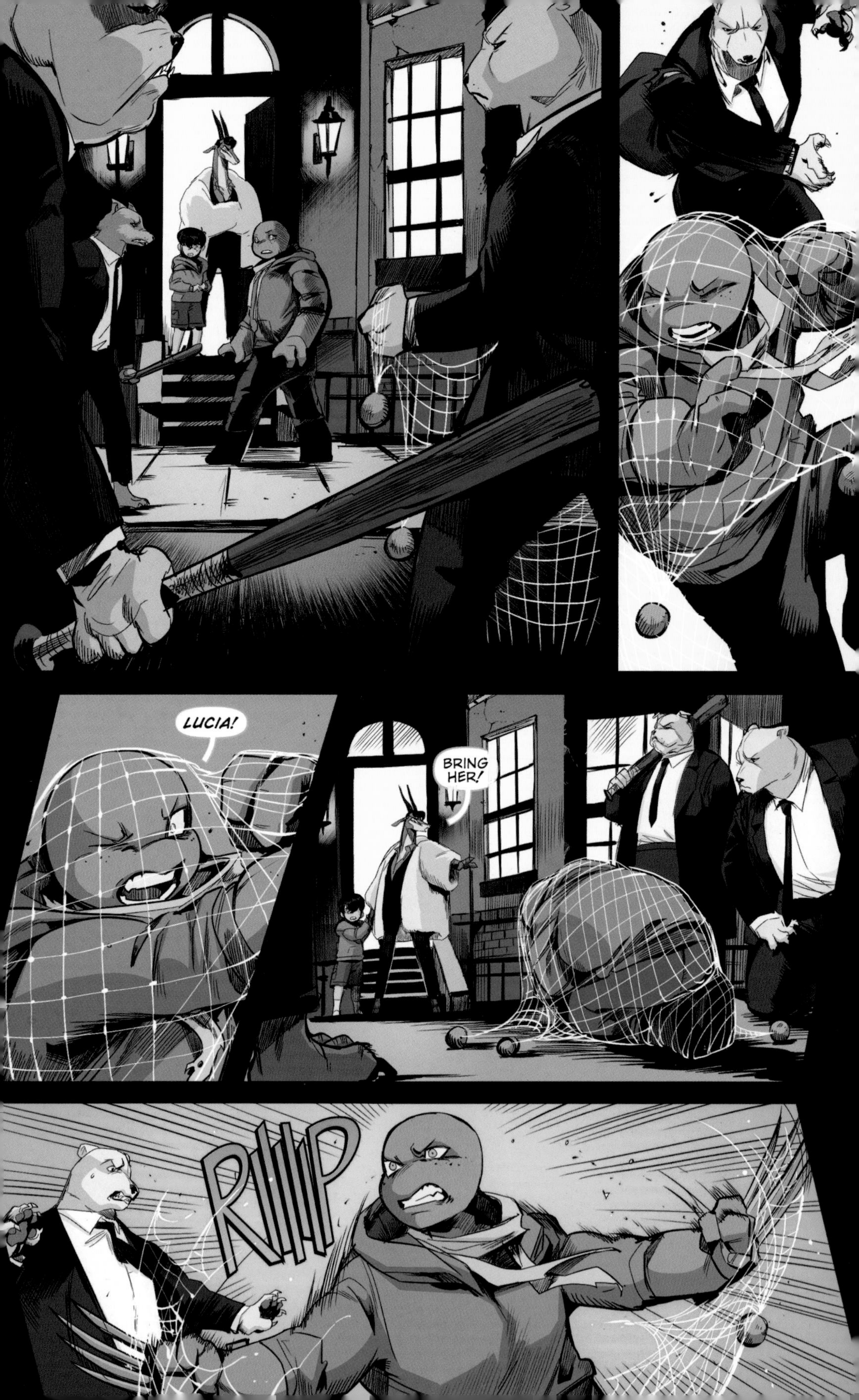
LUCIA!
BRING HER!
RIIIP

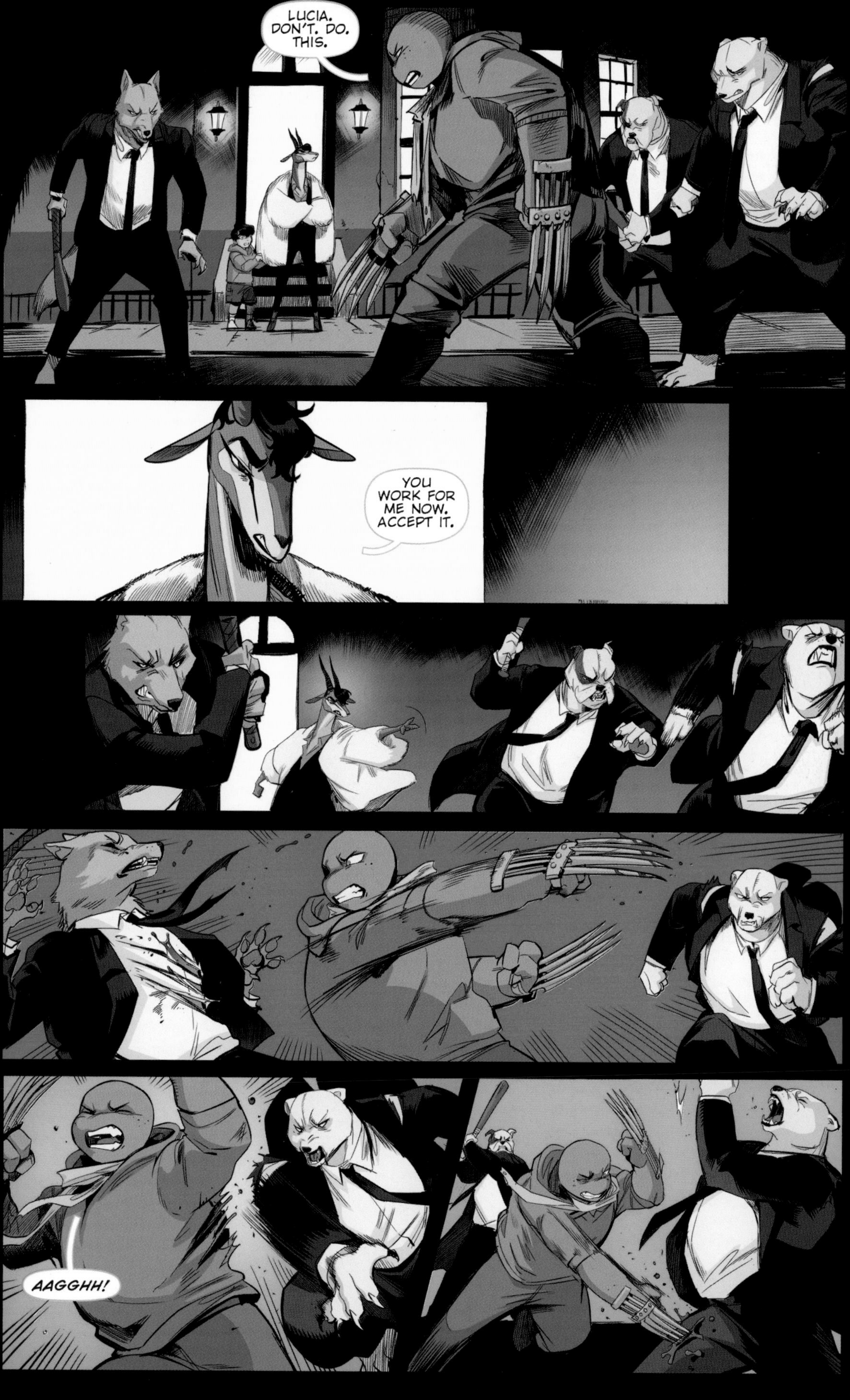
LUCIA. DON'T. DO. THIS.
YOU WORK FOR ME NOW. ACCEPT IT.
AAGGHH!

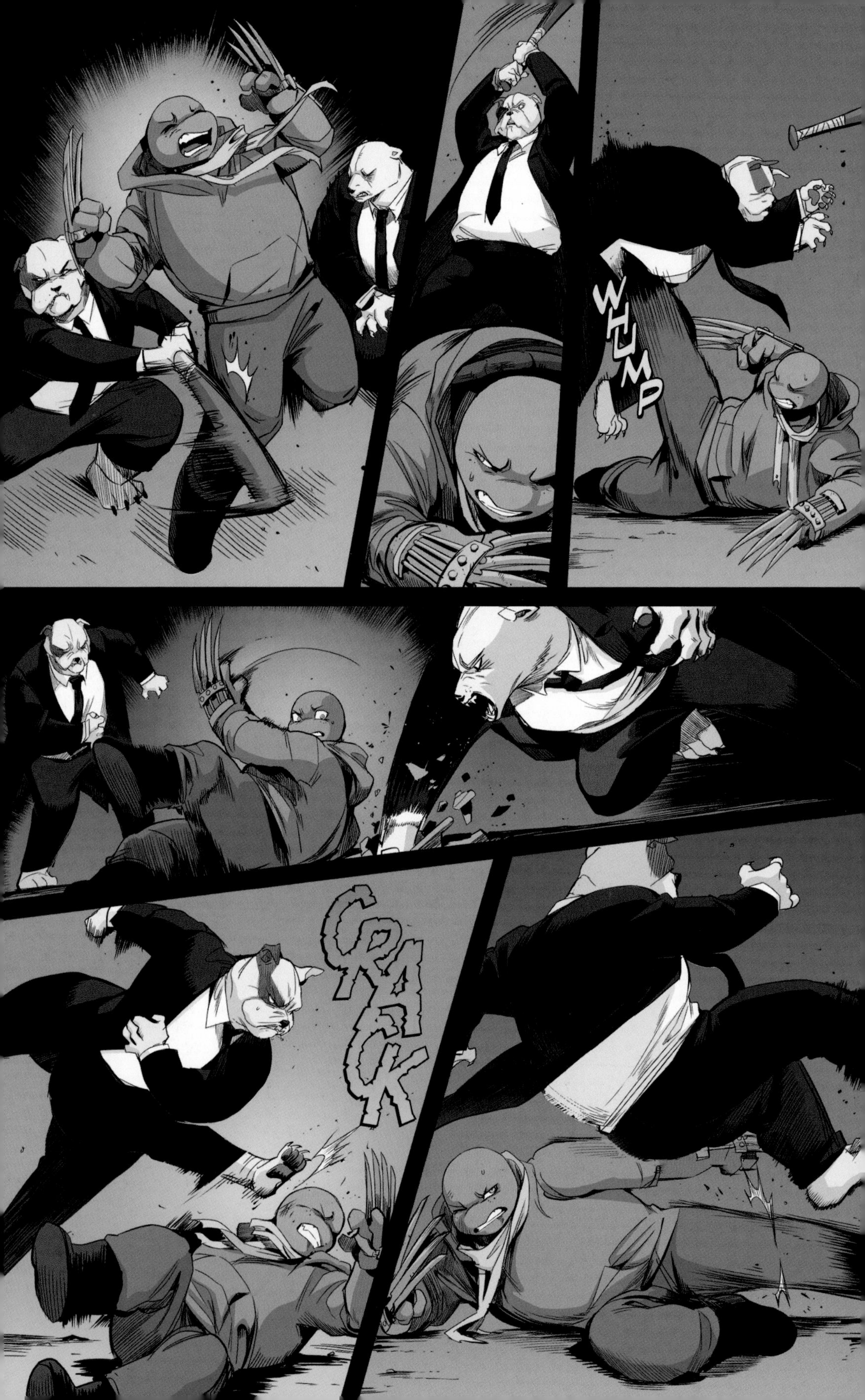
WHUMP
CRACK

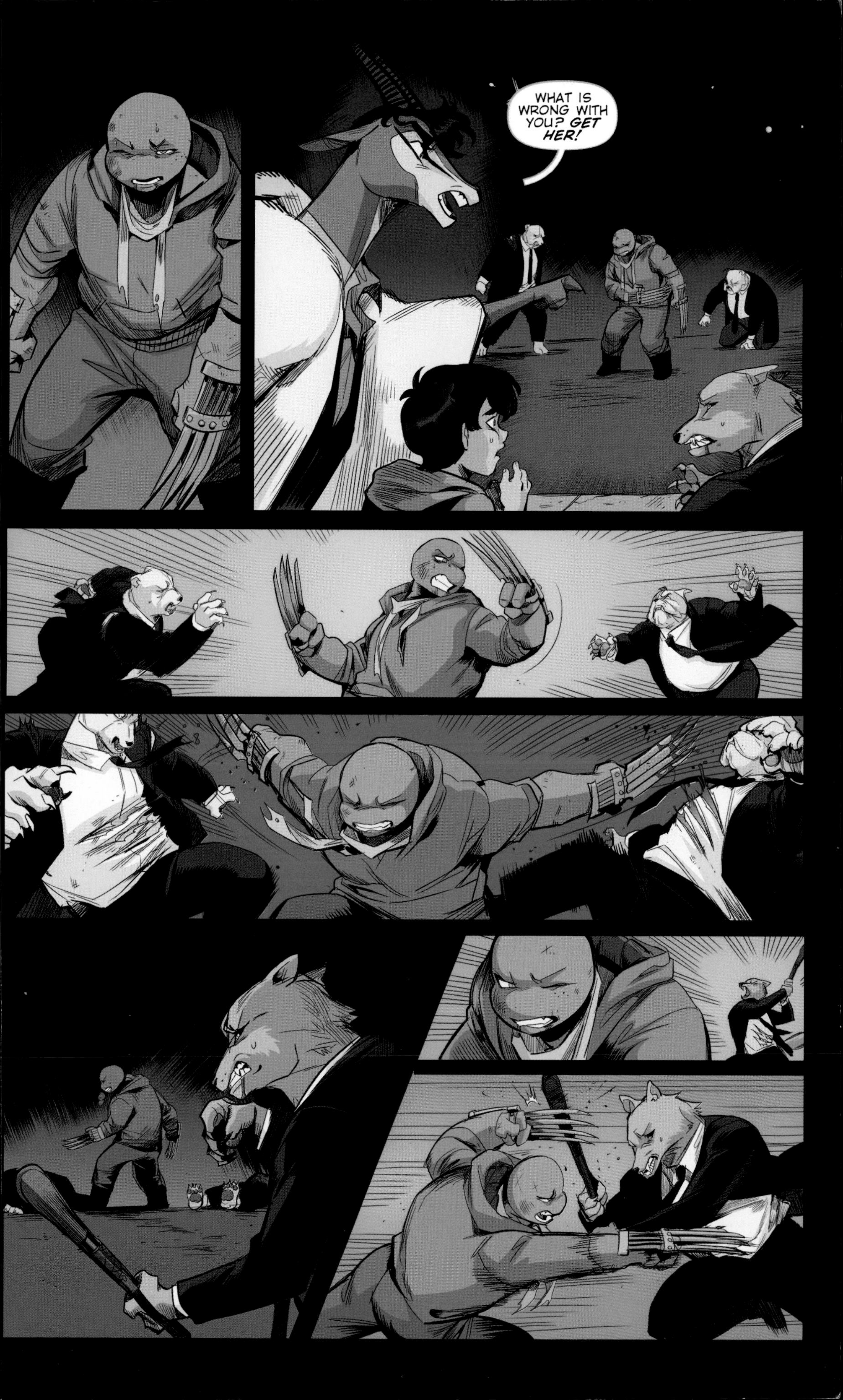
WHAT IS WRONG WITH YOU? GET HER!

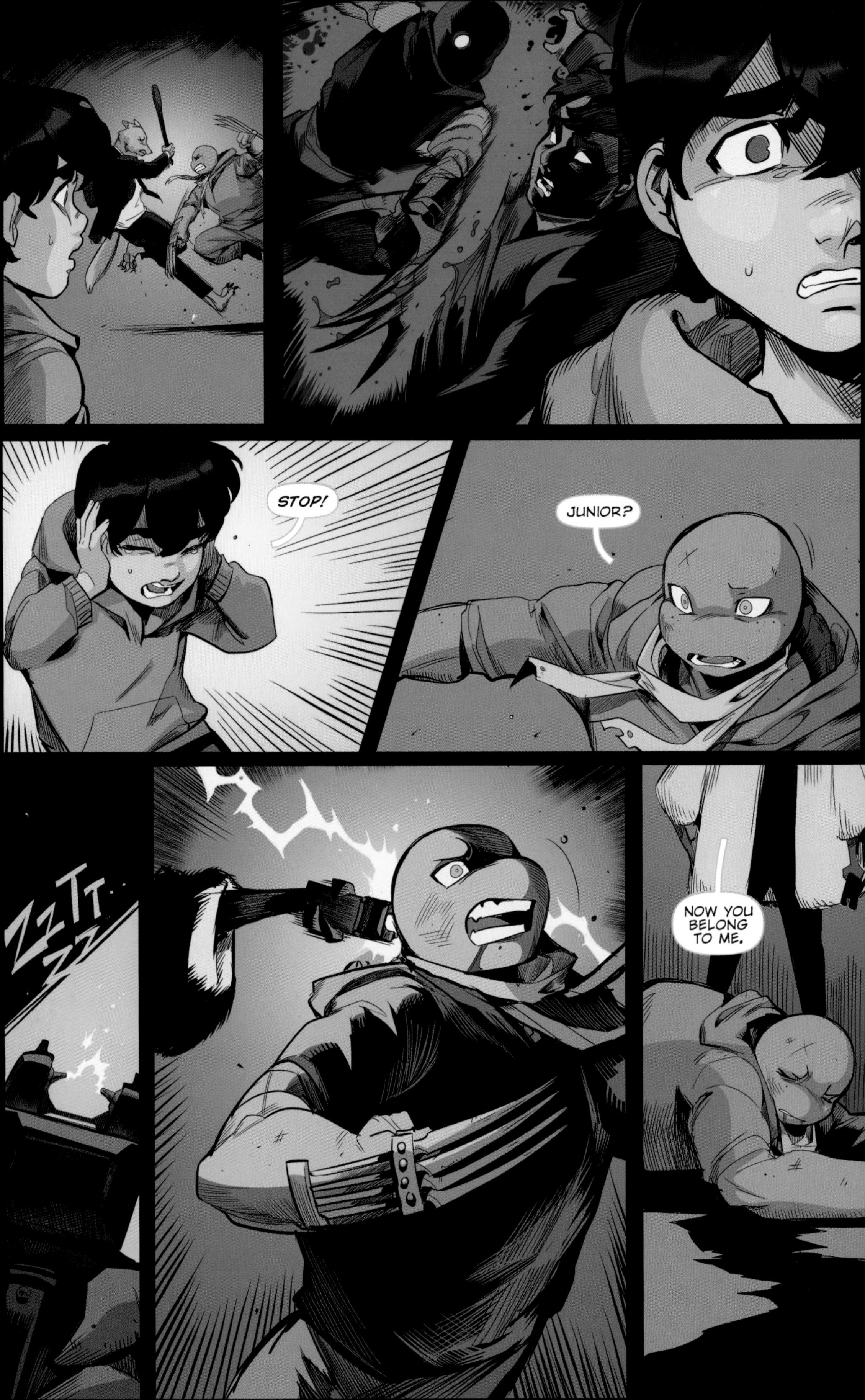
STOP!
JUNIOR?
ZZTT...
ZZ
NOW YOU BELONG TO ME.

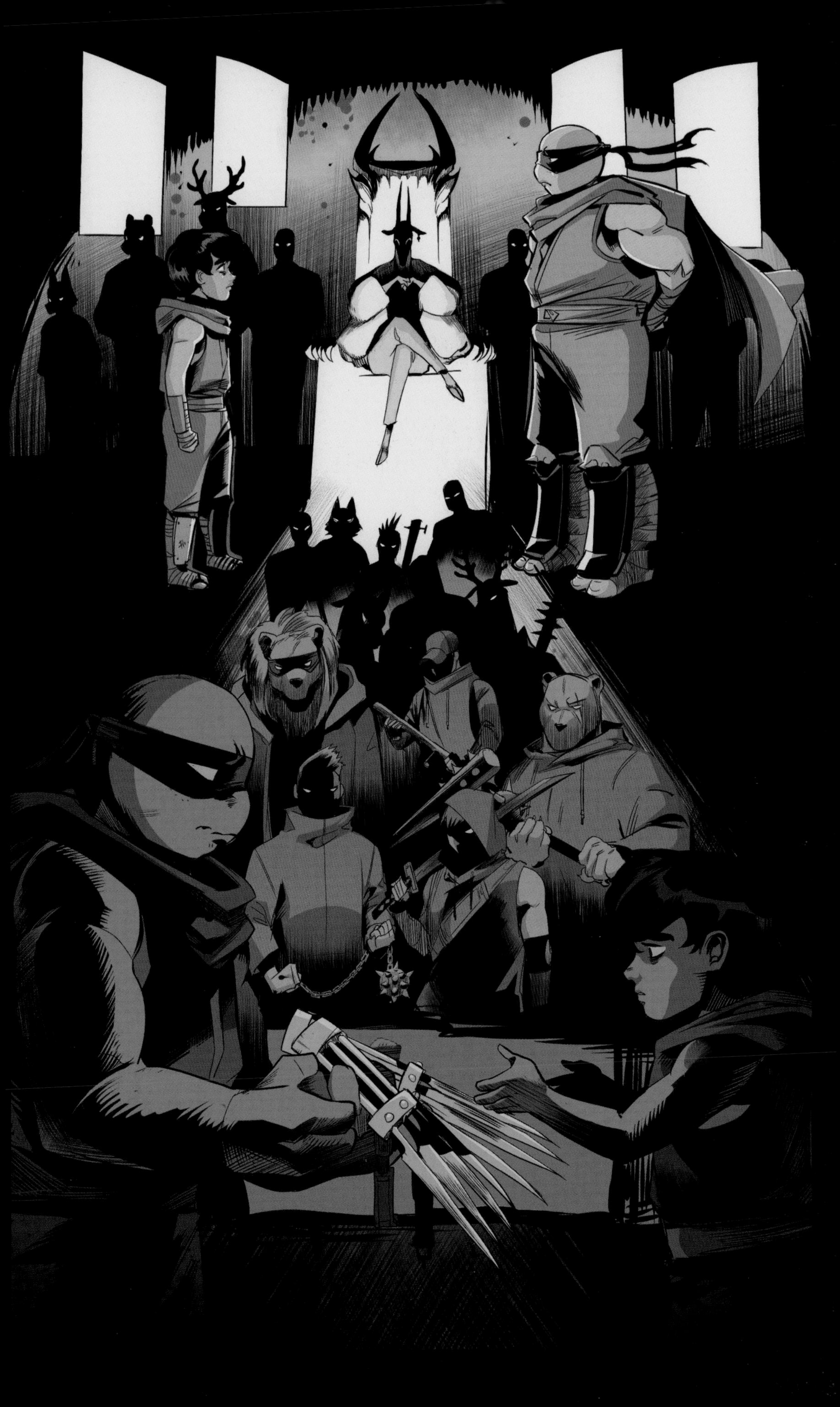

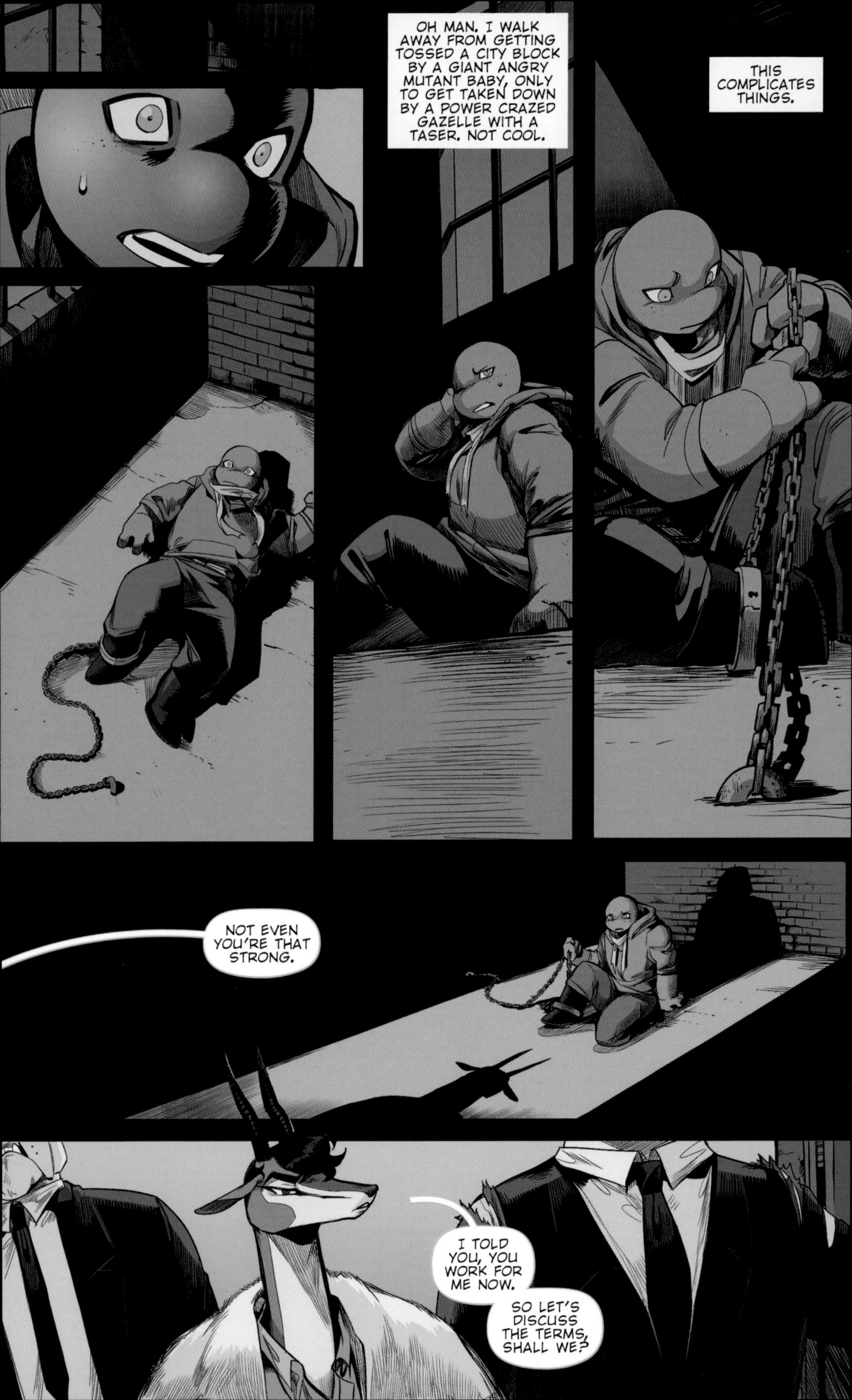
OH MAN. I WALK AWAY FROM GETTING TOSSED A CITY BLOCK BY A GIANT ANGRY MUTANT BABY, ONLY TO GET TAKEN DOWN BY A POWER CRAZED GAZELLE WITH A TASER. NOT COOL.
THIS COMPLICATES THINGS.
NOT EVEN YOU'RE THAT STRONG.
I TOLD YOU, YOU WORK FOR ME NOW.
SO LET'S DISCUSS THE TERMS, SHALL WE?

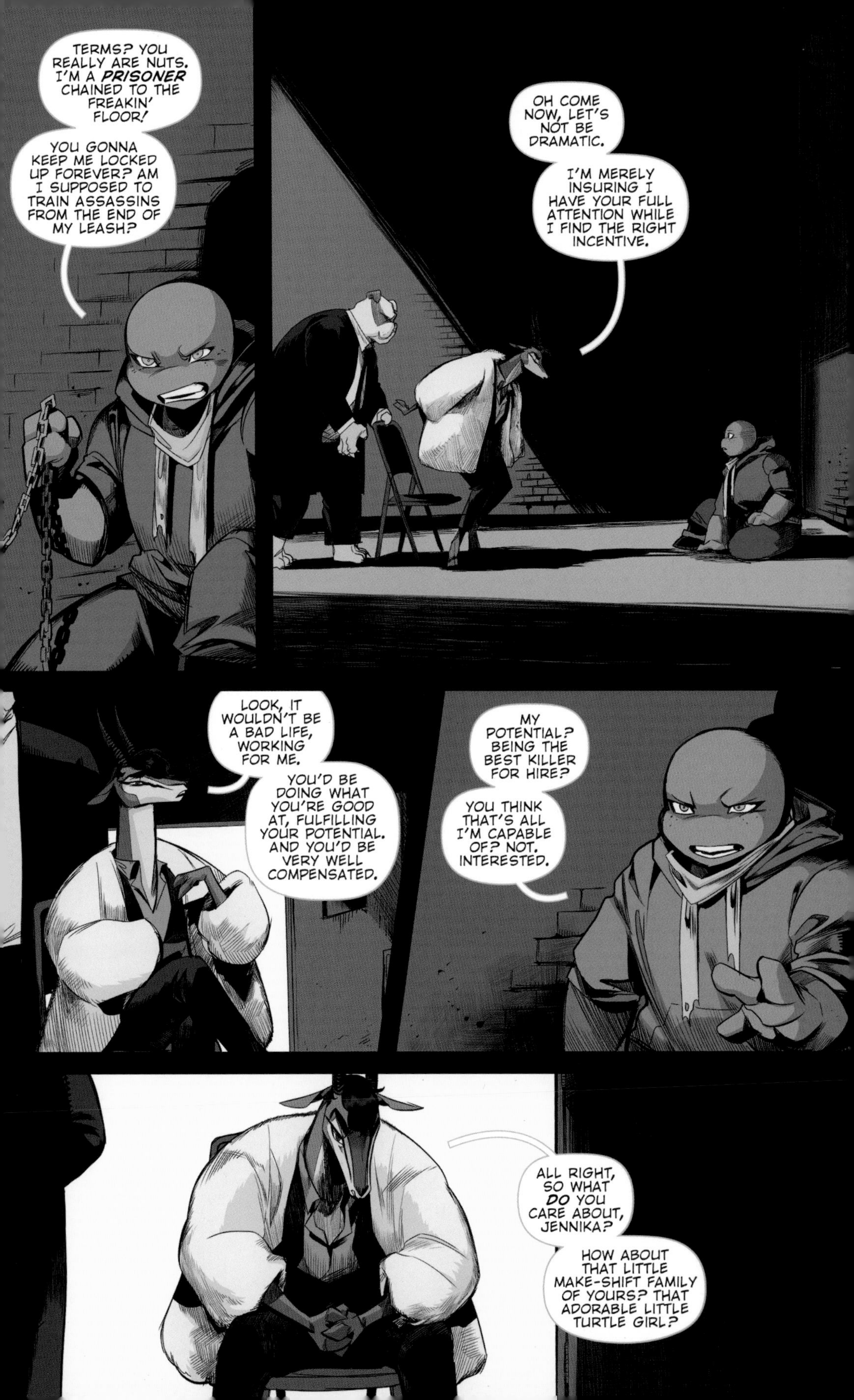
TERMS? YOU REALLY ARE NUTS. I'M A *PRISONER* CHAINED TO THE FREAKIN' FLOOR!
YOU GONNA KEEP ME LOCKED UP FOREVER? AM I SUPPOSED TO TRAIN ASSASSINS FROM THE END OF MY LEASH?
OH COME NOW, LET'S NOT BE DRAMATIC.
I'M MERELY INSURING I HAVE YOUR FULL ATTENTION WHILE I FIND THE RIGHT INCENTIVE.
LOOK, IT WOULDN'T BE A BAD LIFE, WORKING FOR ME.
YOU'D BE DOING WHAT YOU'RE GOOD AT, FULFILLING YOUR POTENTIAL. AND YOU'D BE VERY WELL COMPENSATED.
MY POTENTIAL? BEING THE BEST KILLER FOR HIRE?
YOU THINK THAT'S ALL I'M CAPABLE OF? NOT. INTERESTED.
ALL RIGHT, SO WHAT *DO* YOU CARE ABOUT, JENNIKA?
HOW ABOUT THAT LITTLE MAKE-SHIFT FAMILY OF YOURS? THAT ADORABLE LITTLE TURTLE GIRL?

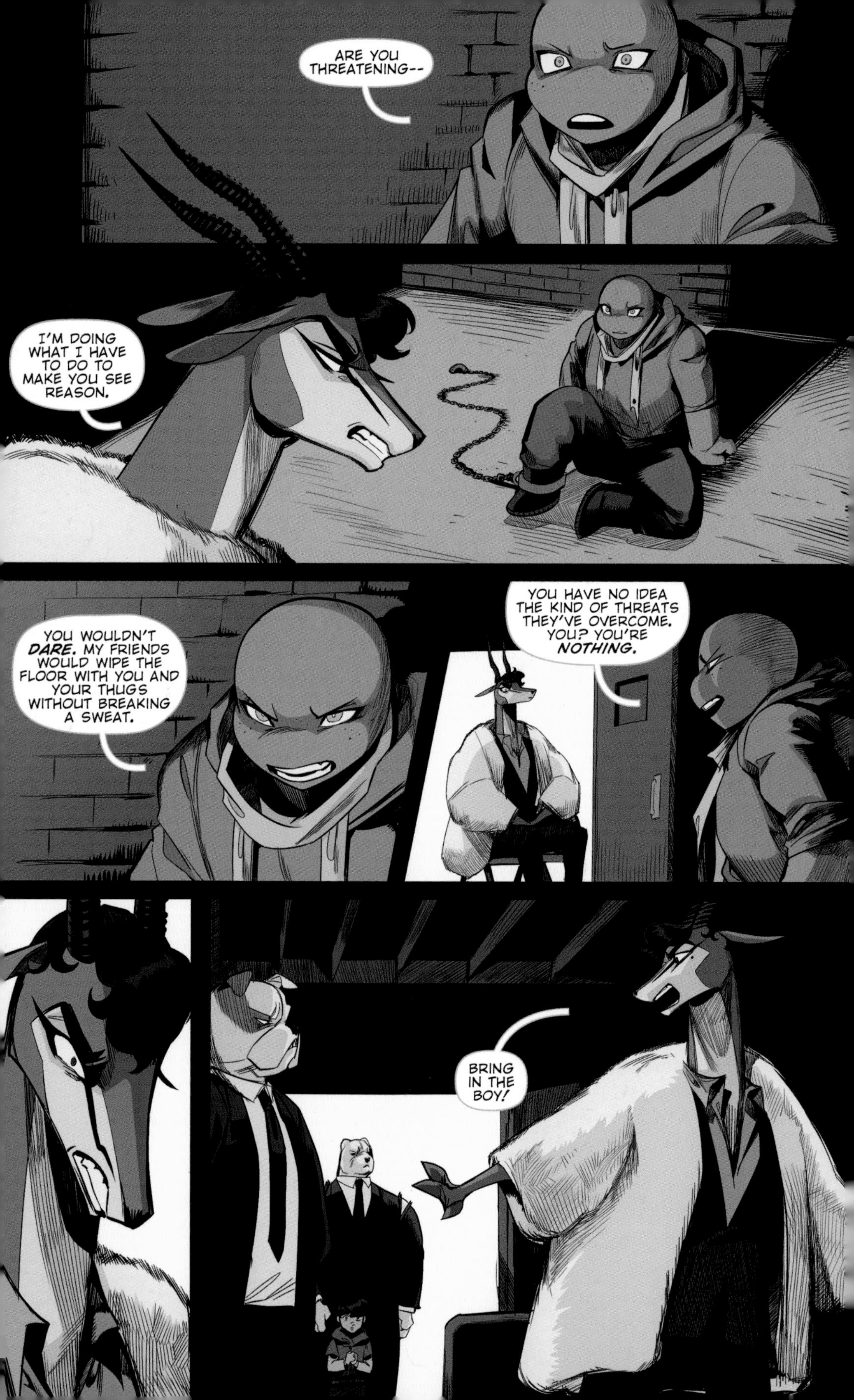
ARE YOU THREATENING--
I'M DOING WHAT I HAVE TO DO TO MAKE YOU SEE REASON.
YOU WOULDN'T *DARE*. MY FRIENDS WOULD WIPE THE FLOOR WITH YOU AND YOUR THUGS WITHOUT BREAKING A SWEAT.
YOU HAVE NO IDEA THE KIND OF THREATS THEY'VE OVERCOME. YOU? YOU'RE *NOTHING*.
BRING IN THE BOY!

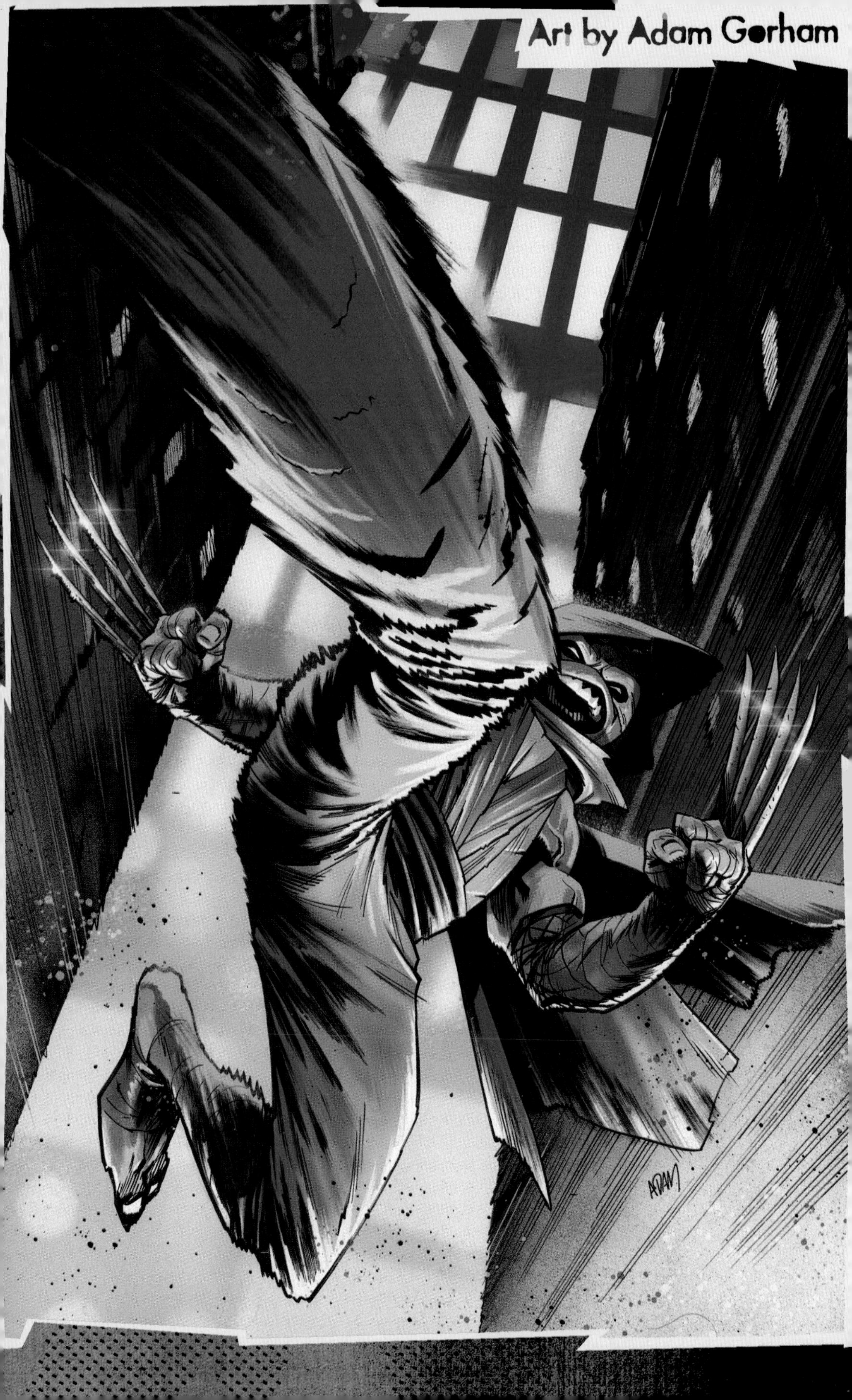
ADAM

Art by Adam Gorham

Art by Jodi Nishijima

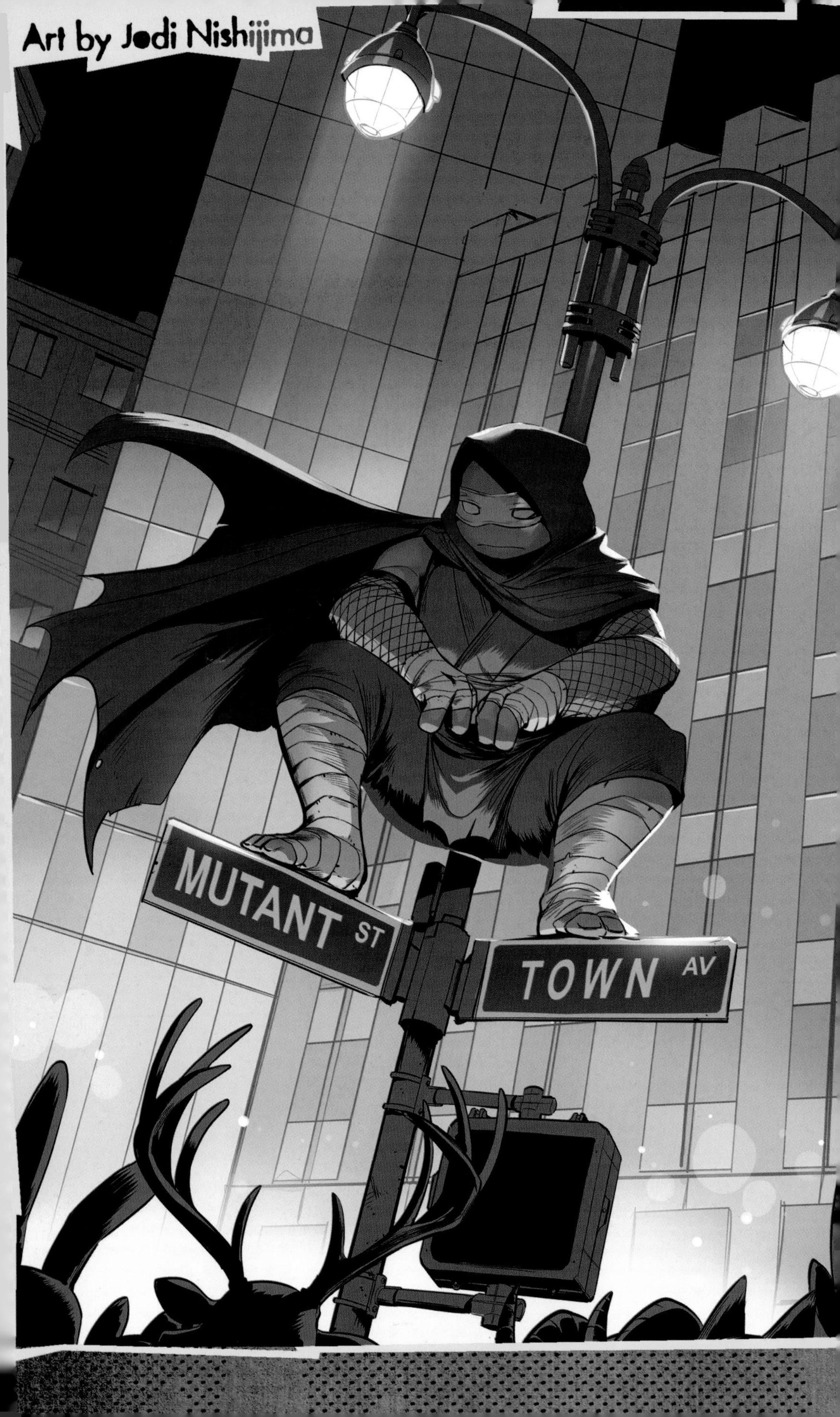
MUTANT ST
TOWN AV

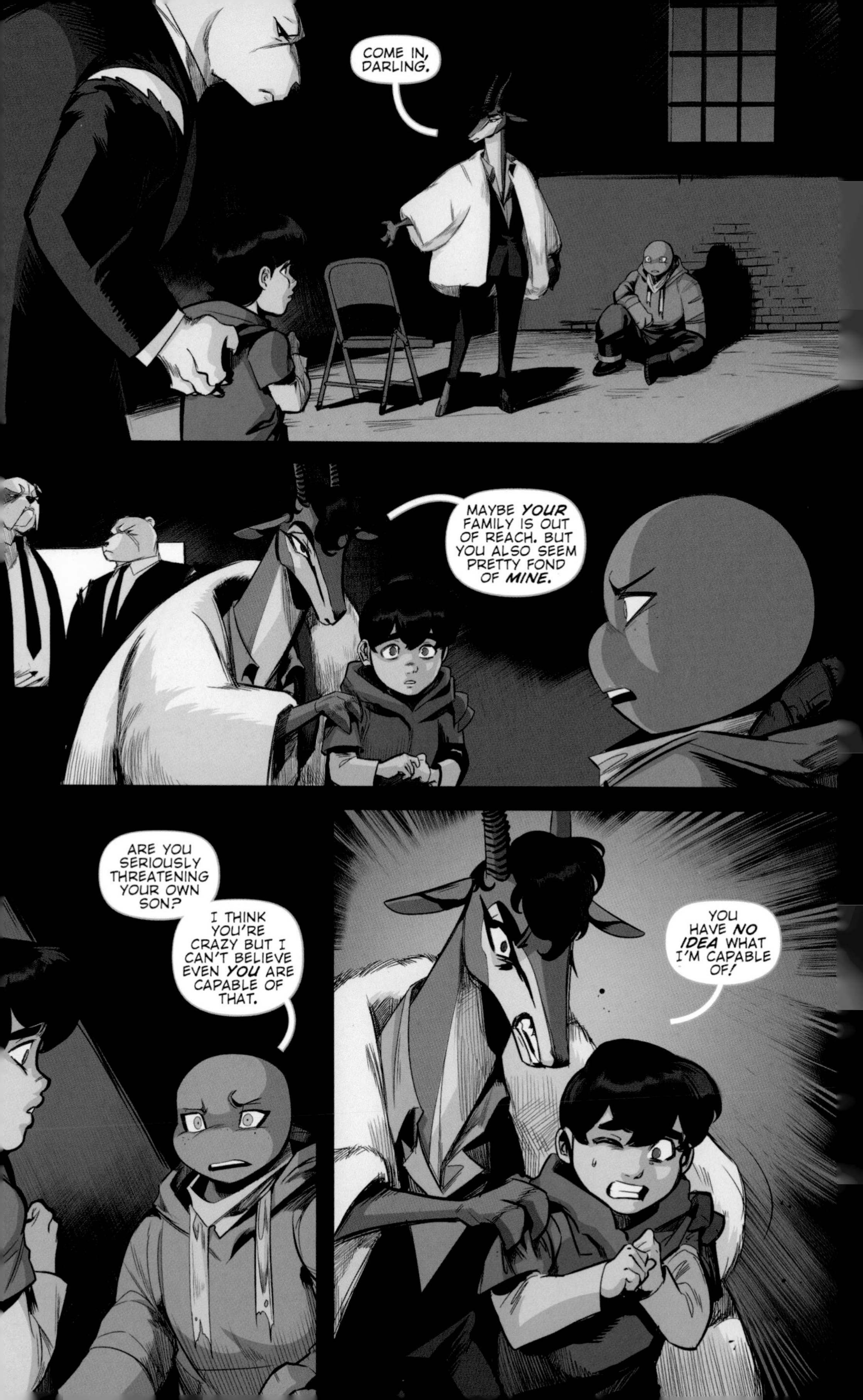
COME IN, DARLING.
MAYBE YOUR FAMILY IS OUT OF REACH. BUT YOU ALSO SEEM PRETTY FOND OF MINE.
ARE YOU SERIOUSLY THREATENING YOUR OWN SON?
I THINK YOU'RE CRAZY BUT I CAN'T BELIEVE EVEN YOU ARE CAPABLE OF THAT.
YOU HAVE NO IDEA WHAT I'M CAPABLE OF!

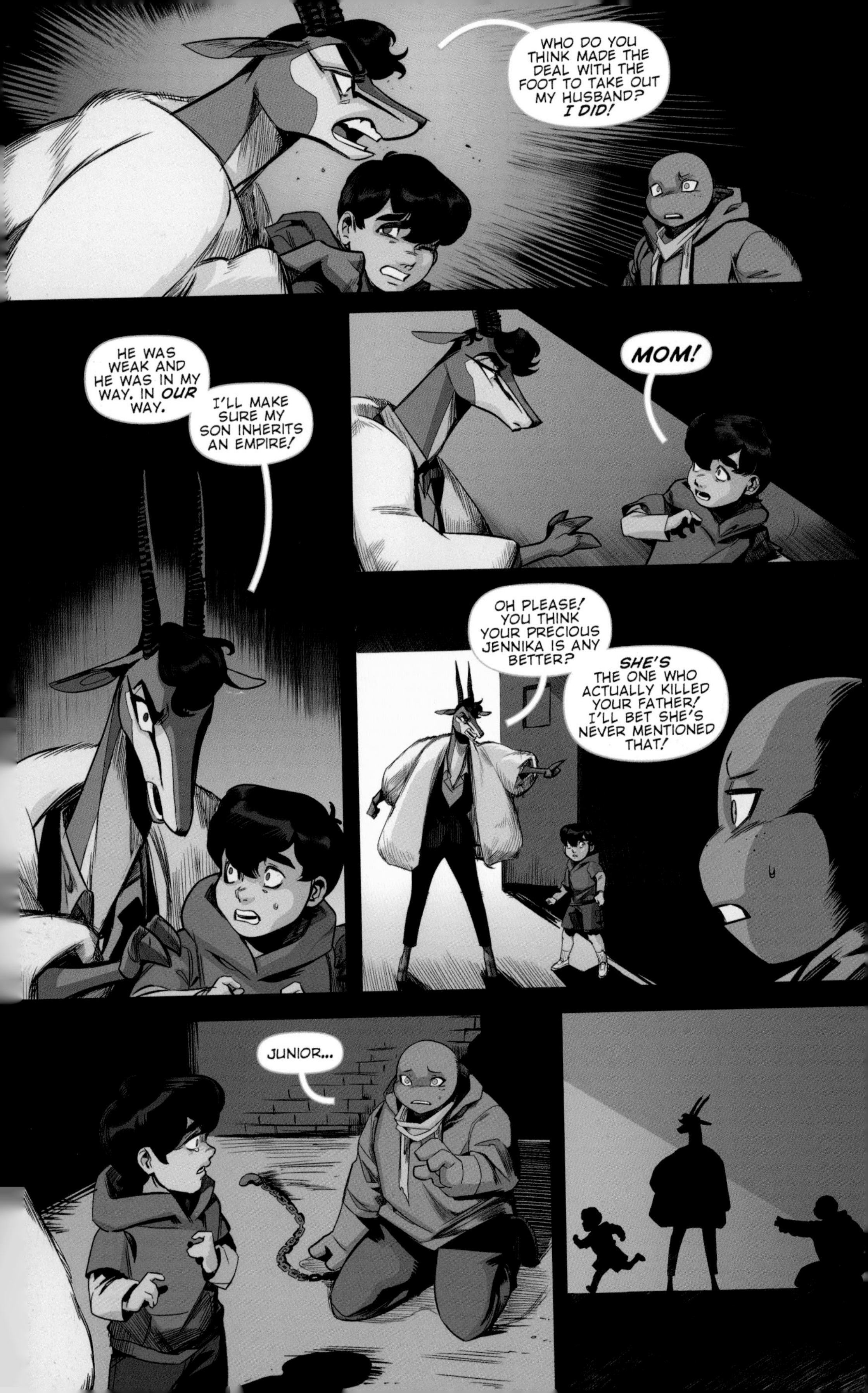

WHO DO YOU THINK MADE THE DEAL WITH THE FOOT TO TAKE OUT MY HUSBAND? *I DID!*
HE WAS WEAK AND HE WAS IN MY WAY. IN *OUR* WAY.
I'LL MAKE SURE MY SON INHERITS AN EMPIRE!
*MOM!*
OH PLEASE! YOU THINK YOUR PRECIOUS JENNIKA IS ANY BETTER?
*SHE'S* THE ONE WHO ACTUALLY KILLED YOUR FATHER! I'LL BET SHE'S NEVER MENTIONED THAT!
JUNIOR...

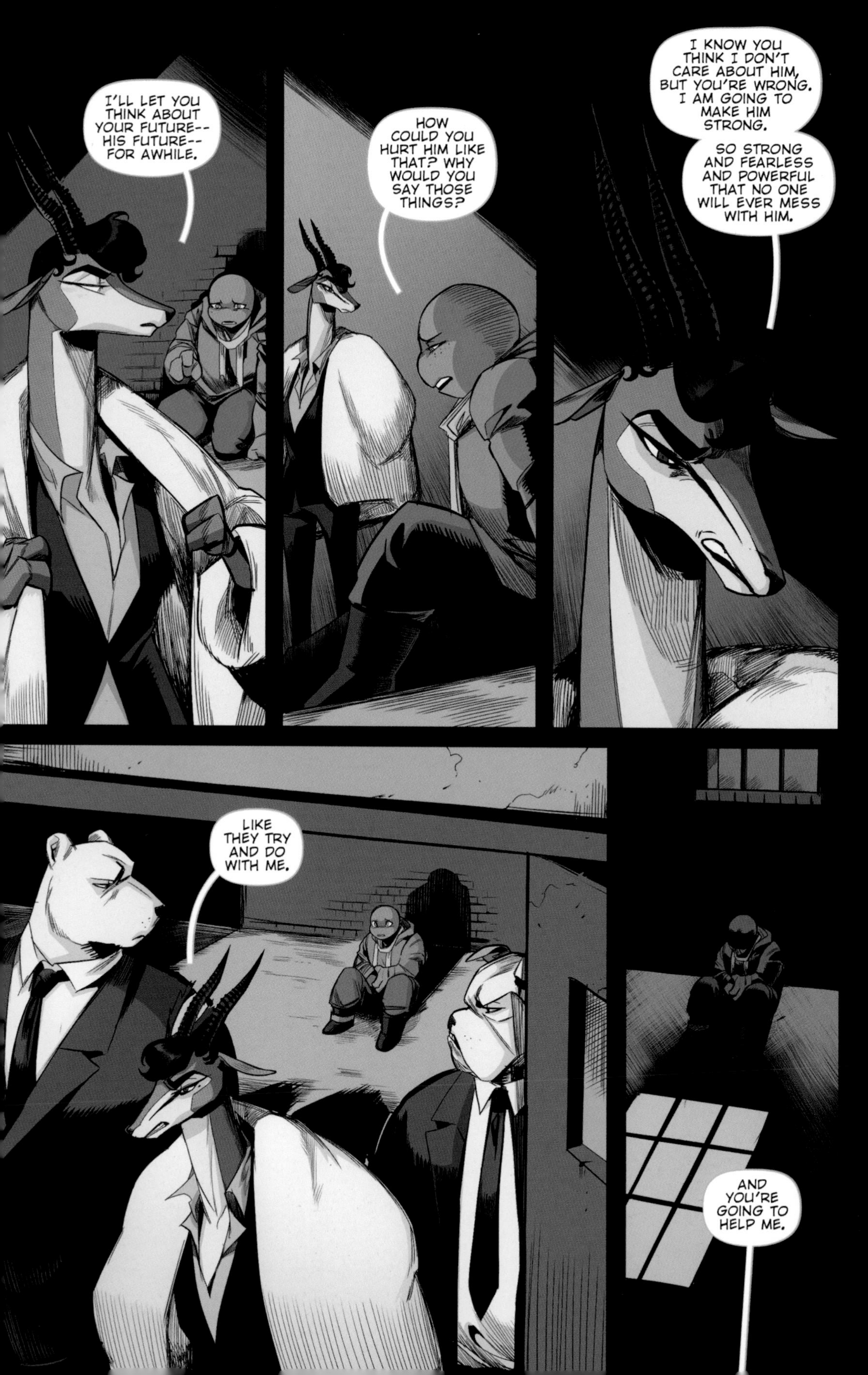
I'LL LET YOU THINK ABOUT YOUR FUTURE-- HIS FUTURE-- FOR AWHILE.
HOW COULD YOU HURT HIM LIKE THAT? WHY WOULD YOU SAY THOSE THINGS?
I KNOW YOU THINK I DON'T CARE ABOUT HIM, BUT YOU'RE WRONG. I AM GOING TO MAKE HIM STRONG.
SO STRONG AND FEARLESS AND POWERFUL THAT NO ONE WILL EVER MESS WITH HIM.
LIKE THEY TRY AND DO WITH ME.
AND YOU'RE GOING TO HELP ME.

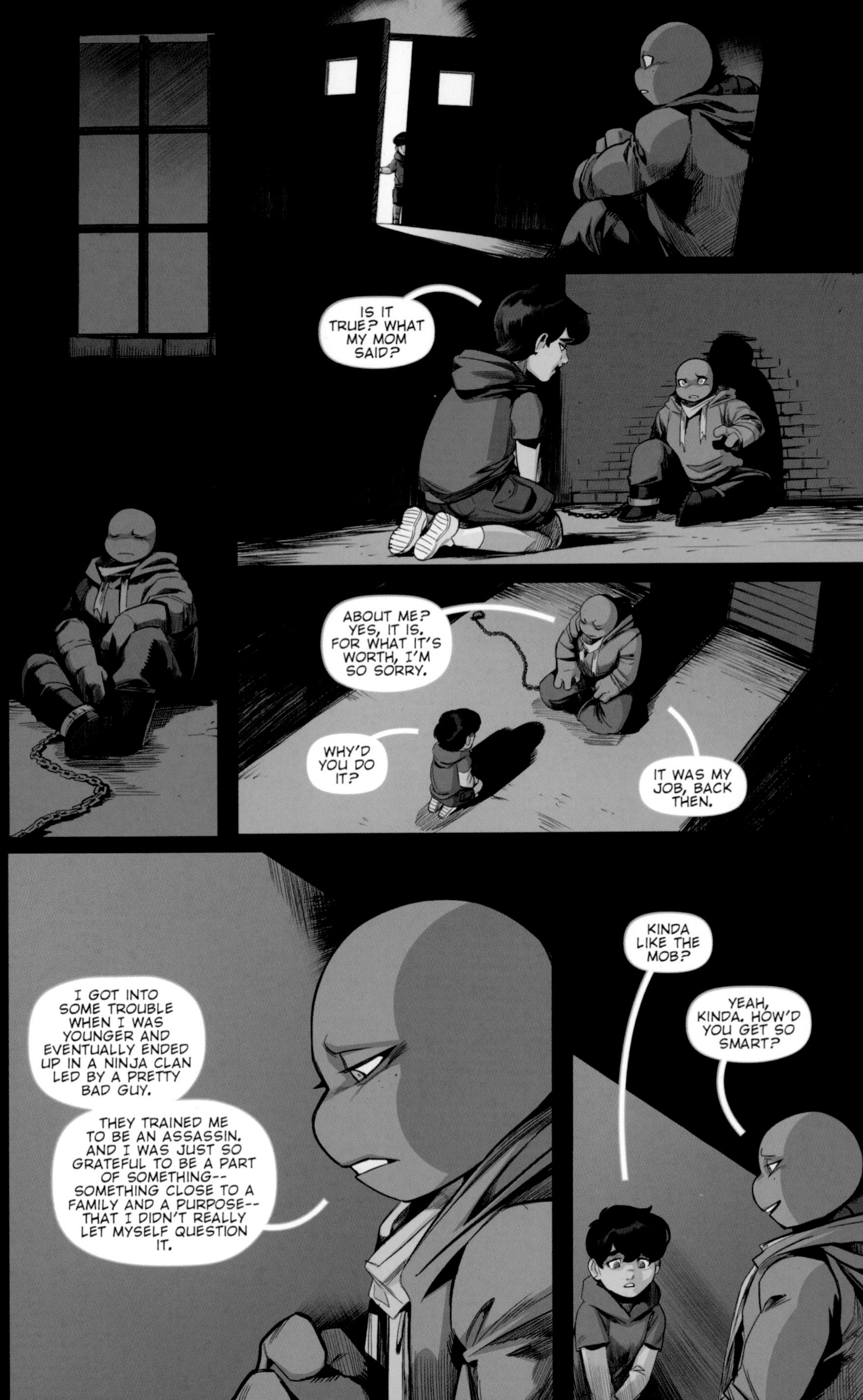
IS IT TRUE? WHAT MY MOM SAID?
ABOUT ME? YES, IT IS. FOR WHAT IT'S WORTH, I'M SO SORRY.
WHY'D YOU DO IT?
IT WAS MY JOB, BACK THEN.
I GOT INTO SOME TROUBLE WHEN I WAS YOUNGER AND EVENTUALLY ENDED UP IN A NINJA CLAN LED BY A PRETTY BAD GUY.
THEY TRAINED ME TO BE AN ASSASSIN. AND I WAS JUST SO GRATEFUL TO BE A PART OF SOMETHING-- SOMETHING CLOSE TO A FAMILY AND A PURPOSE-- THAT I DIDN'T REALLY LET MYSELF QUESTION IT.
KINDA LIKE THE MOB?
YEAH, KINDA. HOW'D YOU GET SO SMART?

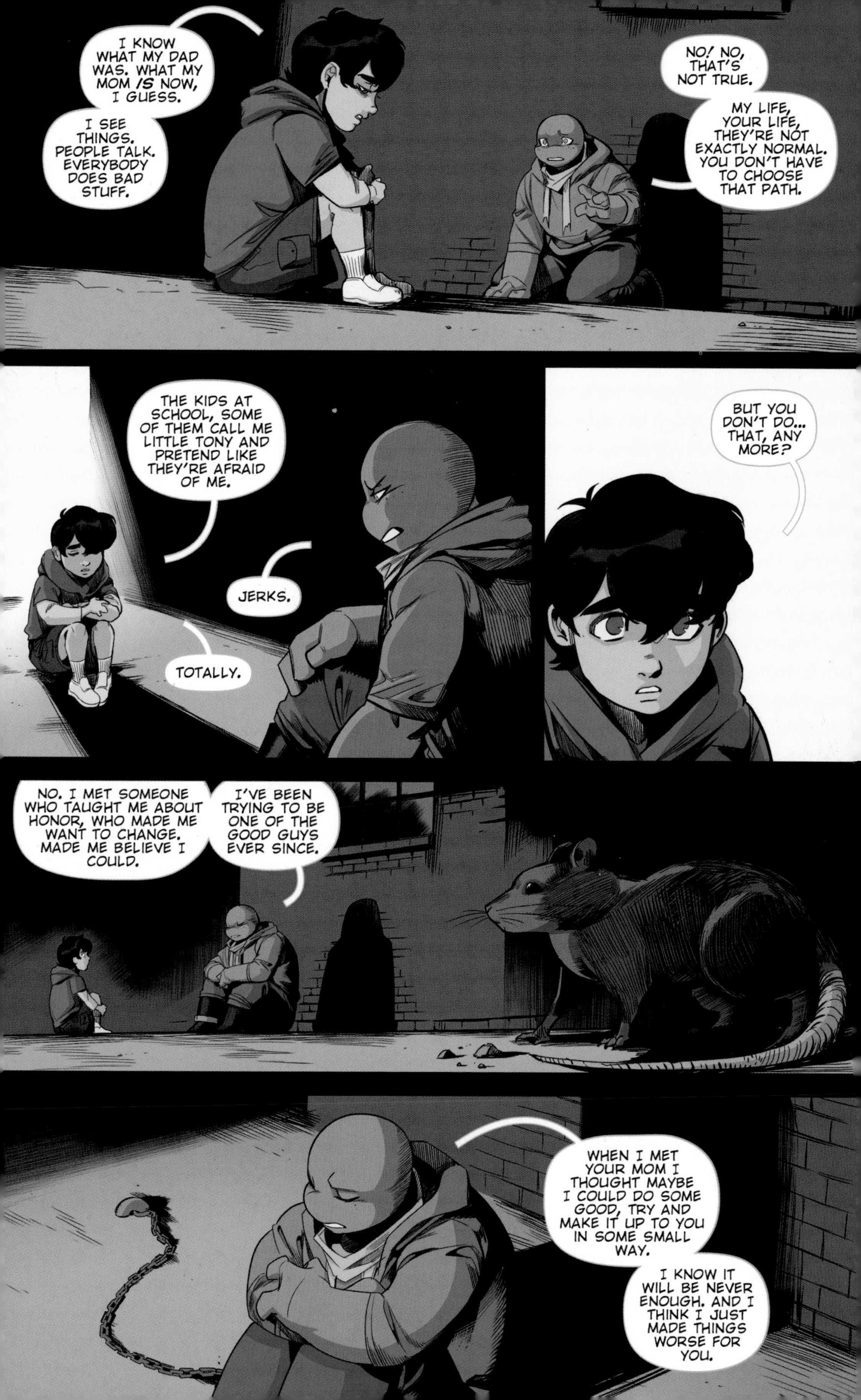
I KNOW WHAT MY DAD WAS. WHAT MY MOM *IS* NOW, I GUESS.
I SEE THINGS. PEOPLE TALK. EVERYBODY DOES BAD STUFF.
NO! NO, THAT'S NOT TRUE.
MY LIFE, YOUR LIFE, THEY'RE NOT EXACTLY NORMAL. YOU DON'T HAVE TO CHOOSE THAT PATH.
THE KIDS AT SCHOOL, SOME OF THEM CALL ME LITTLE TONY AND PRETEND LIKE THEY'RE AFRAID OF ME.
JERKS.
TOTALLY.
BUT YOU DON'T DO... THAT, ANY MORE?
NO. I MET SOMEONE WHO TAUGHT ME ABOUT HONOR, WHO MADE ME WANT TO CHANGE. MADE ME BELIEVE I COULD.
I'VE BEEN TRYING TO BE ONE OF THE GOOD GUYS EVER SINCE.
WHEN I MET YOUR MOM I THOUGHT MAYBE I COULD DO SOME GOOD, TRY AND MAKE IT UP TO YOU IN SOME SMALL WAY.
I KNOW IT WILL BE NEVER ENOUGH. AND I THINK I JUST MADE THINGS WORSE FOR YOU.

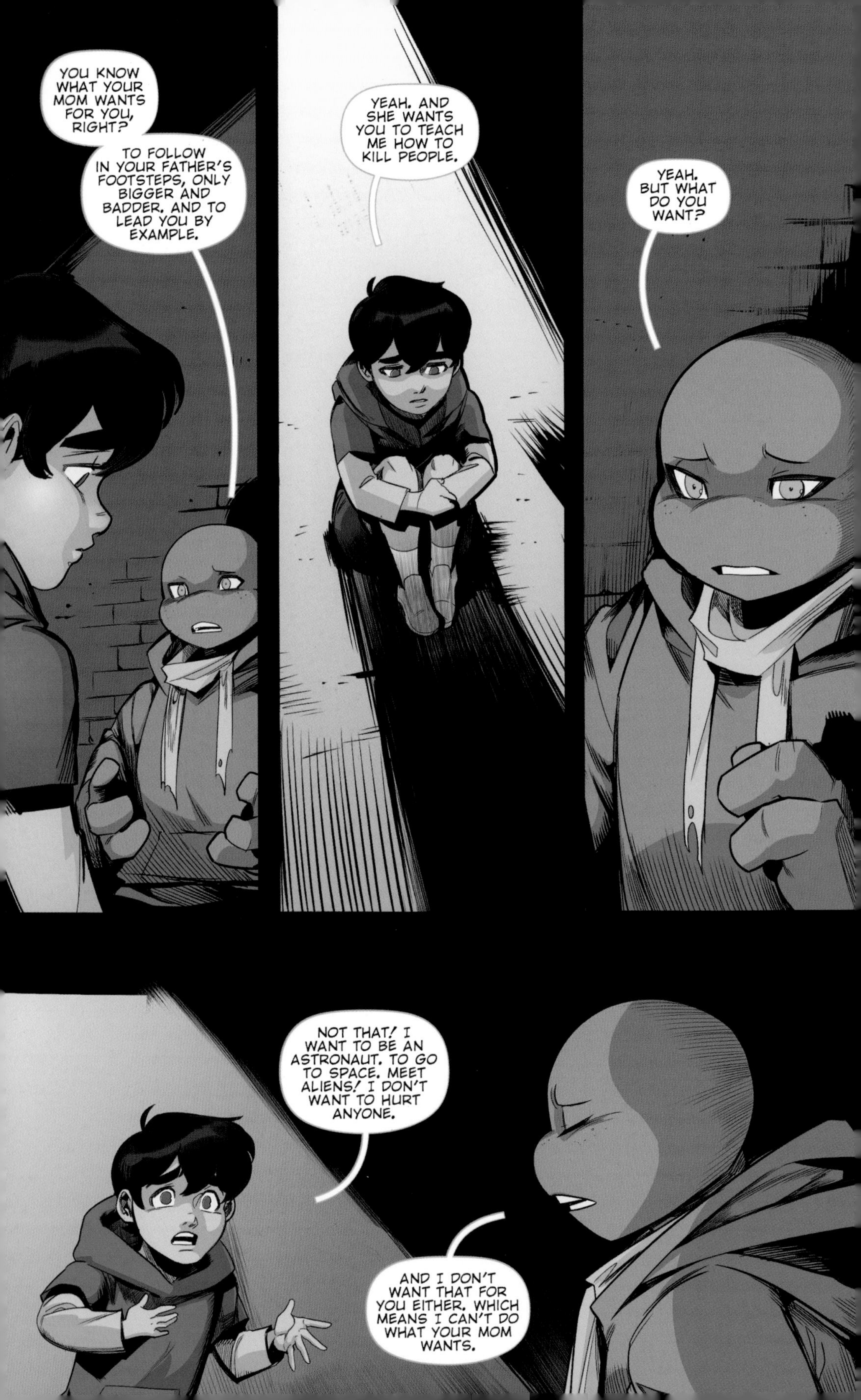
YOU KNOW WHAT YOUR MOM WANTS FOR YOU, RIGHT?
TO FOLLOW IN YOUR FATHER'S FOOTSTEPS, ONLY BIGGER AND BADDER. AND TO LEAD YOU BY EXAMPLE.
YEAH. AND SHE WANTS YOU TO TEACH ME HOW TO KILL PEOPLE.
YEAH. BUT WHAT DO YOU WANT?
NOT THAT! I WANT TO BE AN ASTRONAUT. TO GO TO SPACE. MEET ALIENS! I DON'T WANT TO HURT ANYONE.
AND I DON'T WANT THAT FOR YOU EITHER. WHICH MEANS I CAN'T DO WHAT YOUR MOM WANTS.

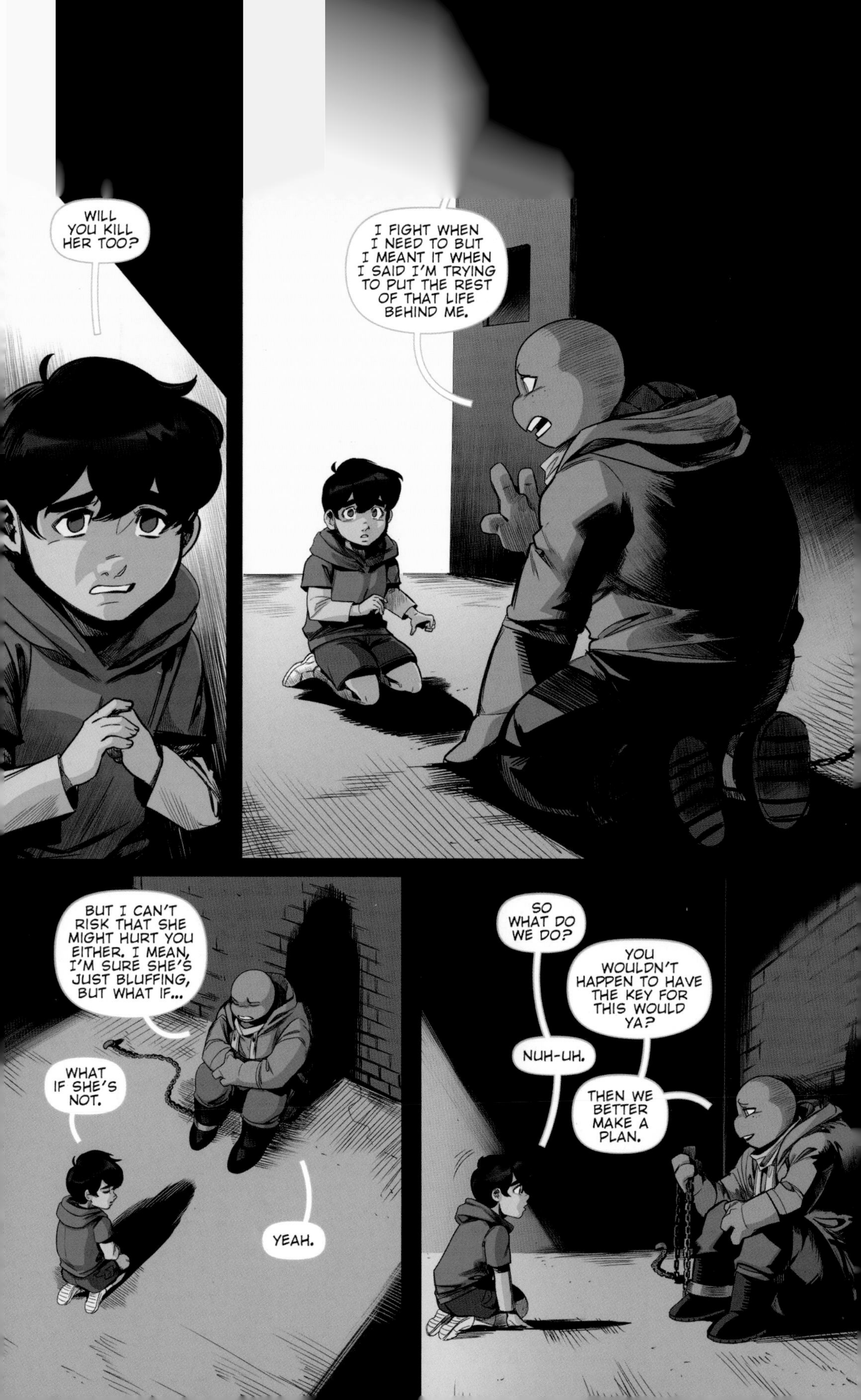
WILL YOU KILL HER TOO?
I FIGHT WHEN I NEED TO BUT I MEANT IT WHEN I SAID I'M TRYING TO PUT THE REST OF THAT LIFE BEHIND ME.
BUT I CAN'T RISK THAT SHE MIGHT HURT YOU EITHER. I MEAN, I'M SURE SHE'S JUST BLUFFING, BUT WHAT IF...
WHAT IF SHE'S NOT.
YEAH.
SO WHAT DO WE DO?
YOU WOULDN'T HAPPEN TO HAVE THE KEY FOR THIS WOULD YA?
NUH-UH.
THEN WE BETTER MAKE A PLAN.

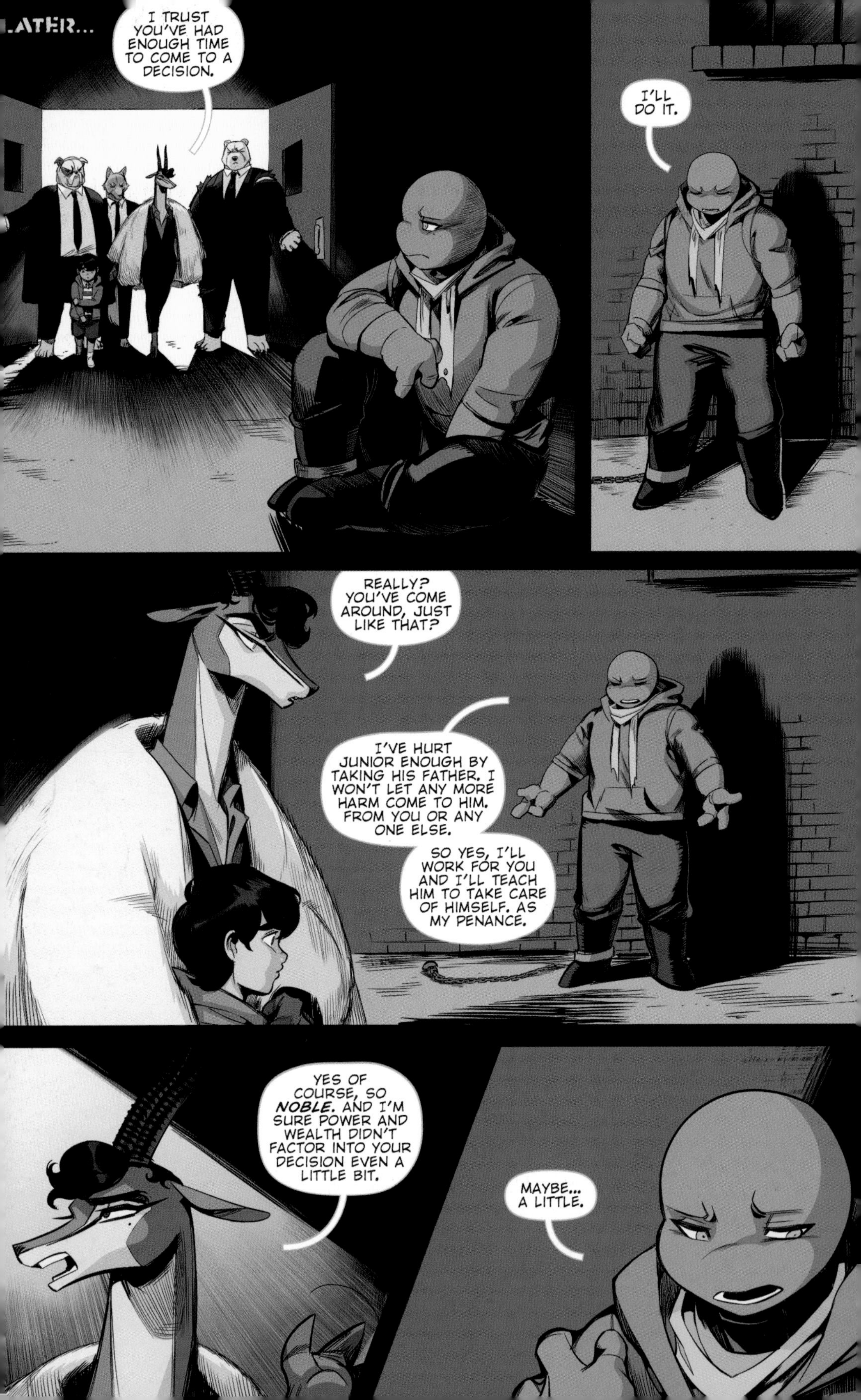
LATER...
I TRUST YOU'VE HAD ENOUGH TIME TO COME TO A DECISION.
I'LL DO IT.
REALLY? YOU'VE COME AROUND, JUST LIKE THAT?
I'VE HURT JUNIOR ENOUGH BY TAKING HIS FATHER. I WON'T LET ANY MORE HARM COME TO HIM. FROM YOU OR ANY ONE ELSE.
SO YES, I'LL WORK FOR YOU AND I'LL TEACH HIM TO TAKE CARE OF HIMSELF. AS MY PENANCE.
YES OF COURSE, SO NOBLE. AND I'M SURE POWER AND WEALTH DIDN'T FACTOR INTO YOUR DECISION EVEN A LITTLE BIT.
MAYBE... A LITTLE.

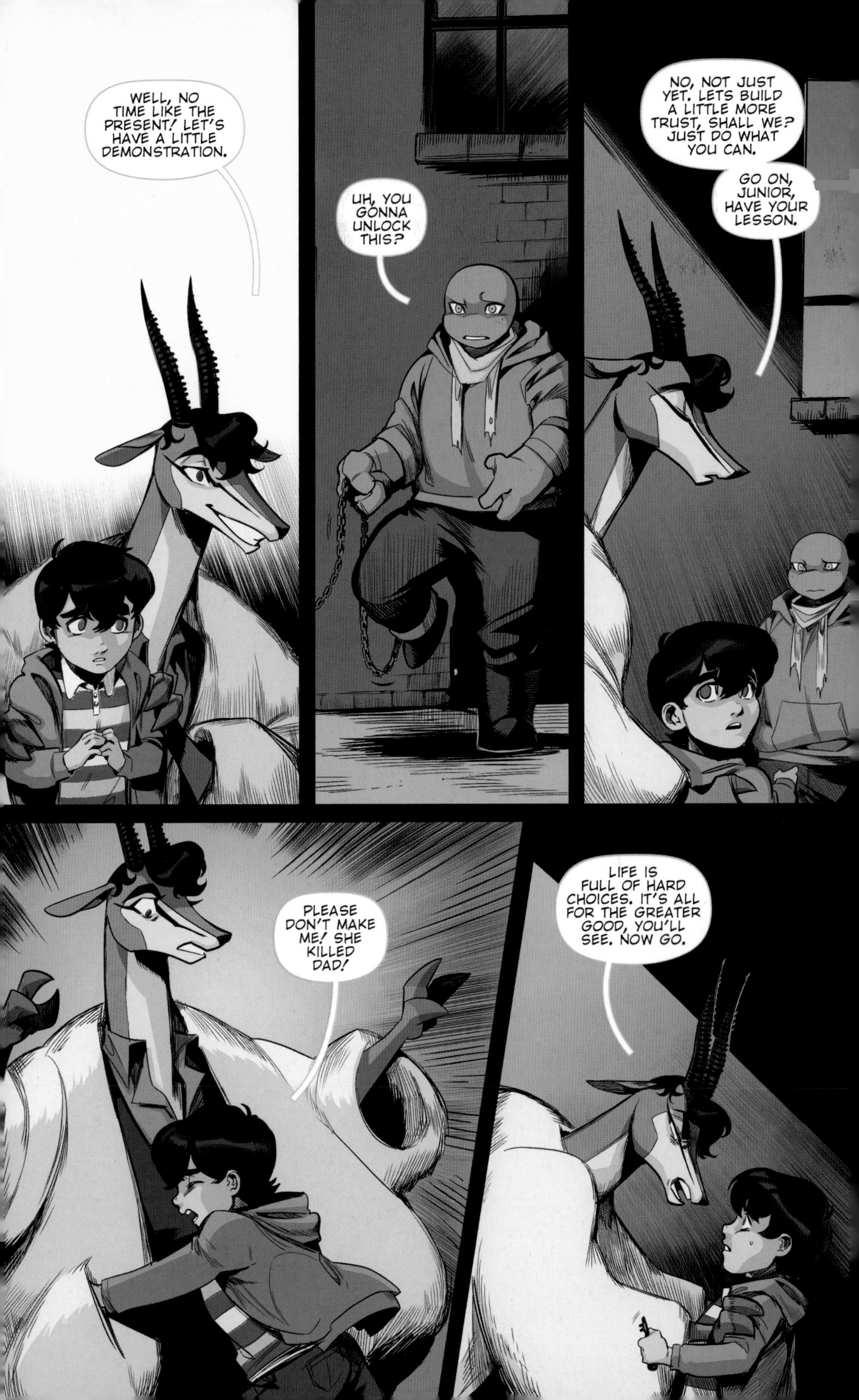
WELL, NO TIME LIKE THE PRESENT! LET'S HAVE A LITTLE DEMONSTRATION.
UH, YOU GONNA UNLOCK THIS?
NO, NOT JUST YET. LETS BUILD A LITTLE MORE TRUST, SHALL WE? JUST DO WHAT YOU CAN.
GO ON, JUNIOR, HAVE YOUR LESSON.
PLEASE DON'T MAKE ME! SHE KILLED DAD!
LIFE IS FULL OF HARD CHOICES. IT'S ALL FOR THE GREATER GOOD, YOU'LL SEE. NOW GO.

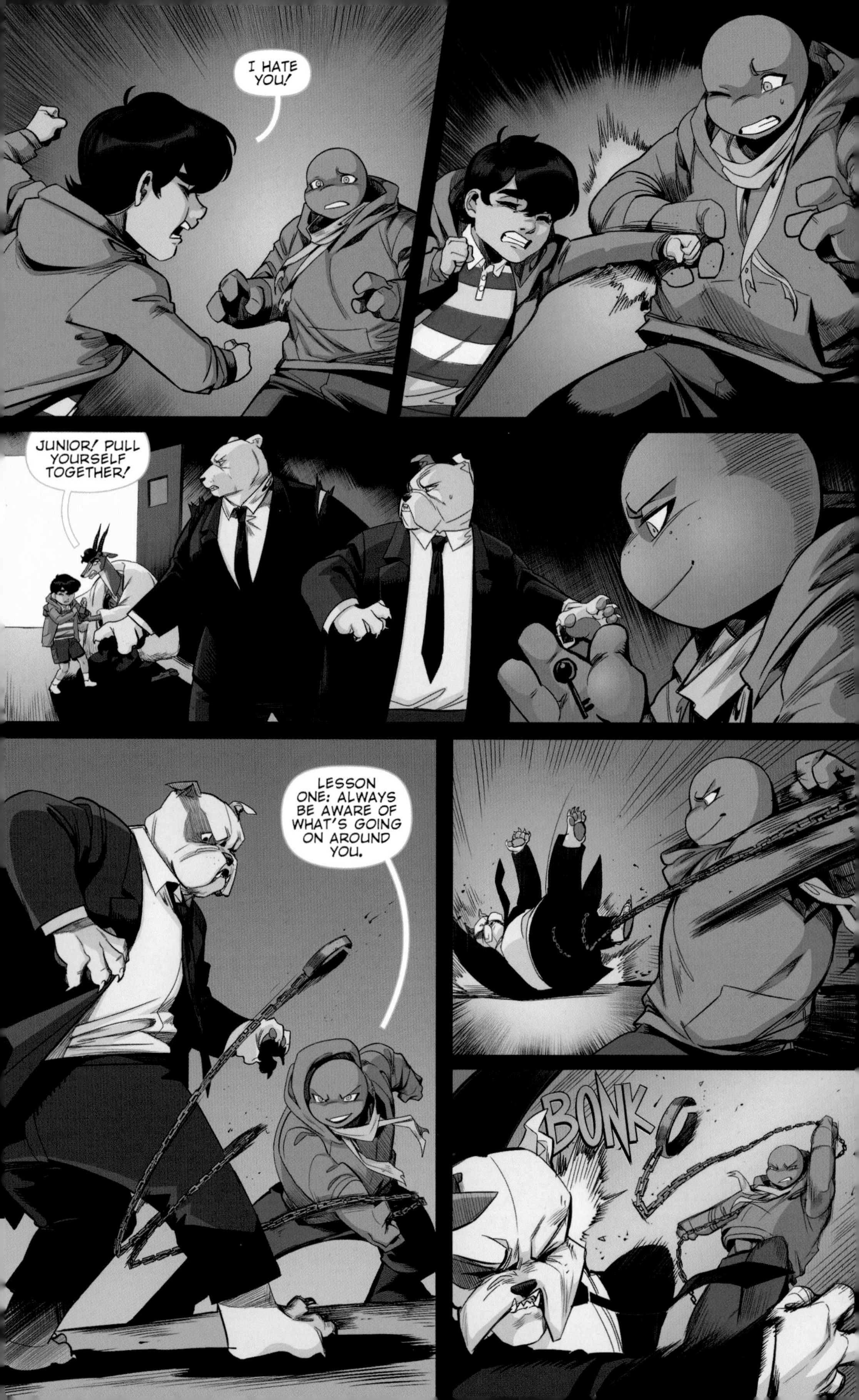
I HATE YOU!
JUNIOR! PULL YOURSELF TOGETHER!
LESSON ONE: ALWAYS BE AWARE OF WHAT'S GOING ON AROUND YOU.
BONK

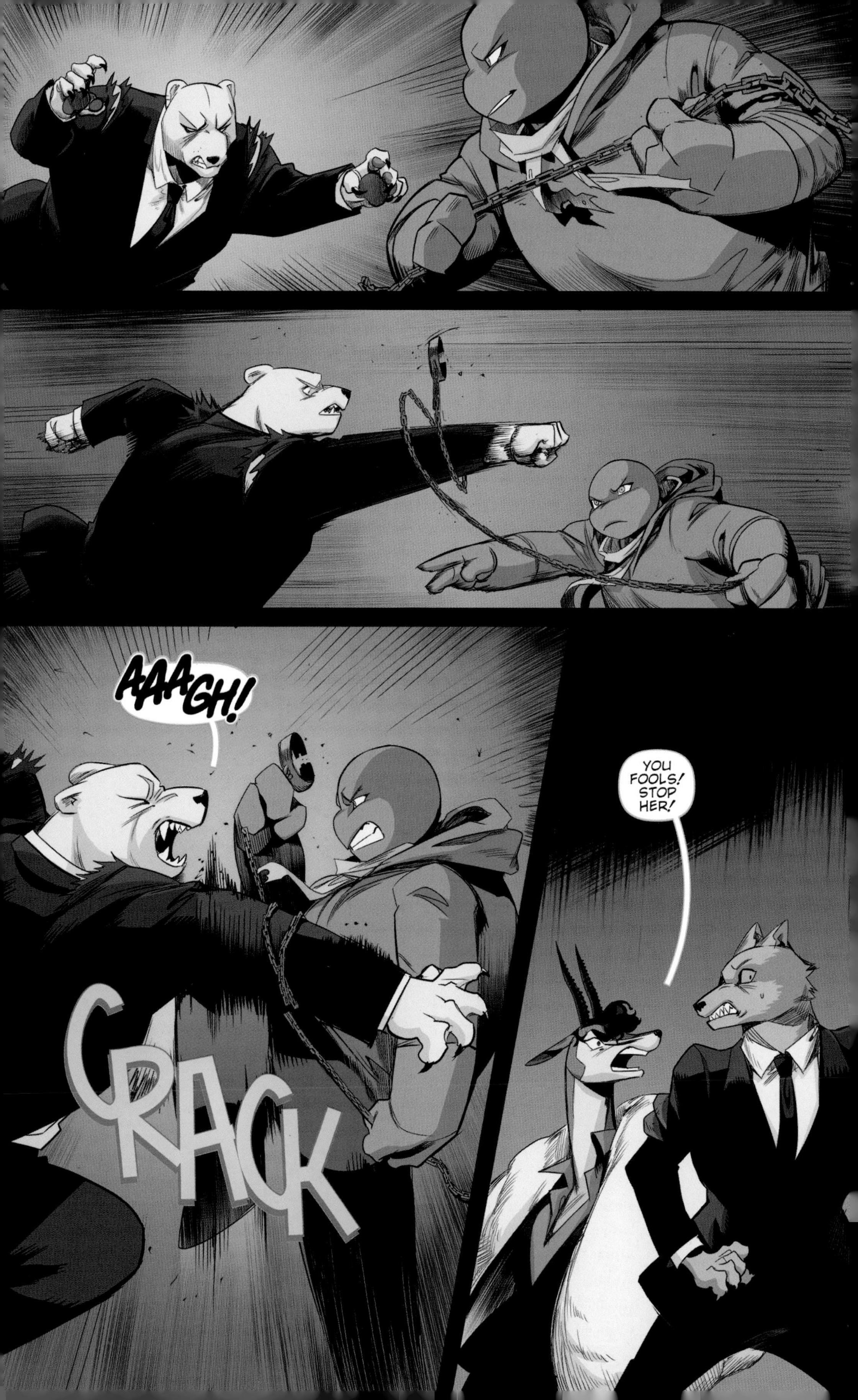

AAAGH!
CRACK
YOU FOOLS! STOP HER!

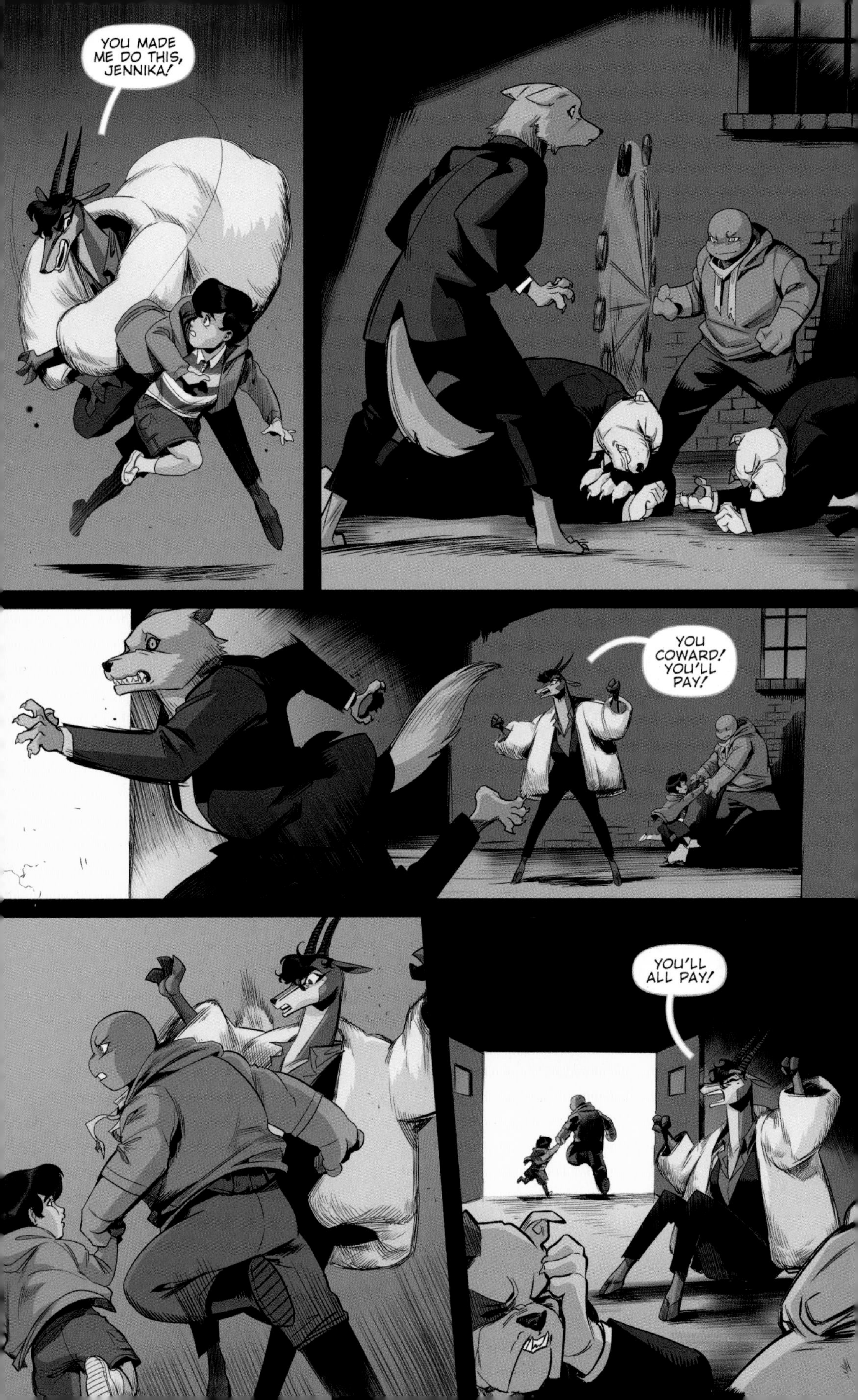
YOU MADE ME DO THIS, JENNIKA!
YOU COWARD! YOU'LL PAY!
YOU'LL ALL PAY!

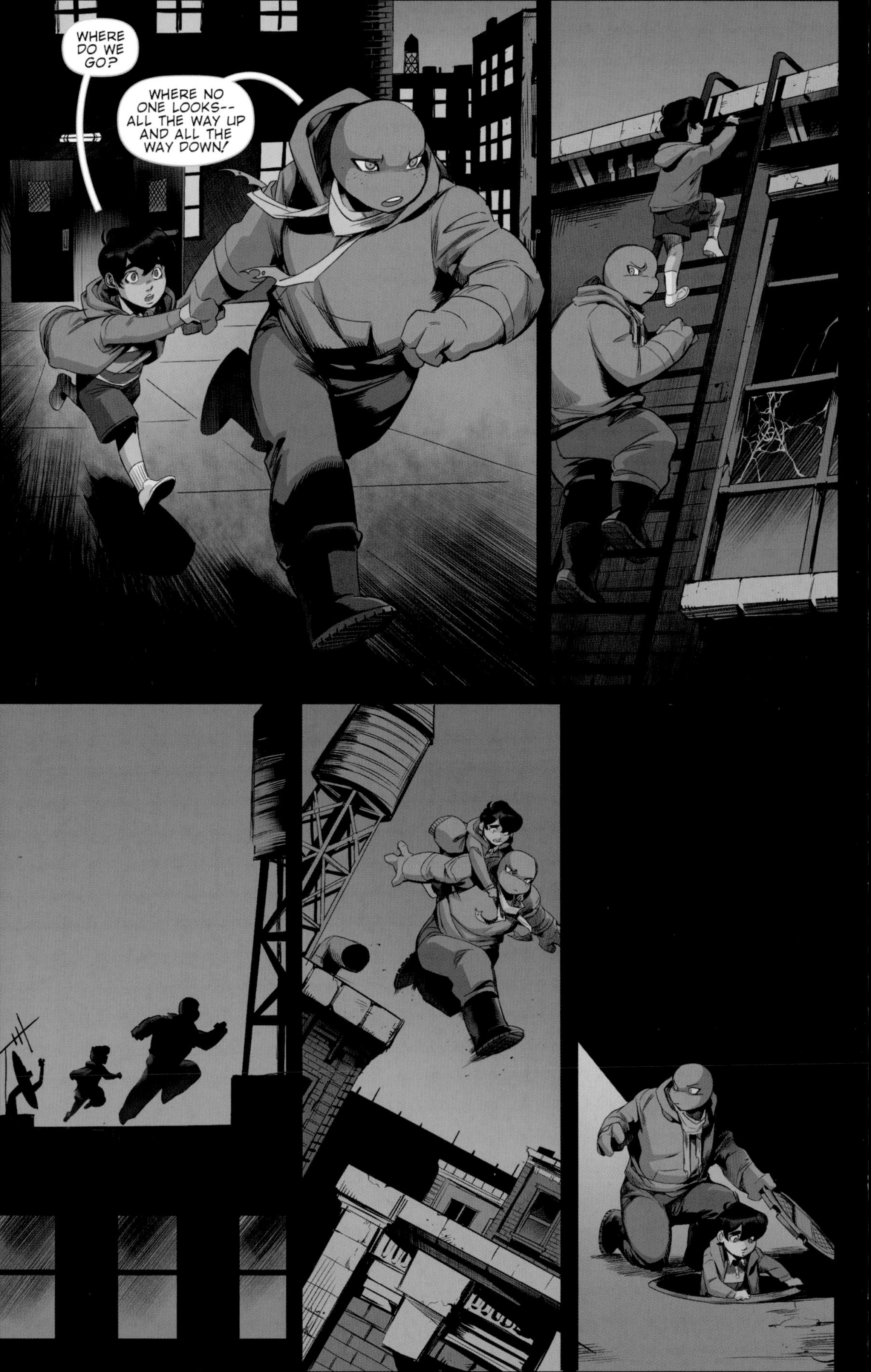
WHERE DO WE GO?
WHERE NO ONE LOOKS-- ALL THE WAY UP AND ALL THE WAY DOWN!

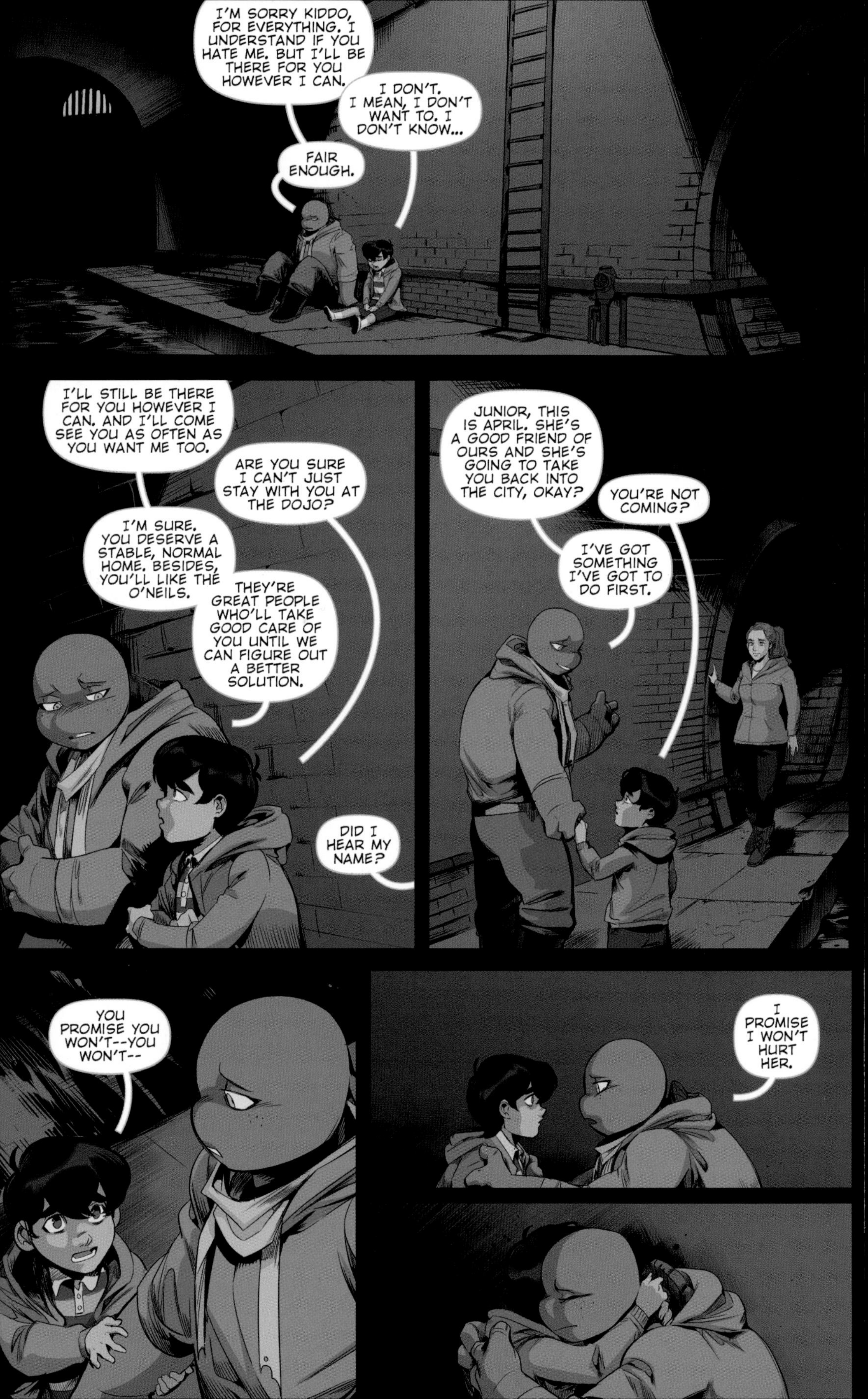
I'M SORRY KIDDO, FOR EVERYTHING. I UNDERSTAND IF YOU HATE ME. BUT I'LL BE THERE FOR YOU HOWEVER I CAN.
I DON'T. I MEAN, I DON'T WANT TO. I DON'T KNOW...
FAIR ENOUGH.
I'LL STILL BE THERE FOR YOU HOWEVER I CAN. AND I'LL COME SEE YOU AS OFTEN AS YOU WANT ME TOO.
ARE YOU SURE I CAN'T JUST STAY WITH YOU AT THE DOJO?
I'M SURE. YOU DESERVE A STABLE, NORMAL HOME. BESIDES, YOU'LL LIKE THE O'NEILS.
THEY'RE GREAT PEOPLE WHO'LL TAKE GOOD CARE OF YOU UNTIL WE CAN FIGURE OUT A BETTER SOLUTION.
DID I HEAR MY NAME?
JUNIOR, THIS IS APRIL. SHE'S A GOOD FRIEND OF OURS AND SHE'S GOING TO TAKE YOU BACK INTO THE CITY, OKAY?
YOU'RE NOT COMING?
I'VE GOT SOMETHING I'VE GOT TO DO FIRST.
YOU PROMISE YOU WON'T--YOU WON'T--
I PROMISE I WON'T HURT HER.

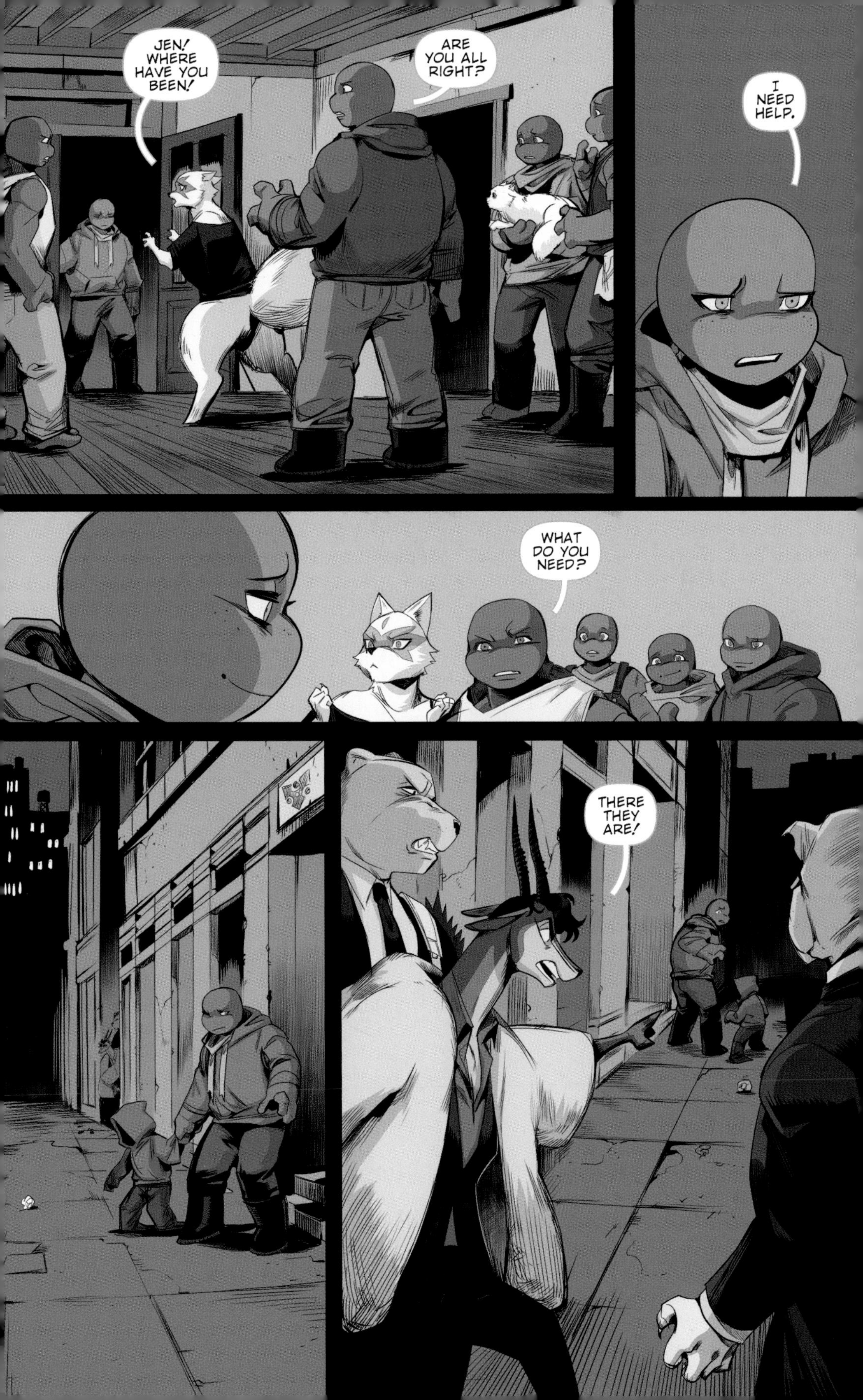
JEN! WHERE HAVE YOU BEEN!
ARE YOU ALL RIGHT?
I NEED HELP.
WHAT DO YOU NEED?
THERE THEY ARE!

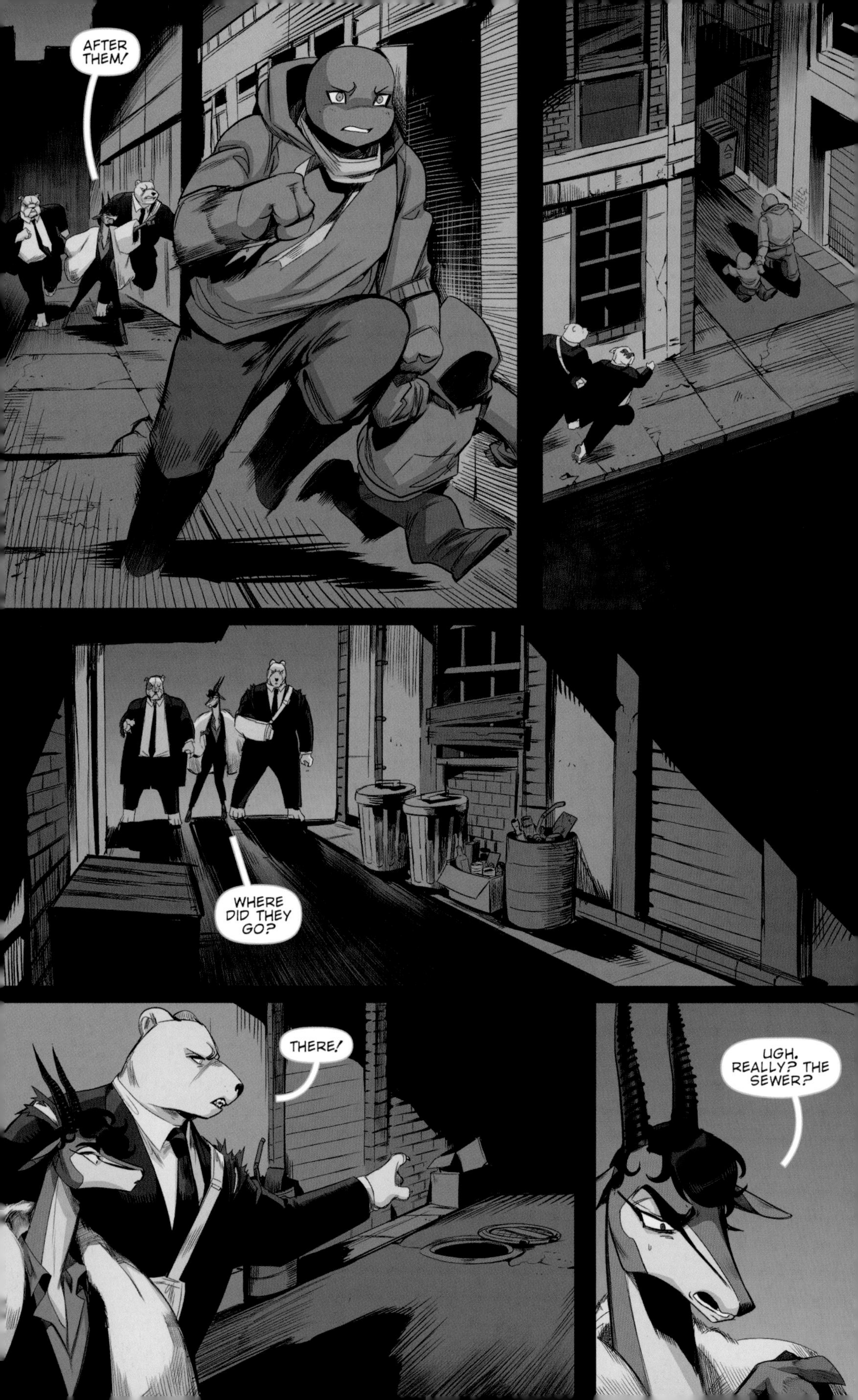
AFTER THEM!
WHERE DID THEY GO?
THERE!
UGH. REALLY? THE SEWER?

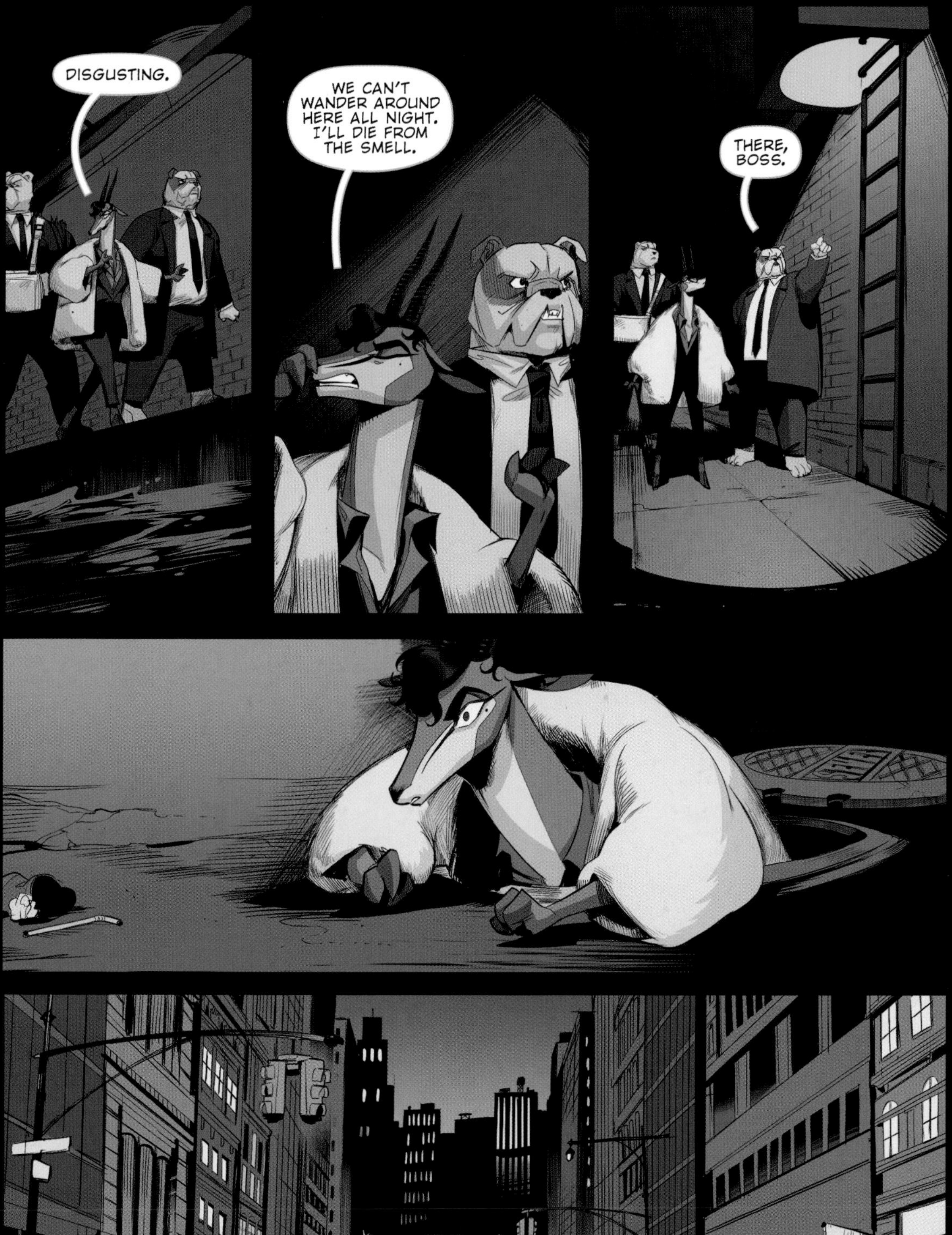
DISGUSTING.
WE CAN'T WANDER AROUND HERE ALL NIGHT. I'LL DIE FROM THE SMELL.
THERE, BOSS.

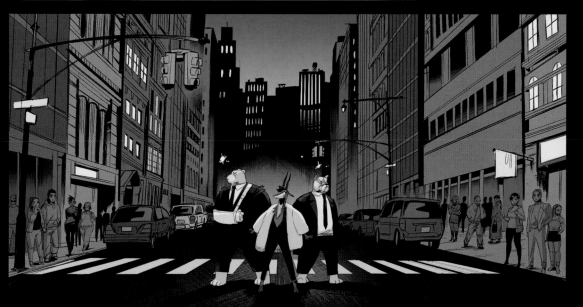

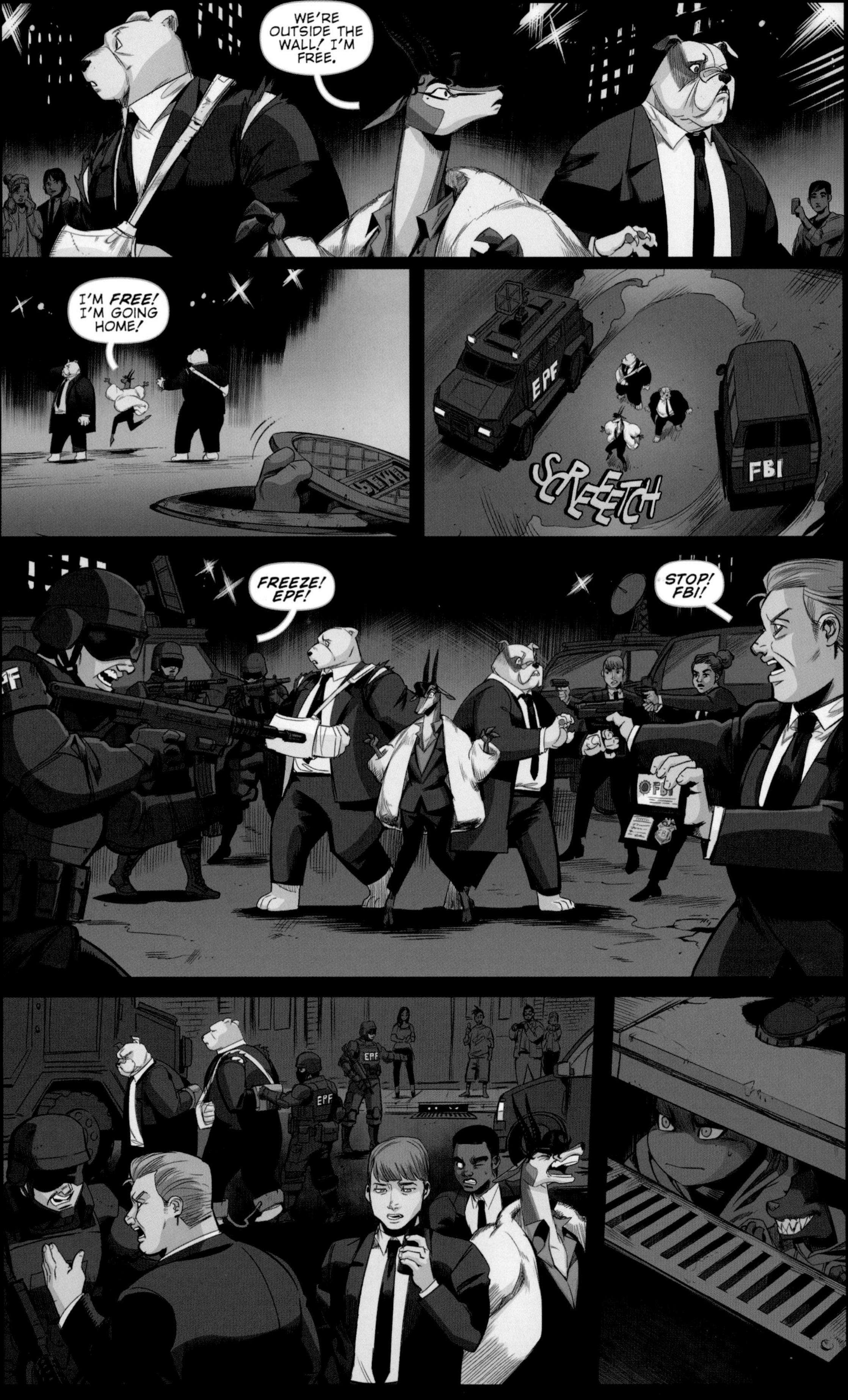
WE'RE OUTSIDE THE WALL! I'M FREE.
I'M FREE! I'M GOING HOME!
EPF
FBI
SCREEETCH
EPF
FREEZE! EPF!
STOP! FBI!
FBI
EPF
EPF

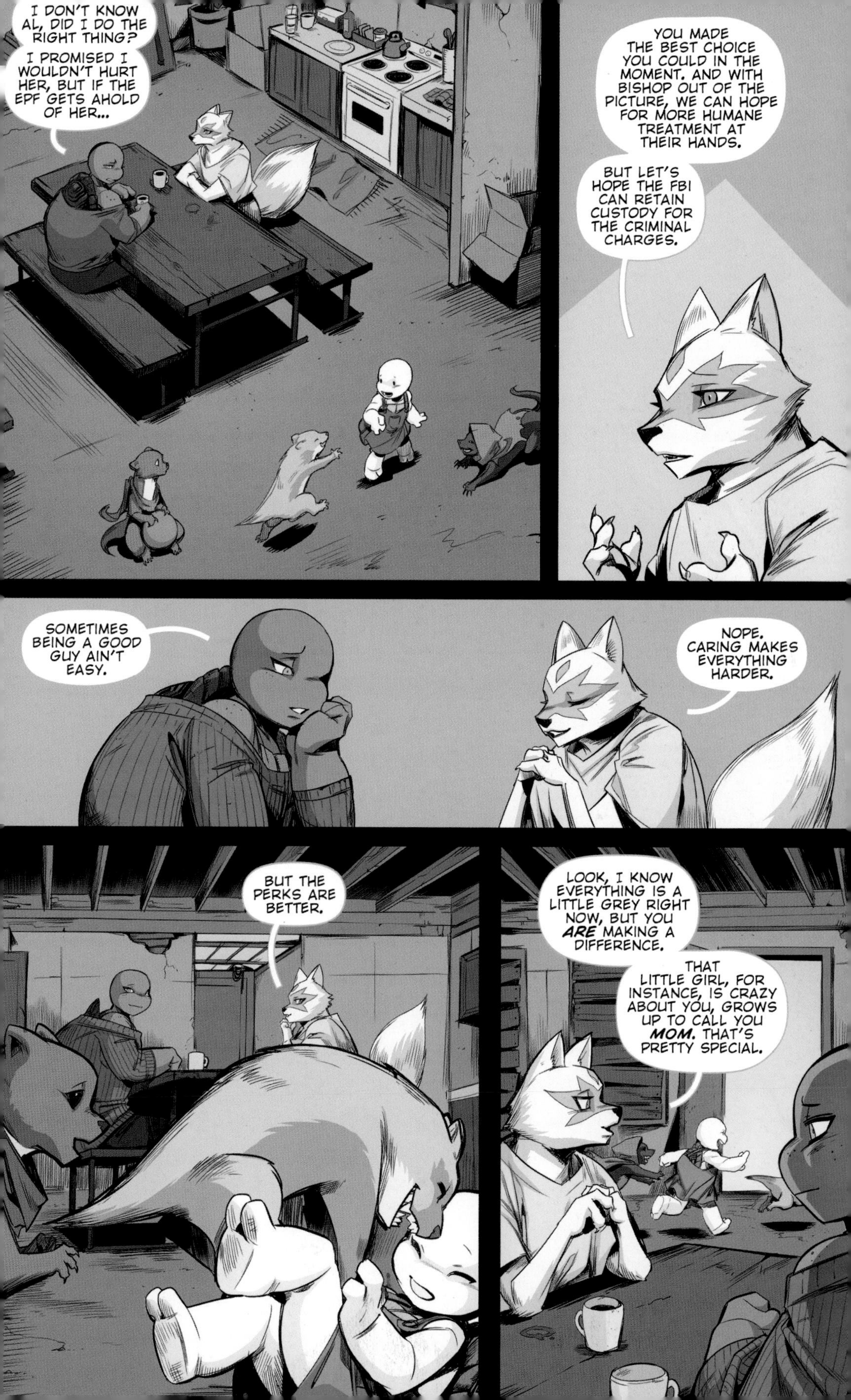
I DON'T KNOW AL, DID I DO THE RIGHT THING?
I PROMISED I WOULDN'T HURT HER, BUT IF THE EPF GETS AHOLD OF HER...
YOU MADE THE BEST CHOICE YOU COULD IN THE MOMENT. AND WITH BISHOP OUT OF THE PICTURE, WE CAN HOPE FOR MORE HUMANE TREATMENT AT THEIR HANDS.
BUT LET'S HOPE THE FBI CAN RETAIN CUSTODY FOR THE CRIMINAL CHARGES.
SOMETIMES BEING A GOOD GUY AIN'T EASY.
NOPE. CARING MAKES EVERYTHING HARDER.
BUT THE PERKS ARE BETTER.
LOOK, I KNOW EVERYTHING IS A LITTLE GREY RIGHT NOW, BUT YOU ***ARE*** MAKING A DIFFERENCE.
THAT LITTLE GIRL, FOR INSTANCE, IS CRAZY ABOUT YOU, GROWS UP TO CALL YOU ***MOM***. THAT'S PRETTY SPECIAL.

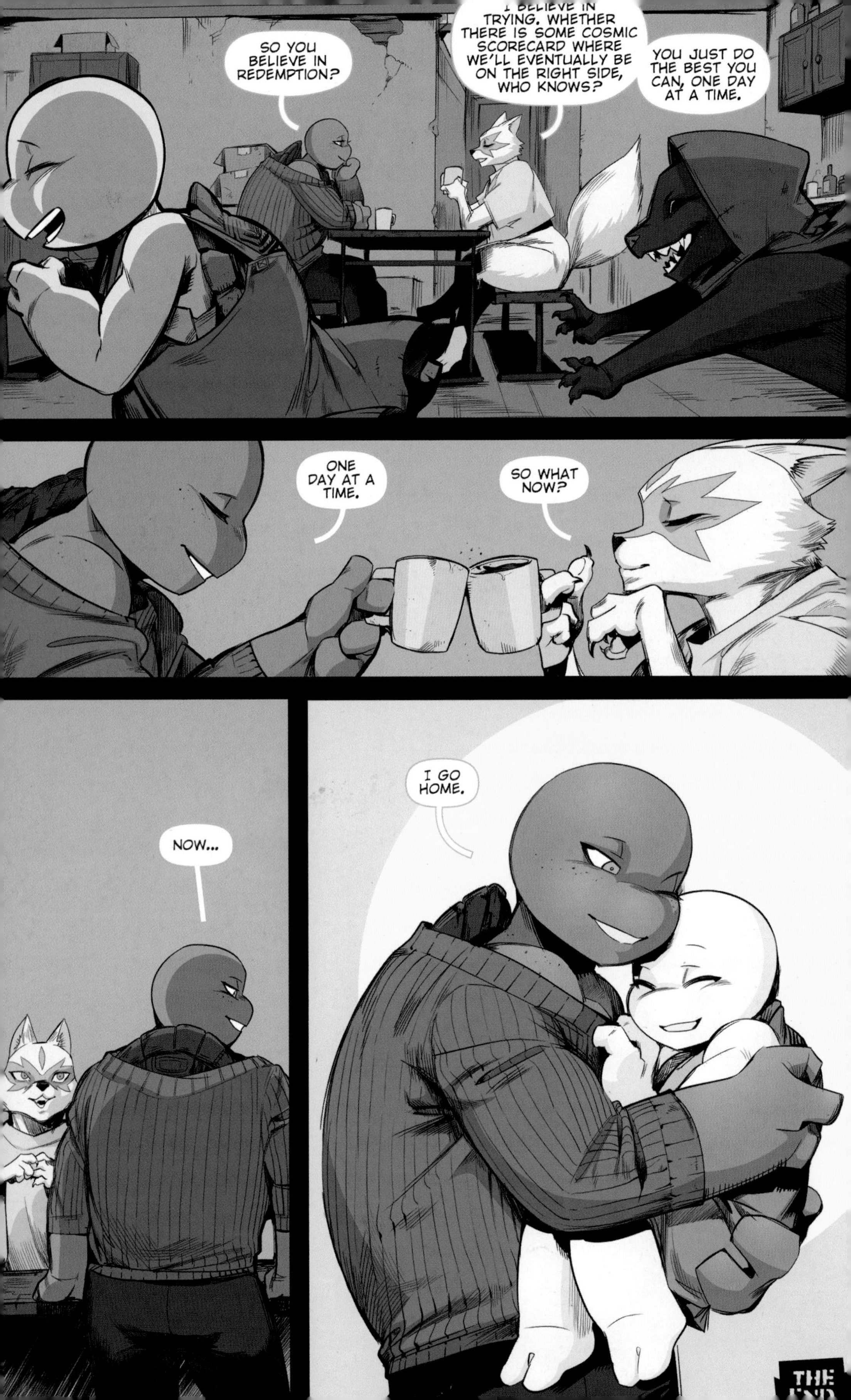
SO YOU BELIEVE IN REDEMPTION?
I BELIEVE IN TRYING. WHETHER THERE IS SOME COSMIC SCORECARD WHERE WE'LL EVENTUALLY BE ON THE RIGHT SIDE, WHO KNOWS?
YOU JUST DO THE BEST YOU CAN, ONE DAY AT A TIME.
ONE DAY AT A TIME.
SO WHAT NOW?
NOW...
I GO HOME.
THE

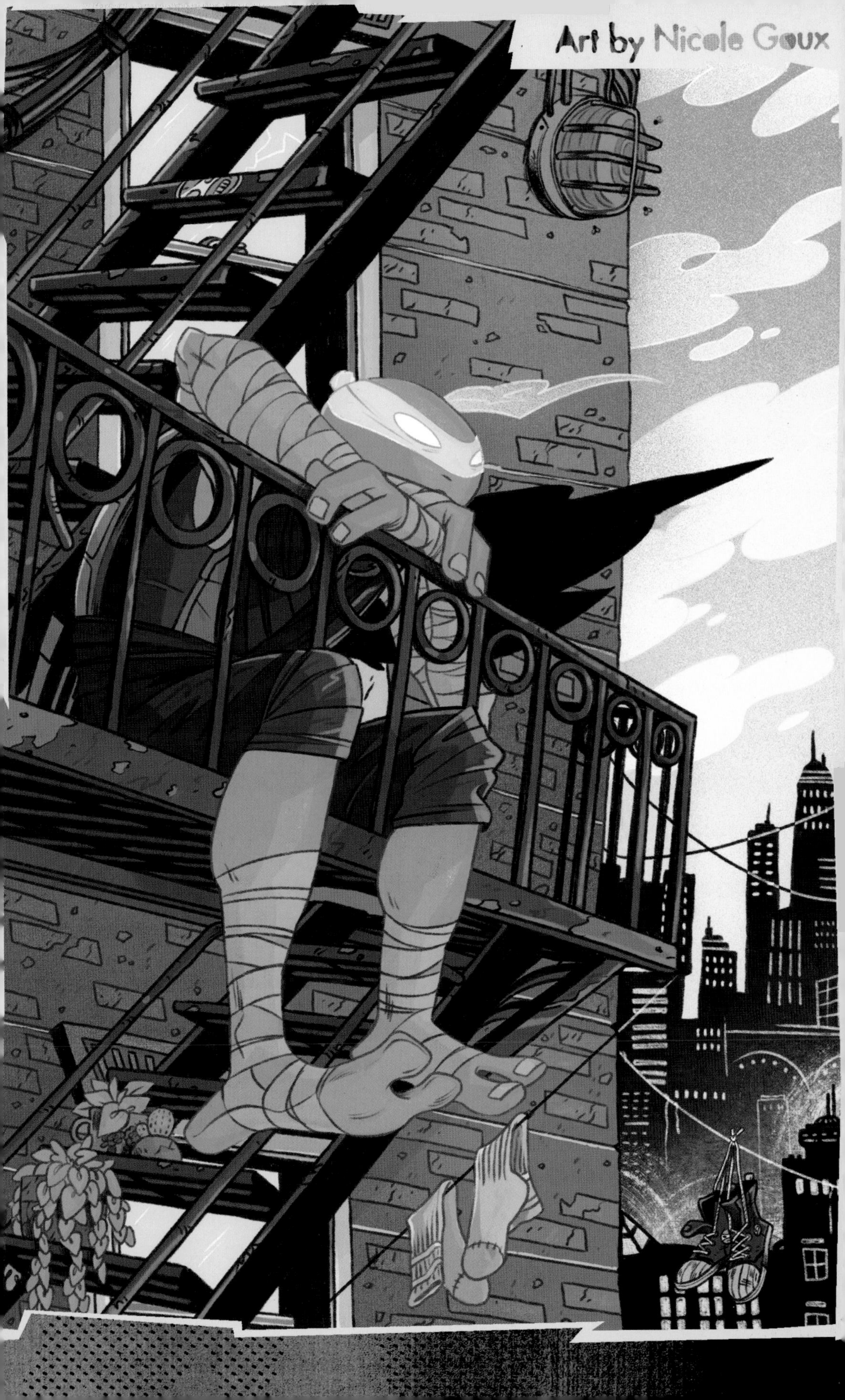
Art by Nicole Goux

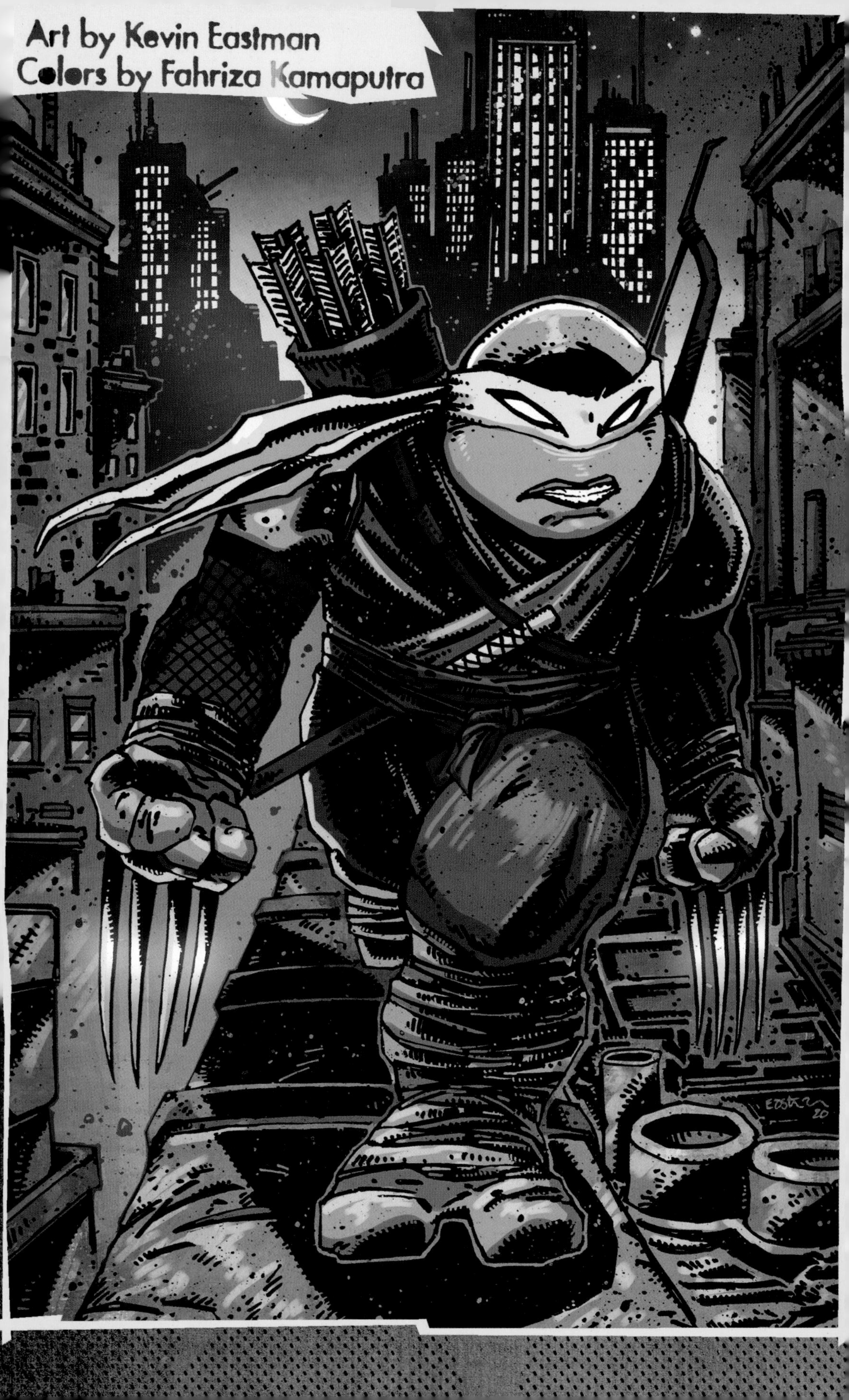
Art by Kevin Eastman
Colors by Fahriza Kamaputra